Publications of the John Gower Society

XIV

JOHN GOWER IN MANUSCRIPTS AND EARLY PRINTED BOOKS

Publications of the John Gower Society

ISSN   0954-2817

Series Editors
R.F. Yeager (*University of West Florida, emeritus*)
Alastair J. Minnis (*Yale University, emeritus*)

Editorial Board
David R. Carlson (*University of Ottawa*)
Helen Cooper (*University of Cambridge*)
Siân Echard (*University of British Columbia*)
Andy Galloway (*Cornell University*)
Brian W. Gastle (*Western Carolina University*)
Linne Mooney (*University of York*)
Peter Nicholson (*University of Hawaii*)
Derek Pearsall (*Harvard University*)
Russell A. Peck (*University of Rochester*)
Ana Sáez-Hidalgo (*University of Valladolid*)
Nicholas Watson (*Harvard University*)

This series aims to provide a forum for critical studies of the poetry of John Gower and its influence on English and continental literatures during the late Middle Ages and into the present day. Although its main focus is on the single poet, comparative studies which throw new light on Gower, his work and his historical and cultural context are also welcomed.

Proposals or queries should be sent in the first instance to the series editors or to the publisher, at the addresses given below; all submissions will receive prompt and informed consideration.

R.F. Yeager, Professor of English, *emeritus*
University of West Florida
byeager@uwf.edu

Alastair J. Minnis, Douglas Tracy Smith Professor, *emeritus*
Yale University
alastair.minnis@yale.edu

Boydell & Brewer Limited, PO Box 9, Woodbridge, Suffolk, IP12 3DF, UK

Previously published volumes in this series are listed at the end of this volume.

JOHN GOWER IN MANUSCRIPTS AND EARLY PRINTED BOOKS

Edited by
Martha Driver, Derek Pearsall and R. F. Yeager

D. S. Brewer

© Contributors 2020

All Rights Reserved. Except as permitted under current legislation
no part of this work may be photocopied, stored in a retrieval system,
published, performed in public, adapted, broadcast,
transmitted, recorded or reproduced in any form or by any means,
without the prior permission of the copyright owner

First published 2020
D. S. Brewer, Cambridge

ISBN 978-1-84384-553-9

D. S. Brewer is an imprint of Boydell & Brewer Ltd
PO Box 9, Woodbridge, Suffolk IP12 3DF, UK
and of Boydell & Brewer Inc.
668 Mt Hope Avenue, Rochester, NY 14620–2731, USA
website: www.boydellandbrewer.co.uk

A CIP catalogue record for this book is available
from the British Library

The publisher has no responsibility for the continued existence or accuracy
of URLs for external or third-party internet websites referred to in this book,
and does not guarantee that any content on such websites is, or will remain,
accurate or appropriate

This publication is printed on acid-free paper

CONTENTS

List of Illustrations — vii

Acknowledgements — xi

List of Contributors — xiii

List of Abbreviations — xvii

Introduction — 1

PART I: IN MANUSCRIPT

1 John Gower's Scribes and Literatim Copying — 13
   Wendy Scase

2 Looking for Richard: Finding "Moral Gower" in Oxford,
   Bodleian Library, MS Hatton 92 — 33
   Stephanie L. Batkie

3 A State above All Other: The Recensions of *Confessio Amantis*
   and the Anthropology of Sovereignty — 55
   Robert Epstein

4 What Lies Beneath — 71
   Karla Taylor

5 Earthly Gower: Transforming Geographical Texts and Images in
   the *Confessio Amantis* and *Vox Clamantis* Manuscripts — 89
   Amanda J. Gerber

6 Paratextual Deviations: The Transmission and Translation of
   Gower's *Confessio Amantis* in the Iberian Peninsula — 113
   Tamara Peréz-Fernández

Contents

7 "Mescreantz," Schism, and the Plight of Constantinople: Evidence for Dating and Reading London, British Library, Additional MS 59495   131
David Watt

8 John Shirley and John Gower   153
Margaret Connolly

PART II: IN PRINT

9 Gower between Manuscript and Print   169
Siân Echard

10 Gower from Print to Manuscript: Copying Caxton in Oxford, Bodleian Library, MS Hatton 51   189
Aditi Nafde

11 A Caxton *Confessio*: Readers and Users from Westminster to Chapel Hill   201
Brian W. Gastle

12 English Poets in Print: Advertising Authorship from Caxton to Berthelette   219
Julia Boffey

13 In Praise of European Peace: Gower's Verse Epistle in Thynne's 1532 Edition of Chaucer's *Workes*   231
Yoshiko Kobayashi

14 George Campbell Macaulay and the Clarendon Edition of Gower   247
A. S. G. Edwards

Bibliography   263

Index   289

ILLUSTRATIONS

Frontispiece: Glasgow, University of Glasgow, MS Hunter 59 (T.2.17), fol. 6v. By permission of University of Glasgow Library, Special Collections.   xviii

LOOKING FOR RICHARD: FINDING 'MORAL GOWER' IN OXFORD, BODLEIAN LIBRARY, MS HATTON 92

Fig. 2.1 Detail of Hatton 92 fol. 104r, reprinted with permission of The Bodleian Libraries, University of Oxford.   37

EARTHLY GOWER: TRANSFORMING GEOGRAPHICAL TEXTS AND IMAGES IN THE *CONFESSIO AMANTIS* AND *VOX CLAMANTIS* MANUSCRIPTS

Fig. 5.1 Frankfurt am Main, Universitätsbibliothek Johann Christian Senckenberg Frankfurt am Main, MS Barth. 110, fol. 26r. By permission of Universitätsbibliothek Johann Christian Senckenberg Frankfurt am Main.   97

Fig. 5.2 Collegeville, Minnesota, St. John's University, MS Steiner 54 [HMML Pr. No. SJRB 00102], fol. 20v, the "T-O diagram". Photo courtesy of the Hill Museum and Manuscript Library, Saint John's University, Minnesota, USA. Published with permission of the Hill Museum and Manuscript Library, Saint John's University, Minnesota, USA. All rights reserved.   98

Fig. 5.3 *De orbis indagacione facta per Iulium Cesarem,* San Marino, California, Huntington Library, MS HM 19960, fol. 13v. This item is reproduced by permission of The Huntington Library, San Marino, California.   99

Illustrations

Fig. 5.4	Glasgow, University of Glasgow, MS Hunter 59 (T.2.17), fol. 6v. This image is reproduced by permission of University of Glasgow Library, Special Collections.	101
Fig. 5.5	Rodrigo Jiménez de Rada's *Historia Gothica*, San Marino, California, Huntington Library, MS HM 1034, fol. 9. This item is reproduced by permission of The Huntington Library, San Marino, California.	102
Fig. 5.6	*Vox Clamantis* and Other Latin Poems, San Marino, California, Huntington Library, MS HM 150, fol. 13v. This item is reproduced by permission of The Huntington Library, San Marino, California.	103
Fig. 5.7	Oxford, Bodleian Library, MS Laud Misc. 719, fol. 21r. By permission of The Bodleian Libraries, University of Oxford.	104
Fig. 5.8	London, British Library, Cotton MS Tiberius B. v, fol. 29r. © The British Library Board.	105

GOWER BETWEEN MANUSCRIPT AND PRINT

Fig. 9.1	The end of the table of contents, and the opening of the *Confessio Amantis*, in William Caxton's 1483 printing. By permission of the Chapter of Worcester Cathedral.	177
Fig. 9.2	Oxford, Bodleian Library, MS Fairfax 3, folio 37v. By permission of The Bodleian Libraries, University of Oxford.	178
Fig. 9.3	London, British Library, MS Stowe 950, folio 35r. © The British Library Board.	179
Fig. 9.4	Oxford, Bodleian Library, MS Hatton 51, folio 7r. By permission of The Bodleian Libraries, University of Oxford.	182
Fig. 9.5	Thomas Berthelette's printing of the *Confessio Amantis*, in the second (1554) edition. By permission of Rare Books and Special Collections, the University of British Columbia.	183

Illustrations

A Caxton *Confessio*: Readers and Users from Westminster to Chapel Hill

Fig. 11.1a   Unidentified leaf fragment removed during restoration. Incunabula 532.5. Rare Book Collection, Wilson Special Collections Library, UNC-Chapel Hill. By permission of Wilson Special Collections Library, UNC-Chapel Hill.   208

Fig. 11.1b   Detail of a complete human figure drawn on unidentified leaf. Incunabula 532.5. Rare Book Collection, Wilson Special Collections Library, UNC-Chapel Hill. By permission of Wilson Special Collections Library, UNC-Chapel Hill.   208

Fig. 11.1c   Detail of partially cut and partially embossed human figure on unidentified leaf. Incunabula 532.5. Rare Book Collection, Wilson Special Collections Library, UNC-Chapel Hill. By permission of Wilson Special Collections Library, UNC-Chapel Hill.   208

Fig. 11.2   Opening lines of "Nutbrown Maid" added to bottom margin of fol. 043r. Incunabula 532.5. Rare Book Collection, Wilson Special Collections Library, UNC-Chapel Hill. By permission of Wilson Special Collections Library, UNC-Chapel Hill.   212

The editors, contributors and publisher are grateful to all the institutions and persons listed for permission to reproduce the materials in which they hold copyright. Every effort has been made to trace the copyright holders; apologies are offered for any omission, and the publisher will be pleased to add any necessary acknowledgement in subsequent editions.

ACKNOWLEDGEMENTS

The editors wish to thank Ana Sáez-Hidalgo for many quiet efforts to bring this book to fruition which otherwise would go unsung.

CONTRIBUTORS

Stephanie L. Batkie is a Teaching Associate Professor of English at The University of the South in Sewanee, Tennessee. Her research and publication interests focus on Gower, Langland, and Chaucer, along with Anglo-Latin poetry of the later Middle Ages. Along with Matthew Irvin, she is working on a new edition and translation of Gower's *Vox Clamantis*.

Julia Boffey is Professor of Medieval Studies in the Department of English at Queen Mary, University of London. Her interests include Middle English verse, especially lyrics and dream poetry, and the relationships between manuscript and print in the late fifteenth and early sixteenth centuries.

Margaret Connolly is Senior Lecturer in Medieval Studies at the University of St Andrews where she teaches paleography, codicology, and Middle English literature. She is the author of *John Shirley: Book Production and the Noble Household in Fifteenth-Century England* (1998) and *Sixteenth-Century Readers, Fifteenth-Century Books* (2019), and has published critical editions with the Early English Text Society and the Middle English Texts series, as well as a volume in the Index of Middle English Prose series. She has also co-edited several volumes of essays on later medieval manuscripts.

Martha W. Driver is Distinguished Professor of English and Women's and Gender Studies at Pace University in New York City. A co-founder of the Early Book Society for the study of manuscripts and printing history, she writes about illustration from manuscript to print, book production, and the early history of publishing. In addition to publishing some seventy-five articles in these areas, she has edited twenty-five journals over twenty-two years, including *Film & History: Medieval Period in Film* and the *Journal of the Early Book Society*. Her books about pictures include *The Image in Print: Book Illustration in Late Medieval England* (2004) and *An Index of Images in English MSS, fascicle four*, with Michael Orr (2007). She contributed to and edited *Preaching the Word in Manuscript and Print in Late Medieval England: Essays in Honour of Susan Powell* with Veronica O'Mara (2013). Her most recent essay appeared in *Poetica* in 2018, "The Curious Case of a De Worde Edition in the Morgan Library & Museum".

Siân Echard is Professor of English at the University of British Columbia. She has published widely on John Gower, Anglo Latin literature, manuscript studies, and the history of the book.

Contributors

A. S. G. Edwards, FSA, FEA, holds visiting positions at the University of Kent and at University College, London and at King's College, London. He writes occasionally about Middle English and early modern books and manuscripts.

Robert Epstein is Professor of English at Fairfield University. His research interests center on the application of economics, anthropology, and social theory to Middle English literature. He is the author of *Chaucer's Gifts: Exchange and Value in the Canterbury Tales*, and co-editor with Craig E. Bertolet of *Money, Commerce, and Economics in Late Medieval English Literature*.

Brian W. Gastle is Professor of English at Western Carolina University where he teaches medieval British literature, research methodology, and professional writing courses. He is co-editor of the *MLA Approaches to Teaching the Poetry of John Gower* (2011) and *The Routledge Research Companion to John Gower* (2017), and he has authored a number of articles and chapters, and presented repeatedly at national and international conferences on the texts of Gower, Chaucer, Margery Kempe, and others. He also serves as webmaster for the John Gower Society (www.johngower.org).

Amanda J. Gerber is Lecturer of Medieval and Renaissance Literature at the University of California, Los Angeles. She is the author of *Medieval Ovid: Frame Narrative and Political Allegory* (2015). Her monograph, entitled *Narrating Science in Chaucer's England*, will be published in 2020 and addresses how late medieval writers explored scientific knowledge through their classical literary studies.

Yoshiko Kobayashi is Professor of English Language and Literature in the Graduate School of Arts and Sciences at the University of Tokyo. She has written in both English and Japanese on Geoffrey Chaucer, John Gower, John Leland, and Edmund Spenser. Her most recent publications on Gower include chapters in *The Routledge Research Companion to John Gower* (2017) and *John Gower: Others and the Self* (2017).

Aditi Nafde is Lecturer in Medieval Literature at Newcastle University with research interests in fifteenth-century book history. She is an AHRC Early Career Leadership Fellow and PI on a project entitled "Manuscripts after Print c.1450–1550: Producing and Reading Books during Technological Change".

Derek Pearsall was Professor of English at the University of York, 1965–85, and after that Professor of English at Harvard University, 1985–2000. His books include *John Lydgate* (1970), *Piers Plowman: An Edition of the C-Text* (1978; rev. 2008), *The Canterbury Tales: A Critical Study* (1985), *The Life of Geoffrey Chaucer* (1992), *Gothic Europe* (2001), and *Arthurian Romance: A Short Introduction* (2003).

Contributors

Tamara Pérez-Fernández is Assistant Professor at the University of Valladolid. Her main field of research is the textual transmission of the works by Geoffrey Chaucer and John Gower, with a focus on the paratextual material and the role of the scribes. As part of the research project "Exile, Diplomacy, and Textual Transmission: Networks of Exchange between the Iberian Peninsula and the British Isles", funded by the Spanish *Ministerio de Ciencia, Innovación y Universidades*, she has written about Anglo-Spanish relations in the late Middle Ages and the early modern period.

Wendy Scase has published widely on medieval English literature and its manuscripts. She is currently completing a major book about the visual semiotics of medieval written English. Her other current research interests include social contexts for scribal copying, and medieval news. She co-edits *New Medieval Literatures*. She is Geoffrey Shepherd Professor of Medieval English at the University of Birmingham and a current holder of a Leverhulme Trust Major Research Fellowship.

Karla Taylor teaches medieval literature at the University of Michigan, with special interests in Chaucer, Gower, Anglo-Italian cultural and literary relations, and narrativity. Author of *Chaucer Reads the 'Divine Comedy'*, she is finishing a book on Chaucer, Gower, and their early readers.

David Watt is an Associate Professor in the Department of English, Theatre, Film and Media at the University of Manitoba. His teaching and research interests focus on late medieval literature and manuscript studies. He is the author of *The Making of Thomas Hoccleve's Series* and has served as guest editor for a special issue of *Florilegium* – the journal of the Canadian Society of Medievalists – on the topic of medieval manuscripts in Canada.

R. F. Yeager is Professor of English, University of West Florida, *emeritus*. He is president of the International John Gower Society, editor of *JGN The John Gower Newsletter*, and with Alastair Minnis, series editor for the John Gower Society Monograph Series. His current research includes English recusant writings, especially in Spain, the scribes and limners of late fourteenth-century Norwich, and a literary biography of John Gower.

ABBREVIATIONS

CA	John Gower, *Confessio Amantis*
CB	John Gower, *Cinkante Balades*
Confisyon	*Confisyon del Amante* (Castilian translation of *Confessio*)
CT	Geoffrey Chaucer, *Canterbury Tales*
CTr	John Gower, *Cronica Tripertita*
IPP	John Gower, "In Praise of Peace"
LA	*Livro do Amante* (Portuguese translation of *Confessio*)
LALME	*Linguistic Atlas of Late Mediaeval English*
MED	*Middle English Dictionary*
MO	John Gower, *Mirour de l'Omme*
NIMEV	Boffey and Edwards, *A New Index of Middle English Verse*
ODNB	*Oxford Dictionary of National Biography*
STC	*Short Title Catalogue*
TC	Geoffrey Chaucer, *Troilus and Criseyde*
Tr	John Gower, *Traitié selonc les auctours pour essampler les amantz marietz*
VC	John Gower, *Vox Clamantis*

FRONTISPIECE. Glasgow, University of Glasgow, MS Hunter 59 (T.2.17), fol. 6v. By permission of University of Glasgow Library, Special Collections.

INTRODUCTION

Martha W. Driver, Derek Pearsall and R. F. Yeager

THE STUDY OF THE poetry of John Gower originated, one might fairly say, with the careful scrutiny of manuscripts and early printed books. G. C. Macaulay, Gower's first and still foremost comprehensive editor, grounded his four-volume edition of the poet's *oeuvre* (1899–1902) in a meticulous examination of the full complement of Middle English, Anglo-French, and Latin copies of Gower's work known to him, both in manuscript and black letter. Much later, John Fisher likewise spent significant time with the manuscripts while producing the first scholarly monograph in English devoted entirely to Gower's work, his *John Gower: Moral Philosopher and Friend of Chaucer* (1964). Ironically, perhaps, these pioneers may have done their work a bit too well: for decades, past the middle of the last century, with but a few notable exceptions scholarly studies of Gower's poetry relied primarily on Macaulay and Fisher for paleographic and bibliographical details. Clearly, this was hardly sustainable practice.

A great deal of the credit for broadening the focus of scholarship to include the manuscripts and early printed editions of poets like Gower must go to the Early Book Society. Since its founding in 1987, the Early Book Society through biennial conferences and (since 1997) *JEBS* – the *Journal of the Early Book Society* – has been indispensable in bringing about the present resurgence of interest in manuscripts, incunabula, the scribes and printers who made them, and the libraries – ecclesiastical, common, and private – that housed them. Given the converging concerns of the Early Book Society and the Gower Society, the overlapping of many of their members, and their contemporaneity (the Gower Society was founded in 1984), it hardly seems surprising, in retrospect, that the two would find occasion to co-sponsor an international meeting – as they did in 2017.

In that year, the Fifteenth Biennial Conference of the Early Book Society and the IV International Congress of the John Gower Society convened jointly on the grounds of Durham University with the purpose of combining their members' wide-ranging expertise to establish new approaches to the materiality of Gower's work. The fourteen essays collected here represent substantial evidence of the profound success of that shared enterprise. Each of them when presented in Durham in early form prompted significant, helpful comment; each contributor has put this to full use, revising and expanding those briefer, orally delivered versions to transform them into print-worthy chapters of value and distinction that add importantly to what we know about Gower's poetry, its presentation, and its reception.

The essays are organized around two major headings: "In Manuscript" and "In Print." Chapters within these divisions appear roughly in chronological order, early to latest. Wendy Scase's essay, "Gower's Scribes and Literatim Copying," is the first of seven essays in the opening section, "In Manuscript." Scase challenges the established wisdom that the nearly unique homogeneity of copies of Gower's *Confessio Amantis* is the result of scribal attempts to replicate his *Mischsprache* (in Angus MacIntosh's term) – his mixture of Suffolk and Kentish dialects. Instead, she argues, the so-called "literatim" Gower manuscripts, which include Oxford, Bodleian Library MS Fairfax 3 and San Marino, Huntington Library MS EL 26.A.17 (*olim* Stafford), are better explained as the scribes' response to his meter. Gower produced his notably regular meter by strictly counting syllables, a practice uncommon in fourteenth-century England. For Scase, the most accomplished scribes who copied Gower's manuscripts became sophisticated judges of when to proceed letter-by-letter ("literatim"), the better to preserve significant variant forms, and when looser transcription would suffice. She assesses their work on Gower's manuscripts as here-to-fore unrecognized evidence of scribes taking a major step forward, "an innovative and creative development and implementation of scribal practices of dialectal tolerance and constraint long practiced in the copying of traditional rhymed Middle English verse."

In the chapter following, Stephanie L. Batkie similarly probes received wisdom when she goes "Looking for Richard: Finding 'Moral Gower' in Oxford, Bodleian Library, MS Hatton 92." "Moral Gower" is perhaps the best-known (and least generally understood) epithet applied to Gower. Rather than glancing back yet again to Chaucer's *Troilus and Criseyde* for insight, Batkie asserts that in fact "Hatton 92 offers us perhaps the clearest picture of 'moral Gower' we have." For scholars of Gower, Hatton 92 is of special interest, as the sole witness to a separate circulation of the *Cronica Tripertita*, Gower's Latin poem justifying Richard II's deposition and Henry IV's accession. Her meticulous reconstruction of the assemblage of the manuscript by several scribes from many diverse texts centers on the presence and treatment in MS Hatton 92 of Gower's most political poem. She reads the manuscript "compilationally," to show that its compilers structured "a precise set of interpretive priorities for the text involving authority and exemplaric reading, while occluding others concerned with the nature of political critique. As a result," Batkie contends, "Hatton 92 supplies a particular picture of what exactly it means to read 'moral Gower,' and allows us to question what our own priorities are when it comes to his Latin work."

The following four essays, by Robert Epstein, Karla Taylor, Amanda J. Gerber, and Tamara Peréz-Fernández, all make aspects of manuscripts of the *Confessio Amantis* their primary subject. Epstein's contribution, "A State Above All Other: The Recensions of *Confessio Amantis* and the Anthropology of Sovereignty," revisits Gower's transference of allegiance from Richard II to Henry IV – a shift that for long has stirred volatile critical debate, even prompting accusations of "turncoat" from some. This shift is played out across the three (more likely two) versions of the *Confessio*, termed "recensions" by Macaulay. For most participants in the ongoing argument, two questions have been central: when did Gower change his mind about Richard, and why? Epstein's adversarial inquiry brings him to add a third: not when, or why, but *if* – a question he answers in the negative. Drawing on recent theoretical work on kingship and sovereignty by the anthropologists Marshall Sahlins and David Graeber, Epstein contends that "the seemingly shifting political philosophy of the *Confessio* manuscripts evinces neither inconsistency nor radical evolution in Gower's thought"; rather, for Epstein, "the Lancastrian recension develops and extends the philosophy of kingship inherent in the Ricardian text."

In her essay, "What Lies Beneath," Karla Taylor also re-examines Gower's ideas about right rulership. She suggests that the re-dedications of the poem to Henry IV, manifest in manuscripts that include the late "recensions," can be understood in terms of, and evince, Gower's struggles with Wycliffian positions on *dominium*. Her main text is the "Tale of the Two Coffers" from *Confessio* Book V. Her argument leads from a thoughtful envisioning of the several roles in the tale of fortune, merit, and grace (via comparisons with treatments in Boethius, Dante, Boccaccio and Shakespeare) to a recognition that Gower's evolving concept of right rulership evoked many of Wyclif's, and so brought Gower disconcertingly close to heresy. Taylor portrays Gower struggling internally "to differentiate his thinking from Wycliffite ideas that were perhaps too close for comfort." The "Tale of the Two Coffers" in her view exemplifies this struggle, depicting "a Wycliffite polity at odds with everything Gower seeks to accomplish in the *Confessio Amantis*: the reformation of the individual subject who learns to make better ethical choices, and the reformation of the polity with the help of a poet who, rather than holding his tongue, instead writes a poem initially to advise a king, later revised to address a broader polity as 'a bok for Engelondes sake'." For Taylor, then, the manuscript "recensions" reflect an unnoticed aspect of Gower's late state of mind: not just his change of allegiance from Richard II to Henry IV, but also – no less importantly – his philosophical ambivalence at the proper meaning of *dominium*. "One might consider," she remarks, "the possibility that the revised third recension ending articulates not so much a vision of ideal *dominium* as an uneasy *ex post facto* philosophical justification for Gower's shift in allegiance. The new ending is preoccupied with grace, the crucial unknowable factor of Wycliffite *dominium*."

Amanda J. Gerber's essay, "Earthly Gower: Transforming Geographical Texts and Images in the *Confessio Amantis* and *Vox Clamantis* Manuscripts," comes next after Taylor's. Gerber grounds her argument in the texts of the *Confessio Amantis* and *Vox Clamantis*, but her central focus is on the Gower-as-archer "portraits" in manuscripts of the *Vox Clamantis* (Glasgow, University of Glasgow, MS Hunter 59 (T.2.17), San Marino, Huntington Library, MS HM 150, Oxford, Bodleian Library, MS Laud Misc. 719, London, British Library, MS Cotton Tiberius A.iv.) – or more specifically, on the configurations of the *mappae mundi* depicted therein. These "portraits" have seldom been considered more than incidentally, but Gerber contends that in fact they offer important insight into Gower's informed use of a range of geographical references and allusions in his verse. She identifies Gower's technique as "geo-historical exegetics," a method she traces to Euhemerus' attempts in the late fourth century BC to "reinterpret mythology as historical events that occurred in specific geographical locations." Thus in her view, for Gower, "physical" geography – the accurate status of actual places that clearly interested Chaucer – is of less significance than what Gerber calls "textual" geography: that is, descriptions in the *Confessio* and the *Vox Clamantis* calculated to deliver "exegetical approaches that generate multivalent readings of the historical events depicted." Underpinning her argument is 1) a detailed discussion of medieval approaches to maps, both their formulations and their specific uses, purposefully supported by examples from ancient and medieval manuscripts; and 2) analyses of illustrative passages from the *Confessio* and the *Vox*, the *Visio* portion in particular, that "generate multivalent readings of the historical events." By showing the close interrelationship of the "archer portraits" in four manuscripts, and contextualizing them within the traditions of *mappae mundi*, Gerber's chapter offers fresh insight into Gower's poetic practice, and breaks new ground ahead of what undoubtedly will be invigorated scrutiny of these images.

The next essay, "Paratextual Deviations: The Transmission and Translation of Gower's *Confessio Amantis* in the Iberian Peninsula," by Tamara Pérez-Fernández, shifts discussion forward into the fifteenth century, and from England to Portugal and Spain, where the *Confessio* was translated first into Portuguese prose and then into Castilian. Noting that "the rendering of a text into another language inevitably brings forward modifications that range from lexical variation, to content adaptation, or changes in the layout introduced to conform to a new geographical and cultural context," Pérez-Fernández closely scrutinizes the treatment of the Latin commentaries (generally considered Gower's own) that occur in the Middle English manuscripts of the *Confessio*, either in the margins (e.g., Oxford, Bodleian Library, MS Fairfax 3) or variously incorporated into the text columns. Much of this Latin paratextual apparatus was eliminated by the Portuguese and Castilian translators: all the Latin verse headings to sections of the poem were cut, and a great many of the prose commentaries. What they left, they translated and variously included. In Madrid, Real Biblioteca MS II-3088, which contains the Portuguese translation of the *Confessio*, the *Livro do Amante*, some three hundred and fifty prose commentaries, shortened and written in red, occur in the text column preceding the relevant tales. The Castilian version, the *Confisyon del Amante*, exists as well in a single copy, Madrid, Biblioteca de El Escorial g-II-19. There too, prose commentaries are interpolated into the text and while neither written in red nor direct translations, it is clear these were for the most part derived from the Portuguese. Yet there are differences: Pérez-Fernández finds "omissions and some additions unique to the Castilian summaries," and also intriguing variations in a table of contents written in Castilian but attached to both the Portuguese and Spanish manuscripts. Her chapter is thus an exploration of deviation, first by the two Iberian manuscripts from their Middle English exemplar, and subsequently from each other. She finds new clues regarding the lost English manuscript that was translated into Portuguese, allowing us to position it more clearly within the textual tradition of the *Confessio*. At the same time, the examples of deviations in the Castilian and Portuguese manuscripts establish links between the *Livro do Amante* and the *Confisyon del Amante* that have so far been overlooked. Lastly, some of the divergences that are unique to the *Confisyon* hint at the cultural background of the Castilian readers of Gower's work at the end of the fifteenth century, and how that background places it amid a specific literary scene. Such conclusions must resonate significantly for Gower's readers in all three languages.

David Watt next turns attention away from manuscripts of the *Confessio Amantis* and the *Vox Clamantis* to focus on one that may have belonged to Gower himself: London, British Library, MS Additional 59495 (*olim* Trentham). Watt's immediate concern in his essay, "'Mescreantz', Schism, and the Plight of Constantinople: Evidence for Dating and Reading London, British Library, Additional MS 5949," is to determine a date for the manuscript, which contains poems of Gower's in Anglo-French, Latin, and Middle English known to have been written across a decade or more. Noting that the presence of laudatory verses to Henry IV indicates that those at least were written after 1399 – hence assuring a *terminus a quo* – Watt focusses on a poem with potentially identifiable political allusions, the Middle English "To King Henry IV In Praise of Peace," to set a *terminus ad quem*. His argument is that, while portions of "In Praise of Peace" advise Henry to avoid renewing the war with France, "success" alone would not have rendered both poem and the manuscript containing it ineffectual for Gower, as has recently been claimed. Rather, Watt finds other passages at the heart of the poem expressing Gower's urgent concern with schism in Christendom. For Gower, the divided church not only causes war, but also allows heretics and other "mescreantz" to flourish. Importantly, Watt argues strongly that Gower intends "schism" in "In Praise of Peace" to refer to more than one schism, reaching back to the first split between Rome and Constantinople. This reading has direct consequences for the dating of BL MS Additional 59495, since for Watt, "The diction Gower uses when articulating these concerns suggests that he knew of the diplomacy that culminated in the Greek Emperor, Manuel II Palaeologus, arriving in England at the end of

1400 and staying until early 1401 in order to seek help for the defense of Constantinople against the Ottoman Turks." In an essay that traces relevant elements of Gower's diction through his Anglo-French as well as Middle English work, Watt asserts that the opportunity the Greek Emperor's visit offered for Henry to heal the greater schism extends the relevance of the poem and manuscript at least into 1401, if not somewhat farther.

In the final essay of the volume's first section, "John Shirley and John Gower," Margaret Connolly investigates the attribution to Gower of a poem beginning "Passe forþe þou pilgryme" that the scribe Shirley entitled 'Balade moral of gode counseyle' in what is now Oxford, Bodleian Library MS Ashmole 59, compiled by Shirley in the 1440s. Although G. C. Macaulay rejected Shirley's attribution, citing a variety of linguistic and metrical grounds, Connolly surmises that "The question of the authenticity of 'Passe forþe þou pilgryme' might therefore bear revisiting." Her essay describes and discusses Shirley's manuscript and its relationship to the poem's two other witnesses, Oxford, Bodleian Library, MS Rawlinson C. 86, and British Library, MS Additional 29729, the latter written in the 1550s by the historian and antiquary John Stow. Although Stow "had handled" Bodleian Library MS Ashmole 59, Shirley's copy, somewhat inexplicably he attributed the poem to Benedict Burgh – an error that Connolly sorts out, as it may have influenced Macaulay's judgment. In this and other ways, Connolly explores what can be pieced together of Macaulay's thought process that likely led to his dismissal of the poem as "full of lines that Gower would not have written" – an assessment that Connolly clearly finds unconvincing.

Siân Echard's chapter follows. Appropriately titled "Gower between Manuscript and Print," it serves as a bridge, ably connecting the volume's first section, with its focus on Gower's works in manuscripts, to the second, "In Print," where contributors' attention shifts to Gower as he appeared in early printed editions. Indeed, for Echard, much is to be made of the different Gowers readers perceive when they encounter him in "the bokes that be wrytten" – as Gower's second printer, Thomas Berthelette, designated manuscripts – and the printed copies that issued from his press, and William Caxton's blackletter Gower before him. She "explores how the unique features of Gower's *oeuvre* were often muted, redirected, or lost entirely, when the medieval poet's work encountered the strictures and expectations of early print." Echard stresses that Gower was intensely aware of himself as a trilingual poet writing for a trilingual readership; he was also, as she demonstrates here, so "deeply conscious of the materiality of the poetic word" that to some degree he wrote with the ways and means of manuscript production in mind. But Gower's first printers had their own ideas for displaying his work, ones which did not always accord with his. (Nor, Echard points out, is it only Caxton and Berthelette who modify Gower with their editions: G. C. Macaulay's is transformative as well.) Dividing her essay into two sections, "Language" and "Dialogue by Design,"

Echard discusses a broad variety of changes wrought on Gower's careful self-presentation, including the early printers' emphasis on the *Confessio Amantis* and Gower's Englishness, their various treatments of the Latin verse and prose therein, the impact of appended tables of contents, and a foregrounding of the stories over the dialogic frame. From Caxton and Berthelette to the present, the overall *mise-en-page* in print, Echard makes abundantly clear, has had consequences at every level: "Printerly gestures... overwrite Gower's anxious curation of his *auctorite* [...]. [His] presentation of his larger poetic project as a conversation in many languages, with many books, is bounded and muted by the gestures – routine, deliberate, or some combination of both – of print."

Aditi Nafde, whose essay "Gower from Print to Manuscript: Copying Caxton in Oxford, Bodleian Library, MS Hatton 51," comes next, looks more deeply into a single interrelationship of manuscript and printed text. The scribe of MS Hatton 51 (ca. 1500) took Caxton's 1483 printed edition as his exemplar, seeking to copy it exactly. As Nafde notes, the practice "was not unusual. As the number of printed books in circulation grew, it became increasingly typical for scribes to use them as exemplars." In the early years of print culture, there was a "happy co-existence of manuscript and print, the ongoing production of manuscripts after the introduction of print, and the prevalence of manuscript-print hybrid books." The Hatton 51 scribe was both thoughtful and meticulous, seeking to replicate Caxton's book exactly. The resultant copy thus contains a variety of elements uncharacteristic of manuscripts with manuscript exemplars. These include some features that, while labor-saving for the printer, required extra work for the scribe. The placement of the speaker-markers in the column rather than in the margin, where a scribe naturally (and more easily) would put them, is an example. The scribe also copied printer's errors, both small ones, like an obvious typographical blunder, and large ones, requiring significant adjustments to the foliation, and the reproduction of textual gaps, demanding juggling of another kind. More arresting, perhaps, is the presence of Caxton's prologue in MS Hatton 51, still retaining the printer's first-person pronouns. Yet the scribe clearly understood the reaches of his medium, and quite consciously put its strengths to good advantage. "Printing in two colors," Nafde points out, "was difficult and expensive and so comparatively rare in England. Caxton's c.1477 edition of *The Canterbury Tales*, for instance, was printed with gaps awaiting the colored initials that were later filled in by rubricators and decorators." The Hatton 51 scribe could easily and with relatively little expense effect such finishing by hand. Most of the large initials are his own, replicating those that Caxton himself copied from his manuscript exemplar(s). The scribe "also uses different colors of ink and sizes of script to distinguish between the Latin and English texts, disregarding the single color and size of type in his print exemplar." Arguably, the Hatton 51 scribe deliberately combines elements of both manuscript and print to improve upon both media. "Books such as Hatton 51," Nafde demonstrates, "go further still to suggest that scribal practices were not just co-existing with print but being altered by it."

A little known but important copy of Caxton's edition is the focus of Brian W. Gastle's chapter, the next following Nafde's. In "A Caxton *Confessio*: Readers and Users from Westminster to Chapel Hill," Gastle offers the first full physical description in print of the volume, provides what can be known about its modern ownership history, and – based on marginal notations and traceable signatures on its cover and pages, as well as materials incorporated into the binding – speculates on its early provenance, including perhaps time in Spanish hands. This copy, currently in the library of the University of North Carolina at Chapel Hill, is one of the few remaining with Caxton's original binding. It is nearly complete, lacking primarily several pages at the end. (With the permission of the university, Gastle has photographed and made available images of the extant volume on the John Gower Society website, https://johngower.org/caxton-confessio-unc-ch-532-5/.) Among other items used as filler, the binding contained an indulgence printed by Caxton in 1481 for "Giovanni dei Gigli, a papal nuncio, [who] appears to have commissioned the printing...in order to collect revenue for a war against the Turks who had attacked Otranto. The copy found in this binding is one of only four extant, all recovered from other bindings, and this copy is the only one with its opening lines intact." Infrequently sought out by scholars, the Caxton *Confessio*, UNC-CH Incunabula 532.5, has significant value – as Gastle amply demonstrates – as an important witness to the printer's product and practice.

For obvious reasons, the editions of his work by Caxton (1483) and Berthelette (1532 and 1554) are at the center of every study of Gower in print. Julia Boffey, in her essay "English Poets in Print: Advertising Authorship from Caxton to Berthelet," pulls back from granular examinations like Nafdi's and Gastle's to view these first editions in the larger context of English print culture at the end of the fifteenth and in the early decades of the sixteenth centuries. Her particular concern is "to situate the 1532 *Confessio* in that landscape, outlining some of the forms of attention given to authorship in English books printed before 1532, and concentrating especially on discernible continuities and innovations in the printing of poetry in English." She finds that while Caxton's Gower was in fact significantly more bilingual – in addition to the Latin apparatus of the English *Confessio Amantis*, his book contains the short Latin poems "Quam cinxere freta," "Quia unusquisque," "Eneidos, bucolis," "Est amor," and "Orate pro anima" – it was in a relatively understated way. The Latin poems in Caxton's edition have the appearance of an afterthought, as if included merely to fill out the final pages. Some fifty years later, Berthelette presents a Gower both as a humanist and pronouncedly English. Boffey compares his edition to Thynne's of Chaucer, also published in 1532, and finds similar emphases there on Englishness and authorship. But "this interest was not new." As she shows in the body of her essay, treatments of work

Introduction

of authors contemporary with Berthelette, including Skelton, Barclay, and Copland, make for illuminating comparison with Berthelette's presentation of Gower – as do, in a different way, the contemporary laureation of Chaucer and Lydgate side-by-side with Gower. In this, Boffey explains, Berthelette's *Confessio* "took its place among a succession of printed titles whose publishers seem to have been especially concerned to construct and promote a history of poetry written in English, and (in Gower's words) 'for Engelondes sake'."

The next essay, "In Praise of European Peace: Gower's Verse Epistle in Thynne's 1532 Edition of Chaucer's *Workes*," by Yoshiko Kobayashi, follows Boffey more than merely sequentially. Seeking to discover how Gower's poem became included in William Thynne's *Workes of Geffray Chaucer*, she, like Boffey, connects Gower's "In Praise of Peace" with the flowering of humanism and the promotion of the English language during the early years of Henry VIII. Initially citing Leland's description of a "humanist" Gower in his *De viris illustribus* and his special interest in "In Praise of Peace" as "important evidence of the fascination that the poem held for a Tudor humanist with close connections with the royal court," Kobayashi adds Thynne and Brian Tuke, Richard Pace and Thomas More – and pointedly, the printer Thomas Berthelette – to a list of similarly placed men sharing Leland's view of Gower's poem. This interest stemmed from the view held by all these in common that the Christian world was under severe threat from several directions: an ongoing conflict between England and France; tensions and eventually hostilities between France and the Holy Roman Empire; the predations of the Ottoman Turks; and certainly Henry VIII's "great matter" – his desire for a divorce from Katherine of Aragon – which portended another Schism no less great than the earlier one Gower describes in "In Praise of Peace." Agreeing with Greg Walker, who sees Thynne's inclusion of "In Praise of Peace" in his 1532 *Workes* as an intentional intervention, and timely, Kobayashi argues that against this backdrop Gower's century-old plea for universal peace seemed relevant, even prescient. She expands upon Walker's observations in the body of her essay, however, showing that while "Thynne and Tuke's edition asserts the contemporary relevance of Gower's poem [...] the question of why 'In Praise of Peace' appealed to such people as Tuke and Leland demands further exploration." Gower's poem became, in her view, a recognized part of "the peace discourse developed among Henry VIII's humanist officials and their friends during the decades leading up to the publication of Thynne's volume." In doing so, Kobayashi successfully offers "fresh perspectives on the Tudor reception of Gower's poetry."

Even on the slightest consideration, it seems altogether fitting that a volume of this kind should close with reflections on Gower's great modern editor, and the four-volume edition, in three languages, that he produced single-handedly between 1895 and 1902. A. S. G. Edwards' concluding essay, "George Campbell Macaulay and the Clarendon Edition of Gower," by providing such a reflection, also goes far toward redressing a remarkable oversight: as Edwards discovered, "George Macaulay remains elusive to posterity. His death was marked by a single obituary. He does not appear in either the *Dictionary of National Biography* or the *Oxford Dictionary of National Biography*." Edwards' assessment here of Macaulay's achievement is succinct and sensitive:

> In total the [edition] just crept over the 2500 pages..., weighing in at 2519 pages of which 2178 were text, the rest prefatory matter or annotation. For an individual to accomplish so much so speedily was in itself a notable achievement. It may seem the more so since it was undertaken by someone who had had no prior experience of editing medieval texts, who had never held an academic post, and who had had to support himself and a large family throughout this undertaking, and for some time before and after it, without regular employment. And more than a century after its completion Macaulay's edition of Gower remains the standard one. Indeed, in the current academic climate it is hard to see how it could be replaced.

Painstakingly researched, the essay unearths previously undiscovered sources (e.g., *The Clerkenwell News and Daily Intelligencer* of 1901), piecing together what little can be known of the man behind the work. No less importantly, Edwards draws upon his own lifetime of experience with textual scholarship to offer a thoughtful, and thorough, assessment of Macaulay's edition.

This volume, then, offers the state-of-the-art: a rich representation of what scholars of Gower's poetry and book history can do when brought together to focus simultaneously on the same topics. Looking back and forward, the essays it contains have been carefully assembled with a clear eye to showcase a fertile diversity, and with the hopeful expectation of contributing to new research, and especially of stimulating further collaborative study of this kind.

Part I

IN MANUSCRIPT

CHAPTER 1

JOHN GOWER'S SCRIBES AND LITERATIM COPYING*

Wendy Scase

CERTAIN MANUSCRIPTS OF JOHN Gower's *Confessio Amantis* have long been famous for the high quality of their texts. G. C. Macaulay characterized the Fairfax manuscript (Oxford, Bodleian Library, MS Fairfax 3, the base manuscript for his edition) "as a practically accurate reproduction of the author's original text," stated that British Library, Harley MS 3869 is "copied very faithfully from the Fairfax manuscript itself," and viewed the Stafford manuscript (San Marino, Huntington Library, EL 26.A.17) as "in most places [...] absolutely the same [as Fairfax], letter for letter."[1] Not all manuscripts measured up to Macaulay's high standards; he found that "in correctness of text and spelling [Oxford, Bodleian Library, MS Laud Misc. 609] is decidedly inferior;" while a "careless third hand" in Geneva, Fondation Bodmer, MS 178 (known to Macaulay as the manuscript of J. H. Gurney) displays "at least twenty variations in spelling" compared with Fairfax in the space of ten lines.[2] The carefulness of Fairfax, Stafford, and Harley 3869, among others, continues to be remarked upon. Since its inception in the 1950s, the Middle English Dialect Project, whose fruits have been published in the *Linguistic Atlas of Late Mediaeval English* (henceforth *LALME*) and elsewhere, has given us a vocabulary to think about such manuscripts and

---

* This essay represents work from my project Crafting English Letters: A Theory of Medieval Scribal Practice. I am most grateful to the Leverhulme Trust for a Major Research Fellowship to carry out this work and to the organizers and participants of the Early Book Society/Gower Conference at Durham (2017) for the opportunity to present a paper on this material and to benefit from their feedback. I am also grateful to the anonymous reader and to Martha Driver, Derek Pearsall, and R. F. Yeager for their feedback on this essay.
[1] George C. Macaulay, Introduction to *The English Works of John Gower*, ed. George C. Macaulay, 2 vols., EETS e.s. 81–82 (London: Kegan Paul, Trench, Trübner and Co., 1900–01), I, vii–clxxiv (xciii, xciv, cliii).
[2] Macaulay, Introduction to *The English Works*, I, cxlix, clxii.

their scribes.[3] Angus McIntosh, instigator of the project, proposed three "types" of scribal response to an exemplar not in the scribe's own dialect:[4]

A. He may leave it more or less unchanged, like a modern scholar transcribing such a manuscript. This appears to happen only somewhat rarely.

B. He may convert it into his own kind of language, making innumerable modifications to the orthography, the morphology, and the vocabulary. This happens commonly.

C. He may do something somewhere between A and B. This also happens commonly.

Developed by Michael Benskin and Margaret Laing, McIntosh's Type A is called "literatim" copying, while Type B is "translation" copying.[5] Texts of Type C, having elements of both methods, are said to be in mixed languages (*Mischsprachen*). Using the analytical terms of *LALME*, Michael Samuels and Jeremy Smith characterized Gower's own language as a *Mischsprache* that combines forms from Suffolk (where Gower had family ties) and Kent (where Gower lived for some of his youth).[6] Smith has observed that "An unusually high proportion of the texts of the *Confessio Amantis* can be shown to be in whole or in part *literatim* copies, i.e. letter-for-letter reproductions of exemplars."[7] These literatim copies preserve the mixture of dialect forms thought to reflect Gower's own idiolect.

The literatim copies of the *Confessio* have puzzled scholars. We are used to careless scribes (and the trope of the sloppy scrivener reinforces the

---

[3] Michael Benskin, Margaret Laing, Vasilis Karaisko, and Keith Williamson, *An Electronic Version of a Linguistic Atlas of Late Mediaeval English* (Edinburgh: The University of Edinburgh, 2013), http://www.lel.ed.ac.uk/ihd/elalme/elalme.html [revised online edition of Angus McIntosh, Michael L. Samuels, and Michael Benskin, *A Linguistic Atlas of Mediaeval English*, 4 vols. (Aberdeen: Aberdeen University Press, 1986)].

[4] Angus McIntosh, "Word Geography in the Lexicography of Medieval English," *Annals of the New York Academy of Sciences* 211 (1973): 55–66; repr. in *Middle English Dialectology: Essays on some Principles and Problems*, ed. Angus McIntosh, Michael L. Samuels, and Margaret Laing (Aberdeen: Aberdeen UP, 1989): 86–97 (93). Cf. *LALME*, General Introduction, 3.1.3.

[5] Michael Benskin and Margaret Laing, "Translations and *Mischsprachen* in Middle English Manuscripts," in *So many people longages and tonges: Philological Essays presented to Angus McIntosh*, ed. Michael Benskin and Michael L. Samuels (Edinburgh: Middle English Dialect Project, 1981), 55–106. Cf. *LALME*, General Introduction, 3.1.2; 3.5.1–5.

[6] Michael L. Samuels and Jeremy J. Smith, "The Language of Gower," *Neuphilologische Mitteilungen* 82 (1981): 294–304, repr. in *The English of Chaucer and his Contemporaries*, ed. Jeremy J. Smith (Aberdeen: Aberdeen University Press, 1988), 13–22. Cf. Jeremy J. Smith, "John Gower and London English," in *A Companion to Gower*, ed. Siân Echard (Cambridge: D. S. Brewer, 2004), 61–72 (63).

[7] Smith, "John Gower and London English," 70.

stereotype), but the careful scribes who appear to replicate Gower's own usage very accurately present difficulties.[8] For some, the primary question is what control Gower had over his scribes. Macaulay believed that the best early manuscripts of the *Confessio Amantis* were supervised by Gower himself, and were products of a scriptorium.[9] Fisher surmised that Gower must have used scribes at the Priory of St Mary's Overey.[10] In a famous essay, A. I. Doyle and Malcolm Parkes argued that the manuscript evidence did not support the idea that Gower used a scriptorium.[11] Building on their work and that of Macaulay, Peter Nicholson has argued persuasively that the *Confessio* as we have it in its various shapes and versions "was shaped by [...] scribes and editors [...] following Henry's accession."[12] In light of such work, our understanding of the relations between Gower and the *Confessio* scribes has become much more nuanced.[13] R. F. Yeager states that Gower "*somehow* insisted that the forms [of spelling and grammar] he chose appear

---

[8] For the trope see Daniel Wakelin, *Scribal Correction and Literary Craft: English Manuscripts 1375–1510* (Cambridge: Cambridge University Press, 2014), 28–32. Elsewhere, Wakelin points out that "sameness and consistency [among Middle English scribes generally] deserve as much study as do variation and change" ("Writing the Words," in *The Production of Books in England 1350–1500*, eds. Alexandra Gillespie and Daniel Wakelin (Cambridge: Cambridge University Press, 2011), 34–58 (53).

[9] Macaulay, Introduction to *The English Works*, I, cxxx.

[10] John H. Fisher, *John Gower: Moral Philosopher and Friend of Chaucer* (New York: New York University Press, 1965), 60, 93.

[11] A. Ian Doyle and Malcolm B. Parkes, "The Production of Copies of the *Canterbury Tales* and the *Confessio Amantis* in the Early Fifteenth Century," in *Medieval Scribes, Manuscripts, and Libraries: Essays presented to N. R. Ker*, ed. Malcolm B. Parkes and Andrew G. Watson (London: Scolar Press, 1978), 163–210. Cf. Malcolm B. Parkes, "Patterns of Scribal Activity and Revisions of the Text in Early Copies of Works by John Gower," in *New Science out of Old Books: Studies in Manuscripts and Early Printed Manuscripts and Early Printed Books in Honour of A. I. Doyle*, ed. Richard Beadle and Alan J. Piper (London: Scolar, 1995), 81–121 (98) and Derek A. Pearsall, "The Manuscripts and Illustrations of Gower's Works," in *A Companion to Gower*, ed. Siân Echard (Cambridge: D. S. Brewer, 2004), 73–97 (93).

[12] Peter Nicholson, "Poet and Scribe in the Manuscripts of Gower's *Confessio Amantis*," in *Manuscripts and Texts: Editorial Problems in Later Middle English Literature*, ed. Derek A. Pearsall (Cambridge: D. S. Brewer, 1987), 130–42 (141).

[13] The question of Gower's relation with manuscripts of his Latin and French works has also been reopened recently with Sebastian Sobecki's argument that Gower's own hand occurs (writing Latin) in London, British Library, Cotton MS Tiberius A.IV and London, British Library, Additional MS 59495 (see "*Ecce patet tensus*: The Trentham Manuscript, *In Praise of Peace*, and John Gower's Autograph Hand," *Speculum* 90.4 (2015): 925–59). For a recent overview of scholarship on the Middle English Gower manuscripts see Joel Fredell, "John Gower's Manuscripts in Middle English," in *The Routledge Research Companion to John Gower*, ed. Ana Sáez-Hidalgo, Brian Gastle, and R. F. Yeager (Abingdon and New York: Routledge, 2017), E-book.

from under the pens of most of the scribes who worked on his copying."[14] Derek Pearsall suggests that the stability of the text of the *Confessio* and the "extreme regularity of the spelling system that lay persistently before them in their exemplars" caused scribes to find "their own spelling habits 'constrained'."[15]

Other problems relate to output at the level of the individual scribe. It has been observed that a scribe who copies Gower literatim will happily "meddle" and intervene when copying other authors. Kerby-Fulton and Justice, for example, write that the famous Scribe D's "care with the text of Gower stands in marked contrast to his relatively free treatment of Langland in the Ilchester *Piers*, not to mention what seems the almost unconstrained meddling with Chaucer in the Harley [7334] *Canterbury Tales*."[16] They see the apparent difference in the scribe's "concern with [...] textual integrity" as driven by a sense that the *Confessio* was a "classic [...] of the vernacular canon."[17] Smith uses Scribe D as a case study when he seeks to explain the exceptional adoption of a literatim practice by Gower scribes in relation to the history of standardization of written English: "Gower's usage became [...] a 'standard' or 'type' [...] it seems that scribes and other copyists during the fifteenth century were seeking some authoritative reference point on which to base their usage, but a clear model to follow had not yet emerged."[18]

---

[14] R. F. Yeager, *John Gower's Poetic: The Search for a New Arion* (Cambridge: D. S. Brewer, 1990), 3, my italics.

[15] Pearsall, "The Manuscripts," 94–95.

[16] Kathryn Kerby-Fulton and Steven Justice, "Scribe D and the Marketing of Ricardian Literature," in *The Medieval Professional Reader at Work: Evidence from Manuscripts of Chaucer, Langland, Kempe and Gower*, ed. Kathryn Kerby-Fulton and Maidie Hilmo, English Literary Studies 85 (Victoria, BC: University of Victoria, 2001), 217–37 (224). Cf. Kerby-Fulton's discussion of Scribe D's "apparent penchant for scribal meddling" with Chaucer and Langland manuscripts even though "Scribe D does not meddle at all with his Gowers" (Kathryn Kerby-Fulton, "'Langland in his Working Clothes'? Scribe D, Authorial Loose Revision Material, and the Nature of Scribal Intervention," in *Middle English Poetry: Texts and Traditions: Essays in Honour of Derek Pearsall*, ed. Alastair J. Minnis (York: York Medieval Press, 2001), 139–67 (144, 154)). For Scribe D see Doyle and Parkes, "The Production of Copies" and further below.

[17] Kerby-Fulton and Justice, "Scribe D," 224.

[18] Smith, "John Gower and London English," 70–71; cf. Jeremy J. Smith, "Spelling and Tradition in Fifteenth-Century Copies of Gower's *Confessio Amantis*," in *The English of Chaucer and his Contemporaries*, ed. Jeremy J. Smith (Aberdeen: Aberdeen University Press, 1989), 96–113 (99). Kerby-Fulton's and Justice's argument for Scribe D's responsibility for the "meddling" in the Ilchester *Piers* depends on their acceptance of Smith's claim that South West Midland forms in Scribe D manuscripts "suggest that he was an immigrant to the capital from that area" (see Jeremy J. Smith, "The Trinity Gower D-Scribe and his Work on Two Early *Canterbury Tales* Manuscripts," in *The English of Chaucer and his Contemporaries*, ed. Jeremy J. Smith (Aberdeen: Aberdeen University Press, 1989), 51–69 (59)); they argued that the interventions were marked by these

In this essay I propose to offer a different way of analyzing the so-called literatim Gower manuscripts and of formulating and addressing the problems associated with literatim output. I will suggest that the scribes' practice is more productively thought about not as a response to Gower's dialectal *Mischsprache*, but as a response to his *meter*. I will suggest that Gower's scribes copy literatim when meter requires, and the best develop a sophisticated practice that distinguishes metrically significant variant forms from other variants. This practice was, I shall suggest, developed in an attempt (more probably, attempts) to solve the problems that Gower's meter – and any Middle English meter based on strict syllable counting – posed in an age of manuscript transmission and linguistic variety. I will propose that this practice could be viewed as an innovative and creative development and implementation of scribal practices of dialectal tolerance and constraint long practiced in the copying of traditional rhymed Middle English verse.

My proposal runs counter to long-held, and still current, views of scribal responses to meter. Simon Horobin has argued for many cases in Chaucer manuscripts where scribes do not seem aware of or concerned with meter.[19] While Daniel Wakelin finds that scribes correct visual form (stanza layouts, for example) and rhyme, he also provides many examples of scribes who appear not to understand metrical form, such as the Lydgate scribe who is "completely deaf to the sound-patterning."[20] Were the very careful Gower scribes exceptional? To what extent might they have been involved in developing their practice? Could scribal shaping of the *Confessio* text (scribes' involvement in the updatings and different "recensions") have extended to the development of a scribal practice for reproducing it? Research that has built on the Doyle and Parkes essay has provided us with a great deal more information about some of these early scribes and the other manuscripts they copied.[21] In the last part of this essay before the conclusion, I will suggest that there is evidence that the contribution of such scribes extended to innovation in scribal practice more widely.

---

forms and therefore Scribe D must be responsible for them (rather than an editor or a previous scribe). However, Simon Horobin and Dan Mosser subsequently called into question Smith's analysis of Scribe D's origins, suggesting that the South West Midland forms might be attributable to literatim copying (Simon Horobin and Daniel Mosser, "Scribe D's SW Midlands Roots: A Reconsideration," *Neuphilogische Mitteilungen* 3/106 (2005): 289–305).

[19] Simon Horobin, *The Language of the Chaucer Tradition* (Cambridge: D. S. Brewer, 2003), 100, 102–03, 108–09.

[20] Wakelin, *Scribal Correction and Literary Craft*, 217–45; quotation at 243.

[21] See for example, Linne R. Mooney, "Chaucer's Scribe," *Speculum* 81.1 (2006): 97–138; Linne R. Mooney, Simon Horobin, and Estelle Stubbs, *Late Medieval English Scribes*, Version 1.0 (York: University of York, 2011), https://www.medievalscribes.com; and Linne R. Mooney and Estelle Stubbs, *Scribes and the City: London Guildhall Clerks and the Dissemination of Middle English Literature 1375–1425* (York: York Medieval Press, 2013).

Gower's Meter and Literatim Scribal Practice

The metrical regularity of Gower's verse has long been remarked upon.[22] Gower appears to have aimed for strict observance of syllable count in both French and English. As Macaulay remarked, there is scarcely a "superfluous syllable" in the *Confessio Amantis* and the French verse is strictly counted too.[23] Recent quantitative, comparative studies have demonstrated empirically that Gower's metrical strictness was new and experimental. Duffell and Billy provide statistics to prove that Gower's metrical practice contrasts considerably with that of previous poets who composed syllabic verse in English as well as, to a lesser extent, with that of Chaucer. They claim that "Gower's English octosyllables are extremely regular in both syllable count and rhythm: all his lines contain exactly eight syllables and 99 percent of them are iambic throughout", whereas Marina Tarlinskaja's data shows that earlier short-line verse poems "were only roughly octosyllabic: barely 70 percent of lines have exactly eight syllables."[24] Only 84 percent of Chaucer's short verse lines comprise eight syllables; Gower's long lines are also much more regular than Chaucer's decasyllabic lines "in both rhythm and syllable count."[25]

What challenges would a new, strictly-counted and sometimes regularly iambic English verse have confronted scribes with? How far were they successful in solving them? It is well recognized that Middle English verse of all kinds was vulnerable to linguistic variations across time and dialect. Variations in sound could spoil rhyme and alliteration.[26] Variations in inflexional morphology could damage rhyme too, and could spoil meters that relied on syllable count and patterns of stressed and unstressed syllables. In traditional rhymed verse, convention allowed variant forms to

---

[22] John Burrow, "Gower's Poetic Styles," in *A Companion to Gower*, ed. Siân Echard (Cambridge: D. S. Brewer, 2004), 239–50 (241).

[23] Macaulay, Introduction to *The English Works*, I, cxxi; George C. Macaulay, Introduction to *The French Works*, in *The Complete Works of John Gower*, ed. George C. Macaulay, 4 vols. (Oxford: Clarendon Press, 1899–1902), vol. I, xi–lxxxvii (xliv–xlv).

[24] Martin J. Duffell and Dominique Billy, "From Decasyllable to Pentameter: Gower's Contribution to English Metrics," *The Chaucer Review* 38, no. 4 (2004): 383–400 (384–85), citing Marina Tarlinskaja, *English Verse: Theory and History* (The Hague: Mouton, 1976), 89, 256; cf. Martin J. Duffell, *A New History of English Metre* (London: Maney for the Modern Humanities Research Association, 2008), 89–92.

[25] Duffell and Billy, "From Decasyllable to Pentameter," 384, 394. Of course, these statistics may show us more about the manuscripts than the poets; contrasting the regularity of Gower's verse with the rougher quality of Chaucer's, John Burrow adds the caveat that the contrast only holds good "if the Chaucer manuscripts are to be trusted" (Burrow, "Gower's Poetic Styles," 241). Tarlinskaja's statistics probably also tell us more about editions than about manuscripts: Tarlinskaja based her analysis on Skeat's *Complete Works of Chaucer* (1844) and R. Pauli's edition of Gower's *Confessio* (1857).

[26] Cf. *LALME*, General Introduction, 3.3.5–6.

be preserved if rhyme demanded it. Scribes – and we must assume readers – were tolerant of rhymes that only worked in other dialects, taking care to preserve them. An example occurs in the Vernon manuscript copy of the *Northern Homily Cycle Legend of St Eustace* (Oxford, Bodleian Library, MS Eng. Poet.a.1, fol. 183r, col. a):

>Þat tale þat þei in myn hous told
>And þenne may we beo siker and bold
>Þat þey vre sones beoþ baþe
>And Eustas let calle hem raþe
>And whon þei come boþe hym biforen   5
>He asked hem wher þei weore boren

The rhyme-word "raþe" (quickly, line 4) requires the Northern "baþe" (both, line 3). Mid-line, where the rhyme will not be affected, the scribe writes "boþe" (line 5), presumably the form he is used to, but in rhyme position he writes the Northern variant with long *a*. Indeed, it is clear from the manuscript that the scribe at first wrote the form he was more used to in rhyme position, later correcting it to preserve the rhyme. Analyzed in the terms of *LALME*, the Vernon scribe's output is translated in relation to the Northern exemplar (whether proximate or several texts removed) mid-line, but is literatim in rhyme position.

Gower's Middle English verse hugely increased the amount of linguistic variation that scribes were required to attend to. Strict syllable counting and sound patterning required attention to the whole line. The pressures that Gower's meter placed on scribes must have been intensified by morphological changes and variation. Simon Horobin lists those changes and variants that affected the scribes of Chaucer's work.[27] A famous case, and the subject of much controversy, is the *-e* inflexion on monosyllabic adjectives in "weak" positions such as after a possessive pronoun or a determiner. By *c.* 1400 the *-e* inflexion on weak adjectives had ceased to be pronounced in the spoken language.[28] According to Samuels, dialect variation in this usage was long-standing: observance of *-e* was associated with "conservative dialects" of the rural South Midlands and South East, though it was lost in some London language types from the mid fourteenth century.[29] The adverb inflexion *-es* could be *-e* or dropped entirely.[30] The

---

[27] Horobin, *The Language of the Chaucer Tradition*, 96–113.
[28] Horobin, *The Language of the Chaucer Tradition*, 97; cf. Roger Lass, "Phonology and Morphology," in *The Cambridge History of the English Language, Volume II, 1066–1476*, ed. Norman Blake (Cambridge: Cambridge University Press, 1992), 23–155 (115–16).
[29] Michael L. Samuels, "Chaucerian Final '-E'," *Notes and Queries* 217 (1972): 445–48, repr. in *The English of Chaucer and his Contemporaries*, ed. Jeremy J. Smith (Aberdeen: Aberdeen University Press, 1988), 7–12 (9).
[30] Horobin, *The Language of the Chaucer Tradition*, 106.

infinitive ending could be *-e* or *-en*, with implications for syllable count where *-e* could be elided when followed by a vowel or unaspirated *h*.[31] The infinitive could be preceded by *to* or *for to*. The third person present plural verb could end *-e* or *-en*.[32] Gower scribes, too, had to be alert to the dangers of using the forms and spellings of the language they were used to in place of the forms used by Gower (they had to be alert to the dangers of "translating," in *LALME*'s terminology).

But the crucial point, I suggest, about the pressures on the Gower scribes is that Gower's meter *depends* on variant forms. Some of the forms on which it depends have contributed to the analysis of Gower's language as a *Mischsprache* that mixes elements associated with Kent (for example, contracted third person present verbs, such as *makþ* (makes) and spellings such as *hiere* (hear/ here) and *oghne* (own)), with elements associated with Suffolk and its environs (such as *or ... or* (either ... or)).[33] That such forms are very often *crucial* to the meter is proved by Smith's report that he and Samuels deduced that they were authorial ("Gowerian") because they were required by the meter: "the Gowerian origins of certain forms [...] were *supported* by metrical evidence."[34]

However, Gower's Middle English verse is much more linguistically mixed, and a rather different kind of *Mischsprache*, than the *LALME* focus on its disparate dialect forms suggests. In his account of Gower's language, Macaulay gives many examples of words in the *Confessio* that occur in forms with different numbers of syllables. Many nouns have an optional final *-e: help/helpe; sor/sore; falshed/falshede*.[35] Gower often inflects adjectives with *-e*, following the weak adjective rules (e.g. *the grete hert*), but there are exceptions; likewise *-e* varies when the adjective is uninflected (e.g. *low/lowe*).[36] Some possessive and relative pronouns can be monosyllabic or bisyllabic (*our/oure*; *which/whiche*).[37] Forms of the third-person present singular verb occur where the inflexion *-eth* is contracted so that it does not form a separate syllable alongside forms where the inflexion counts as a syllable (*drawth/draweth*).[38] Before a vowel or an unaspirated *h*, final *-e* is elided, so its presence or otherwise does not affect the meter, but in other cases these variations are exploited by Gower for the syllable count and pattern of accents.

---

[31] Horobin, *The Language of the Chaucer Tradition*, 107.
[32] Horobin, *The Language of the Chaucer Tradition*, 111.
[33] Smith, "John Gower and London English," 62–63; cf. Samuels and Smith, "The Language of Gower," 16–17.
[34] Smith, "John Gower and London English," 62–63; cf. Samuels and Smith, "The Language of Gower," 16–17.
[35] Macaulay, Introduction to *The English Works*, I, cviii.
[36] Macaulay, Introduction to *The English Works*, I, cx.
[37] Macaulay, Introduction to *The English Works*, I, cxliii.
[38] Macaulay, Introduction to *The English Works*, I, cxiv.

This enormous degree of variety, essential for Gower's metrical purposes, must have placed considerable demands on scribes. The following passage, transcribed from the Fairfax 3 manuscript (fol. 9v), illustrates this:[39]

>   This worþi prest þis holy man
>   To me spekende þus began
>   And seide benedicite   205
>   Mi sone of the felicite
>   Of loue and ek of all þe wo
>   Thov schalt þee schriue of boþe tuo
>   What þou er this for loues sake
>   Hast felt let nothing be forsake   210
>   Tell pleinliche as it is befalle
>   And wiþ þat word I gan doun falle
>   On knees and wiþ devocioun
>   And with full gret contricioun
>   I seide þanne Dominus   215
>   Min holi fader Genius
>   So as þou hast experience
>   Of loue for whos reuerence
>   Thov schalt me schriuen at þis time
>   I prai þe let me noght mistime   220
>   Mi schrifte for I am destourbed
>   In al myn herte and so contourbed
>   That I ne may my wittes gete
>   So schal I moche þing forʒete
>   Bot if þou wolt my schrifte oppose   225
>   Fro point to point þanne I suppose
>   Thei[40] schal noþing be left behinde
>   Bot now my wittes ben so blinde
>   That I ne can miseluen teche
>   Tho he began anon to preche   230
>   And wiþ his wordes debonaire
>   He seide to me softe and faire
>   Thi schrifte to oppose and hiere
>   Mi sone sone I am assigned hiere. (*CA* I.203–34)

Several optional -*e* endings are required by the meter as counted syllables, for example "spekende" (line 204), "seide" and "þanne" (line 215), "moche" (line 224), "seide" (line 232). The optional endingless infinitive "schriue" (line 208) permits elision with the following "of," preserving the syllable

---

[39] I have modernized word division. As punctuation is not the subject of my analysis here, I have not transcribed it. Book and line references are to John Gower, *Confessio Amantis*, in *The English Works of John Gower*, ed. George C. Macaulay, 2 vols., EETS, e.s. 81–82 (London: Kegan Paul, Trench, Trübner and Co., 1900–01).

[40] Macaulay reads "Ther": John Gower, *Confessio Amantis*, ed. Macaulay.

count, whereas the alternative *-en* infinitive ending "schriuen" (line 219) is required to prevent elision with the following "at." "To preche" (line 230), rather than *prechen* or *for to preche(n)*, preserves the syllable count and stress on the rhyme word. The possessive with optional nasal "Min" (line 216) prevents elision with "holi," as it does before "herte" (line 222); where it is unnecessary, the alternative spelling without the nasal ending is used ("my schrifte" (line 225), "my wittes" (line 228)). The Gowerian spellings "hiere" (here, line 234) and "hiere" (hear, line 233) preserve eye-rhyme.

For accurate transmission, then, Gower's verse relied on sensitivity to his meter and great care with regard to spelling. Whereas scribes of traditional short-line rhymed Middle English verse were able to translate an exemplar into another spelling system and dialect, provided they took care to maintain the rhyme, scribes of syllabic verse had to pay much more attention to preserving linguistic variants if they were to avoid damage to the meter. Given that spellings and forms must vary according to the demands of the meter, it was not feasible to translate into a more familiar system, only adopting literatim practice in rhyme position. Gower's syllabic verse, I would argue, *required* intensive literatim reproduction.

Moreover, if we view literatim practice as "letter-by-letter" copying of alien dialect forms, in the terms of *LALME*, we shall miss the subtleties of the scribes' practice and, too, miss the relation of their work with the practice of the scribes of the traditional Middle English short-line verse, described in *LALME* terms as translation. We shall also miss the opportunity to assess their accomplishments in relation to one another and, in some cases, across their other outputs.

LITERATIM SCRIBAL PRACTICES IN *CONFESSIO AMANTIS* MANUSCRIPTS

Oxford, Bodleian Library, MS Fairfax 3

We have already encountered the output of the main Fairfax 3 scribe, and the way he operates, in the analysis above of the passage from Book I. It is worth adding that the scribe seems to have been actively reviewing his output and seeking to improve its encoding of the meter. Macaulay notes corrections "where a final *e* seems to be deliberately erased for the sake of the meter or before a vowel, as I. 60 'get' for 'gete', III. 2346 'trew' for 'trewe', VI. 1359 'I red' for 'I rede', VII. 1706 'ffyf' for 'ffyue', or where an *e* has been added afterwards, as II. 3399 'deþe', III. 449 'bowe', V. 1269, 3726, 5265, 'whiche'."[41] Corrections of this kind might suggest a scribe who is thinking hard about variant spellings, and working to eliminate unnecessary and superfluous endings. They might suggest, too, that the scribe is engaged in a dynamic process of learning, discovery, and development of practice.

---

[41] Macaulay, Introduction to *The English Works*, I, clix.

In the sample passage analyzed above, there are signs that some words may have been corrected by the main hand as he went along (scraped parchment; positioning of a word slightly out of alignment; darker ink), for example "softe" (232), "Thei" (227), and a little later in the text "godesse" (235). It is possible that some of these corrections were motivated by the scribe's attention to encoding meter. Despite his close attention, however, he allows "sone sone" to stand, adding excess syllables at line 234.

Oxford, Bodleian Library, MS Bodley 902

Compared with the Fairfax 3 text, the *Confessio* in Bodley 902 is an equally careful, though somewhat different, literatim output. The scribe writes "spekende" (line 204, fol. 8v, col. a), "seide" and "thanne" (line 215), "moche" (line 224), "seide" (line 232). He uses the optional endingless infinitive "schriue" (line 208), and the alternative *-en* infinitive ending "schriuen" (line 219), the possessive with optional nasal "Myn" (line 216) preventing elision with "holy," and "myn" before "herte" (line 222); where it is unnecessary, the alternative spelling without the nasal ending is used ("my schrifte" (line 225), "my wittes" (line 228)). This text, though, appears to make a firmer distinction between variants that are necessary for the meter and those which are not, much as the scribes of the translated rhymed verse texts copy literatim in rhyme position but translate mid-line. Whereas the scribes of the traditional verse prioritize line-end rhyme, the Bodley 902 scribe is alert to the distinction between crucial and non-crucial variants mid-line too. He has the Gowerian spellings "hiere" (here, line 234) and "hiere" (hear, line 233), preserving eye-rhyme. But for a mid-line example he reads "Stondende as stoones heer and þere," where Fairfax reads "hiere" (at I. 428). Both *heer* and *hiere* are evidently monosyllables, so the Gowerian spelling is of no consequence mid-line. The Bodley 902 scribe also seems to be trying to push the system for encoding counted syllables further than Fairfax. Where Fairfax reads "þanne" (line 226), Bodley 902 reads "þan." Since "þanne" falls before a vowel the elision rule should mean that it is harmlessly monosyllabic. But the *-ne* ending is superfluous and potentially ambiguous; Bodley 902 is unambiguous. Another example of this rationalization of the spelling occurs at line 211, where Fairfax reads "Tell pleinliche as:" Bodley 902 tidies up with "Tel pleinly as."

Oxford, Bodleian Library, MS Bodley 294

Bodley 294, thought to have been copied by the same scribe as Bodley 902, is equally successful at encoding the meter (my readings are from fol. 9r). The optional *-e* endings required by the meter as counted syllables, for example "spekende" (line 204), "sayde" and "thanne" (line 215), "sayde" (line 232), appear. For bisyllabic "moche" (line 224), Bodley 294 has the even less ambiguous bisyllabic "mochil." The optional endingless infinitive "schriue" (line 208) and the metrically necessary alternative *-en* infinitive ending "schryuen" (line 219) are used, as are the optional forms "To preche" (line 230), "Myn" (lines 216, 222) and the alternatives "my schrifte" (line 225), "my wittes" (line 228). Unambiguously monosyllabic "þan" (line 226) and unambiguously bisyllabic "pleinly" (line 211) appear as in Bodley 902. For the Gowerian spellings "hiere" (here, line 234) and "hiere" (hear, line 233) in Fairfax 3 and Bodley 902, Bodley 294 reads "heere" and "heere," preserving eye-rhyme but dispensing with the metrically unnecessary Gowerian spelling even in rhyme position.

Oxford, Bodleian Library, MS Bodley 693

The text of Bodley 693 is broadly similar, though the scribe is perhaps a little less sure by comparison with the two Bodley manuscripts analyzed above. Bodley 693 drops the unnecessary Gowerian *hiere* spellings at lines 233–34, reading "here/here" instead, preserves the Gowerian present participle in "spekende" (line 204), but drops the *-e*, leaving the line a syllable short (my readings are from fols. 8v–9r). In line 211, where Fairfax has "Tell pleinliche," Bodley 693 reads "telle pleinliche," potentially giving the line a superfluous syllable. Otiose and ambiguous *-e* endings occur in "Þer schal nothing be lefte be hinde" (line 227; Fairfax reads "Thei schal nothing be left be hinde") and "Þo he began anone to preche" (230; Fairfax reads "Tho he began anon to preche"). This scribe may be using prominent word-terminal flourishes where he feels that an optional *-e* has been dropped for the sake of the meter (for example, "all" in line 207, where Bodley 902 and 294 read "al"). This scribe understands that it is necessary to copy literatim those variants where meter might be affected, and he knows that optional inflexions and spellings must be watched closely; he is simply less good than the scribe of Bodley 902 and 294 at discerning occasions when it matters.

Cambridge, Trinity College, MS R.3.2

The scribe attributed with copying Bodley 902 and Bodley 294, as will be well known to many, has been attributed with several other Middle English manuscripts and he is identified as the Scribe D who, as I mentioned above, was a case study in Jeremy Smith's work on literatim scribes and whose literatim characteristics have been contrasted by Kerby-Fulton and others with his work on Chaucer and Langland manuscripts. In my analysis of Bodley 294 and Bodley 902, I have argued that these manuscripts comprise literatim output when it is important for meter, but not when it is unnecessary. These manuscripts are like those of the traditional Middle English short-line rhymed verse in this respect, except that the scribe is obliged to have regard to optional variants across the line to maintain the meter instead of just in rhyme position. Furthermore, my analyses of Bodley 693 and Fairfax 3 have suggested that others shared his general aim and practice, though differed in the details of its implementation and in the degree of skill they displayed in doing so.

A good opportunity for investigating further the degree to which scribes contemporary with Scribe D shared this practice is provided by the *Confessio* manuscript Cambridge, Trinity College, MS R.3.2, for here Scribe D's hand appears alongside the hands of four other scribes. Doyle and Parkes first distinguished five hands in the manuscript, labelled them A–E, dated their work sometime in the period 1408–26, and located them most probably in London. They identified three of the hands (B, D, and E) in further manuscripts, and identified Scribe E as Thomas Hoccleve.[42] Mooney and Stubbs extended the canon of work attributed to these scribes by Doyle and Parkes and suggested that B and D were London scriveners, both of whom may have had associations with the London Guildhall. Mooney identified Scribe B as Adam Pinkhurst and Mooney and Stubbs have identified Scribe D as John Marchaunt.[43] They also suggested that Gower himself may have been associated with the Guildhall and may have been known to some of the *Confessio* scribes.[44] These identifications of B and D have not gone unquestioned, but whatever the precise identities of the scribes, we can say with some confidence that though working independently, these scribes belonged to a network, linked through whoever co-ordinated the production of the manuscript, and one of them at least – if we accept the Hoccleve identification – was probably based in London.[45] Their exemplar (or exemplars) does not survive and we can only make limited inferences about it. Further, direct comparison is impossible since they all, of course, copy different material. However, we can compare their outputs using an adaptation of the method I employed above.

Scribe D in Cambridge, Trinity College, MS R.2.3 copied quires 9 (fols. 66r–73v); 14 (fol. 113, col. b, line 15, 3rd word–121v); and 15–19 (fols. 122r–147v).[46] Macaulay thought his hand "neater and better" than

---

[42] Doyle and Parkes, "The Production of Copies," 170, 177, 182–85.
[43] Mooney, "Chaucer's Scribe;" Mooney and Stubbs, *Scribes and the City*, 38–85.
[44] Mooney and Stubbs, *Scribes and the City*, 137.
[45] Contributions to these debates include Jane Roberts, "On Giving Scribe B a Name and a Clutch of London Manuscripts from c. 1400," *Medium Ævum* 80.2 (2011): 247–70 and Lawrence Warner, "Scribes, Misattributed: Hoccleve and Pinkhurst," *Studies in the Age of Chaucer* 37 (2015): 55–100 and *Chaucer's Scribes: London Textual Production, 1384–1432* (Cambridge: Cambridge University Press, 2018), especially 115–33.
[46] For characteristics of the scribes' hands that enable them to be identified individually across manuscripts see Doyle and Parkes, "The Production of Copies," 206–23 and the entries in Mooney, Horobin, and Stubbs, *Late Medieval English Scribes*; for Scribe B see also Mooney, "Chaucer's Scribe", and Mooney and Stubbs, *Scribes and the City*, 66–85, and for Scribe D see *Scribes and the City*, 38–65. My analysis in this paper attends to rather different features: those that may enable us to compare the scribes' responses to their Gower exemplar. Identifications of scribal stints are based on Doyle and Parkes, "The Production of Copies," 168–85.

those of Scribes A and B.[47] Scribe D's hand has been discerned in thirteen literary manuscripts, including eight of the *Confessio* and two of the *Canterbury Tales*, Oxford, Corpus Christi College, MS 198 and British Library, MS Harley 7334. In order to assess his response to Gower's meter in Cambridge, Trinity College, MS R.3.2, I use as an example a passage from Book VII, lines 1–26 (fol. 99r, col. b). Scribe D observes the Gowerian spelling "matier" (line 25) but elsewhere has "matere" rhyming with "here" (lines 7–8). He uses the optional third-person present plural verb inflexion *-n* to prevent elision with the following *h* ("sitten," line 8) and the contracted singular present verb form "seist" (line 11) where it is a metrical requirement. A nasal on the possessive is used to prevent elision with a following vowel "thin ere" (line 18; cf. "thi time," line 13). Final *-e* often has to be pronounced, for example "loue" (line 8), "shryue" (line 9), "suche" (line 12). However, a final *-e* is missing from "thenk" (line 24) unless this is the force of the prominent tail on *k*. Dittography in the form of "somdel somdel" has been allowed to stand uncorrected, creating a decasyllabic line (line 6). Perhaps the scribe is more alert to deficiencies of rhyme than he is to those of meter, as erroneous "april" has been altered to "aprise" to maintain the rhyme with "wise" (and the sense) (lines 11–12). His output is similar to that in Bodley 902 and 294, though perhaps slightly less careful and unambiguous.

Scribe A copied quires 1 (fols. 1r–8v); 7 (fols. 50r–57v); 10 (fols. 74r–81v); 11 (fols. 84v–89v only); 13 (fols. 98r–105v); and 14 (part, fols. 106r–113r, col. b, line 15, second word). Macaulay views this scribe as "rather less correct [i.e. less close to the readings of Fairfax] and less good in spelling than the others [i.e. less close to Gower's inferred spellings]."[48] Scribe A's hand has not been identified in other manuscripts. I use as my example Book III, lines 34–60 (fol. 5v, col. b). Scribe A's output does not reproduce all distinctive Gowerian forms and spellings, but it usually observes variants needed for meter. For example, the scribe observes the *-e* inflexion on "ovne" required for the meter in "Saue onlich of myn ovne thoght" (line 42) but not the Gowerian spelling *oghne* as in Fairfax (fol. 47r, col. a). His present participle is *-ing*: ("al waking," line 51) instead of Gower's *-ende*. His substitution here makes no difference to the meter: both forms are bisyllabic (*-e* in Fairfax is followed by a vowel). He uses the infinitive in *-e* where required for rhyme and meter ("answere," line 53). He uses the bisyllabic variant *gamen* to preserve the syllable count and iambic meter unambiguously ("That how so that the gamen goth," line 35, cf. line 38, "game"), the variant "withouten" to guard against elision and damage to the meter ("She seith me nay withouten othe," line 55), and varies "my seluen" with "my self" (lines 43, 49) for metrical purposes. But his output

---

[47] Macaulay, Introduction to *The English Works*, I, clv.
[48] Macaulay, Introduction to *The English Works*, I, clv.

is not entirely systematic nor accurate. He misses the Gowerian contraction of "makþ" (line 37) required by the iambic meter, reading "And al makith loue wel y wot;" perhaps he reads "loue" as a monosyllable and uses -*ith* to make up the syllable count.

Scribe B copied quires 2–4 (fols. 9r–32v). I use as my example Book IV, lines 1–24 (fols. 20v, col. b–21r, col. a). Doyle and Parkes identified Scribe B as the scribe of the Ellesmere and Hengwrt manuscripts of the *Canterbury Tales* and a fragmentary *Troilus and Criseyde*.[49] A further four literary manuscripts have since been associated with this scribe, who has been identified by Mooney as Adam Pinkhurst.[50] Macaulay views the hand as good in spelling but less neat than others.[51] Commenting on his punctuation at Book III, lines 631–38 (fol. 9r), Parkes observes "the scribe has perceived subtle rhythms in the lines [...] and has punctuated the verse accordingly."[52] Samuels comments, "as a copyist of Gower, this scribe is very unusual in that he translates his Gower exemplar thoroughly (with a few notable exceptions)."[53] Samuels does not develop the point about the exceptions. Arguably, as in the outputs discussed already, where meter does not matter, Scribe B translates; for example, *here* is spelt "heere" (line 7) rather than Gowerian *hier* (cf. Fairfax 3, fol. 62r, col. b). But where meter would be affected, Scribe B observes Gowerian forms, notably the contracted third-person present singular ("stant," line 18). The weak adjective ending -*e* is preserved with its metrical effect in "The firste point" (line 3), "this ilke thyng" (line 21) and "my goode fader" (line 18). The infinitive "to procede" (line 1) is used rather than the alternative *proceden*, and the variant "To leuen" (line 2) rather than *toleue*. The scribe is not completely accurate. Uncontracted, bisyllabic "wissheth" (line 12) is required by the meter but "bryngeth" (line 14) introduces a superfluous syllable (Fairfax has "bringþ"). In the last couplet in the passage, "this" rhymes with itself; perhaps the scribe has misread a *y* in his exemplar as a thorn. Some spellings are ambiguous: "thanne" in line 16 is bisyllabic, but in line 13 a monosyllabic pronunciation is required. The practices of Scribes A and B are therefore rather similar to those of Scribe D. Both broadly observe variants required by the meter, though not all Gowerian forms and spellings.

Scribe C copied quire 4, added leaf (fol. 33); quires 5–6 (fols. 34r–49v); 8 (fols. 58r–65v); and 12 (fols. 90r–97v). I use as my example passage

---

[49] Doyle and Parkes, "The Production of Copies," 170.
[50] Mooney, "Chaucer's Scribe;" Mooney and Stubbs, *Scribes and the City*, 68–69.
[51] Macaulay, Introduction to *The English Works*, I, clv.
[52] Malcolm B. Parkes, *Pause and Effect: An Introduction to Medieval Punctuation in the West* (Aldershot: Scolar, 1992), 107.
[53] Michael L. Samuels, "Chaucer's Spelling," in *Middle English Studies presented to Norman Davis*, ed. D. Gray and E. G. Stanley (Oxford: Clarendon Press, 1983), 17–37, repr. in *The English of Chaucer and his Contemporaries*, ed. Jeremy J. Smith (Aberdeen: Aberdeen University Press, 1988), 23–37 (25).

Book V, lines 1–26 (fol. 42r, col. b). Macaulay viewed this hand as "neater and better" than those of Scribes A and B.[54] Scribe C retains the Gowerian construction *or ... or* (line 7). He observes the rule about weak adjectives ("hihe," line 1, "scharpe," line 17); however, in line 20 "hihe" requires a bisyllabic pronunciation even though it is not weak. Scribe C corrects his work, replacing "money" with "pes" (line 12), repairing both meter and sense. Elsewhere, though, the scribe does not appear to have attempted to smooth the meter: line 14 is short of a syllable because of "all;" "auarice" requires to be pronounced with four syllables in line 8; and the uncontracted rhyme verbs "encloseþ [...] supposeþ" (lines 21–22) mean these lines each have nine syllables. Line 26 also appears to have one syllable too many. A little later, he preserves the Gowerian *ie* spelling ("fiele" (*feel*), fol. 42v, col. b, V. 103, "And grope and fiele al aboute") but drops a syllable in this line; compare "Þat ȝe me tolden hiere to fore," fol. 42v, col. b, V. 107. (Does he believe that *fiele* has a bisyllabic pronunciation?) Compared with Scribes A, B, and D, Scribe C is less skillful at distinguishing between forms that are necessary for the meter and forms that are not.

Scribe E copied quire 11 (fols. 82r–84r, col a, only, Book V, 7083–7498).[55] Scribe E has been identified as the poet Thomas Hoccleve, copyist of his own poetic works and professional clerk of the Privy Seal.[56] My example passage is Book V, lines 7373–99 (fol. 83v). Scribe E observes the use of the weak adjective ("hir grete wordes," line 7385). He drops the *-e* when the weak adjective already has two syllables ("hir wrongful dedes," line 7386). He uses the infinitive in *-e* where a syllable is needed and there is no danger of elision ("mighte," line 7382). As is the case with the other scribes, his *-e* is ambiguous however: sometimes it must be pronounced ("more," line 7379, "bothe," line 7380), but on other occasions it must not ("thoughte," line 7377).

Despite the likelihood that the five Trinity Gower scribes were working independently of one another, they all display awareness of a distinction between variants that are necessary to the meter and those which are not. It is this distinction which, arguably, drives their preservation of Gowerian forms and their production of literatim output, not a sense of the authority of Gowerian language. We have also seen that the search for a solution to the problems of encoding and transmitting syllabic meter was a dynamic process in which scribes engaged. Their spelling helps the reader, but it is not always enough: on many occasions readers must work out the meter of the line for themselves. The scribes and their employers must have all been familiar with this process and its limitations. These characteristics are not confined to the Trinity manuscript but are also found in the Fairfax manuscript, Bodley 902, Bodley 294, and Bodley 693.

---

[54] Macaulay, Introduction to *The English Works*, I, clv.
[55] Macaulay believed that this hand and Scribe C were the same person (Introduction to *The English Works*, I, cliv).
[56] Doyle and Parkes, "The Production of Copies," 182–85.

Literatim *Confessio* Scribes' Non-Gower Outputs

In the final section of my analysis I propose to return to the problem of whether Gower manuscripts are somehow different from manuscripts of the other major contemporary Middle English authors. How far was knowledge of this scribal practice shared? Can we link it with outputs in other contemporary literary manuscripts? Space limitations preclude anything more than a brief outline of some avenues for investigation; I will illustrate some of these with reference to the non-Gower Middle English outputs of Trinity Gower Scribe D and Trinity Gower Scribe E.

As noted earlier, Scribe E has been identified as the poet Hoccleve. This scribe's understanding of and principles regarding the encoding of syllabic verse are deducible from the copies he made of his own poetry. Judith Jefferson has examined Hoccleve's holographs to determine his metrical practice, concluding that his lines are decasyllabic but perhaps not iambic pentameters.[57] Jefferson's analysis however also provides data for the system that Hoccleve uses to *encode* decasyllabic meter. Burrow summarizes the rules succinctly: Hoccleve's autographs do not contain "merely orthographic *e*'s;" they are always to be pronounced except where elided, and "Hoccleve does his best to represent [...] optional deletions in his written forms [...] 'mamende' for 'me amende' [...] 'theffect' for 'the effect'."[58] Hoccleve's holographs sometimes carry corrections that repair syllable count, change rhythms and improve rhymes. His corrections draw on linguistic variants, for example, the deletion of "þat" in phrases such as *after that* where it is superfluous.[59] By contrast, according to Burrow the earliest scribal copy of the *Series*, Oxford, Bodleian Library, MS Selden supra 53, "fails the syllable test in 231 out of 574 lines."[60] Burrow notes that "in the majority of the mismetred lines [...] the Selden scribe could claim to have written the same words as in the original, though in a different form [...] yet such formal manifestations of the 'gret diversite in English and in writyng of oure tonge', though they do not affect sense, can disturb metre just as much as do substantive variants," suggesting that this shows us "scribal mismetring in action."[61] But perhaps we should not too hastily assume that poets are sensitive to meter and innovate in the writing down of poetry while scribes are not and do not. Hoccleve the poet who corrects

---

[57] Judith Jefferson, "The Hoccleve Holographs and Hoccleve's Metrical Practice," in *Manuscripts and Texts: Editorial Problems in Later Middle English Literature*, ed. Derek A. Pearsall (Cambridge: D. S. Brewer, 1987), 95–109 (109).
[58] John Burrow, "Scribal Mismetring," in *Middle English Poetry: Texts and Traditions: Essays in Honour of Derek Pearsall*, ed. Alastair J. Minnis (York: York Medieval Press, 2001), 169–79 (171).
[59] Wakelin, *Scribal Correction and Literary Craft*, 293.
[60] Burrow, "Scribal Mismetring," 172.
[61] Burrow, "Scribal Mismetring," 173, 175.

his holographs is also (if the identification of the hand is correct) Hoccleve the scribe who copied part of the *Confessio* with skillful attention to meter and who in his manuscripts of his own poetry tries to improve the encoding of syllabic Middle English verse.

Scribe D, too, has a reputation for being interested in encoding the meter of poets other than Gower. Horobin observes that variants in his *Canterbury Tales* in Harley 7334 (a famously metrically smooth text) "could represent attempts to restore [metrical] regularity," though he is skeptical about scribes' ability to understand meter.[62] Kerby-Fulton suggests that Scribe D's interventions in the *Canterbury Tales* in Harley 7334 show that he was "counting syllables," suggesting that perhaps "he derived his severity about syllable count in the accentual-syllabic line from Gower who is equally severe."[63] Solopova is prepared to go even further, suggesting that metrical smoothing in the manuscript is associated with the imposition of a spelling system and morphology designed to encode the meter unambiguously. She argues that "on the whole the scribe intended all the vowels he spelt to be pronounced."[64] In one of her examples, the Hengwrt manuscript reads "A frere wol entremette hym euermo," while Harley 7334 drops the two instances of superfluous and ambiguous final *-e*, reading "frer wil" and "entremet him." Like Scribe E, Scribe D appears to be seeking to find ways that other syllabic poetry, not simply that of Gower, can be encoded and transmitted without ambiguity or damage to the meter.

Conclusion

In this essay I have proposed a new way of thinking about Gower's literatim scribes. I have suggested that the analysis of Gower's text as a dialectal *Mischsprache* that is copied literatim by its scribes requires revision. The text of the *Confessio* is not just a *Mischsprache* in that it combines dialect variants. It also mixes together many other examples of linguistic variant, both orthographic and morphological. This high degree of linguistic variation is integral to the new kind of syllabic meter that the *Confessio* uses. Scribes already had available a tradition of observing dialect variation in the literatim copying of rhyme in traditional Middle English verse, but this practice had to be intensified and developed to meet the demands of syllabic meters. Preserving the traditional Gowerian dialect forms was but a by-product of this practice. The best scribes developed, and continued to think about, ways of encoding syllable counts unambiguously, and could

---

[62] Horobin, *The Language of the Chaucer Tradition*, 108–09.
[63] Kerby-Fulton, "'Langland in his Working Clothes'?," 146.
[64] Elizabeth Solopova, "Chaucer's Metre and Scribal Editing in the Early Manuscripts of the *Canterbury Tales*," *The Canterbury Tales Project Occasional Papers* 2 (1997): 143–64 (151).

distinguish between places where literatim reproduction of variants was required and places where it was unnecessary. The *Confessio* manuscripts are witness to a dynamic process in which scribes engage in trying to improve their outputs. But this process was not confined to copies of Gower: manuscripts of other authors also testify to it. It looks as if certain, perhaps networked, scribes who copied Middle English authors in London were engaged in this process. Whether they were alone, or whether others too – perhaps elsewhere – tried to find solutions to the problem of syllabic meter remains to be investigated.[65]

---

[65] I am investigating other traditions of copying verse as part of the project cited in n. 1.

CHAPTER 2

LOOKING FOR RICHARD: FINDING "MORAL GOWER" IN OXFORD, BODLEIAN LIBRARY, MS HATTON 92

Stephanie L. Batkie

WHENCE "MORAL GOWER"? WE have, of course, the (in)famous dedicatory lines of Chaucer's *Troilus and Criseyde*:

> O moral Gower, this book I directe
> To the and to the, philosophical Strode,
> To vouchen sauf, ther need is, to correcte,
> Of youre benignities and zeles good. (V.1856–69)[1]

We also have the numerous critical accounts, both documentary and deconstructive, that have addressed the ramifications and durability of the epithet in scholarly conversations about Gower and his writings.[2] I, however, would like to place this persistent label not in the work of Gower's friend, nor in Gower's corpus directly, but in the rather less exalted pages of MS Hatton 92. The manuscript is of note to Gower scholars inasmuch as it contains a copy of the *Cronica Tripertita* (the Z-text), which, as an early witness to the poem, serves as the base manuscript for the most recent edition of the text, edited by David Carlson.[3] MS Hatton 92 is an eclectic compilation, including

---

[1] Geoffrey Chaucer, *The Riverside Chaucer*, ed. Larry D. Benson, et al., 3rd ed. (Boston: Houghton Mifflin, 1986).
[2] For versions of each approach, see (as two out of many examples): R. F. Yeager, "'O Moral Gower': Chaucer's Dedication of *Troilus and Criseyde*," *The Chaucer Review* 19, no. 2 (1984): 87–99, and Diane Watt, *Amoral Gower: Language, Sex, and Politics* (Minneapolis: University of Minnesota Press, 2003).
[3] John Gower, *Poems on Contemporary Events: The Visio Anglie (1381) and Cronica Tripertita (1400)*, ed. David R. Carlson, trans. A. G. Rigg (Toronto: Pontifical Institute of Mediaeval Studies, 2011). For Carlson's proposed stemma for the *Cronica* manuscripts, see David R. Carlson, "Gower on Henry IV's Rule: The Endings of the *Cronica Tripertita* and Its Texts," *Traditio* 62 (2007): 207–36. An alternate stemma, based on scribal rather than revision patterns, is offered by Parkes: "Patterns of Scribal Activity and Revisions of the Text in Early Copies of

the condemnation of a rare English heresy concerning Mary Salome and the *Trinubium Annae*, a series of epistles and verses exchanged between two church officials regarding said heresy, two moralized excerpts from Ovid in prose and verse, axioms on a range of moral subjects, a collection of Latin metrical proverbs, a series of fables and parables from an array of authors, and a copy of the statutes of an unnamed Bishop of Winchester. Among these we also find Gower's versified account of the last days of Richard's reign, coupled with several of his shorter Latin poems ("H. aquile pullus," "O recolende," "Rex celi deus," and a fragment of "Quicquid homo scribat").[4] The manuscript does not contain the *Vox Clamantis*, as MS Hatton 92 is the only extant version of the *Cronica* that survives decoupled from Gower's longer Latin work. The presence of Gower's unaccompanied poem in this miscellany is something of an unexpected one, and while some effort has been made to streamline the transition between the *Cronica* and the surrounding materials, the difference between the verse-chronicle and its neighbors is striking. Moreover, as the manuscript as a whole is written in a series of highly abbreviated fifteenth-century hands, on parchment that has been well-used, and with binding effects that seem opportunistic rather than intentional, the physical object of MS Hatton 92 does not inspire one with a sense of unity and interpretive purpose, nor does it give a sense of a complete and completed text.[5]

But it is nevertheless here where I would like to locate the specter of "moral Gower," and I do so for several reasons. The relationship between the *Cronica* and the *Vox* is one that, while understudied, nevertheless poses a raft of questions for readers of Gower's Latin. If, for example, we read the *Vox* as examining the estates from an impossible and shifting point of reference, in which no one place, not even the stance of the author, is free from critique, then the *Cronica* deepens this question while raising the

---

Works by John Gower," in *New Science out of Old Books: Manuscripts and Early Printed Books, Essays in Honour of A. I. Doyle*, ed. Richard Beadle and A. J. Piper (London: Scolar Press, 1995), 81–121.

[4] The portion of *Quicquid homo scribat* is the same as the Trentham version of the poem (lines 9–12) rather than what we see in the two other versions found elsewhere (manuscripts C, H, G, and S). For the complete text of all three versions, see *John Gower: The Minor Latin Works*, ed. and trans. R. F. Yeager (Kalamazoo, MI: Medieval Institute Press, 2005), 46. A fuller description of the content of MS Hatton 92 can be found in the *Summary Catalogue* for the Bodleian Library, entry no. 4073. See also Macaulay's description in the preface to his edition of Gower's Latin works: *The Complete Works of John Gower*, ed. G. C. Macaulay, 4 vols., IV (Oxford: Clarendon Press, 1899–1902).

[5] The manuscript is compiled from a fifteenth-century manuscript and a thirteenth-century manuscript. The first part comprises all of the texts apart from the statutes, which appear at the end of the compilation on parchment that is slightly smaller in size. The bulk of the manuscript contains several scribal hands. The *Cronica* includes two of these, one for the main text, and another for the marginal notes and the first folio of the Prologue (see below).

stakes for its answer.[6] Implicit in the jointure of the two texts is the question of what "ground" the nobility, or Parliament for that matter, stands upon in relation to a king they believe to be descending into tyranny. In a similar fashion, the interactions between the speaking "I" and his subject matter are often shifting and unstable – he appears at once to be an eyewitness, a dreamer, a chronicler, an allegorist, and a subject.[7] The poem is thus also an experiment in legal precedent, making a case for extraordinary action taken on both the part of the crown and the Lords Appellant. It couches its criticism of Richard in elevated and moralistic terms, but its relationship to Parliamentary sources is complex, careful, and deeply invested in questions of narrative, temporal structure, and legal standing.[8] Furthermore, the structure of the poem itself, written in disyllabic Leonines, speaks to a shift in Gower's approach to language from his earlier Latin efforts. David Carlson has termed the style of the poem "unparalleled," "original," and "highly mannered," noting that "Gower sustained what was for others fundamentally a lyric style over the course of lengthy historical ennarration."[9] An experiment in form, style, legal argument, and political critique, then, the

---

[6] Here, we might think of the famous images of Gower *qua* archer, shooting his arrows at the globe from an undefined and even ungrounded position.

[7] This is a large topic, and beyond the scope of this essay. To take an example: Andrew Galloway has questioned Gower's use of the dream-vision genre in the *Visio* (Book 1 in most manuscripts of the *Vox Clamantis*), expanding the reading of the text beyond a simple allegorical representation of the uprising, focussing instead on the status of the dreamer-narrator and his own moral and authorial standing. Following suit, Ian Cornelius has recently argued that "No longer an archer who takes aim at immorality from afar, the poet now impersonates it. He becomes an 'implicated speaking presence,' present within and compromised by the secular happenings he narrates." Both readings productively complicate the way we should read the idea of exemplarity and authorship in the form, and in Gower's works at large. The same work might also be performed for the *Cronica*'s relationship to the *Vox*, as well as for the position of its narrator. Galloway, "Reassessing Gower's Dream Visions," in *John Gower, Trilingual Poet: Language, Translation, and Tradition*, ed. Elisabeth Dutton, John Hines, and R. F. Yeager (Cambridge, UK: D. S. Brewer, 2010), 288–303; Cornelius, "Gower and the Peasants' Revolt," *Representations* 131 (2015): 22–51, quote at 27.

[8] For a thorough exploration of the relationship between the two sources, see David R. Carlson, "The Parliamentary Source of Gower's *Cronica Tripertita* and Incommensurable Styles," in *John Gower, Trilingual Poet*, ed. Dutton, Hines, and Yeager, 98–111. For the Record and Process itself, see *The Deposition of Richard II: The Record and Process of the Renunciation and Deposition of Richard II and Related Writings*, ed. David R. Carlson (Toronto: Pontifical Institute of Medieval Studies, 2007).

[9] Carlson, "Incommensurable Styles," 98. For an argument about the *Vox*'s stylistic tendencies as designed to speak to a wider public readership, see David R. Carlson, "The Invention of the Anglo-Latin Public Poetry (circa 1367–1402) and Its Prosody, Especially in John Gower," *Mittellateinisches Jahrbuch* 39 (2004): 3984–06.

Cronica is rife with complexities and interest, both inside and outside of Gower studies.

Yet the other (and perhaps more familiar) mode in which to read the text is to bypass these complexities and adopt a resolutely exemplaric eye: the abstract critiques of the *Vox* are enacted and made temporal and specific in the *Cronica*'s account of Richard's final years. In this reading, the poem becomes akin to a fable, an *historia* that asks us to see precepts of moral or ethical action in narrative forms. This is the mode, I will argue, in which the scribes and readers of MS Hatton 92 approached the text, and its inclusion in the manuscript speaks to their interest in emphasizing an exemplaric hermeneutic, both in the poem's treatment in the collection and in the material conditions of the manuscript as a whole. As the primary text in the manuscript concerned with political events rather than religious doctrines or moralizing aphorisms, the problem of the *Cronica* in MS Hatton 92 is the problem of how the historical reads against the allegorized truths of classical voices or the wisdom of ecclesiastical officials, not Gower's more polyvalent approach to political commentary. The text's performance of heraldic personification offers one potential bridge to other texts in the manuscript, but such formal considerations do not satisfactorily explain the presence of real, and relatively recent, political figures in an assemblage which seems to focus its primary attention on a trans-historical perspective. If, however, we read the poem's presence in MS Hatton 92 compilationally, following Arthur Bahr's example for others of Gower's texts, we find a scribal approach to historical events and the reading thereof that resonates with the strongly exemplaric and moralizing agenda of the collection as a whole.[10] With this perspective in mind, I argue that MS Hatton 92 offers us perhaps the clearest picture of "moral Gower" we have. The manuscript, as we shall see, structures a precise set of interpretive priorities for the text involving authority and exemplaric reading, while occluding others concerned with the nature of political critique. As a result, MS Hatton 92 supplies a particular picture of what exactly it means to read "moral Gower," and allows us to question our own priorities when it comes to his Latin work.

***

To begin, a metaphor. As a material object, the *Cronica* of MS Hatton 92 is marked by incompleteness. The text of the poem is reproduced without

---

[10] See, specifically, Bahr's attentive reading of the Trentham Manuscript (now London, British Library, MS Additional 59495). "I define *compilation*, not as an objective quality of either texts or objects, but rather as a mode of perceiving such forms so as to disclose an interpretably meaningful arrangement, thereby bringing into being a text/work that is more than the sum of its parts." *Fragments and Assemblages: Forming Compilations of Medieval London* (Chicago: University of Chicago Press, 2013), 3.

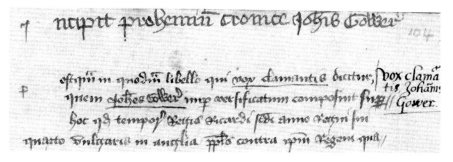

FIGURE 2.1. Detail of Hatton 92 fol. 104r, reprinted with permission of The Bodleian Libraries, University of Oxford.

overt omissions and in a clear hand, but the pages also present readers with an unfinished project of illumination and decoration in a fashion not uncommon among similar manuscripts. At the head of each new section of the poem, or every thirty lines or so, we are confronted with a small, square space that has been left empty, anticipating future decoration. Within the resulting gap hangs a ghostly letter, the first of the following word, as a place-holder for the unfinished design which would presumably both elevate the visual appeal of the manuscript and offer readers a guide to the text by creating verse divisions for the unfolding action of the poem (see Figure 2.1). Due to this planned (but incomplete) illumination program, each of the faint, abandoned guide-letters appears detached from the word it is intended to introduce; it floats free of the text of which it would otherwise be a part. At the same time, the small, still-visible letters nevertheless ground the encircling empty space, thus creating within each small square an overlay of both absence and possibility. We feel the lack of the projected decoration as well as the imagined prospect of its presence.

These present but absent capitals offer a compelling representation of the larger gaps that open in the text when we consider its place in this particular manuscript. Even though the embellished letters are absent, we are made aware of their trace by the empty space they would occupy and the ghostly place-holders that have been left behind. In the same way, we might think of the unexpected presence of the political within the otherwise moralistic compilation, and consider how the inclusion of Gower's historical reporting makes felt the tenuous links between his poem and the works that surround it. On the one hand, much of the manuscript (apart from the opening text on the Salomitic heresy) spends its energy on universal truths culled from aphoristic sayings and Ovidian commentary. On the other, Gower's pointed political commentary, populated as it is by figures both named and allegorically figured, is marked by its attention to specific events unfolding in measurable time and space. This shift from inclusive truths to time-bound chronicle therefore opens a political space in the manuscript that is present, but which is also marked (like the capitals in the *Cronica*) by a kind of

37

absence in its immediate textual surroundings; the surrounding folios are more interested in maxims like, "Pride has many daughters: suffocate the mother and you will have no daughters" (fol. 132^v), or in allegorized readings of fables and tales than in temporal, political critique.

The *Cronica* itself raises and negotiates these same questions of absence and presence, of history and exemplum. If MS Hatton 92's inclusion of the *Cronica* feels odd to readers, it is in large part because we are used to encountering the poem as physically connected to the *Vox*, and therefore as part of Gower's wider political vision. The question as to why Richard's deposition and downfall comes hard on the heels of the *Vox*'s larger commentary in the first place is the question of how to read the presentation of particular, historical events within an otherwise devotional or moralizing mien. The question as to why MS Hatton 92 includes the *Cronica* is much the same.

The opening of the poem spans one of the manuscript's openings, with the initial section of the prologue appearing on folio 103^v and the other on folio 104^r. At the top of the second page, two pieces of marginal material have been added by later readers. The first, written in a sixteenth-century hand, spans the top of the page and reads, "Incipit prohemium Cronice Iohannis Gower" [Here begins the preface of the Chronicle of John Gower]. In essence, this note repeats an earlier appearance of Gower's name, added by the same reader as part of the text at the bottom of the previous folio, which reads "Incipit cronica Johannis Gower de tempore Regis Ricardi secondi vsque ad secundum annum Henrici quarti" [Here begins the chronicle of John Gower concerning the time of King Richard the Second up to the second year of Henry the Fourth.][11] The second piece is a marginal note written in another Early Modern script in the right-hand margin, directly next to the opening lines of the prologue: "Vox clamantis Johannis Gower" [The crying voice of John Gower]. To supplement all of this, it appears that the same hand responsible for the "Vox clamantis" note has also underlined "vox clamantis" and "Iohannis Gower" in the prologue text itself.[12]

The author's name is therefore highlighted three separate times at the outset of the poem by later readers of the text. But more urgently, the briefer "Vox clamantis Johannis Gower" side-note also brings the ghost of the absent *Vox* into the *Cronica*'s opening lines. The immediate suggestion is to read this emendation as a titular reference to the missing *Vox*, reinforcing the origin of the accompanying *Cronica* text, which appears much as it does elsewhere, beginning with "Postquam in quodam libello qui vox clamantis

---

[11] N.B. This inclusion only appears in Hatton 92, not in the other copies of the *Cronica* that appear alongside the *Vox Clamantis*.

[12] This hand belongs to a fairly active reader of at least pieces of the manuscript. Similar name-based annotations and correlating underlining occur throughout the Salomite material: fols 4^v, 10^v, 15^r, 15^v, 27^r, 30^v, 31^v, 32^r, 32^v, and 37^r. There is also a marginal "3" in the *Cronica* (fol. 114^v) indicating the beginning of the third section of the poem that may also be the work of the same annotator.

dicitur quem Iohannis Gower nuper versificatum composuit..." [After in which little book which is called *Vox Clamantis* that John Gower recently composed in verse...] But to encounter this note absent the *Vox* itself is to experience a kind of textual disorientation, in which we start to hear things which are not there. The "disembodied *Vox*" of the note conjures a relationship between the two texts, but the manuscript as a whole does not facilitate the same. How, then, are we to take this reference to a text that most readers of this particular iteration of the poem did not have access to, even if the original scribe likely did?[13]

Like the guide-letters in MS Hatton 92, the political present is located in the *Cronica*, but is also not-yet-present in the *Vox*; the longer poem paradoxically looks forward to and makes space for Richard *qua* tyrant, but it does so only after the fact, once the *Cronica* is already in place.[14] To take a small example, throughout the *Cronica*, Richard is described as erratic, sliding, and deceitful. These are the precise terms with which Fortune is extensively described in Book 2 of the *Vox*, wherein Gower excoriates her for her untrustworthy behavior, setting the stage for his corrective vision of the various estates to which the poem will attend. Fortune is "inconstans animi" [inconstant of soul] (*VC* 2.94), she has an "aspectum duplum" [double face] (*VC* 2.103), and "leues oculi sint ictus" [the glance of her eye is

---

[13] N.B. It is unlikely that the annotator of the "Vox Clamantis" note is confused as to the title of the text itself; the lines to which the annotation is connected are those describing how the completed poem entitled "Vox clamantis" was written prior to the chronicle which is about to unfold. The passage follows a common "then...now" pattern familiar elsewhere in Gower's Latin writings: "Postquam in quodam libello qui vox clamantis dicitur quem Iohannis Gower nuper versificatum composuit [...] iam in hac presenti cronica, que tripertita est..." This same annotator is also (as previously mentioned) responsible for the note at the bottom of the previous folio, which reads "Incipit cronica Johannis Gower de tempore Regis Ricardi secondi..." This earlier note suggests that the reader is, at the very least, clear about the difference between the two poems.

[14] For the moment, I am excluding the *Visio* from this analysis. It is worth noting, however, that the only extant version of the *Vox* without the *Visio* (Oxford, Bodleian Library, MS Laud 719) also does not contain the *Cronica*. It is also important to recognize that the letter to the king in Book 6 of the *Vox* is the primary way Richard is present in the longer poem, but the structure of this section is quite different from what we see in the *Cronica*. Rather than read the boy-king Richard as an exemplum in the *Vox*, we are encouraged to see these sections of Book 6 as a mirror for princes – an arguably different form than what we see in the later text. Richard is addressed directly in the *Vox*, but there are few moments of specificity apart from discussing his age – the advice is political, but not necessarily historical. Exemplary rulers abound in the section (Saul, Hector, Alexander, David, etc.), but are used as instruction in their own right. For more on the relationship between the *fürstenspiegel* tradition and exemplarity, see Larry Scanlon, *Narrative, Authority, and Power: The Medieval Exemplum and the Chaucerian Tradition* (Cambridge, UK: Cambridge University Press, 1994), 81–134.

fickle] (*VC* 2.111) – all qualities Richard too possesses in Gower's account.[15] Moreover, as things go from bad to worse in the *Cronica* and Richard starts eliminating Appellant Lords, we are brought back to the (un)fortunate language from the beginning chapters of the *Vox*:

> O quam fortuna stabilis non permanet vna
> Exemplum cuius stat in ordine carminis huius
> Rex agit... (*CTr* 2.29–31)
>
> [O! How fortune remains steadfast in not a single place.
> An example of this stands in the course of this song:
> The king acted...]

We should certainly read the *Cronica*'s references to Fortune and to duplicity in granting or rescinding worldly favors in light of similar descriptors in the *Vox*, drawing together the extensive complaints against fickle Fortune in the *Vox* and a monarch who has seemingly abandoned right rule in the *Cronica*. But I would also argue that once we encounter Richard's characterization it becomes difficult not to read Fortune's description in the earlier poem in light of Richard's manifestation in the latter. The two characterizations collapse into one another, strengthening the relationship between the moral imperatives that populate the *Vox* and Gower's reading of the proximate political events of his chronicle. If, then, we are to read in an exemplaric mode, it is not just that we should see Fortune in the figure of Richard, but that we begin to see the anticipation of Richard in the personification of Fortune.[16]

Reading across the jointure between the poems in this way, we find that the presence of the *Cronica* necessarily changes the conditions of signification the *Vox* establishes for the later poem. Without the *Cronica* (or, by extension, without the *Visio*), the *Vox* is a different text, and in those manuscripts in which both *Cronica* and *Vox* are visible, the political critique of the *Cronica* is anticipated and made possible within the form of the *Vox*'s

---

[15] All quotations from the *Vox Clamantis* taken from Macaulay's edition, *The Complete Works of John Gower*, IV.

[16] In another example, in the *Vox* Gower complains (in a relatively rare use of the first person) of corrupt priests: "Hij gestant celi claues. intrant nec et ipsi/ Nos nec inire sinunt quos sine lege regunt/ Nec populi mentes doctrine vomere sulcant" [They bear the keys of heaven, but they enter not;/ Ruling without law, they grant us no entry,/ Neither do they till people's minds with doctrine's plough] (*VC* 3.1053–55). The same "ruling without law" echoes a similar complaint against Richard at *CTr* 2.235–37: "Non satis est regem mundi deflectere legem/ Vt periant gentes sub eo sine lege manentes/ Sed magis in Christum seuit..." [It is not enough that the king might bend worldly law/ Such that the people, enduring underneath him, might perish without the law--/ But he raged even more against Christ] (fol. 112^v).

universal complaint. In the same fashion, the *Cronica* without the *Vox* is also a different animal – one that presents challenges and opportunities of its own.

MS Hatton 92, of course, embodies those challenges. The question of things present and things absent, things remembered and things reimagined, and things recorded and things repeated fills the opening lines of the *Cronica*; indeed, the poem begins by pointedly establishing a series of strong ties to the *Vox*, and specifically to the upheaval of 1381:

> Ricardi Regis oritur transgressio legis,
> Quo fortuna cadit et humus retrograda vadit
> Quomodo surrexit populus quem non bene rexit
> Tempus adhuc plangit super hoc quod cronica tangit
> Libro testante stat cronica scripta perante
> Est alibi dicta transit nec ab aure relicta
> Audistis mira vulgaris que tulit ira
> Omnibus in villis timuit vir iustus ab illis. (*CTr* I.5–12)

> [The violation was born of King Richard's law,
> Where fortune fell and the earth rushed backwards.
> Just so, the people, who had not been ruled well, rose up.
> Furthermore, the time still laments what this chronicle touches;
> As the book bears witness, the previously written chronicle stands.
> Elsewhere it is spoken – it passed not unheeded by the ear:
> You have heard the astonishing things the common people brought in their wrath;
> In every village, the just man trembled before them.]

The purpose of this passage is to establish a pattern of behavior for Richard, which argues for his unfitness for rule even while acknowledging the terrifying outcomes of his errors, culminating in the bloodshed and destruction we see allegorized in the *Visio Anglie*. The next lines in the *Cronica* continue the theme:

> Rex induratum cor semper habet neque fatum
> Tale remordebat semper mala quin faciebat. (*CTr* I.13–14)

> [The king's heart was always hard, and this misfortune did not
> Disturb him in the least; in fact, always he committed evil deeds.]

The text goes on to describe how Richard continued to accept advice from overly-youthful counsellors and how this leads him to ill-considered and ill-received actions towards his barons, looking forward to the Appellant crisis and, eventually, to the events of 1399. But in so doing, it joins what we are about to read in the *Cronica* to not only the earlier stirrings of unrest but also to Richard's persistent errors as a monarch, making this opening not only a revisitation of earlier causes of political turmoil, but also something of a revision of how we read the violence of 1381. Just as Richard's rule is questionable in 1399, so too was it in 1381, when the people "non bene rexit" [had not been ruled well]. The terrible events (*mira*) of the *Visio* are in no way negated, before which just men legitimately quake with fear (*timuit vir iustus*), but they have a different flavor here. Not unrelenting, mindless horror, but rather a terrifying (if predictable) response to an unfit ruler.

But Gower is careful to cast this revisionist history in light of current events, contextualizing his backward glances by keeping readerly attention focused on the goal at hand: Richard's behavior in the present. In a move that joins his text to other political chronicles and prophecies, Gower opens the poem with a date-riddle, setting the scene for where and when the events are about to take place:

> Tolle caput mundi C ter et sex lustra fer illi
> Et decies quinque cum septem post super adde
> Tempus tale *nota* quia tunc fuit Anglia *mota*
> Dum stat *Commotus* Ricardus amore *remotus*. (*CTr* I.1–4, emphasis mine)[17]

> [Take the head of mundus, bring three Cs and six five-year spans, and to these
> Add five tens with seven more after that –
> *Note* such a time because thereupon was England *moved*,
> When *Tempestuous* Richard stands from love *removed*.]

The answer to the riddle places us in 1387 (M+CCC+30+50+7), and the lines characterize the year by Richard's uneasy temperament.[18] Beyond the date, the opening of the text formally establishes how the chronicle will account for the trials England is about to undergo: Gower asks us as readers to note (*nota*) Richard's instability (*commotus*), which both severs him (*remotus*) from love (either of the people, or from his love for them)

---

[17] N.B. The capitalization of "commotus" in line 4 is found in MS Hatton 92, and I have chosen to represent it here to give the titular impression the term seems to carry for the scribe.

[18] Gower includes a possible bit of wordplay here. In the opening line, a *lustrum* is a five-year timespan, as dictated by the period between Roman census-takings – the beginnings of which were marked by purifying (*lustrum*) sacrifices. However, *lustro* as a verb is also used to describe the coursing of the sun through the signs of the zodiac in Ovid's tale of Philomela (*Met.* 6.571): "Signa deus bis sex acto lustraverat anno" [The god had brightened twice six signs with the year being completed]. In this way, the slippage between the noun-form (*lustrum*) and the possible second-person imperative verb form (*lustra* – the form which the other verbs [*tolle, fer, adde*] take in the passage) offers an echo not just of the riddling found in medieval political writing, but of Gower's favorite classical poet as well. (Ovid translation taken from Bartolo A. Natoli, *Silenced Voices: The Poetics of Speech in Ovid* [Madison: University of Wisconsin Press, 2017], 72.)

and which will lead to turmoil (*mota*) for the country at large. The leonine form highlighted above draws these effects together and underscores the structural nature of the causality Gower accentuates – we cannot talk about England's present troubles without speaking first of Richard's present (but also past) character.

The result of this juxtaposition of 1387 and 1381 complicates how the poem establishes its contexts and content, even as it strengthens connections between the *Visio* and the *Cronica*. The initial date-riddle gives us the distinct impression of being placed, as readers, in a moment of punctual specificity as the imperative verbs of the lines (*tolle, fer, adde*) enliven the chronicle as part of our present experience. We construct the date for ourselves as we read, and we place ourselves in the appointed year as instructed. Just as we get comfortable in this chronicled "present," however, the text shifts back to reminisce about earlier difficulties in Richard's reign, and the verb tenses follow suit. Over the next several lines, the verbs move from the present tense (the times lament, the chronicle touches, the book testifies) to the past (things were said, the just man trembled, you have heard), slipping easily from the one to the other. The hinge between the two fields is the "previously written book" which nevertheless "stands" in the present and, if we look to the dating move at the outset, will move into the future as it relates events that are, as of the first lines of the poem, yet to come. Moreover, this temporal structure is muddied further inasmuch as the poem itself is written after Henry's ascent in 1399, thereby troubling further the relationship between the present-tense verbs used to describe the durability of the book itself with the recently-past events described therein.

This temporal play allows Gower to straddle the bridge between the past and the present as he re-casts earlier events to speak to more recent circumstances, and in so doing it offers a view as to how Gower imagines his writings moving into the future, beyond the pages he inscribes. His book (having been written before) stands now, but it will also, of course, stand in the future, carrying its own present (and present tense) along with it. Much as the language of the opening passage negotiates between present and past in textual terms, it also works between the permanent and the ephemeral, between what remains behind and what disappears in time. We see this most clearly in the use of images (and verbs) of writing and of speech. As above:

> *Tempus adhuc plangit* super hoc quod *cronica tangit*
> *Libro testante stat cronica scripta perante*
> Est *alibi dicta* transit nec *ab aure relicta*
> *Audistis* mira vulgaris que tulit ira
> Omnibus in villis timuit vir iustus ab illis. (*CTr* I.8–12, emphasis mine)

[Furthermore, *the time still laments* what this *chronicle touches*.
As *the book bears witness*, the *previously written chronicle stands*.
Elsewhere it was spoken – it passes *not unheeded by the ear*:

>*You have heard* the astonishing things the common people brought in
>   their wrath;
>In every village, the just man trembled before them.]

As with the present and the past, the line between writing, speech, reading, and audition is a fluid one. Chronicles are written (*scripta*) in (and about) earlier times, and they remain (*stat*) to offer testament (*testante*) in the present. But testimony might be written or spoken, and a deliberately auditory quality is gathered and repeated here: the things which the chronicle reports are spoken (*dicta*) of beyond the province of the pages themselves.[19] Consequently, the way Gower presents this speaking makes it unclear if the people are currently speaking about what he has written, spreading it to others, or if he records what has already been spoken elsewhere (*alibi*), as he so often claims in the *Visio*, the *Vox*, and the *Cronica*. Whichever way we choose to read the line, Gower highlights the volume with which these tidings are received, and he reiterates using the second person verb *audistis* (you will hear) that their aural reception is particularly vigorous and memorable. And so, even though the chronicle touches (*tangit*) on its subject matter in a notably tactile metaphor, it is now the larger times (*tempus*) which cry out (*plangit*) audibly in their distress.[20]

Just as the passage complicates the relationship between what is present and what is looked back upon in the poem, just as 1381 is present here but also remembered and re-imagined by 1387, the juxtaposition of the permanence of text and the ephemeral (but seemingly escalating) resonance of speech defines the parameters by which Gower understands his chronicle form. The opening of the poem toys with the continued presence of news retold and the increasing temporal absence of the events themselves: events are transient, but they leave far more permeant effects in their wake; the wonders themselves have passed, but books and speech about them linger on. Gower finds political moments stretching forward in an unending chain of causality: Richard is an inconstant ruler from his youth, thus his laws inevitably lead to rebellion again and again. Just so, we might look forward to the subsequent effects of his eventual deposition as being similarly unavoidable, even if we do not yet know how they will manifest themselves. In this way, the looking backward at the beginning of this poem is an act of finding and (re)inscribing absent causes that are (re)presented in the light of what we are about to hear, even as that finding persists as an always-present action.

---

[19] We find another unexpected tense-shift here: from the past-tense *dicta* (had been spoken) to the present-tense *transit nec* (does not pass).

[20] To add to this collection of speech, writing, and action, Gower chooses *fero* (*tulit*) to describe the wrathful violence the commons bring to the country. We should certainly take this as "to bring" or "to bear," but we might also hear an echo of "to report" or "to tell" in the choice as well.

This back-and-forth motion similarly structures some of the larger, thematic ligatures between the *Cronica* and the *Vox* as it draws the one into conversation with the other – when both poems are present. The temporal references at the outset encourage readers to move between the two, thereby strengthening exemplary readings that, like the Fortune/Richard connection, create pathways between the reported events of the *Cronica* and the moralizing truths of the estates complaint in the *Vox*. For exemplaric readers, the critiques of the *Vox* stand as a stabilizing heuristic for the *Cronica*, a text which speaks of fleeting things made permanent only through textual or oral repetition: Richard's actions find renewed life in their varied consequences and in memory of them, but they themselves pass quickly away. By contrast, the nature of something like Fortune is (rather paradoxically, in this case) unchanging and eternal. And in this juncture is, I would argue, where we encounter "moral Gower." A reading of this sort casts history as exemplarity, a move familiar to readers of the *Traitié*, which Gower ends with the sentiment "Exemplo veteri poterunt ventura timeri" [We may fear what is to come by the example of what is past],[21] or indeed to readers of the *Vox* itself, which opens with "Scripture veteris capiunt exempla futuri" [The ancient's writings hold the future's examples] (*VC* Pro.1). Past events not only continue causal chains, but they become exempla by which we read history into the present, and the past is useful inasmuch as it makes this causality visible and, perhaps (in the case of a figure like Richard), avoidable. In this, Gower's attention to political pasts is different from the commentaries on Ovidian stories in a manuscript like MS Hatton 92 only in that he offers his commentary as part of the telling rather than as interventions after the fact.

The scribes and readers of MS Hatton 92 take this relationship to heart and capitalize on it in the presentation of the poem, but they must manage to do so without the benefit of the *Vox* itself. The problem with the *Vox*'s absence is that Gower's carefully curated resonances become unmoored in the manuscript inasmuch as references to previously-written chronicles can only induce reflection on the past, not a return to an earlier page. There is no textual grounding to work from here, and any looking back to 1381, for example, must occur without the *Visio* preceding it. Like the missing capitals peppering the text, the space opened by the lack of the other poems makes them paradoxically present in the gap their absence opens. It is at this point where the scribe and subsequent readers of Hatton 92 intervene, stabilizing and underscoring their reading from the outset. They do so in two ways: the first method uses the *Vox* not as a text *per se*, but as an authorizing impulse that lends political authority to the *Cronica*, whereas

---

[21] Line and translation taken from John Gower, *The French Balades*, ed. and trans. R. F. Yeager (Kalamazoo, MI: Medieval Institute Publications, 2011), 32–33.

the second emphasizes exemplaric reading through material intervention in the opening sections of the poem.

In the first place, at least one reader of MS Hatton 92 worked to establish a link between the authoritative voice of the *Vox* and the political complaint of the *Cronica*. To return to the marginal "Vox clamantis" note, we might read this as an instance in which the reader responsible attempts to call up the kinds of conjoined reading between the two texts described above, despite the fact that readers would not have access to those very readings. The other option is that we take the note as calling up not the poem, but rather the *vox* of the *Vox*: what we hear in the *Cronica* is the crying-out of John Gower, drawing his presence into the text as a form of prophetic, political complaint. In this reading, the note makes present a voice rather than denotes the lack of a physical text. In the way that an annotation above the second moralized Ovid, to take one example, places "John of Garland" (fol. 70^v) as a heading for the commentary that follows (Garland's own *Integumenta* on Ovid), the note at the beginning of the *Cronica* performs a corresponding identifying and authorizing function.[22] A similar phenomenon is also found in a series of *sententiae,* which are presented in the manuscript with careful rubrications giving the purported authors' names neatly arranged in the margin adjacent to each individual maxim (fol. 132^r–140^v).[23] Alternatively, in the pages just following the *Cronica* appear a series of aphorisms on love, which are indexed in the margins according to what topic each passage addresses (On wrath, On consolation, etc.) (fol. 125^v–131^v).[24] Following this pattern, the marginal *vox clamantis* (rather than the *Vox Clamantis*) becomes an epithet, characterizing Gower's authoritative, speaking form rather than his other, materially-absent work.

We cannot know if the reader responsible for the "Vox clamantis" note was familiar with the *Vox*, or if he made the note only as a reference to Gower's arguably better-known Latin work. As such, we cannot know for certain if he is drawing on the links between the two poems discussed above, or if he simply means to conjure the kind of voice responsible for a poem like the *Vox* as part of his understanding of the complaints of the *Cronica*. But for this later reader, the opening of the *Cronica*, Gower's previous work on the *Vox*, and the multiple mentions of Gower's name in the first folios of the poem establish Gower's voice as embodying *auctoritas*, much in the way Maurice appears in his treatment of the Salomites, or as does the

---

[22] Unlike the marginal annotations of the *Cronica*'s opening folios, this note is scribal, in the same hand as the Ovidian text and commentary. Moreover, this section of the manuscript is in a different hand from that responsible for the Gower texts, or its corresponding annotations.

[23] As with the Ovidian material, these rubrications are scribal, and in a different hand from either the Ovid or the Gower pieces.

[24] Another instance of scribal (rather than readerly) annotation, in a hand that does not correlate to any of the other examples given above.

classicizing wisdom of Ovid, as does the patristic authority of the Church Fathers.[25] As previously mentioned, the note is accompanied by underlining in the text that corresponds to the annotation itself: the reader has marked out "vox clamantis" and "Iohannes Gower" in the same ink as his marginal emendation, echoing the two phrases in the order in which they appear in the original lines.

Gower's text has two scribal hands in evidence: one for the verses of the poem itself, and another for the authorial annotations explaining the heraldic allegory. Whereas the scribal program of these two hands records John Gower as the author of the present work several times over in the first few pages of the manuscript, the later, readerly note re-inserts the missing *Vox* into the manuscript in a more visible manner. The note and the underlining indicate that, at least for one reader, the connection between the two texts was meaningful, even if the *Vox* only exists as a trace or, more accurately, as a form of political voicing that remains present in the poem which follows. As a stabilizing technique, the note figures Gower as the voice of complaint, authorizing his reporting of the *Cronica*'s events by calling to mind the kind of critique associated with him. It is a legitimizing move, and one that contextualizes the events of the poem through the lens of political commentary. But, absent the *Vox* in the manuscript, its primary effect is to emphasize the authoritative persona the note-taker associates with the crying-out voice of the *Vox* rather than any deliberate connection to the specifics of the text itself. The annotator calls up Gower as an acknowledged, authorizing presence, aligning him with the other masterful voices the manuscript valorizes in its rubrications, arrangement, and marginal notes.

While this question of authority is likely one both original scribes were also attentive to, their strategy for managing the absent *Vox* takes a different shape from that of the reader-annotator. Rather than shoring up any accrediting claim of an author-persona the missing poem might call

---

[25] Maurice in particular makes his case against the heretics he condemns through his learned knowledge of Hebrew, and he offers a detailed linguistic analysis of the differences in stress patterns of pronunciations of Salome's name. He presents himself as an eminent authority on the subject, and his case depends on a mixture of academic performance and invective. See the analysis provided by M. R. James, who agrees with Maurice's arguments, even though he laments the manner with which he presents them. "Indubitably Prior Maurice was on the side of truth and common sense: the Salomite position was totally indefensible [...]. But so disastrous a writer is he that one almost wishes he had been in the wrong. The prolixity and above all the repetitiousness in which he indulges makes the transcriber's spirit faint within him. He is fairly obsessed with Salome and with the depravity of those who err on the subject, and he would have been a bold man who ventured into Maurice's presence even to breathe her name." "The Salomites," *Journal of Theological Studies* 35 (1934): 290–91. See also note 12 above for the "Vox clamantis" reader's interest in the *Cronica* and Maurice's writings.

into question, the scribal program used for the *Cronica* seeks to construct an "appropriate" framework for readers approaching the beginning of the text.[26] Rather than concerning themselves with epithets, they rather encourage and foreground the exemplary nature of the *Cronica*, establishing the grounds by which we should interpret the events depicted absent the fulsome critique of the *Vox*'s estates complaint. Jean-Pascal Pouzet notes that the prologue to the text seems to have been added to the blank pages preceding the *Cronica,* presumably in an attempt to fit it more elegantly into the rest of the manuscript.[27] Such a move is in keeping with the material history of the collection: much of the exemplary material – the Aesopic tales, the moralized fables, a tale of Balaam and Josaphat – are found at the ends of gatherings, indicating that they are later emendations to the original composition of the manuscript.[28] Like these, the prologue texts to the *Cronica* seem to also be the result of a scribe attempting to both ease the way into the text and to tie it to the exemplary focus the manuscript developed over its compilation.

More than the fact of its placement in the gatherings of the manuscript, the *Cronica*'s prologue is noteworthy in that it is constructed from re-ordered pieces of the opening to the text we find represented in All Souls 98 (among others), the manuscript Macaulay uses as the base text for his edition of Gower's Latin corpus. In the All Souls manuscript, the *Cronica* and the *Vox* are linked by four elements, all of which also appear in MS Hatton 92: 1) a prose passage outlining what events the subsequent chronicle will treat upon and which moves us from the *Vox* to the later events of the *Cronica*, 2) a verse description of the tripartite nature of the poem's *ordinatio*, 3) a marginal prose note that expands upon the role of divine judgment in bringing about the events in question, with an emphasis on the tripled structure, and finally 4) the opening lines of the poem itself, along with the opening action of the narrative.

---

[26] It is worth noting that the program of authorial attribution discussed here, though clearly something the manuscript as a whole is interested in, is specific to the two main scribes of Gower's poem. It appears that the scribe of the main text and the scribe of the annotations were working close to the same time, with the annotations added after the main text was completed. With that said, the manuscript as a whole seems to have been assembled from several different sources and contains multiple hands – none of which could be said to be responsible for the entirety of the texts included in the collection.

[27] Jean-Pascal Pouzet, "Southwark Gower: Augustinian Agencies in Gower's Manuscripts and Texts – Some Prolegomena," in *John Gower, Trilingual Poet*, ed. Dutton, Hines, and Yeager, 11–24, at 20.

[28] These additions appear to have all been added at the same time by the same scribe, who does not appear to be the same as the scribes responsible for the *Cronica*. Apart from the possible inclusion of the thirteenth-century statutes at the end of the manuscript, they are likely some of the latest additions to the miscellany.

Each of these sections finds a place in MS Hatton 92 but in a different arrangement. In fact, apart from the fact that each ends, as we might expect, with the beginning lines of the poem, the MS Hatton 92 passages appear in the inverse order from that we find in MS All Souls 98: the marginal note (the third item, above) comes first, included as a prose text that begins at the top of the folio, followed by the verse description of the poem (the second item) and finally the longer, historical explanation in prose (the first item).

Prologue arrangement by text

All Souls 98 (S-text)
1) prose outline of the chronicled events
2) tripartite structure described in verse
3) marginal prose note on divine judgment
4) opening of the poem

Hatton 92 (Z-text)
1) marginal prose note on divine judgment (no longer in the margin)
2) tripartite structure described in verse 2a) *additional note identifying Gower as the author of the chronicle (see above)*
3) prose outline of the chronicled events
4) opening of the poem

If we consider the function of each textual unit, the All Souls manuscript opens with a section dedicated principally to the chronicle form. The prose outline marks temporal incidents and the names of critical characters as structuring elements of both this passage as well as the poem to come. We read about the events "tempore regis Ricardi secondi anno regni sui quarti" [in the time of Richard II, in the fourth year of his reign], and "anno eiusdem regis decimo" [in the tenth year of that same king]. The passage refers to itself as a *cronica* twice, and pointedly names the Duke of Gloucester and the Earls of Arundel and Warwick, along with the heraldic designations (the swan, the horse, and the bear) by which they will be known in the main text. In so doing, it signals the shift from the political complaint of the *Vox* into the historical narrative of the *Cronica*, with the clear assertion that the chronicle-form will be structured by temporal action and defined, named figures.

By contrast, the poem's arrangement in MS Hatton 92 favors exemplarity over chronicle, inasmuch as the scribes open the text with a nod to the tripartite heuristic the poem will employ, articulating the complaints Gower will level against the crown and his sorrow over the lamentable end of the Appellant Lords in light of a larger, moralized reading. The text opens with what is initially a marginal note in S, promoting it to text in its own right. In the All Souls manuscript, the note begins in the right-hand margin of the page (fol. 116^r), but rapidly sprawls beneath it, its final two lines extending all the way across the page to the left-hand margin, even with the beginnings of the rest of the text. The hand is small, clearly distinguishing itself as marginal, but the note forcefully intrudes upon the body of the verse, appearing as a visual divider between the brief prose prologue and the beginning of Part 1 of the text, which itself is defined further by a large capital. In MS Hatton 92, the text appears without distinction, simply serving as the opening of the work:

> *Opus humanum* est inquirere pacem et persequi eam hoc enim fecerunt hii tres proceres de quibus infra fit mencio ubi fides interfuit. *opus inferni* est pacem turbare iustosque regni interficere. hoc enim Ricardus tirannice contra deum et homines facere non timuit. *opus in Cristo* est deponere superbos de sede et exaltare humiles. hoc enim deus fecit. odiosum Ricardum de solio suo proiecit et pium henricum omni dileccione gratissimum cum Gloria sublimari constituit. (Pro., emphasis mine)

> [*The work of human affairs* is to seek out and pursue peace; indeed, this these three noblemen did, of whom mention is made below, when faith was in their midst. *The work of hell* is to throw peace into turmoil and to destroy the just men of the realm; indeed, this Richard did not fear to do, tyrannically against God and against men. *The work in Christ* is to cast down the proud from their seat and lift up the humble; indeed, this God did. The hateful Richard he threw down from his throne and caused the pious Henry to ascend in glory, beloved in the goodwill of all.]

Richard and Henry are named, but the noblemen in question remain anonymous. There are no dates or temporal markers, and the focus of the passage is in the move from *opus humanum*, to *opus inferni*, to *opus in Cristo*. This is not political time, but anagogical time. Qualitative markers also abound: the passage is full of "peace," "faith," and "goodwill," and the text is careful to characterize Richard as a "hateful" tyrant while depicting "pious" Henry ascending "in glory," "beloved in the goodwill of all." The anagogical flavor to the summary and its pointed reading of the two primary figures of Richard and Henry prepare readers to approach the text itself in a similar vein – that of historical exemplum rather than political reportage.

The next element in Hatton 92 repeats and deepens this structure, re-relating what is to come in the poem in terms that echo the preceding prose passage:

> Ista *tripertita* sequitur que mente *perita*
> *Cronica* seruetur. nam pars qui prima *videtur*.
> Est opus *humanum*. pars illa secunda *prophanum*.
> Est opus *inferni*. pars tercia iura *superni*.
> Est opus in *Cristo*. vir qui bene sentit in *isto*.
> Scire potest *mira*. quid amor sit quid sit et *ira*.
> Est tamen hoc *clamor* omnia vincit *amor*. (Pro.1–7, emphasis mine)

[With a *skillful* mind might this following *tripartite*
Chronicle be *preserved*, for the part which *is seen* first
Is the work of *man*; the second part, a *profane*
Work of hell is; the third part, in the justice *of heaven*,
Is a work done in *Christ*. In such, the man who perceives well
Can know *wonders*, what is love and what is *wrath*.
Nevertheless, *this cry* is: "*Love* conquers all things."]

The leonine pairings in the passage are especially opportune. "Cronica" in the second line is syntactically divided from its modifying "tripertita" in the first to allow the deliberate, tripled structure to be sonically reflected in the skillful (*perita*) mind – a tongue-in-cheek gesture that encompasses both the encouraged diligence of the reader and an air of self-congratulation on the part of the poet. This poetic skill and call for preservation is subsequently joined to that which will immediately be seen (*seruetur/videtur*) in the physical text at hand. But it is in the following lines that we move back to the complaint form, wherein the human is linked with the profane (*humanum/profanum*), and the threat of hell is balanced out by the promise of the power of the divine (*inferni/superni*). And perhaps in the most telling moment of sonic conflation, the wonders of the text are ominously balanced with wrath (*mira/ira*), a move which is only softened by the claim that the clamor of the poem is, at its heart, one of love (*clamor/amor*) – no longer a *vox clamantis*, then, but a *vox amantis*. As such, the poet assures us that even though the text will focus on heavenly wrath, it will end with love and redemption, joining this work, in the end, with Christ's salvific grace (*Cristo/isto*). Like in the prose note *qua* introduction, the structure of earth/hell/heaven predominates, but here the verse form is used to draw stronger connections between this heuristic and the interpretive attention initiated by the text. The passage invites us to read the events of 1387 to 1399 with a critical, commentator's eye before we encounter the details of the material itself.

The prologue-scribe of MS Hatton 92 thus privileges exemplarity by promoting commentary on the coming verses, reading the events described through a moral or devotional lens, and saving the more ostensibly chronicle-based framing for later.

Prologue arrangement by function

All Souls 98 (S-text)	**Hatton 92 (Z-text)**
1) Chronicle	1) Exemplarity
2) Exemplarity	2) Exemplarity 2a) *added identifying note*
3) Exemplarity	3) Chronicle
4) Text	4) Text

This organization was clearly a scribal decision, and likely one made after the manuscript was assembled; the recalibration of the poem via this prologue material marks the most dramatic intervention into the text as well as the most eloquent evidence as to how the poem was used and interpreted by readers of this particular collection. In it we see the negotiation of the absent *Vox* through the reordering of passages: rather than emphasize a move to the historical from the outset as we see in MS All Souls 98, the text now substitutes a moralizing heuristic through a doggedly anagogical turn, mitigating the specificities of the chronicle-form with the immediate establishment of a larger temporal frame in which we are to understand the figures, their actions, and their allegorical import.

This choice to privilege exemplaric reading at the cost of all other possibilities in MS Hatton 92 has two primary effects. First, it brings the *Cronica* in line with the other texts of the manuscript, allowing their interest in moralized and moralizing reading to stand in effectively for the heuristic the *Vox* would have provided. In this, the inclusion of the *Cronica* speaks not to its appearing out of place in the compilation, but rather to the ways in which it has been successfully reclaimed by the manuscript's priorities. Second, it carries with it ramifications for how the rest of the poem functions within these priorities. I have focused primarily on the opening folios of the poem here, but the contexts established by the material conditions of the text shift our approach to any number of other elements. The position of the speaker, for example, is now enfolded into the structures of the exemplaric form, thereby modifying how we read his moments of first-person narration when we come across them in the text. How are we to relate to his ostensible performances of fear, sorrow, or hope? Similarly, as the idea of the historical takes on new resonances, I would argue that the relationship between the heraldic figurations of the key players and the authorial notes that "translate" the allegories within the text also find a different purchase here than in other iterations of the work. We might also look with interest to the shorter poems that conclude Gower's section of the collection, in which we find poems celebrating Henry – do they trouble or extend the exemplary mode, and what does this mean for how fifteenth-century readers of the manuscript contextualized the political events they themselves might be adjacent to, or participating in? In this way, the exemplaric mode of MS Hatton 92 might preempt some readings of Gower's work even as it opens others.

I would like to suggest that the "moral Gower" of MS Hatton 92 is the one with whom we, as scholars, have been acquainted for quite some time. When it comes to Gower's Latin poetry, we seem to readily accept this designation, even as we feel quite comfortable pushing back against it in, say, his Middle English writing. This is not to say that exemplarity does not find a place in the *Vox*, the *Cronica*, or the *Visio*. But to read it at the exclusion of other possible concerns is to render the poems (and the poet) as single-minded, defined and confined by a performance of untroubled authority that forecloses other, less imperious versions of the texts. It simplifies the complex negotiation performed by both the *Vox* and the *Cronica* and creates a picture of Gower as a Latin poet who becomes easy to define but difficult to value. "Moral Gower" is in this way a bit like Hatton 92's version of Richard: present but still absent, a trace that is readable but not completely accessible. As such, the version of the *Cronica* in Hatton 92 is singular, reflecting the interests and priorities of the community for which it was made. I do not think it unexamined, but I do think it deliberate. In the same fashion, as modern scholars of Gower's works, we too bring our own versions of symptomatic reading with us, reflective as they are of the ground or grounds on which we ourselves stand. As of now, that ground has felt quite stable when it comes to Gower's non-English works. I would like to suggest, however, that this ground, like the exemplaric reading we see in this manuscript, is a choice rather than a given.

CHAPTER 3

A STATE ABOVE ALL OTHER: THE RECENSIONS OF *CONFESSIO AMANTIS* AND THE ANTHROPOLOGY OF SOVEREIGNTY

Robert Epstein

As Siân Echard makes clear in her essay in this volume, editors of *Confessio Amantis* have always given what is now commonly known as the "third recension" pride of place. William Caxton seems to have known only this version. Thomas Berthelette noted the textual variants, and sought to justify his following of Caxton's edition. G. C. Macaulay printed the earlier recension beneath the later, with asterisks before the line numbers to indicate their variance; Russell Peck maintained these conventions.[1]

Echard further notes that editors have had many reasons for these choices. Chief among these would seem to be the assumption that the latest version must represent Gower's final choices and therefore have greater authority. Recent scholarship, however, has called into question the hierarchy of recensions, both in terms of their number and their chronology. There seems to be nearly as much textual variation within each of the three groupings that Macaulay identified as recensions as there are among them.[2] And scholars have shown that there is little manuscript evidence to support the editorial model of Macaulay and Fisher, in which a version of the poem from the late 1380s was revised twice by Gower, the second and

---

[1] On the manuscripts of *Confessio Amantis*, see, in addition to Echard's present essay, *The Complete Works of John Gower*, ed. G. C. Macaulay, 4 vols. (Oxford: Clarendon, 1899–1902), II.cxxvii–cxxxviii; John H. Fisher, *John Gower, Moral Philosopher and Friend of Chaucer* (New York: New York University Press, 1964), 303–07; *Confessio Amantis*, ed. Russell A. Peck, 3 vols. (Kalamazoo: Medieval Institute Publications, 2003–06), I.36–37; Derek Pearsall, "The Manuscripts and Illustrations of Gower's Work," in *A Companion to Gower*, ed. Siân Echard (Cambridge: D. S. Brewer, 2004), 73–97; Joel Fredell, "John Gower's Manuscripts in Middle English," in *The Routledge Research Companion to John Gower*, ed. Ana Sáez-Hidalgo, Brian Gastle, and R. F. Yeager (London: Routledge, 2017), 91–96.

[2] See Fredell, "John Gower's Manuscripts in Middle English."

more substantial revision in about 1392.[3] Peter Nicholson and Joel Fredell have made strong cases that all manuscripts of the *Confessio* and their textual variations are products of the early Lancastrian period.[4]

The issue is by no means resolved, however, and Macaulay's classifications and editorial choices still predominate in the Gowerian critical discourse.[5] It is all the more important, therefore, to ask why the conventional representation of the *Confessio* text persists. Macaulay's innovation of printing, at the start of the Prologue and at the conclusion of Book VIII, the so-called third recension above and the first recension beneath it, constructs the text as a dyad. One version preserves the dedications to Richard II in the Prologue and the conclusion, and the narrative of the meeting on the Thames at which Richard requests the composition of the poem. This is superseded by a recension that removes these passages, dedicates the poem to "Engelond," and includes praise of Henry of Lancaster. The most popular explanation for this radical political revision has been that it represents Gower's reaction to Richard's budding absolutism.[6] In prioritizing the third recension, are editors betraying a preference for a Gower who seems to have evolved into a judicious critic of monarchical authoritarianism?

Some critics have seen Gower as an advocate of divinely ordained and absolute monarchical authority, but as Conrad van Dijk has observed, "more recent criticism has turned increasingly to his theoretical discussions of the constitutional basis of kingship."[7] Focusing on Gower's "Mirror for Princes," Book VII of *Confessio Amantis*, these readers have found that Gower sees the king as subject to the law, rather than a law unto himself. James Simpson maintains that "constitutionalism is implicit in the subtle psychology of the poem" and "occasionally explicit in the political narratives," and that the "reformation of kings in the *Confessio* often takes the form of proud kings

---

[3] On the conventional ordering and dating, see Peck's introduction to the *Confessio*, 36.

[4] See by Peter Nicholson, "The Dedications of Gower's *Confessio Amantis*," *Mediaevalia* 10 (1988): 159–80; "Poet and Scribe in the Manuscripts of Gower's *Confessio Amantis*," in *Manuscripts and Texts: Editorial Problems in Later Middle English Literature*, ed. Derek Pearsall (Cambridge: D. S. Brewer, 1987), 130–42; and "Gower's Revisions in the *Confessio Amantis*," *Chaucer Review* 19 (1984): 123–43. See also Joel Fredell, "The Gower Manuscripts: Some Inconvenient Truths," *Viator* 41 (2010): 231–50; Terry Jones, "Did John Gower Rededicate His *Confessio Amantis* before Henry IV's Usurpation?" in *Middle English Texts in Transition: A Festschrift Dedicated to Toshiyuki Takamiya on His 70th Birthday*, ed. Simon Horobin and Linne R. Mooney (York: York Medieval Press, 2014), 40–74.

[5] Fredell summarizes responses to the challenges to the conventional typology and chronology in "Inconvenient Truths," 231 n. 3 and 237 n. 24.

[6] See George B. Stow, "Richard II in John Gower's *Confessio Amantis*: Some Historical Perspectives," *Mediaevalia* 16 (1993): 3–31. See also Fredell, "Inconvenient Truths," 236–37.

[7] Conrad van Dijk, *John Gower and the Limits of the Law* (Cambridge: D. S. Brewer, 2013), 90.

recognizing that they are subject to the same laws as their subjects."[8] Most recently, in a groundbreaking essay, Matthew Giancarlo has demonstrated "Gower's importance as a pivotal figure in the English discourse of governmentality" and his "creativity as a constitutionalist writer."[9] In Giancarlo's analysis, the goal of the regimentation of the king, as in *Confessio* VII, is "to bring royal power in consonance with the *regimen recte* of justice and thus to constitute kingship through its operation and *scola*."[10]

There are, however, significant difficulties with such an evolutionary interpretation of the relationship between the Ricardian and Lancastrian recensions. One is timing. If we accept the standard timeline, the first recension dates to 1386 to 1390, and the third recension, with its Lancastrian revisions, to 1392 to 1393. This cannot but seem a brief interval for such a radical change of authorial perspective in an otherwise extremely stable text.[11] Moreover, the changes between the recensions seem to mark more than just a shifting of Gower's allegiances. In its praise of the king, the Ricardian recension itself displays absolutist inclinations. The king commands, and Gower seems eager to comply: "And thus upon his comandyng / Myn hert is wel the more glad / To write so as he me bad" (*CA* Pro.*54–56). In fact, Gower says, there is no alternative: "For that thing may nought be refused / Which that a king himselve bit" (Pro.*74–75).[12]

Van Dijk finds evidence for both absolutist and constitutionalist interpretations in the *Confessio*, a tension that he sees playing out in the moral ambiguity of Gower's judicial exempla, particularly in Book VII. "Gower desires equitable justice from the king and for that reason places him above the law," van Dijk finds, "but he worries about the king abusing his power, and thus in the very section on Justice (as well as elsewhere), he reinforces the rigorous application of the law."[13] This apparent conflict within Gower's political philosophy seems to many readers not only to shape the poem and especially Book VII, but also to inform the evolution of the poem through its several recensions.

In this essay, I revisit the recensions to contend that the seemingly shifting political philosophy of the *Confessio* manuscripts evinces neither inconsistency nor radical evolution in Gower's thought. Drawing on recent

---

[8] James Simpson, *Sciences and the Self in Medieval Poetry: Alan of Lille's Anticlaudianus and John Gower's* Confessio amantis (Cambridge: Cambridge University Press, 1995), 282.

[9] Matthew Giancarlo, "Gower's Governmentality: Revisiting John Gower as a Constitutional Thinker and Regiminal Writer," in *John Gower: Others and the Self*, ed. Russell A. Peck and R. F. Yeager (Cambridge: D. S. Brewer, 2017), 225–59 (226).

[10] Giancarlo, "Gower's Governmentality," 238.

[11] The remarkable uniformity of the poem's text across its numerous manuscripts is emphasized by Pearsall, "Manuscripts," 80.

[12] Quotations of *Confessio Amantis* are taken from Macaulay's edition.

[13] Van Dijk, *Gower and the Limits of the Law*, 138.

contributions to the anthropological theory of kingship and sovereignty, I will argue that the Lancastrian recension develops and extends the philosophy of kingship inherent in the Ricardian text.

Kingship is, of course, a hallmark Gowerian preoccupation.[14] But in addition to being a mode of government and an element of political theory, it is also an anthropological phenomenon. The historian Francis Oakley has shown that kingship is the most ancient and the most widespread form of human government, and demonstrated "the remarkable degree to which archaic and pagan notions of sacral kingship succeeded in acclimatizing themselves to the alien religious conditions prevailing alike in the Byzantine east and the Latin west."[15] Gower's conceptions and depictions of kingship, while drawing on rarified intellectual traditions and while engaging with the brass tacks of political "practique" and contemporary controversy, also participate in the broader story of the emergence and persistence of monarchical structures in the history of human society.

The theories of kingship I am referring to appear in the recently published collaboration of Marshall Sahlins and David Graeber.[16] At the core of their argument is the assertion that kingship arises out of ritual.[17] Sahlins and Graeber assert that kingship originates as a social expression of "cosmic polity." Whereas it is often assumed that humans have constructed hierarchical pantheons as extensions of their own terrestrial forms of government, Sahlins and Graeber say that the opposite is the case, that "kings are imitations of gods rather than gods of kings."[18]

This conception contrasts markedly with more dominant models, from the Marxist to the sociobiological, which assume hierarchical power relations and political domination to be inherent and originary to human society or even

---

[14] See, among other sources, George R. Coffman, "John Gower in His Most Significant Role," in *Elizabethan Studies and Other Essays in Honor of George F. Reynolds*, ed. E. J. West (University of Colorado Studies, Series B 2.4, Boulder, CO: 1945), 52–61; Russell A. Peck, *Kingship and Common Profit in Gower's Confessio Amantis* (Carbondale: Southern Illinois University Press, 1978); Kurt Olsson, *John Gower and the Structures of Conversion: A Reading of the* Confessio Amantis (Cambridge: D. S. Brewer, 1992).

[15] Francis Oakley, *Kingship: The Politics of Enchantment* (Oxford: Blackwell, 2006), 108.

[16] David Graeber and Marshall Sahlins, *On Kings* (Chicago: Hau Books, 2017).

[17] Sahlins's and Graeber's central premise revives an argument of the now relatively obscure British anthropologist A. M. Hocart. Hocart maintained that kingship originated in ritual – that is, that royal status and privilege grew out of religious practice, that in fact gods were invented as extensions of kings and not vice versa. The political realm and the sovereign authority of kings developed subsequently, and incidentally rather than intentionally or necessarily. See *Kings and Councillors: An Essay in the Comparative Anatomy of Human Society*, ed. Rodney Needham (Chicago: University of Chicago Press, 1970 [1936]); *Kingship* (London: Oxford University Press, 1969 [1927]).

[18] Graeber and Sahlins, *On Kings*, 2–3.

to the human species.[19] To Sahlins and Graeber, kingship is not functional, in that societies needed god-like figures to exercise sovereign power over all other individuals so as to maintain order or to secure power or resources; rather, kingship, the origins of the political, is simply an extension of ritual performance. Sahlins extends his view of kingship with his key concept of the "stranger-king."[20] He observes that virtually all cultures that develop a mode of divine kingship have justified the institution with mythologies of the king as originally foreign. The king is figured as coming from beyond society, and therefore as superseding the normal bounds of society. Thus, for Sahlins, the king is a "meta-human."

In this view, the king's status as both foreign and divine entails inevitable conflict with those he rules. The king and his subjects are locked in and defined by an inescapable antagonism. Such struggle between ruler and ruled is not unfamiliar to us. It is commonly conceived as the conflict between a king's claim to "divine right" and a democratic insistence on the common humanity of all and a secular basis for government. Or, as in the constitutionalist readings applied to Gower, it is perceived in the contrast of absolutist claims of divinely ordained monarch and the philosophical principle that the king must be subject to human law.[21] But in "stranger-king" formations, both sides, the king and the people, agree on the god-like qualities of the king. The fundamental struggle, therefore, is between what Sahlins and Graeber term "divine kingship" and "sacred kingship." These may sound synonymous, but there is a crucial distinction. "Divine kingship," which perhaps found its fullest expression in Stuart political theology and the principle of the "divine right of kings," maintains that the god-like nature of the king grants him innate and inviolable authority to command and act in the political realm. "Sacral kingship," which Sahlins and Graeber see as the original principle of kingship in all societies, maintains that the king's divinity is expressed in his sacredness, which is observed in ritual; far from granting the king autonomous political agency, sacrality intentionally walls the king off from direct political command, which is imagined as potentially sullying to his meta-human nature. As Sahlins and Graeber describe it, these two ways of imagining the nature of the king define a struggle between king and people:

---

[19] Sahlins has characterized these views as the "quaint Western concept that domination is a spontaneous expression of the nature of society." Marshall Sahlins, "The Stranger-King: or Dumézil among the Fijians," *The Journal of Pacific History* 16 (1981): 107–32 (109).

[20] Sahlins has been developing the "stranger-king" model since the early 1980s; see "The Stranger-King, or Dumézil among the Fijians." Part of his intention was to demonstrate that native groups were not exhibiting infantile folly or inherent servility when they welcomed colonial outsiders as kings.

[21] On the development of "absolutist polity," see David Wallace, *Chaucerian Polity: Absolutist Lineages and Associational Forms in England and Italy* (Stanford: Stanford University Press, 1997).

> In practice, divine kingship is the essence of sovereignty: it is the ability to act as if one were a god; to step outside the confines of the human, and return to rain favor, or destruction, with arbitrariness and impunity.... To be "sacred," in contrast, is to be set apart, hedged about by customs and taboos; the restrictions surrounding sacralized kings... are ways not only of recognizing the presence of unaccountable divine power, but also, crucially, of controlling and limiting it.[22]

From the king's perspective, his divinity grants him unlimited power and unrestricted command; from the people's perspective, the king's sacrality requires rituals to "protect" him, which function actually to separate him from human contact and to delimit his powers of command. The king seeks to exercise and justify his power to command; the people seek to isolate and circumscribe the king with ritual and sacred imagination to delimit and contain this potentially dangerous autonomy. Thus, king and people are locked "in a continual chess game... in which the king and his partisans attempt to increase the divinity of the king, and the popular factions attempt to increase his sacralization."[23]

David Graeber takes this formulation one step further, to explain the origins not just of social inequality, but of "sovereignty," which he sees as the generalized claim of the right to exercise power over others, beyond and above the law. Graeber sees this sovereign power as being the defining feature not only of the king, but also generally of the State – the entity to which people, in familiar Hobbesian terms, have granted the authority to rule and dominate them; he notes that "sovereign" is both a synonym for a monarch and also an adjective denoting an independent state. He hypothesizes, therefore, that the power of the sovereign and the authority of the sovereign state share an ontogeny. Graeber posits "that monarchies – and by extension, modern states – are marked by a kind of primordial, constitutive war between king and people."[24] The people have many strategies for containing the power of the king. One of these is the sacred isolation and containment that Sahlins refers to. Graeber calls this "adverse sacralization": "the imposition of elaborate taboos that deny the mortal qualities of the king, cut him off from regular contact with his subjects, and often, imprison him in a carefully bounded physical space (village, compound, palace)."[25] The people can also deputize authorities to perform ritual containment of the king; these, Graeber notes, are often clown figures in carnivalesque performances, of the sort familiar from Mikhail Bakhtin's analyses.[26] These satirical figures of carnival can develop into what Graeber calls "clown-police,"

---

[22] Graeber and Sahlins, *On Kings*, 7–8.
[23] Graeber and Sahlins, *On Kings*, 8.
[24] Graeber, *On Kings*, 398.
[25] Graeber, *On Kings*, 460.
[26] See M. M. Bakhtin, *Rabelais and His World*, translated by Hélène Iswolsky (Cambridge, MA: MIT Press, 1968).

their authority to restrict power and to enforce popular behaviors expanding and extending beyond carnival season. In its most extreme form, "adverse sacralization" can take the form of symbolic, or even real, regicide.

Ultimately, Graeber says, one or the other side in this struggle will win. Either the king will establish independent authority, and found a monarchy, or the policing forces will establish independent and perpetuating powers, rooted in their ritual control of the king. But, in either case, the consequence is the establishment of the State and its "sovereign" exercise of power.

The seeming contradictions within *Confessio Amantis*, and the differences between its recensions, then, might best be understood not as the conflict between absolutism and constitutionalism, but rather as the tension between "divine" and "sacred" kingship.

The sacral conception of kingship is especially apparent in Book VII.[27] Genius implies near the beginning that the rule of the good king is analogous to God's divine governance:

> Bot ther is on above the Sonne,
> Whos time nevere was begonne,
> And endeles schal evere be;
> That is the god, whos mageste
> Alle othre thinges schal governe,
> And his beinge is sempiterne. (*CA* VII.99–104)

Nonetheless, Gower's regimen for the prince, as Giancarlo shows, evinces a constitutionalist vision of kingship, in which the legitimacy of the king requires his disciplinary submission to justice, and law is supreme over monarch, surpassing any one king. And, as van Dijk demonstrates, "The attempt to resolve the difficult relations between king and law results in the creation of judicial exempla that show a certain amount of vacillation and apparent contradiction."[28] But it is not merely law or governmentality that

---

[27] It should be acknowledged that the historical and contemporary world societies that Sahlins and Graeber study are not fourteenth-century England and generally do not produce books of moral or amatory verse. On the other hand, both Sahlins and Graeber insist that the kingship patterns that they describe are something like universal. More specifically, both of them see affinities in the patterns and mythologies of kingship in ancient Semitic and Greco-Roman sources; both authors dwell extensively on examples from the Western tradition, particularly Aeneas and Romulus. Graeber explains that he deliberately avoids extensive engagement with medieval kingship only because sovereignty in that period becomes too complicated by the imbrication of divine kingship with the theologies of the major world religions. See Sahlins and Graeber, 462. For the history of kingship in the Christian West, Graeber defers to historians like Francis Oakley, whose historical studies of sacred kingship dovetail nicely with Graeber's and Sahlins' theories. See Oakley, "The Sacrality of Kingship in Medieval and Early Modern Europe: Papal, Imperial, National," in *Kingship*, 108–31.

[28] Van Dijk, *Gower and the Limits of the Law*, 92.

delimits royal power in Book VII. Simpson has noted, for instance, that the tale of the Sultan Darius "in particular succinctly encapsulates the forces which might constrain a king."[29] In this tale, which Gower borrows from 1 Esdras, Darius asks three counselors to determine what is strongest: the king, wine, or woman? The first counselor makes the case for the king:

> the strengthe of kinges
> Is myhtiest of alle thinges.
> For king hath pouer over man,
> And man is he which reson can,
> As he which is of his nature
> The moste noble creature
> Of alle tho that god hath wroght:
> And be that skile it semeth noght,
> He seith, that eny erthly thing
> Mai be so myhty as a king.
> A king mai spille, a king mai save,
> A king mai make of lord a knave
> And of a knave a lord also:
> The pouer of a king stant so,
> That he the lawes overpasseth;
> What he wol make lasse, he lasseth,
> What he wol make more, he moreth;
> And as the gentil faucon soreth,
> He fleth, that noman him reclameth;
> Bot he al one alle othre tameth,
> And stant himself of lawe fre. (*CA* VII.1825–45)

The king is divinely ordained; his power to command is unlimited; his status exceeds that of all men, and he can determine the status of all other men. He wields god-like authority over life and death. He is above the law and stands as a law unto himself. These are precisely the powers that Graeber sees implicit in divine kingship. But this expansive vision of kingly power is immediately undermined by the other responses to Darius. The second counselor argues that wine is more powerful than the king: it can take away reason, or make the fool wise; it can make a man blind or make the blind man see; and so on. The third counselor says that woman is clearly the most powerful, as both the king and the vintner come from woman, and both are subject to the woman's thrall, and further "Among the men is no solas, / If that ther be no womman there" (*CA* VII.1900–01). The description of the supreme power of the king is revealed to be ironic, as the exemplum's true moral is the king's incapacity. The apparently cosmic power of the king is trumped by the sublunary powers of alcohol or the generative female body.

---

[29] Simpson, *Sciences and the Self*, 282.

Like the forces of sacral kingship, this exemplum works to delimit the king's agency and to restrict his very life.

Many of the exempla in Book VII function in this manner. They focus on the consequences of monarchical overweening, on the dangers of excessive agency, or on the positive results of the king's inaction. An impoverished knight shames Julius by reminding him of the knight's service in his military campaigns (*CA* VII.2061–2114). Another poor knight, Antigonus, asks King Cinichus for a gift that in the king's views "passeth / His povere astat" (*CA* VII.2123–24); when the knight requests a more modest donation, Cinichus says that "To yive a man so litel thing / It were unworschipe in a king" (*CA* VII.2129–30). This, according to Genius, exemplifies largess, but it certainly seems to expose the self-serving emptiness of royal dignity. Two students leave school. One, Arisippus, pursues "vein honour and worldes good" (*CA* VII.2255); the other, Diogenes, stays home with his books. When Arisippus, having grown rich through flattery, encounters Diogenes in his garden, he remarks that if Diogenes knew how to pick his words to please a prince, he would not have to gather herbs. Diogenes responds that if Arisippus knew how to pick his words better, he would know the uselessness of princely favor won through flattery (*CA* VII.2217–2317). Such exempla question not just whether the king's will is inviolable or if his actions are delimited by law, but whether the king's royal status is best manifested in action at all. It seems, at points, as if the king is most kingly when he does nothing.

In another exemplum, a king asks his steward and his chamberlain what his subjects think of him. Both flatter him, telling him he is considered honorable and wise. But the king's fool, hearing this, laughs, and tells the king that if he were so naturally wise, he would not need to seek the advice of counselors. The king, Genius tells us,

> ...merveille hadde,
> What that a fol so wisly spak,
> And of himself fond out the lack
> Withinne his oghne conscience:
> And thus the foles evidence,
> Which was of goddes grace enspired,
> Makth that good conseil was desired.
> He putte awey the vicious
> And tok to him the vertuous. (*CA* VII.3998–4007)

Here, then, is a "policing clown," who has license to reveal "hou al the poeple seith" (*CA* VII.3982) and their true antagonism toward the king, and who thereby appropriates not only aristocratic status but also the divine associations of rule and the authority to command the king.

Genius concludes with stories of Lucrece (*CA* VII.4754–5124) and Virginia (*CA* VII.5131–5306.) These aptly illustrate the virtue of Chastity, but they are also republican foundation myths. Far from demonstrating the value of kingship, they served the Romans as examples of the inevitable corruption of monarchism and the liberation of overthrowing kings. As a result, Book VII consistently shows why science, wisdom, and ethics are important to the success of the king, but it is much less clear why a successful king is essential to a nation. Kingship is simultaneously divinely ordained and politically marginal. Gower, by way of Brunetto Latini, offers a typology of royal "Practique," but it makes kingship appear impracticable.

Indeed, as Giancarlo observes, many of Gower's exempla suggest that "sovereign authority... is most firmly established and powerfully affirmed by the self-extinguishing of the persona of regal-judicial presence: constitution requires self-negation, even suicide."[30] For instance, there is the tale of the Roman consul Carmidotirus, who, forgetting his own ban on weapons in the Senate, enters the chamber while wearing his sword, and being made aware of the error, promptly kills himself (*CA* VII.2845–88). Ultimately, Giancarlo says, justice hinges "not just upon the law's separation from the law-giver, but on the actual disappearance of his regal person," even his "literal or symbolic death."[31] This conclusion conforms to Graeber's view of sacred kingship, which also culminates in symbolic or even actual regicide. In another brief exemplum, "The Emperor and the Masons" (*CA* VII.2412–31), an emperor, on the day of his coronation, encounters the masons building his tomb, who ask him what he would like engraved on it. The monarch is dead from the moment he rules.

I would suggest, in fact, that Book VII as a whole is not about the power of the king but rather about the containment of the latent claims of divine kingship, by means of what Graeber calls "adverse sacralization," the ritualized modes of using the divine status of the king to contain and delimit his functional political power. This educational program can be delineated by non-noble pedagogues – from Aristotle to Gower – and it is applicable to the microcosmic individual as well as the macrocosmic monarch. And the exempla give the impression that the *speculum principis* is designed to keep the king from hazards of agency, not just from immoral action.

One form that "adverse sacralization" can take, according to Graeber, is "abstraction," by which, essentially, the king's sacredness is figured as so idealized that it removes him from ordinary interaction with the remainder of the human world. Graeber discusses the *reth*, the divine king of the Shilluk kingdom of Africa, and the subject of famous studies by Sir James Frazer. The *reth*, Graeber explains, was expected to maintain a state of physical purity and perfection. But such perfection, Graeber says, alienates the *reth* from the realm of the human:

> In this sense, the king is indeed an abstraction or transcendental principle: the ideal-typical human. [...] Insofar as the *reth* is the

---

[30] Giancarlo, "Gower's Governmentality," 242.
[31] Giancarlo, "Gower's Governmentality," 243.

embodiment of the nation, and of humanity as a whole before the divine powers, he is a generic human; insofar as he is the generic human, he must be the perfect human; insofar as he is an image of humanity removed from time and process, he must be preserved from any harmful transformation until the point where, when this becomes impossible, he must be simply destroyed and put away. In this sense, the king's body is less a fetish than itself a kind of microutopia, an impossible ideal.[32]

I would suggest that Gower's Book VII, like the bodily perfection of the Shilluk king, renders the ideal king as an ethical abstraction, an avatar of ethical perfection that no real human – not Alexander, not Richard II, not even assiduous Amans – could fully emulate. To imagine that the true king will embody the qualities taught in Book VII of the *Confessio* is to "destroy and put away" the king, to abstract him into impotence and impossibility. The purpose of such texts is perhaps not so much to provide a practical education for princes, as it is to abstract sacral kingship into irrelevance.

As Giancarlo explains, the constitutionalist reading of Gower places him in the High Medieval tradition of what Ernst Kantorowicz calls "law-centered kingship," when jurists worked to translate the absolutist ideals inherent in divine kingship into law.[33] Eventually, the Early Modern period would deploy the "abstract physiological fiction" of the "king's two bodies" to transmogrify these legal conventions into the authority for the secular state.[34] But in late-medieval constitutionalism like Gower's, Giancarlo says, "The king is made by the law as the law is made by justice as enforced by the king, who is both above and under the Law but who is not therefore bifurcated or made into 'two bodies.' He remains, as yet, integral and one."[35]

---

[32] Graeber, "The Divine Kingship of the Shilluk," *On Kings*, 132. It will be noted that Graeber's language here evokes Kantorowicz's analysis of the early modern legal principle of the "king's two bodies." Ernst H. Kantorowicz, *The King's Two Bodies: A Study in Mediaeval Political Theology* (Princeton: Princeton University Press, 1957). Graeber (*On Kings*, 69) notes that related medieval intellectual history probably influenced E. E. Evans-Pritchard when he was formulating his early and influential anthropological analysis of the Shilluk. See *The Divine Kingship of the Shilluk of Nilotic Sudan* (Cambridge: Cambridge University Press, 1948). Graeber also remarks that some more recent anthropological studies have explicitly applied Kantorowicz's work to Shilluk kingship. See William Arens, "The Divine Kingship of the Shilluk: A Contemporary Reevaluation," *Ethnos* 44 (1979): 167–81; Burkhard Schnepel, *Twinned Beings: Kings and Effigies in Southern Sudan, East India and Renaissance France* (Göteborg: Institute for Advanced Studies in Social Anthropology, 1995).
[33] On late-medieval "law-centered kingship," see Kantorowicz, *The King's Two Bodies*, 87–192.
[34] Kantorowicz, *The King's Two Bodies*, 4.
[35] Giancarlo, "Gower's Governmentality," 234.

From the perspective of anthropological theory, however, we can trace a somewhat different narrative, one in which king and people are formed in binary tension, and in which the seeds of modern state sovereignty inhere in the apparently constitutionalist poetry of Gower.

Graeber and Sahlins define divine kingship largely by the king's assumption of the prerogative to command; the forces of sacramental kingship, in contrast, work to wall the king off from direct command. It is notable, therefore, that the Ricardian version of the *Confessio* Prologue depicts the poem as a whole as a royal command performance. As I noted at the start, Gower emphasizes the king's irresistible power to command his subjects: "For that thing may nought be refused / Which that a king himselve bit" (*CA* Pro.*74–75).

At the same time, the poem is concerned with the king's virtue – both that of the ideal king imagined in Book VII, and that of the present King Richard in the Prologue and Book VIII of the first recension. The motivation of this concern is not primarily to make the king rule in a way that is beneficial to people or nation – as we have noted, there are few instances showing this – but more because personal and political vices threaten the security of a king's rule. Such vices are, fundamentally, unsafe. In his prayer at the end of Book VIII in the first recension, Gower declares Richard the embodiment of the kingly ideal – "In his persone it mai be schewed / What is a king to be wel thewed" (*CA* VIII.*2991–92) – and he asks God to keep this royal paragon safe: "The hihe god, him overspradde / Of his Justice, and kepte him so, / That his astat stood evere mo / Sauf, as it oghte wel to be" (*CA* VIII.*3002–05). Here is the seeming paradox: in the Ricardian recension Gower praises Richard's divine royalty and acknowledges his absolute authority to command, but in the Lancastrian recension he erases Richard in reaction to his absolutism. In Graeber's model of adverse sacramentality, however, limitations on the king's agency and command are figured as ways of protecting his sacral being.

This brings us to an even more challenging paradox, one central to anthropological analysis as well as to the political philosophy engaged in the *Confessio*, and indeed to English history in Gower's time and after. Van Dijk notes that in Book VII of the *Confessio*, the king seems "simultaneously above the law and subject to the law." He concludes that Gower "espouses personal kingship but does everything he can to ensure that the king will *uphold* the law."[36] But what if the king does not uphold the law? What if he succumbs to the vice of tyranny and presses his divine authority to command beyond the limits of the licit? Can it be legal to remove a king?[37]

---

[36] Van Dijk, *Gower and the Limits of the Law*, 137–38. Emphasis Van Dijk's.

[37] As Graeber notes, even revolutions that end monarchy in the name of law are extra-judicial in their authority: "The notion of popular sovereignty might seem to depart from the logic of transgression so evidenced in other forms of sovereign power, but in fact it does not: the legitimacy of systems of constitutional law

This is an ancient and intractable problem, and not one readily solved by a new theoretical paradigm. But it might help to clarify the issues if we were to see the roots of the paradox in a universal, mutually constitutive struggle between people and king, which is only partly overlaid by law. The adherents of the sacral king seek to "protect" the king by isolating and disempowering him, the fullest expression of which, according to Sahlins and Graeber, is regicide. Gower can be seen to perform an imaginary and symbolic regicide, anticipating the real usurpation and regicide, by erasing from his text the king whom he has praised as divinely ordained and indomitable in his will.

The third recension praises and commends Henry of Lancaster, both in the Prologue – "I sende unto myn oghne lord, / Which of Lancastre is Henri named: / The hyhe god him hath proclamed / Ful of knyhthode and alle grace" (*CA* Pro.86–89) – and at the end of Book VIII in the Latin dedication. Readers have naturally found here, despite the chronological difficulties, Gower's anticipation of a more amenable rule of the Lancastrian king. And there might well be justification for believing that Gower perceives Henry as the "stranger-king." This is not to say that Henry is a foreigner (though, throughout history, the English monarch is the least English Englishman – and in order to vie for the throne Henry had to return from exile in France). But despite subsequent Lancastrian claims he was never in the direct line to inherit the throne. Henry would hold the promise of being outside of, of potentially transcending, the legacies of command and resistance that had already complicated Richard's reign.

Gower, however, does not welcome Henry as a prospective king. Rather, he praises him for his chivalrous dedication to holiness and justice: "The hyhe god him hath proclamed / Ful of knyhthode and alle grace" (*CA* Pro.88–89). Gower may not be exchanging one king for another; instead, he may be idealizing Henry of Lancaster as the embodiment of the divinely ordained knighthood that can restrict the power of the king (as in fact it, and he, did, well before Richard's ultimate deposition.)

This does not mean that Gower is a proleptic republican.[38] Nor is he a partisan of baronial independence. The excision of Richard from the Book VIII conclusion leaves Gower space to address the estates, including the First Estate, which he figures as "chevalerie" (*CA* VIII.3007), but he admonishes them for their gratuitous retinues and the rivalrous conflicts amongst themselves: "And in som part to ben amendid, / That of here large retenue / The lond is ful of maintenue… / Wher of the poeple is sore oppressid: / God graunte it mote be redressid" (*CA* VIII.3010–12, 3019–20). Nor, despite his warnings against tyranny (*CA* Pro.49; 8.3076), does Gower assert that Richard is a tyrant, or even, like Nebuchadnezzar, a giant with feet

---

is derived from 'the people,' but the people conveyed that legitimacy through revolution, American, French, etc.—that is, through acts of illegal violence" (*On Kings*, 463 n.78).

[38] A point made forcefully by Giancarlo, "Gower's Governmentality," 254.

of clay. The case may instead be that Gower does believe that kingship is divine and that the political operation of a divinely empowered individual – a "meta-human" – must necessarily be circumscribed.

What is most significant, I believe, is what takes Richard's place when he is banished from the third recension. It is not Henry of Lancaster, who is mentioned only briefly in the Prologue and in the closing dedication, and not in royal terms. Rather, what takes the place of Richard II is England and the English people. "A bok for king Richardes sake" (*CA* Pro.*24) becomes "A bok for Engelondes sake" (*CA* Pro.24). The concluding prayer for Richard becomes a prayer for the English people – "Parce precor, Criste, populus quo gaudeat iste" [Spare I pray, O Christ, the people in order that they may rejoice] – and for the "locus beatus" of England. Gower emphasizes again that he "undirtok / In englesch for to make a book" (*CA* VIII.3107–08). The final colophon directs the book to the Count of Derby with the hope "ut ista Iohannis / Perpetuis annis stet pagina grata Britannis" [that this page of John remain for all time pleasing to the Britains].

What is this "Engelond" that emerges in the imaginative absence of Richard II, and what constitutes the "people"? Gower's emergent nationalism, verging on ethno-nationalist identity, could be seen as an expression of what Sahlins calls the "residual authority retained by the underlying native people" when they receive a stranger-king.[39] I do believe that "the people" Gower is conscious of in his prologue and conclusion, especially in the third recension, are the corporate resistance to royal authority, sacral in reaction to claims of divinity, emerging as sovereign statehood. "What we call 'the social peace'," Graeber says, "is really just a truce in a constitutive war between sovereign power and 'the people' or 'nation' – both of whom come into existence, as political entities, in their struggle against each other."[40]

In his remarks on the First Estate in the Prologue to the *Confessio* (present in all recensions), Gower, as is his habit, evokes an ideal condition of a remote and hazy past:

> Justice of lawe tho was holde,
> The privilege of regalie
> Was sauf, and al the baronie
> Worschiped was in his astat;
> The citees knewen no debat,
> The poeple stod in obeissance
> Under the reule of governance,
> And pes, which ryhtwisnesse keste,
> With charite tho stod in reste. (*CA* Pro.102–10)

---

[39] Graeber, *On Kings*, 230.
[40] Graeber, *On Kings*, 136.

There is no king here. And even the "baronie" and, earlier, "knyhthode" (99) are only vaguely imagined. The "governaunce" that the "poeple" stand in "obeissance" to seems to be simply a generalized conception of the state. But in the conclusion of this section Gower makes it clear that this state derives its authority from divinity, conceived in explicitly monarchical terms:

> Bot thilke lord which al may kepe,
> To whom no consail may ben hid,
> Upon the world which is betid,
> Amende that wherof men pleigne
> With trewe hertes and with pleine,
> And reconcile love ayeyn,
> As he which is king sovereign
> Of al the worldes governaunce,
> And of his hyhe porveaunce
> Afferme pes betwen the londes
> And take her cause into hise hondes,
> So that the world may stonde appesed
> And his godhede also be plesed. (*CA* Pro.180–92)

In the third recension's conclusion, after addressing the three estates, Gower turns to kingship:

> Ther is a stat, as ye schul hiere,
> Above alle othre on erthe hiere,
> Which hath the lond in his balance:
> To him belongith the leiance
> Of Clerk, of knyght, of man of lawe;
> Undir his hond al is forth drawe
> The merchant and the laborer;
> So stant it al in his power
> Or forto spille or forto save.
> Bot though that he such power have,
> And that his myghtes ben so large,
> He hath hem noght withouten charge,
> To which that every kyng ys swore. (*CA* VIII.3055–68)

Gower emphasizes the king's god-like power over life and death, and his authority over Church, nobility, and even law. And yet the king must govern with justice "So that ther be no tirandise, / Wherof that he his poeple grieve" (*CA* VIII.3076–77). It is precisely because the king is in his very conception divine and meta-human that there is a general need among the ruled for a sacral restriction on his agency.

The "stat... Above alle othre" (*CA* VIII.3055–56) that Gower refers to is, explicitly, kingship. As Gower imagines it, the king is a meta-human being whose divine status calls for sacral containment in the political realm. I would suggest, then, that this "state above all other" is simultaneously the state, in the most fundamental political sense – an imagined and created entity granted meta-human authority over the lives of the people it rules, via a tacit mysticism borrowed from kingship, claiming transcendent authority in order to disseminate moral guidance, justify legal authority, and inspire (or enforce) unity. The *Confessio* offers evidence for Graeber's hypothesis: that the divinity of the king entails his sacral restriction and containment; that the people and the king are locked in a perpetual and mutually constitutive struggle; that the king's attempts to turn ritual authority into political command are a contingent but always potential route to autocratic power; that popular resistance to royal autonomy is the genesis of state sovereignty.

Ultimately, then, it seems appropriate that Gower's editors – first Caxton and Berthelette, and later Macaulay and Peck – have prioritized the third recension of the *Confessio*, while also displaying the major variations of the first recension. The changes thereby demonstrated, profound though they are, reveal neither a revolution nor an evolution in his political thought, but rather a logical extension of the philosophy of kingship inherent in it from the start. More broadly, we might conclude that what looks like a distinctly medieval moment in the *Confessio* – the weakness of the central monarch, the persistence of baronial rivalry – might in fact be its most modern moment – the supplanting of the sacral king by the state apparatus originally invented to contain him.

CHAPTER 4

WHAT LIES BENEATH

Karla Taylor

THE STORY OF A king who devises a lesson for his discontented courtiers in "The Tale of the Two Coffers" poses a conundrum for John Gower's devotion to "plain" referentiality – a direct, or at least reliable, relationship between what you see and what you get, expressed in the *Confessio Amantis*' recurrent rhyme between the visible "visage" and the intentions of the hidden "corage" (*CA* Pro.111–12).[1] Although rarely the overt topic of the narratives in the collection, the problem of reference reveals a habit of mind that helps to map out Gower's understanding of and attitude toward major tensions in the civil society for which he wrote the poem. The two coffers in this story thwart the transparency of ethical, visual, and linguistic reference to which the *Confessio* frequently adverts. Their contents are hidden by identical appearances not merely deceptive, but opaque and incommunicative. In representing the choice between the two coffers as a consequence of both fortune and individual ethical character, the tale also participates in another recurrent confusion in the poem, discussed by Russell Peck and Matthew

---

[1] John Gower, *Confessio Amantis*, V.2273–2390, in G. C. Macaulay, ed., *The Complete Works of John Gower* (Oxford: Clarendon Press, 1899–1902). Translations from Latin marginalia from Russell A. Peck, ed., with Latin translations by Andrew Galloway, *Confessio Amantis*, 3 vols., 2nd ed (vols. 1–2) (Kalamazoo: Medieval Institute Publications, 2004–13). The rhyme of *visage* and *corage* appears eleven times in the *Confessio*, of which nine instances are relevant to this problem of reference: Pro.111–12, Pro. 447–48, I.715–16, II.1923–24, II.2671–72, IV.2405–06, VII.3545–46, VIII.1203–04, VIII.2405–06. See below, 11 ff. With the exception of three occurrences in Chaucer's "Clerk's Tale," the rhyme (and the analogous close proximity in prose) is otherwise vanishingly rare in the texts assembled in the Corpus of Middle English Verse and Prose, https://quod.lib.umich.edu/c/cme/. Consulted 15 May 2018.

Irvin: that between "'chance' and 'pourveance.'"[2] These threads have led me to the central design of the tale as well as its place in Book V's examination of avarice and possession in both politics and love. Working from the problem of reference and the role of fortune in delivering a lesson in ethical choice, I shall argue that the story explores Gower's tentatively skeptical thinking about kingship and secular *dominium*; further, its peculiarities may be explained as Gower's effort to differentiate his thinking from Wycliffite ideas that were perhaps too close for comfort.

"The Tale of the Two Coffers" is a perverse story. It concerns a "wise king" (*CA* V.2388) whose discontented older courtiers grumble constantly about his failure to reward them with the advancement they believe is their due owing to their lengthy service. Their situation recalls that of workers who labor all day in the Parable of the Vineyard, only to see those who arrive late to the task receive the same penny.[3] Like the vineyard laborers, who expect to be paid more than the latecomers, they reason from a principle of equity, a fair ratio of service and recompense. But the resemblance between parable and tale is only partial, for these courtiers receive nothing at all:

> Some of long time him hadden served,
> And thoghten that thei have deserved
> Avancement, and gon withoute;
> And some also ben of the route
> That comen bot a while agon,
> And thei avanced were anon. (*CA* V.2277–82)

Although the tale presents their plight neutrally – or perhaps encourages at least momentary sympathy for the injustice implied by their privation – the Latin marginal summary sides against them:

---

[2] The terms are from *Confessio*, VI.325–26. See Russell A. Peck, *Kingship and Common Profit in Gower's* Confessio Amantis (Carbondale: Southern Illinois University Press, 1978), 125; and Matthew D. Irvin, *The Poetic Voices of John Gower: Politics and Personae in the* Confessio Amantis (Cambridge: D. S. Brewer, 2014), 229.

[3] Matthew 20:1–16. The principle of equity is voiced by those who work all day: "Venientes autem et primi arbitrati sunt quod plus essent accepturi acceperunt autem et ipsi singulos denarius. Et accipientes murmurabant adversus patrem familias, dicentes hii novissimi una hora fecerunt et pares illos nobis fecisti qui portavimus pondus diei et aestus" [But when the first also came, they thought that they should receive more: and they also received every man a penny. And receiving it they murmured against the master of the house, saying: These last have worked but one hour, and thou hast made them equal to us, that have borne the burden of the day and the heats] (10–12). *Biblia Sacra Vulgata*, translation *Douay-Rheims 1899 American Edition*, Bible Gateway www.biblegateway.com/. Consulted 22 May 2018.

> Hic ponit Confessor exemplum contra illos, qui in domibus Regum seruientes, pro eo quod ipsi secundum eorum cupiditatem promoti non existunt, de regio seruicio quamuis in eorum defectu indiscrete murmurant. (*CA* V.2278 ff.)
>
> [Here the Confessor presents an instructive example against those who, serving in kings' houses, because they were not promoted as seemed appropriate to their own cupidity, indiscreetly grumble about royal service, however much it injures themselves.]

Like the English narrative, the marginal Latin relies on a just ratio of merit and outcome, although it adds a distinctly judgmental slant against ("contra") the courtiers, who are described as ingrates wrong to think they deserve better from the king. Whereas the parable distinguishes between the unearned gift of grace and a fair wage, "The Tale of the Two Coffers" returns insistently to the issue of merit. That it is also shadowed by the economy of grace from the parable is a problem to which I will return at the end of this essay.

Hearing their grumbling, the king devises a lesson for the older courtiers: he sets before them two coffers, identical in every tangible way:

> And al withinne his oghne entente,
> That noman wiste what it mente,
> Anon he let tuo cofres make
> Of o semblance and of o make,
> So lich that no lif thilke throwe
> That on mai fro that other knowe... (*CA* V.2293–98)

One coffer contains gold and precious jewels from his treasury; the other contains stones, rubbish, and straw. Having filled them with his own hands, the king alone knows which is which. The passage above stresses the king's intention as well as the meaning of the choice, which is as opaque as the coffers themselves to everyone but the king. He asks the disgruntled courtiers to agree amongst themselves which coffer to choose, and warns them that any consequences will result from "youre oghne chance / Al only in defalte of grace." Hinting that these consequences will be unwelcome, he disavows all responsibility, saying "That no defalte schal be myn" (*CA* V.2346–47, 2350). His instructions draw on the language of political deliberation and assent: "Now goth togedre of on assent / And taketh youre avisement" (*CA* V.2343–44).[4] As narrative logic requires, the courtiers choose the worthless coffer, whereupon the king draws the lesson he had intended from the beginning: your plight follows not from my injustice, but from your fortune, which is a consequence of your own choice.

---

[4] See too "yerde" (*CA* V.2363, 2366), "assent" (*CA* V.2365), and "commun vois" (*CA* V.2370) later in the tale.

The story thus blurs two antithetical rationales for its outcome: the vagaries of fortune, and the consequences of ethical choice. In presenting the choice, the king adverts to fortune as well as the twin responsibilities of donor and recipient for the outcome:

> Ther schal noman his happ despise;
> I wot wel ye have longe served,
> And god wot what ye have deserved:
> Bot if it is along on me
> Of that ye unavanced be,
> Or elles it be long on you
> The sothe schal be proved nou... (*CA* V.2324–30)

The tale's perversity emerges more clearly from a comparison of its folk motif as it appears in other versions. To modern readers, *The Merchant of Venice* offers probably the most familiar version of a choice among/between containers.[5] In a hermeneutic test designed by her father to discern the worthiest husband, Portia's suitors must choose from among three caskets. Made from gold, silver, and lead, they lure or repel the suitors with riddling inscriptions. The Prince of Morocco, by choosing the gold casket inscribed "Who chooseth me shall gain what many men desire,"[6] reveals an avarice unworthy of Portia. The Prince of Arragon then exposes a hollow self-regard by choosing the silver casket, inscribed "Who chooseth me shall get as much as he deserves" (*Merchant*, II.vii.7, 23). Both suitors assume that the precious materials and appearance of the caskets directly indicate what lies within.

They would have been better served to assume the deceptiveness of such accident. Thus, inside the gold casket is a *memento mori* portrait of "carrion Death, within whose empty eye" is a written scroll warning:

---

[5] Stith Thompson classifies the motif in several different categories. The two most relevant are L211 and D859.5. In L211, a reversal of fortune is brought about by a modest choice; in the three caskets type, "objects from which choice is to be made are hidden in caskets (or the like). The worst looking casket proves to be the best choice." In D859.5, a "magic object to be chosen from among identical worthless objects. Three caskets. Princess offered to man who chooses correctly from three caskets." See Thompson, *Motif-Index of Folk-Literature: A Classification of Narrative Elements in Folktales, Ballads, Myths, Fables, Mediaeval Romances, Exempla, Fabliaux, Jest-Books and Local Legends*, rev. ed. (Copenhagen: Rosenkilde and Bagger, 1955), Vols. 2 and 5. I have consulted the digital version, *Motif-Index of Folk-Literature. Electronic Version* (Charlottesville: InteLex, 2000), http://pm.nlx.com.proxy.lib.umich.edu/xtf/view?docId=motif/motif.02.xml;chunk.id=div.motif.v2.1;toc.depth=2;toc.id=div.motif.v2.1;hit.rank=0;brand=default, consulted 16 April 2018.

[6] *Merchant of Venice*, in *The Riverside Shakespeare*, ed. G. Blakemore Evans *et al.*, 2nd ed. (Boston: Houghton Mifflin, 1997), II.vii.5, 37.

> All that glitters is not gold;
> Often have you heard that told:
> Many a man his life hath sold
> But my outside to behold:
> Gilded [tombs] do worms infold. (*Merchant*, II.vii.63, 65–69)

Likewise, the silver casket contains only "the portrait of a blinking idiot" confronting the Prince with his own folly: "There be fools alive iwis, / Silvered ov'r, and so was this" (*Merchant*, II.ix.54, 68–69). Only Bassanio solves the riddle of misleading appearances. In choosing the lead casket, he shows himself both undeceived by "outward shows" that are "least themselves" and unafraid to risk its ominous inscription: "Who chooseth me must give and hazard all he hath" (*Merchant*, III.ii.73; II.vii.9 and 16). He is rewarded by a picture of Portia, holding a scroll that explicitly articulates the "content and summary of my fortune" as well as the inverse relationship between the appearance of value and genuine worth:

> You that choose not by the view,
> Chance as fair and choose as true!
> Since this fortune falls to you,
> Be content and seek no new. (*Merchant*, III.ii.130, 131–34)

Bassanio not only demonstrates superior character, but also relies on a hermeneutic assumption more effective than that of his rivals, who must indeed be blinking idiots to choose the gold and silver caskets. Since the scrolls so clearly warn against trusting that costly material points to riches within, self-glossing renders the inverse relationship between substance and accidence in *The Merchant of Venice* with limpid clarity.

In Boccaccio's *Decameron*, the same folk-motif appears to different effect. Like Gower's tale, the story of King Alfonso the Wise of Castile and the Florentine knight Ruggieri de' Figiovanni (*Decameron* X.1) stresses both the determinative role of "chance," or fortune, and the prudence of the ruler. Also like Gower's tale, this *novella* makes the key choice between two apparently identical coffers, rather than the three misleading but self-glossing caskets of *The Merchant of Venice*. Here the mercenary Ruggieri resolves to leave the king's service when he is not recompensed with land and wealth according to his merit. The king sends him off with the gift of a mule and (unbeknownst to Ruggieri) a spy. When the mule refuses to urinate in an appropriate place, but then cuts loose in a stream, Ruggieri bitterly compares the gift to its giver. Learning of the comparison from his spy, Alfonso recalls Ruggieri, who repeats his criticism directly: "Signor mio, per ciò ve la assomigliai, perché, come voi donate dove non si conviene e dove si converrebbe non date, cosí ella dove si conveniva non stallò e dove non si convenia sí" [My lord, I compared it to you for this reason, that just as you bestow your gifts where they are inappropriate, and withhold them where they would be justified, so the mule relieved itself, not in the right place, but in the wrong one].[7] The king defends himself by blaming Ruggieri's personal fortune: "il non avervi donato come fatto ho a molti li quali a comparazion di voi da niente sono, non avvenuto perché è io non abbia voi valorosissimo cavalier conosciuto e degno d'ogni gran dono: ma la vostra fortuna, che lasciato non m'ha, in ciò ha peccato e non io" [it was not because I failed to recognize in you a most gallant knight, deserving of the highest honours, that I withheld my bounty from you and bestowed it on many others, who were insignificant by comparison with yourself. The blame rests not with me but with your fortune, which has prevented me from giving you your deserts] (*Decameron* X.1.15). To prove it, he then offers Ruggieri his choice of two apparently identical coffers, one filled with treasure and the other with dirt. Ruggieri, of course, chooses the worthless coffer.

Having proved his point, the king gives Ruggieri the riches anyway. Paramount in Boccaccio's story is Alfonso's magnanimity in overriding Ruggieri's ill fortune. Here the wise ruler acknowledges criticism and then shapes a just outcome; Ruggieri can have no doubt that his transformed condition owes everything to the king's discernment and generosity. Confronted by a deserving retainer who, as a foreigner, is barred from receiving Spanish honors, Alfonso finds a way not only to distinguish himself from fortune – which has dictated the circumstances of Ruggieri's birth – but also to display this difference in a deed both generous and magnificent.[8] Human ingenuity frequently prevails over forces outside individual human control in the *Decameron*; here, Alfonso takes advantage of his opportunity to reverse the amoral, often inimical trajectories of fortune.[9]

---

[7] Giovanni Boccaccio, *Decameron*, ed. Vittore Branca (Torino: Einaudi, 1992), X.1.14. Electronic version Decameron Web, http://www.brown.edu/Departments/Italian_Studies/dweb/texts/DecShowText.php?myID=nov1001&lang=it, consulted 16 April 2018. Trans. G. H. McWilliam, Giovanni Boccaccio, *The Decameron* (London: Penguin, 1972, rpt. 1995), 705.

[8] The stories of the tenth day concern those who act "liberalmente ovvero magnificamente" in love or other spheres, *Decameron*, IX.Conclusione.3.

[9] The ban on expatriation of land and honors of course results from human custom and law, not an impersonal, nonhuman force of the cosmos; see too the case of Cisti the baker (*Decameron* VI.2), who also uses his Florentine ingenuity to prevail over the low social standing dictated to him by fortune. Despite his low birth, Cisti finds exactly the right answer to show the visiting dignitary Geri Spina that he is being unreasonable. Fortune in the *Decameron* is not Boethius' or Dante's minister of divine providence, but most often a personification of all the impersonal circumstances beyond control of human intentionality; humans can nonetheless use their ingenuity to find opportunities to overcome what are sometimes represented as "mistakes" of fortune. See Howard Rollin Patch, *The Tradition of the Goddess Fortuna in Roman Literature and in the Transitional Period*, Smith College Studies in Modern Literature 3.3 (Northampton, MA: Smith College, 1922); Vincenzo Cioffari, "The Conception of Fortune in the *Decameron*," *Italica* 17 (1940): 129–37; Cioffari, "The Function of Fortune in

Fortune in "The Tale of the Two Coffers" is not Boccaccio's figure for the impersonal circumstances beyond the control of human intentionality, whose "mistakes" can nonetheless be overcome by human ingenuity. Unlike Alfonso, Gower's king does not overrule fortune, but rather uses it as the vehicle for his lesson. In the tale's narrative logic, the courtiers desire material advancement – the gifts of fortune – according to their own injured sense of merit; their choice of the worthless coffer instead repays their grudging service to the king according to a principle of equitable justice. But if fortune embodies any principle of justice, then it differs from the figure familiar from many medieval texts and images. Fortune can be Boethius' agent of divine providence, or the Stoics' hard didactic figure who teaches humans not to pin their happiness on the fleeting temporal rewards of wealth, friends, and power.[10] This version of fortune turns her wheel, which kings mount, reign for a moment, and then fall, regardless of individual merit, as the wheel rotates inexorably. Courtiers rise and fall in the same trajectory. Had Gower evoked this familiar figure, the courtiers would have only themselves to thank when fortune behaves like fortune.

Here lies the confusion of "chance" and "pourveance" in "The Tale of the Two Coffers": the king's intended lesson emerges only because the delegated chooser picks the worthless coffer. The story would fall apart if the courtiers actually got the material advancement they covet. Instead, "chance" is aligned with the king's intent; from this we must infer that it is neither random accident nor the amoral, impersonal force beyond human intentionality personified by Boethius and his followers. Rather, it is determined by personal ethical merit, and is thus capable of delivering an ethical lesson.[11]

Dante, Boccaccio, and Machiavelli," *Italica* 24 (1947): 1–13; Teodolinda Barolini, "The Wheel of the 'Decameron'," *Romance Philology* 36 (1983): 521–39; David Wallace, *Chaucerian Polity: Absolutist Lineages and Associational Forms in England and Italy* (Stanford: Stanford University Press, 1997), 156–81; and Patrick Mula, "'Il peccato della fortuna'. La nouvelle X 1 du *Décaméron*," *Lettere italiane* 60 (2008): 43–83.

[10] Dante's divinely ordained "general ministra e duce" who "provede, giudica, e persegnue / suo regno" [the general minister [who] foresees, judges, and pursues her reign], *Inferno* VII, 78, 86–87, is largely Boethian; cited from Charles S. Singleton, ed. and trans., *Divine Comedy*, 6 vols. (Princeton: Princeton University Press, 1970–75), I, 72–75. See too Patch, *Goddess Fortuna*; and Cioffari, "The Function of Fortune."

[11] In the Prologue to *Vox Clamantis*, Book III, Gower differentiates between Fortune (which many blame for their unjust lots in life) and the real determiner of people's fates: personal ethical merit. Prosperity and adversity, he writes in the summary, result "non a fortuna, set meritis et demeritis" [not from fortune, but from merit and demerit]; and the Prologue itself begins: "Cum bona sue mala sit nobis sors tribuenda / Ex propriis meritis..." [Since good or bad fate is dealt to us according to our own merit...].

"The Tale of the Beggars and the Two Pastries," which follows "The Tale of the Two Coffers" (*CA* V.2391–2441), sharpens the point. This tale uses a slightly different version of the choice between two indistinguishable containers. Here no attention is given to the beggars' conduct, good or bad; thus their choice between two pastries, one stuffed with a capon and the other with riches, is entirely fortuitous and utterly amoral. There is no economy of merit and reward, and no principle of justice at stake. As the contrasting second term of a minimal pair, "The Tale of the Beggars and the Two Pastries" precisely isolates the peculiarity of fortune's role in "The Tale of the Two Coffers." When fortune is pressed into service to impart a lesson about the causal relation between conduct and reward, it muddies the roles both of fortune and of ethical choice.

The decisive role of fortune, then, is to render the treatment of ethical choice in "The Tale of the Two Coffers" perverse. Throughout the *Confessio*, from "Tale of Florent" in Book I to Gower's own confession in Book VIII, Genius' direct probing and his stories educate Amans in the processes of ethical choice. But ethical choice – Augustine's pull of desire originating in the senses, delighting the will, and reined in by rational deliberation – necessarily involves reason, the capacity for judging the rightness or wrongness of actions. Unlike the three caskets in *The Merchant of Venice*, with their decipherable hermeneutic and pointed inscriptions, the two coffers in Gower's tale give the courtiers no basis on which to make such a judgment. Because they are identical in appearance, the senses cannot distinguish between them. There is no rational means of knowing or inferring what each opaque, incommunicative coffer might "mean." Although the courtiers freely choose the wrong coffer, then, the tale models only a stripped down, nonsensical parody of ethical choice, without a role for reason and thus drained of the deliberation at the heart of ethics. Fortune too plays a *de minimis* role, since purely random "chance" is pressured by both narrative logic and the king's intent – which, the king implies, also embodies divine intent or "pourveance": "God wot what ye have deserved" (*CA* V.2326). Even if the outcome is just, it cannot result from any genuine ethical choice by the courtiers.

What, then, is Gower trying to accomplish in a tale that seems so thoroughly to undermine the ethical commitments of the whole poem? The problems in the role of fortune as well as the shadowy evocation of grace, I propose, point to a speculative critique of the Wycliffite terms of *dominium*. To sketch in this critique, I now return to the conundrum posed for referential integrity by "The Tale of the Two Coffers," in order to combine it with two of the overt topics of Book V: kingship and possession.

Referential integrity is as constant a concern in the *Confessio* as ethical choice, or the relation of "chance" and "pourveance"; I have argued elsewhere that it is a linguistic version of ethics.[12] It recurs time and again, starting with the Prologue's Golden Age when, Gower writes, rulers were trustworthy because their visible "visages" accurately registered the intangible intentions of their "corages":

> Of mannes herte the corage
> Was schewed thanne in the visage;
> The word was lich to the conceite
> Withoute semblant of deceite... (*CA* Pro. 111–14)

The same untroubled expressive ratio between face and inward intention appears in the Latin verses introducing the Golden Age: "Dum facies hominis nuncia mentis erat" [Then a man's face was the messenger of his mind] (*CA* Pro. after l. 92). Referential integrity is evinced in the ethical rhyme of "visage" and "corage," the most reliable sign of truth – a transparent, decipherable relation between outside and inside – in the poem whose purpose is to restore that relation. In this tale, however, the two coffers are indistinguishable, and no protocol of interpretation, no human rational process, can help a chooser reason from visible sign to inner content.

The two coffers, then, not only parody the processes of ethical choice, but also model the decay of truth in reference in Gower's diminished contemporary world. The failure of linguistic reference was a live topic in the late fourteenth century, argued most compellingly by the theologians and polemicists associated with the Wycliffite movement. The non-referentiality of the coffers' accidence suggests the recurrent Wycliffite idea that truth is truth, regardless of the human words used to refer to it. The problem of the two coffers is not ontological or theological, however, but epistemological – a matter of knowing, interpreting, deciphering the evidence of our accidental world – and thus very much in Gower's own poetic domain. Whereas Gower's purpose was to reform people (and language) so that their "visages" could rhyme with their "corages," Wycliffite writings tended more toward anti-materialist immediacy – a view suggested by the inert indecipherability of the coffers. Impatient with material signs, images, or language, the Wycliffite ideal was not to reform them, but to dispense with them altogether in favor of direct apprehension of God's meaning.[13] This view is most familiar in the translation and interpretation of Scripture, for instance in this passage from a tract supporting vernacular translation of the Bible:

---

[12] See "Inside Out in Gower's Republic of Letters," in *John Gower, Trilingual Poet: Language, Translation and Tradition*, ed. Elisabeth Dutton with John Hines and R. F. Yeager (Cambridge: D. S. Brewer, 2010), 169–81.

[13] For a study of the Wycliffite war on images, see Sarah Stanbury, *The Visual Object of Desire in Late Medieval England* (Philadelphia: University of Pennsylvania Press, 2007).

> Þis trett[yse] þat folewþ proueþ þat eche nacioun may lefully haue holy writ in here moder tunge.
>
> Siþen þat þe trouþe of God stondiþ not in oo langage more þan in anoþer, but who so lyueþ best and techiþ best plesiþ moost God, of what langage þat euere it be, þerfore þe lawe of God written and tauȝt in Englisch may edifie þe commen pepel, as it doiþ þe clerkis in Latyn, siþen it is þe sustynance to soulis þat schulden be saued.[14]

What matters here is not the language expressing "the trouthe of God" but rather the state of virtue of the interpreter – "who so lyueth best." The untrustworthy mediation of language tends to get in the way and lead to error; but God communicates his truth directly to the heart of the good man, whose interpretation is warranted by his moral and spiritual standing. This Wycliffite touchstone resembles the two coffers in the failure of material reference to express moral, ethical, or spiritual standing – which is somehow known even though "no man wiste what it mente." The resemblance is only partial, since Gower's tale suggests not that the good man can discern the "truth" of the coffers – the choosers lack such virtue – but that the choice renders the moral state of the chooser open and public. The choice, like that in *The Merchant of Venice*, discerns the "truth" of the courtiers.

But the problem may not be the hapless courtiers. It may be the king. The partiality of resemblance suggests that the underlying problem is not material reference alone, but also secular *dominium*, or lordship: the justification of possession of things, offices, and political authority by moral and spiritual standing alone. The link between the Wycliffite impatience with linguistic reference and their thinking about secular lordship may be found in the first chapter of the English version of Wyclif's *De officio regis*:

> Syþen witte stondis not in langage but in groundynge of treuthe, for þo same witte is in Laten þat is in Grew or Ebrew, and trouthe schuld be openly knowen to alle manere of folke, trowthe moueþ mony men to speke sentencis in Yngelysche þat þai han gedirid in Latyne, and herfore bene men holden heretikis.[15]

Truth apprehended immediately in the heart of a good man is the basis not only for scriptural interpretation, but also for equally grace-based Wycliffite ideas on *dominium*, which held, as Anne Hudson has succinctly written, that "authority depended not upon the office but upon the righteousness of the man holding the office."[16]

---

[14] Cambridge University Library MS. II.6.26, fols. 41V–46; quoted from Anne Hudson, *Selections from English Wycliffite Writings*, 20, 107.
[15] Hudson, *Selections*, 25, 127.
[16] Hudson, *The Premature Reformation* (Oxford: Oxford University Press, 1988), 315.

The proposition that Gower is thinking through the problem of the coffers with Wycliffite terms – or conversely, thinking through Wycliffite ideas by casting them into the terms of this narrative – helps make sense of the tale's combination of uncommunicative coffers with the king's use of fortune to impart an ethical lesson. Although many of Wyclif's ideas about *dominium* are amply attested elsewhere, only in Wycliffite writings are they linked to problems in linguistic reference. The conviction that grace alone authorizes scriptural interpretation and civil *dominium* was recognized by contemporaries as radical.[17] For Wyclif, secular lordship – both possession and authority – is founded in grace; such *dominium*, if just, necessarily combines possession and political authority.[18] Crucially, a human secular lord has authority only over goods of fortune, not spiritual gifts.[19] Rulers delegate authority over the goods of fortune – wealth, land, and so on – according to "condign" merit: "When a temporal lord lends his subject according to the subject's worthiness, the subject's merit is commensurable with the lord's [...]. Condign merit implies that the meritorious truly deserve the reward, requiring the giver to give it to the merited as something due."[20] Moreover, since the secular lord possesses goods and the authority to distribute them only by virtue of being a steward of God, he confers them by grace.[21] Conversely, then, if the king – whose *dominium* results from his alignment with divine will – withholds goods of fortune, the would-be recipients implicitly lack the requisite condign merit. The disgruntled courtiers' conduct – complaining about the king's failure to reward them – both

---

[17] Stephen E. Lahey, *Philosophy and Politics in the Thought of John Wyclif*, Cambridge Studies in Medieval Life and Thought, Fourth Series (Cambridge: Cambridge University Press, 2003), 67. Grace-based truth in scriptural interpretation was the first proposition condemned at the Council of Constance in 1415. Wyclif's ideas on *dominium* were derived largely from Richard Fitzralph's Augustinian, papalist *De Pauperie Salvatoris* (1356), but differed from Fitzralph's in viewing the created *dominium* of the just secular ruler as the "instantiation" of divine *dominium* (Lahey, 46), a view which became the basis for Wyclif's radical denunciation of clerical possession. For recent discussions of Wycliffite *dominium*, see too Anne Hudson, ed., *Wyclif: Political Ideas and Practice. Papers by Michael Wilks* (Oxford: Oxbow Books, 2000); and Takashi Shogimen, "Wyclif's Ecclesiology and Political Thought," in *A Companion to John Wyclif, Late Medieval Theologian*, ed. Ian Christopher Levy (Leiden and Boston: Brill, 2006), 199–240.

[18] See Lahey, *Philosophy and Politics*, 54.

[19] "Civile dominium est dominium proprietarium active viatoris super bonis fortune plene secundum leges humanas" [Civil *dominium* is the proprietary *dominium* held by the active sojourner over the goods of fortune in full accord with human law] (*De civili dominio*, III.11.178.10, quoted and discussed in Lahey, *Philosophy and Politics*, 112).

[20] Lahey, *Stanford Encyclopedia of Philosophy*, https://plato.stanford.edu/entries/wyclif-political/, summarizing Wyclif, *De civili dominio* III, 178.9–17). Consulted 16 April 2018.

[21] Lahey, *Philosophy and Politics*, 103.

invokes the commensurability of condignity and suggests that they deserve no secular authority or possession delegated by the king owing to their lack of virtue. This is the position suggested by the Latin marginal summary of the story, which accords scant sympathy to the courtiers. Their grumbling suggests the favorite dodge of unrewarded underlings: that amoral fortune has determined the outcome without reference to their merit.[22] They act as if their very lack of advancement proved that they deserved it. The king's lesson is admirably suited to demonstrating that their condition results from their own choice, for it is literally the case: they choose the worthless coffer. Sadly, the metaphorical model works better in fiction than in practice.

But if Wycliffite terms are evoked to expose the courtiers as undeserving, they do not imply that Gower endorses Wycliffite ideas. Rather, as Andrew Cole has written, "Wycliffism is [...] part of the processes of cultural negotiation itself, an emergent fund of ideas, forms, and rhetorics" that were the most powerful contemporary tool to draw upon in thinking about (among many central topics) *dominium*.[23] Since the practical force of Wycliffite *dominium* was intended to divest clerical possessioners, Gower's discussion of the ills of the contemporary Church in the Prologue to the *Confessio* is relevant here, because parts of it sound so much like a Wycliffite critique of clerical possession. After excoriating simony, Gower reverts to his frequent complaint about hypocrisy in which "visage" masks rather than reveals "corage."[24] Thus he characterizes clerical possessioners by the *species pietatis*

---

[22] See Mervyn James, *Society, Politics and Culture: Studies in Early Modern England* (Cambridge: Cambridge University Press, 1986), 13.

[23] Andrew Cole, *Literature and Heresy in the Age of Chaucer* (Cambridge: Cambridge University Press, 2008), 186. See too Alistair Minnis, who makes a parallel argument with respect to Chaucer: "the fact that Chaucer was interested in such issues need not mean that he advocated them in some distinctively Lollard form;" see *Fallible Authors: Chaucer's Pardoner and Wife of Bath* (Philadelphia: University of Pennsylvania Press, 2007), xv.

[24] See *Confessio*, Prologue 442-63, including:

> Ther ben also somme, as men seie,
>   That folwen Simon ate hieles,
>   Whos carte goth upon the whieles
>   Of coveitise and worldes Pride,
>   And holy cherche goth beside,
>   Which scheweth outward a visage
>   Of that is noght in the corage.
>   For if men loke in holy cherche,
>   Betwen the word and that thei werche
>   Ther is a full gret difference.
>   Thei prechen ous in audience
>   That no man schal his soule empeire,
>   For al is bot a chirie feire
>   This worldes good, so as thei telle... (442-55)

that was considered the hallmark of the heretic, even though elsewhere in the *Confessio* he blames "This newe secte of Lollardie" (*CA* Pro.349) for divisions in the Church.[25] Far from endorsing Wycliffite *dominium*, Gower evidently found parallels between his own and Wycliffite ideas unnerving – making it imperative that he work out how to think about them.

Confessio V's focus on problems of possession provides the larger context for how Gower resolved this ambivalence, and why it was so important for him to work through the challenge these emergent ideas posed to his own thinking on secular *dominium*. As elsewhere, he is more concerned with ethics and politics than theology. The explicit topic of Book V is Avarice – obviously connected to *dominium*, which originally in Roman law referred to private possession.[26] Wyclif was not the only thinker to minimize the differences between private possession and the political authority to dispose it. By the fourteenth century *dominium* had acquired a political dimension, including jurisdiction, the authority to possess or delegate possession – and to rule.[27] Thus Dante's *De monarchia* argues with impeccable logic – and terrible psychologic – that since greed (*cupiditas*) is the flaw that most leads humans astray, the universal emperor should be given unbounded sovereignty. With no land beyond his possession or jurisdiction, Dante reasons, the emperor will have no object to covet – leading to the absurd conclusion that his desire itself will also wither away. The emperor's universal *dominium* will thus result in universal justice and peace.[28]

Like Dante's treatise, Book V of the *Confessio* intimately links kingship to possession, beginning with its striking version of Midas' Golden Touch. Here Midas models the processes of ethical choice – the delectation of the will, and the succumbing to temptation – as he first rejects the proffered

---

See too the thorough critique of clerical misdeeds in *Vox Clamantis*, Book III, including especially chapters 2–4, 5–6, 11–12, and 19–21, which concern chiefly the subordination of spiritual care to worldly possessions. *Vox Clamantis*, in G. C. Macaulay, ed., *The Complete Works of John Gower*, Vol. 4: *The Latin Works* (Oxford: Clarendon Press, 1902, rpt. 1968).

[25] Hermann Grundmann, following the inquisitor Bernard Gui, defines *species pietatis* (appearance of devoutness) as: "die sichtbare Wirklichkeit als bloße Maske des wahren Wesens entwerten" ("visible phenomenal reality as a mere mask of true being"); see "Der Typus des Ketzers in mittelalterlicher Anschauung" (Leipzig and Berlin: B. G. Teubner, Sonderdruck, 1927), 96.

[26] According to Janet Coleman, in classical Roman private law, lordship or *dominium* concerned "ownership of corporeal things"; see "Property and Poverty" in *The Cambridge History of Medieval Political Thought, c.350–c.1450*, ed. J. H. Burns (Cambridge: Cambridge University Press, 1988), 607–48 (611). In this essay, Coleman also traces the medieval revival of Roman civil law from the twelfth through fourteenth centuries, especially concerning *dominium* and *possessio*.

[27] See Coleman, "Property and Poverty," and Lahey, *Philosophy and Politics*, 24–64.

[28] *De monarchia* I.x.11–14. Cited from http://etcweb.princeton.edu/dante/pdp/, ed. Pier Giorgio Ricci, trans. Prue Shaw, Edizione Nazionale (Florence: Società Dantesca Italiana, 1965). Consulted 16 April 2018.

rewards of "delit," "worshipe," and "profit" (*CA* V.187–88) and then falls into "coveitise / of gold" (*CA* V.223–24), imagining and taking pleasure in the prospect of using all his new gold for the benefit of his kingdom. His motives closely follow Dante's arguments for the emperor's universal *dominium* in *De monarchia*: to achieve peace and justice. Gold, he thinks to himself, "'can make of hate love / And werre of pes and ryht of wrong'" (*CA* V.238–39). Thus, despite his original rational assessment, he chooses the Golden Touch. It's a disaster. Midas quickly repents his choice, and undoes it. The opening story of Book V thus intertwines avarice with kingship – "lordship" (*CA* V.196) or *dominium* – but subordinates both to the processes of ethical choice, with its possibility of repentance and transformation.

Such subordination is missing from "The Tale of the Two Coffers," where the just outcome is achieved apparently because the king is a good man with immediate access to the source of wisdom and virtue. Three elements of the tale I have touched on – the inert lack of referentiality of the indistinguishable coffers, the role ascribed to fortune, and the centrality of possession – either the advancement the courtiers desire, or the riches at the king's disposal to delegate as he sees fit – suggest that the work of the tale is to figure out how Gower's understanding of kingly authority and just rule differs from the emergent Wycliffite discourse on *dominium*, on grounds both ethical and poetic. It is the systematic exclusion of ethical choice that makes "The Tale of the Two Coffers" so troubling, the king's lesson so empty of the kind of transformation Midas undergoes. The courtiers have no ethical basis for their choice between indistinguishable coffers, no interpretative protocol (such as those in *The Merchant of Venice*) that would guarantee or forbid a relationship between "chance" and "pourveance." We may assume that the king (like Alfonso in *Decameron* X.1) – whose wisdom and "hih prudence" (*CA* V.2289) are carefully limited to his ability to see into his courtiers' resentment – is a just ruler whose *dominium* is real because it is aligned with the divine will – but actually we have no way of knowing whether he is a just king or a tyrant. Michael Wilks cites a contemporaneous objection to Wyclif's theology of *dominium*: that he "had no answer to the objection that he never really made it clear how one was to distinguish between the elect and the damned, so that it was virtually impossible to tell who had a right to rule and possess, and who did not."[29] For this reason, Wycliffite *dominium* may have had radical elements in theory, but lacked practical consequences. Again Wilks: "The practical significance of Wyclif's doctrine of dominion and grace was therefore the reverse of revolutionary. Behind a smokescreen of predestinarian speculation it enabled him to reconstruct the old lay ideal

---

[29] Michael Wilks, "Predestination, Property and Power: Wyclif's Theory of Dominion and Grace," *Studies in Church History* 2 (1965): 223; quoted from Anne Hudson, ed., *Wyclif: Political Ideas and Practice. Papers by Michael Wilks* (Oxford: Oxbow Books, 2000), original pagination.

of a theocratic monarchy and a proprietary church."[30] A subject living under Wycliffite *dominium* cannot discern whether or not the ruler is justified, and thus must obey him as if he were. "The Tale of the Two Coffers" depicts a Wycliffite polity at odds with everything Gower seeks to accomplish in the *Confessio Amantis*: the reformation of the individual subject who learns to make better ethical choices, and the reformation of the polity with the help of a poet who, rather than holding his tongue, instead writes a poem initially to advise a king, later revised to address a broader polity as "a bok for Engelondes sake" (*CA* Pro.24).

The Wycliffite polity in "The Tale of the Two Coffers," with its crucially unknowable grace, complicates the argument that Gower's disenchantment with Richard II by 1392–93 caused him to switch his political allegiance to Henry of Derby and to revise the *Confessio* accordingly.[31] The new version omits the idealized scene of commission in the *Confessio*'s Prologue, including its fulsome obeisance to Richard; and the original ending, with more praise for the king (*CA* Pro.*24–92; VIII.*2940–*3116). In their places Gower substitutes a new dedication to Henry and a new ending (*CA* Pro.16–92; VIII.2940–3172) that outlines Gower's ideal exercise of kingly *dominium*:

> For if a kyng wol justifie
> His lond and hem that beth withynne,
> First at hym self he mot begynne,
> To kepe and reule his owne astat
> That in hym self be no debat
> Toward his God... (*CA* VIII.3080–85)

Like most of the rest of the *Confessio*, the text of "The Tale of the Two Coffers" underwent no revisions that might serve as evidence of a political conversion. But its tense equipoise of sympathy and critique – toward both

---

[30] Wilks, "Predestination, Property and Power," 235.
[31] John H. Fisher offers the standard account of Macaulay's recensions as a political conversion in *John Gower: Moral Philosopher and Friend of Chaucer* (New York: New York University Press, 1964), 119–23; see too Peck, *Kingship and Common Profit*, 8–9; George B. Stow, "Richard II in John Gower's *Confessio Amantis*: Some Historical Perspectives," *Mediaevalia* 16 (1993): 3–31; Lynn Staley, "Gower, Richard II, Henry of Derby, and the Business of Making Culture," *Speculum* 75 (2000): 68–96; and Frank Grady, "Gower's Boat, Richard's Barge, and the True Story of the *Confessio Amantis*: Text and Gloss," *Texas Studies in Literature and Language* 44.1 (2002): 1–15. As Peter Nicholson argues in "The Dedications of Gower's *Confessio Amantis*," *Mediaevalia* 10 (1984): 159–80, there is little internal evidence to support this account. For a cogent account of the intersection of textual evidence with Gower's political orientation, see Joel Fredell, "John Gower's Manuscripts in Middle English," in *The Routledge Research Companion to John Gower*, ed. Ana Sáez-Hidalgo, Brian Gastle, and R. F. Yeager (London: Routledge, 2017), 91–96.

courtiers and king – registers an uneasiness with partisanship of any kind, especially when it comes to claims of grace-based right to rule.

"The Tale of the Two Coffers" rather pointedly implicates Richard. Richard's ideas about kingship appear to have been acquired largely from Giles of Rome's *De regimine principum*, most likely through intermediaries like his tutor Simon Burley and his early favorite Michael de la Pole – both victims of Parliament's efforts in the late 1380s to curb Richard's acts and authority as king.[32] It's thus not surprising that these ideas overlap considerably with the Wycliffite theology of *dominium*, which was also based indirectly (through Fitzralph) on the same tradition of political thought.[33] The representation of the "wise king" acting out of "hih prudence" initially suggests a sympathetic mirroring of Richard's own self-image, which Nigel Saul has described as a new Solomon, a "sage" philosopher-king, modeled on Charles V of France.[34] Moreover, Richard's exalted sense of his own majesty as the divinely-anointed vicar of God on earth, his actions aligned (like those of an ideal Wycliffite secular ruler) with the divine will, makes sense of the tale's strong (if partial) evocation of the Parable of the Vineyard, whose vintner – a stand-in for the king of heaven – distributes his wage as an unearned gift of grace. But in his strategy of elevating late-comers at the expense of those who had labored longer in the kingdom's service, Richard resembled the king in "The Tale of the Two Coffers" more closely than he does the parable's vintner, who gives each the same penny. Once he reasserted his authority to rule in 1389, Richard began once again (as he had early in his reign, notably with Burley, Robert de Vere, and de la Pole) to reward new favorites with land and life-tenure titles. He essentially replaced the traditional councils of the great hereditary nobles with a courtier model of kingship, in which newly elevated favorites owed their positions entirely to the grace and favor of the king.[35]

The overlap between the thirty-three articles in the "Record and Process," the official Lancastrian justification for deposing Richard on grounds of tyranny, and the concerns with *dominium*, *possessio*, and the elevation of late-comers over long-serving courtiers in "The Tale of the Two Coffers," makes the experience of reading them side by side like entering a time warp. The costs of courtier kingship caused the royal household budget to balloon, requiring sometimes forced (and sometimes unrepaid) loans. Richard justified his expropriations by the theory that as king, he retained

---

[32] Janet Coleman, *Medieval Readers and Writers, 1350–1400* (New York: Columbia University Press, 1981), 18, identifies a French translation of *De regimine principum* in Burley's library, which was forfeited when he was appealed and executed for treason in 1388.

[33] Lahey, *Philosophy and Politics*, 24–35; Saul, *Richard II*, 16, 249–50, 449.

[34] Nigel Saul, *Richard II* (New Haven: Yale University Press, 1997), 465.

[35] For an account of Richard's increasingly autocratic courtier kingship after 1389, especially 1389–91, see Saul, *Richard II*, 235–69.

dominium over all possessions anyway, merely delegating them to their apparent owners. At least nine articles concern his attitudes about *possessio* or property – seizure of the hereditary lands of nobles on trumped up charges of treason, extortion of property to pay fees for pardons, cavalier appropriation of crown treasures as personal property, and so on. No fewer than six articles cite his elevation of "unworthy persons" as evidence of misrule. Articles Sixteen and Seventeen cite his exalted view of kingship as above human law.[36] Two articles in particular are eerily foretold in "The Tale of the Two Coffers." Article Twenty-Six charges that whereas private property was protected by ancient law, the king "frequenter dixit et affirmauit quod vita cuiuscumque ligei sui, ac ipsius terre, tenement, bona, et catalla, sunt sua, ad voluntatem suam" [frequently declared that the lives of each of his subjects, together with their lands, tenements, goods, and chattels were his, and subject to his will].[37] And Article Sixteen charges that Richard acted "secundum sue arbitrium voluntatis" [according to his own arbitrary will] in disregarding the laws and customs of the realm, claiming instead that "leges sue in ore suo et aliquoiens in pectore suo, et quod ipse solus posset mutare et condere leges regni sui" [his laws were in his mouth, or, at other times, that they were in his breast; and that he alone could change or make the laws of his kingdom].[38]

To read backwards from the 1399 account justifying the victorious Lancastrians – and to the "Record and Process" one must add Gower's own versification into political narrative in the *Cronica Tripertita* – to a tale written a decade earlier risks mistaking the contingencies of the early 1390s for hardened inevitabilities. While "The Tale of the Two Coffers" is concerned with the issues of possession, merit, and kingship by divine grace that later became the backbone of the case against Richard's tyranny, the terms it uses to explore them are almost pointedly non-partisan. With the king's problematic use of fortune to impart a lesson in ethical merit, Gower both returns to a topic of long-standing concern in his previous poems (especially Book III of *Vox Clamantis*) and draws specifically on a Wycliffite rhetoric about *dominium*. The discomfort it registers with the exercise of

---

[36] See David R. Carlson, *The Deposition of Richard II: "The Record and Process of the Renunciation and Deposition of Richard II" (1399) and Related Writings* (Toronto: Pontifical Institute of Medieval Studies, 2007), Articles One, Five, Thirteen, Fifteen, Eighteen, and Nineteen on giving "bona et possessions [...] ad [...] personis indignis" [goods and property to unworthy persons] (article 1, 29–30); Articles Four, Five, Seven, Twelve, Fourteen, Fifteen, Twenty-One, Twenty-Four, and Twenty-Six on disrespect for property rights; and Articles Sixteen and Seventeen on the claim to be above human law. Translations from Chris Given-Wilson, *Chronicles of the Revolution, 1397–1400: The Reign of Richard II* (Manchester: Manchester University Press, 1993), 168–89.

[37] Carlson, *Record and Process*, 47; Given-Wilson, *Chronicles of the Revolution*, 180.

[38] Carlson, *Record and Process*, 42; Given-Wilson, *Chronicles of the Revolution*, 177–78.

dominium, even by a king also represented sympathetically, points to an alternative explanation of the Henrician revisions to the *Confessio*. Although it can't be proven, one might consider the possibility that the revised third recension ending articulates not so much a vision of ideal *dominium* as an uneasy *ex post facto* philosophical justification for Gower's shift in allegiance. The new ending is preoccupied with grace, the crucial unknowable factor of Wycliffite *dominium*.[39] It posits that right rule proceeds from "rightwisnesse," and asserts that unless a king "hym self amende / Toward his god and leve vice," he will fall into tyranny (*CA* VIII.3069–71). The consequence for a king who does not govern himself is to lose his grace-based legitimacy – his true *dominium*:

> For what kyng sett hym uppon pride
> And takth his lust on every side
> And wil nought go the righte weie,
> Though god his grace caste aweie
> No wondir is, for ate laste
> He schal wel wite it mai nought laste,
> The pompe which he secheth here. (*CA* VIII.3089–95)

Or so Gower supposes: paraphrased, the passage above suggests that it wouldn't be any wonder if God cast his grace aside from a king who strayed from the right way, and in the end, he should recognize that the pomp he seeks is evanescent, like the gifts of fortune. The passage is above all tentative. What it cannot know is what no one can discern in a grace-based Wycliffite polity: whether the ruler has a right to *dominium*. The fundamental problem, posed narratively by "The Tale of the Two Coffers" and politically by Richard II's justifications for his exercise of *dominium*, remains unresolved. Certainly regime change did not resolve it: when Henry IV laid claim to the throne in 1399, he asserted his own claim "þat god of his grace hath sent me [...] to recouer" his rightful inheritance.[40] The confusion that so troubles "The Tale of the Two Coffers" – to treat possession, the king's distribution of the gifts of fortune, merit, and God's grace as reflexes of one another – would not end with Henry's ascension.

---

[39] The word appears seven times in the third recension; see *CA* VIII.2984, 3028, 3046, 3053, 3092, 3099, and 3131; compare three instances in the first recension (*CA* VIII.*2985, *3044, and *3112).

[40] Carlson, *Deposition*, "Henry's Challenge and Acclamation," 58.

CHAPTER 5

EARTHLY GOWER: TRANSFORMING GEOGRAPHICAL TEXTS AND IMAGES IN THE *CONFESSIO AMANTIS* AND *VOX CLAMANTIS* MANUSCRIPTS

Amanda J. Gerber

THE NOW-ICONIC MANUSCRIPT IMAGE of Gower as an archer taking aim at a tripartite earth has attracted attention in relation to the poet's ethical and national concerns, with the latter being likened to the characteristically English militarism of archers at the turn of the fourteenth century.[1] However, the earth that supplies the archer's terrestrial target has remained only a backdrop for modern scholarship, which tends to gravitate towards Gower the socio-political commentator instead of Gower the writer with an impressive command of geography. Chaucerian criticism has fared better on this front, amassing studies of his toponymic references, interest in the Near East, and the diverse geographical areas in which his tales occur.[2] As

---

[1] Maria Wickert, *Studies in John Gower*, 2nd edition, trans. Robert J. Meindl (Tempe, Arizona: Arizona Center for Medieval and Renaissance Studies, 2016), 70. Meindl also refers to Gower's "posture as archer/satirist" in the *Vox Clamantis*. Robert J. Meindl, "The Latin Works," in *The Routledge Research Companion to John Gower*, ed. Ana Sáez-Hidalgo, Brian Gastle, and R. F. Yeager (New York: Routledge, 2017), 348.

[2] Warren Ginsberg, "From Simile to Prologue: Geography as Link in Dante, Petrarch, Chaucer," in *Through a Classical Eye: Transcultural and Transhistorical Visions in Medieval English, Italian, and Latin Literature in Honour of Winthrop Wetherbee*, ed. Andrew Galloway and R. F. Yeager (Toronto: University of Toronto Press, 2009), 145–64; Carol F. Heffernan, *The Orient in Chaucer and Medieval Romance* (Cambridge: D. S. Brewer, 2003); Geraldine Heng, *Empire of Magic: Medieval Romance and the Politics of Cultural Fantasy* (New York: Columbia University Press, 2003); Noel Harold Kaylor, Jr., "The Orientation of Chaucer's *Canterbury Tales*," *Medieval Perspectives* 10 (1995–96): 133–47; Stephen Knight, "Places in the Text: A Topographicist Approach to Chaucer," in *Speaking Images: Essays in Honor of V. A. Kolve*, eds. R. F. Yeager and Charlotte C. Morse (Asheville, NC: Pegasus Press, 2001), 445–61; Miriamne Ara Krummel, "Globalizing Jewish Communities: Mapping a Jewish Geography in

with many topics, Gower's geographical sophistication becomes trivialized when juxtaposed with Chaucer's, a trivialization with certain justifiable premises. Gower has comparatively little interest in the Near East and in detailed settings. Gower also includes fewer geographical references than does Chaucer, and his treatments of these references differ in some respects from each other within his own corpus. In particular, the *Confessio Amantis* tends to treat geographical details as literal locations, whereas the *Visio* that introduces the *Vox Clamantis* infuses them with multiple layers of meaning. Both poems, however, often turn to historical texts for details about the earth's regions.

This reliance on historical texts has prompted modern scholars to treat Gower's geographical references more as abstract concepts than as existing places, implying that Gower's reliance on written traditions contradicts what otherwise might be recognized as actual geographical knowledge. As a result, the few studies produced on Gower's geographical topics tend to address them as *perceptions* of space instead of tangible places. Ethan Knapp's analysis of Egypt's intellectual (particularly astrological) impact on the *Confessio* exemplifies this treatment, as does Kurt Olsson's discussion of place in the *Vox Clamantis*, a discussion that quickly transitions from geographical London to conceptual justice.[3] Although such abstract concepts influence Gower's geographical depictions, his geographical topics also encompass physical locations that helped render subjects historical, instead of purely conceptual. This essay proposes that, in the process of using geographical locations to ground his narratives, Gower appropriates a skeptical tradition dating back to antiquity while also contributing a new sense of mythological meaning. As a result, Gower's comparatively limited interest in physical geography yields a relatively sophisticated engagement with textual geography, resulting in exegetical approaches that generate multivalent readings of the historical events depicted within the *Confessio* and the *Vox Clamantis*. In this way, Gower's poems present an array of

---

Fragment VII of the Canterbury Tales," *Texas Studies in Literature and Language* 50 (2008): 121–42; Kathy Lavezzo, *Angels on the Edge of the World: Geography, Literature, and English Community, 1000–1534* (Ithaca, NY: Cornell University Press, 2006); Kathryn Lynch, ed., *Chaucer's Cultural Geography* (New York: Routledge, 2002); Sylvia Tomasch, "*Mappae mundi* and the 'Knight's Tale': The Geography of Power, the Cartography of Control," in *Literature and Technology*, ed. Mark Greenberg and Lance Schachterle (Bethlehem, PA: Lehigh University Press, 1992), 66–98.

[3] John Ganim also addresses the abstract concept of space in "Gower, Liminality, and the Politics of Space," *Exemplaria* 19 (2007): 90–116. Ethan Knapp, "The Place of Egypt in Gower's *Confessio Amantis*," in *John Gower, Trilingual Poet: Language, Translation, and Tradition*, ed. Elisabeth M. Dutton, with John Hines, and R. F. Yeager (Cambridge: D. S. Brewer, 2010); and Kurt Olsson, "John Gower's *Vox Clamantis* and the Medieval Idea of Place," *Studies in Philology* 84.2 (1987): 134–58.

"geo-historical exegetics," a type of textual explication that ancient scholars developed to reinterpret mythology as historical events that occurred in specific geographical locations.[4] To explore this array, the following pages first address the academic context that supplied these exegetical foundations before turning to the *Confessio*, the *Vox Clamantis*' *Visio*, and the four *Vox Clamantis* archer illustrations with three different geographical representations. The historical interpretations discussed here are not original to Gower but rather place him within an ancient tradition often disseminated through classical literature to medieval writers along with the techniques of Latin composition. Gower, however, goes further by often layering his inheritance to produce unique readings that re-write his own historical moment as part of an ancient geographical and exegetical landscape.

THE SPREAD OF HISTORICAL EXEGESIS

The geographical traditions with which Gower engaged predominantly relied on ancient Roman erudition to define the boundaries and relevance of the observable earth, despite an increasing medieval awareness of the world beyond its climes.[5] The practice now known as cartography tended to reserve its efforts for seafarers' portolan charts; the rest of the period's so-called maps only remotely resembled their modern forms of representation.[6] In fact, the word "map," more specifically *mappa*, was rarely used and referred

---

[4] Maura Nolan mentions one aspect of this experimentation in relation to the *Vox Clamantis*' Boethian tension between experience and authority. Maura Nolan, "The Poetics of Catastrophe: Ovidian Allusion in Gower's *Vox Clamantis*," in *Medieval Latin and Middle English Literature: Essays in Honour of Jill Mann*, ed. Christopher Cannon and Maura Nolan (Cambridge: D. S. Brewer, 2011).

[5] Ptolemy's geographical theories influenced western Europe through his *Almagest* since the twelfth century and through tables of geographic co-ordinates, yet the first Latin translation of *Geographia* did not commence until the Florentine commission at the beginning of the fifteenth century. Patrick Gautier Dalché, "The Reception of Ptolemy's *Geography* (End of the Fourteenth to Beginning of the Sixteenth Century)," in *The History of Cartography*, vol. 3: *Cartography in the European Renaissance*, ed. David Woodward (Chicago: University of Chicago Press, 2007), 285–364. See also O. A. W. Dilke, "The Culmination of Greek Cartography in Ptolemy," in *The History of Cartography*, vol. 1: *Cartography in Prehistoric, Ancient, and Medieval Europe and the Mediterranean* (Chicago: University of Chicago Press, 1987), 177–200 (esp. 190–99).

[6] See, for example, Patrick Gautier Dalché, *Carte marine et portulan au XIIe siècle: le Liber de existencia riverarium et forma maris nostri Mediterranei (Pise, circa 1200)* (Rome: Ecole française de Rome, 1995); and Tony Campbell, "Portolan Charts from the Late Thirteenth Century to 1500," in *History of Cartography*, vol. 1: *Cartography in Prehistoric, Ancient, and Medieval Europe and the Mediterranean*, ed. J. B. Harley and David Woodward (Chicago: University of Chicago Press, 1987), 371–463.

to the cloth on which some maps were drawn, not to the geographical representations themselves. Geographical representations' more customary moniker was *historia*, a categorization that informs the following pages' connection between geographical and historical subjects.[7] The resulting geographical tradition neither resembled its modern incarnation nor even constituted a complete discipline.[8] Geographical knowledge instead entered the medieval corpus indirectly through encyclopedias, chronicles, poems, and scholarship on other texts more than it did through maps like the Hereford *Mappa mundi*.

Gower explicitly addresses the textual inheritance of geographical knowledge in Book VII of the *Confessio*, which begins with encyclopedic classifications of diverse worldly studies from the perspective of Aristotle's supposed lessons for Alexander the Great.[9] After defining different disciplinary pursuits, Book VII initiates an account of the earth's creation, including the divisions of the earth and water:

> So as these olde clerkes spieke
> And sette proprely the bounde
> After the forme of Mappemounde. (*CA* VII.528–30)[10]

Gower's Aristotle recounts a rather standard process of deriving geographical knowledge from "olde clerkes," rather than from contemporaneous explorers or cartographers, for his verbal "Mappemounde."[11] "Olde clerkes," or ancient

---

[7] Harley and David Woodward, eds, *The History of Cartography*, 1, xvi.

[8] According to the *OED*, the first known use of "geography" in English is by John Skelton in 1487. Latin texts also tended not to use the Greek word. According to Natalia Lozovsky, only two Latin texts refer to *geographia*, namely Cicero and Ammianus Marcellinus. Due to inconsistent terminology in the Middle Ages, Lozovsky opts to use the adjective "geographical" instead of the noun when referring to the field's multiple incarnations. This essay adopts her adjectival practice. Natalia Lozovsky, *The Earth is Our Book: Geographical Knowledge in the Latin West ca. 400–1000* (Ann Arbor, MI: University of Michigan Press, 2000), 8–9, n. 4.

[9] For more about the scientific emphases of the *Confessio*'s Book VII, see George Fox, *The Mediaeval Sciences in the Works of John Gower* (Princeton: Princeton University Press, 1931); and James Simpson, *Sciences and the Self in Medieval Poetry: Alan of Lille's* Anticlaudianus *and John Gower's* Confessio Amantis (Cambridge: Cambridge University Press, 1995).

[10] All quotations from the works of Gower are taken from G. C. Macaulay, ed., *The Complete Works of John Gower*, 4 vols. (Oxford: Clarendon Press, 1899–1902); quotation from vol. III.

[11] Even as additional continents were discovered, medieval maps and some Renaissance ones tended to reproduce the same three continents as those identified in antiquity. Regarding the continued use of T-O diagrams, see, for example, Meg Roland, "'After poyetes and astronomyers': Geographical Thought and Early English Print," in *Mapping Medieval Geographies: Geographical Encounters in the Latin West and Beyond, 300–1600*, ed. Keith D. Lilley (Cambridge: Cambridge

authors, commonly supplied the medieval literate class with knowledge of the earth's bounds and divisions. These authors became a pivotal medieval source for the geographical language and graphic representations that were regularly transmitted to interpret ancient events as literal ones.

The *Confessio*'s literal interpretations belong to a general, fourfold method of exegesis: namely, literal, allegorical, moral or tropological, and anagogical interpretations that classical commentaries shared with biblical ones.[12] The literal level of meaning, which is also called historical or euhemeristic meaning, produced the foundation for all exegetical readings. According to medieval scholars like Nicholas of Lyra, the literal level prepared audiences for further studies in allegorical, tropological, and anagogical interpretations.[13] The *Confessio* adapts this practice by narrating literal tales of reputedly historical significance before Genius supplies various interpretations of the tales' ethical import. The historical sense that characterizes many of the *Confessio*'s tales originated in antiquity, derived from the tradition attributed to a Greek skeptic "Euhemerus," who was said to have converted mythic pagan gods into historical figures.[14]

"Euhemerus," like Homer, may not have existed, yet the tradition attributed to him left a lasting mark on ancient mythological traditions.[15]

University Press, 2013), 138–41. Regarding their presumed first use in Sallust's geographical chapter in the *De bello Jugurthino* (86–34 BC), see Catherine Delano Smith and Roger J. P. Kain, *English Maps: A History* (Toronto: University of Toronto Press, 1999), 37.

[12] For more about medieval exegesis, see especially Henri de Lubac, *Medieval Exegesis: The Four Senses of Scripture*, 3 vols., trans. Mark Sebanc and E. M. Macierowski (Grand Rapids, MI: W. B. Eerdmans Pub. Co., 1998–2009); and Alastair Minnis, "*Quadruplex sensus, multiplex modus*: Scriptural Sense and Mode in Medieval Scholastic Exegesis," in *Interpretation and Allegory: Antiquity to the Modern Period*, ed. John Whitman (Leiden: Brill, 2000), 229–54.

[13] Lubac, *Medieval Exegesis*, vol. 1, 1.

[14] The fragmentary text attributed to him, *Sacred Inscription*, unfolds as a travelogue told from the perspective of "Euhemerus" as he visits an island near Arabia, where he encounters engraved monuments commemorating the acts of great kings who came to be known as gods. "Euhemerus" uses these monuments to suggest that pagan mythology originates from a mistaken practice of apotheosizing monumental historical figures. This notion of mistaken practice informed many subsequent studies of ancient mythology and consequently gave rise to the exegetical level of meaning called euhemerism, or the historical sense that eventually came to be applied as the first level of interpretation for the Judeo-Christian Bible. For more about the origins and applications of euhemerism, see Syrithe Pugh, ed., *Mortalizing the Gods from Euhemerus to the Twentieth Century* (New York: Routledge, 2019).

[15] According to Tim Whitmarsh, the *Sacred Inscription*, written around 300 BC, was a philosophical experiment and parody of the Hellenistic ruler cult, but created an influential fiction of mythological historicism. Tim Whitmarsh, *Beyond the Second Sophistic: Adventures in Greek Postclassicism* (Berkeley: University of California Press, 2013), 49–62. For more about Greek skepticism, see

Gower, in particular, though never mentioning "Euhemerus" by name, indicates his indebtedness to the Greek tradition by providing historical readings of his pagan source material.[16] Book V of the *Confessio* supplies an expanded example of euhemerism when Genius the narrator states that the Chaldeans mistook the seven planets and sundry constellations for gods (*CA* V.752–57). By identifying a conflation of natural and supernatural entities, Gower's Genius employs euhemeristic skepticism to reaffirm the historical origins of mythology.[17] Scholars such as John Burrow and Robert Edwards have already observed the importance of historical exegesis for Gower when focusing on his literal readings, convincingly demonstrating Gower's reliance on this level of meaning that provided the foundation for all literary studies, especially Christian studies of ancient mythologies.[18] Nevertheless, the literal level of meaning offered more interpretive complexities than its generic label implies; this level of meaning also retained vestiges of the skepticism of "Euhemerus," especially its characteristic historicization of pagan gods by means of associating them with geographical locations.[19]

Gower's use of geographical references when constructing his historical narratives indicates some awareness of the euhemeristic approach. In the case of Aeolus, a wind god, Gower attributes the god's deified qualities to his point of origin: namely, that he became known as a wind god because of his patrilineal right to Sicily, an island that lay open to the wind (*CA* V.967–80). At times, such geographical reinterpretations emerge almost imperceptibly

---

Whitmarsh, *Battling the Gods: Atheism in the Ancient World* (New York: Alfred A. Knopf, 2015).

[16] The following pages refer to interpretations, paratexts, and poetic adaptations as readings to emphasize that these various levels of narrative transmission begin with readings of mythology, including annotations presented by anonymous readers of the manuscripts discussed below.

[17] As John Kirtland Wright observes, medieval geography was more capacious than its modern incarnation; it included studies of the earth, stars, celestial spheres, cosmology, astronomy, astrology, and theology because all were geocentric. Unlike "Euhemerus," neither Gower nor medieval scholars seemed to confine their mapping to the terrestrial world. John Kirtland Wright, *The Geographical Lore of the Time of the Crusades: A Study in the History of Medieval Science and Tradition in Western Europe* (New York: Dover, repr. 1965), 2.

[18] Burrow calls it the *Confessio*'s "prevailing mode of meaning," which Edwards regards not only as hermeneutics but also as a narrative technique that creates continuity within a mutable world and its divided social realms. This literal continuity may be characteristic of the *Confessio*, but, as will be discussed below, not of the *Vox Clamantis*. John A. Burrow, "Gower's Poetic Styles," in *A Companion to Gower*, ed. Siân Echard (Cambridge: D. S. Brewer, 2004), 239; and Robert Edwards, "Gower's Poetics of the Literal," in *John Gower, Trilingual Poet*, 62.

[19] Regarding the geographical legacy of euhemerism in medieval classical commentaries, see Amanda Gerber, "Grounding the Gods: Geographic Euhemerism in Medieval Europe," in *Mortalizing the Gods from Euhemerus to the Twentieth Century*, ed. Syrithe Pugh (New York: Routledge, 2019).

as part of the mythological narratives themselves. When describing Greek paganism, Genius lists several brief, euhemerized versions of gods and demi-gods, including Pluto swearing by the underworld's rivers:[20]

> Which Pluto hihte, and was the brother
> Of Jupiter, and he fro youthe
> With every word which cam to mouthe,
> Of eny thing whan he was wroth,
> He wolde swere his commun oth,
> Be Lethen and be Flegeton,
> Be Cochitum and Acheron,
> The whiche, after the bokes telle,
> Ben the chief flodes of the helle:
> Be Segne and Stige he swor also. (*CA* V.1104–13)

Genius begins with a fraternal relationship shared by deified and euhemerized accounts of Pluto. Pointedly, Gower then uses this moment to provide a brief geography lesson about the rivers of Hell: Lethe, Phlegethon, Cocytus, Acheron, and Styx. As rivers of the pagan Underworld, these geographical locations challenge euhemerism's typical geographical method for establishing gods as historical personages. The passage instead presents the five rivers as a series of geographical curses equivalent to "By God's wounds." In the process, the pagan god gains a "youthe," much as do some late medieval treatments of Christ's life.[21] Except for the god's childhood, Gower's historical reading of Pluto resembles his mythological reading, reiterating the god's genealogy and geographical context in the Underworld. The rivers of the Underworld particularly gained currency in the Middle Ages, perhaps because Christian lore offered no infernal geography of its own.[22] The result is a Christianized mythology that creates a historical level of meaning separate from the other three exegetical levels: namely, the allegorical, anagogical, and tropological senses.

---

[20] Greek paganism is one of four pre-Christian religions he identifies.
[21] See, for example, Nicholas Love's *Mirror of the Blessed Life of Christ*, or Love's source text, John of Caulibus' (also called Pseudo-Bonaventure's) *Meditationes uitae Christi*. Michael G. Sargent, ed., *Nicholas Love's Mirror of the Blessed Life of Jesus Christ: A Critical Edition Based on Cambridge University Library Additional MSS 6578 and 6686* (New York: Garland, 1992); and John de Caulibus, *Meditaciones vite Christi*, ed. Mary Stallings-Taney (Turnhout: Brepols, 1997).
[22] Dante provides perhaps the most renowned map of the classically delineated Underworld in the *Inferno*. See also variously Jacques Le Goff, *The Birth of Purgatory* (Chicago: University of Chicago Press, 1986); *Otherworld Journeys: Accounts of Near-Death Experiences in Medieval and Modern Times*, ed. Carol Zaleski (New York: Oxford University Press, 1987), esp. 26–96; *Visions of Heaven and Hell before Dante*, ed. Eileen Gardner (New York: Italica, 1989); *The Iconography of Hell*, ed. Clifford Davidson and Thomas H. Seiler (Kalamazoo, MI: Medieval Institute Press, 1992).

Amanda J. Gerber

Visualizing Geographical History

Gower's euhemerized myths had many precedents, not least of which were his classical source materials. Medieval copies of classical poems consistently accumulated marginalia and interlinear glosses that, among other subjects, directed readers' attention to the geographical information stored within their texts. Such paratextual comments functioned as reading aids similar to modern footnotes in that they explained obscure references or defined places mentioned in the primary text. Another sort of paratext consisted of regional diagrams and *mappaemundi*, the latter of which represent either the three known continents or the five climatic zones of the earth. Five-zone *mappaemundi*, or zonal diagrams, developed from Greek antiquity to designate five climates ranging from frigid to torrid.[23] Tripartite *mappaemundi*, or T-O (*orbis terrarum*) diagrams, presented the spherical earth in the shape of an O and the waterways dividing the three known continents in the shape of a T (Figure 5.1). T-O, zonal, and regional diagrams frequently found a home in copies of Virgil's, Ovid's, and Lucan's poetry. These graphic representations of geographical information, like their more numerous discursive variants, supplied context and reading aids for the poems they adorned, often elaborating on the primary source's direct references to places while arranging them so that students might be tested on their contents.[24] Geographical diagrams, with their simple but memorable designs, allowed readers of classical literature to visualize locations while reading about mythological subjects.

Manuscript copies of Ovid's *Metamorphoses* particularly acquired geographical diagrams to accompany Book 1's description of the components of the created world, a description similar to that in the *Confessio*'s Book VII. Zonal diagrams, which were common, directly rendered Ovid's account of creation from chaotic elements to the five ordered zones of habitable and uninhabitable regions, pole-to-pole: frigid, temperate, torrid, temperate, frigid. One such diagram appears in the larger sphere depicted in Figure 5.1 from the thirteenth-century copy of the *Metamorphoses* in Frankfurt-am-Main, Stadt- und Universitätsbibliothek, MS Barth. 110. In fact, one reader considered this zonal information and format so important that he repeated the diagram's outline on the other side of the folio

---

[23] James Evans, *The History and Practice of Ancient Astronomy* (Oxford: Oxford University Press, 1998), 62–63. Zonal diagrams are discussed by Alfred Hiatt, *Terra Incognita: Mapping the Antipodes before 1600* (Chicago: University of Chicago Press, 2008), 78.

[24] Bruce Eastwood makes this point about scientific diagrams, proposing that Carolingian schoolmasters designed them as mnemonics in order to test pupils on the information the graphic designs contained. See *Ordering the Heavens: Roman Astronomy and Cosmology in the Carolingian Renaissance* (Leiden: Brill, 2007), 9 and 424–25.

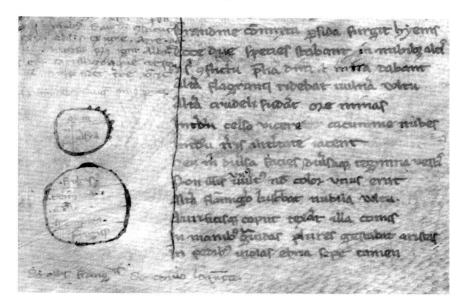

FIGURE. 5.1. Frankfurt am Main, Universitätsbibliothek Johann Christian Senckenberg Frankfurt am Main, MS Barth. 110, fol. 26r. By permission of Universitätsbibliothek Johann Christian Senckenberg Frankfurt am Main.

alongside a more direct reference to Ovid's lines about an unnamed god dividing the earth's regions into five zones to match those of the heavens (I.33–52). Ovid then specifies that these zones include an equatorial zone, two snowy poles, and two temperate zones between that blend frigid and torrid climes. Such diagrams graphically present a literal rendering of the poem, but some annotations further expanded Ovid's geographical lessons. The same producer of the zonal diagram also appended a T-O diagram on the same folio (Figure 5.1). T-O diagrams were the most common graphic representations of geography in the Middle Ages, and, like most graphic representations of the earth, they tended to appear as reading aids within manuscripts, illustrating points supplied by writers and connecting mentioned regions to readers' native Europe, which usually appeared in the bottom right corner of the orb.[25] Most versions preserved the same order of continents, but, as the example in MS Barth. 110 reveals, not even this practice was constant: MS Barth. 110 inverts the most common order for the continents by placing Africa in the top half, Europe in the bottom left quadrant, and Asia in the bottom right, instead of Asia at the top, Africa on the left, and Europe on the right (see Figure 5.2). These variations occur

---

[25] According to Delano-Smith and Kain, geographical mapping originated from biblical commentary traditions that prefaced the historical relevance and locations of Old Testament lore. Delano-Smith and Kain, *English Maps*, 8–9 and 18.

Amanda J. Gerber

FIGURE 5.2. Collegeville, Minnesota, St. John's University, MS Steiner 54 [HMML Pr. No. SJRB 00102], fol. 20v, the "T-O diagram". Photo courtesy of the Hill Museum and Manuscript Library, Saint John's University, Minnesota, USA. Published with permission of the Hill Museum and Manuscript Library, Saint John's University, Minnesota, USA. All rights reserved.

because they do not purport to represent the earth as it exists, but rather to render the earth for textual explication.

The adaptable T-O diagram found a home in many different works during the Middle Ages, including encyclopedias like Isidore of Seville's *Etymologiae*. For example, thirteenth-century Collegeville, MN, Hill Museum and Manuscript Library, MS Steiner 54 (Figure 5.2) provides a traditionally trisected T-O diagram within a reference to the cardinal directions (p[er] orie[n]tem usq[ue] septe[n]t[ri]onem) to illustrate one of its references to the *orbis*. The T-O diagram originates in the work of Ionic philosophers, but the versions that frequented copies of Isidore's *De natura rerum* and *Etymologiae* popularized the form, especially for medieval audiences.[26] Encyclopedic, biblical, and historical traditions alike tended to integrate the T-O design

---

[26] Chet Van Duzer and Ilya Dines explain the importance of Isidore of Seville's *Etymologiae* for establishing thematic mapping traditions, noting similar depictions in other encyclopedic works like Bartholomeus Anglicus' *De proprietatibus rerum*. M. M. Gorman further notes that readers of Isidore's *De natura rerum* were prompted to memorize the contents of diagrams such as the T-O, a mnemonic function that Andy Merrills emphasizes in his study of the repetitive geographical references throughout the *Etymologiae*. Chet Van Duzer and Ilya Dines, *Apocalyptic Cartography: Thematic Maps and the End of the World in a Fifteenth-Century Manuscript* (Leiden: Brill, 2016), 29–30; M. M. Gorman, "The Diagrams in the Oldest Manuscripts of Isidore's 'De natura rerum' with a Note on the Manuscript Traditions of Isidore's Works," *Studi Medievali* 42.2 (2001): 534–41; and Andy Merrills, "Geography and Memory in Isidore's *Etymologies*," in *Mapping Medieval Geographies: Geographical Encounters in the Latin West and*

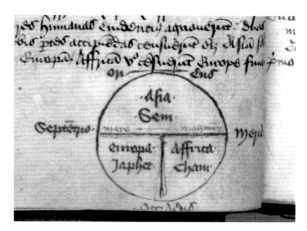

FIGURE 5.3. *De orbis indagacione facta per Iulium Cesarem*, San Marino, California, Huntington Library, MS HM 19960, fol. 13v. This item is reproduced by permission of The Huntington Library, San Marino, California.

with the names of the sons of Noah who reputedly founded each of the three continents. For example, the English compilation of historical works in San Marino, Huntington Library, MS HM 19960 adds the four cardinal directions along with Shem as the heir of Asia, Japhet of Europe, and Ham of Africa (Figure 5.3). By connecting biblical figures to specific regions, the diagram euhemerizes its depicted personages, a process that medieval scholars applied to biblical texts as well as to mythological ones.

Gower demonstrates his indebtedness to this form of reading and interpretation when he adopts the same terminology to describe a tripartite earth:

> Asie, which lay to the Sonne
> Upon the Marche of orient,
> Was graunted be comun assent
> To Sem, which was the Sone eldest;
> [...]
> The brother which was hote Cham
> Upon his part Aufrique nam.
> Japhet Europe tho tok he,
> Thus parten thei the world on thre.
> Bot yit ther ben of londes fele
> In occident as for the chele,

Beyond, 300–1600, ed. Keith D. Lilley (Cambridge: Cambridge University Press, 2013), 45–64.

Amanda J. Gerber

> In orient as for the hete,
> Which of the poeple be forlete
> As lond desert that is unable,
> For it mai noght ben habitable. (*CA* VII.554–57 and 577–86)

Here, Gower follows the usual medieval formula of dividing the world in three and assigning its parts to the three sons of Noah. The passage also integrates aspects of the zonal diagram's division of the earth into five regions, including habitable and uninhabitable sections (Figure 5.1). In this manner, Gower superimposes different types of geographical representations: especially a biblical T-O diagram, zonal diagram, and what approximates a travelogue as he mentions settlements moving from west to east. Such references to biblical figures demonstrate that euhemeristic readings were not the exclusive purview of classical lore.

According to David Woodward, Catherine Delano-Smith, and Roger Kain, medieval scholars developed geographical maps from antiquity to explicate the Judeo-Christian Bible,[27] yet they were also adapted for many allegedly historical works in the Middle Ages. By applying a common euhemeristic method to this geographical representation, Gower places the *Confessio* in the historical company of the Judeo-Christian Bible, chronicles, encyclopedias, and classical poems. These geo-historical designs prove significant for Gower's *Vox Clamantis* as well, so much so that four manuscripts include a *mappamundi* diagram in their Gower-as-archer illustrations.[28] In Glasgow, Glasgow University Library, MS Hunter 59 (T.2.17), produced between 1399 and 1408, a disproportionately large figure thought to resemble Gower aims his bow and arrow at a tripartite earth, an image that directly mirrors the Gower-as-archer illustration in London, British Library, Cotton MS Tiberius A. iv, fol. 9v.[29] These earths, in place of the more common three

---

[27] Delano-Smith and Kain, *English Maps*, 8–9 and 18. The earliest extant world map hails from Babylonia and dates to the sixth or fifth century BC, yet Anaximander of Miletus reputedly drew a world map somewhat earlier: see J. B. Harley and David Woodward, "The Foundations of Theoretical Cartography in Archaic and Classical Greece," in *History of Cartography*, 1, ed. Harley and Woodward, 134.

[28] The illustration features in Glasgow, Glasgow University Library, MS Hunter 59 (T.2.17); London, British Library, Cotton MS Tiberius A. iv; Oxford, Bodleian Library, MS Laud Misc. 719; and San Marino, Huntington Library, MS HM 150.

[29] A. I. Doyle and M. B. Parkes mention that the Hunter manuscript was written before Gower died in 1408. The Cotton Tiberius manuscript was also produced around the same time, that is, between the end of the fourteenth century and the first quarter of the fifteenth century. A. I. Doyle and M. B. Parkes, "The Production of Copies of the *Canterbury Tales* and the *Confessio Amantis* in the Early Fifteenth Century," in *Medieval Scribes, Manuscripts and Libraries: Essays Presented to N. R. Ker*, ed. M. B. Parkes and Andrew G. Watson (London: Scolar Press, 1978), 164 n. 3; Julie Gardham and David Weston, *The World of Chaucer: Medieval Books and Manuscripts* (Glasgow: Glasgow University Library, 2004),

Earthly Gower

FIGURE 5.4. Glasgow, University of Glasgow, MS Hunter 59 (T.2.17), fol. 6v. This image is reproduced by permission of University of Glasgow Library, Special Collections.

FIGURE 5.5. Rodrigo Jiménez de Rada's *Historia Gothica*, San Marino, California, Huntington Library, MS HM 1034, fol. 9. This item is reproduced by permission of The Huntington Library, San Marino, California.

continents, depict three elements: fire in the top left quadrant, earth (in the form of grass) beside it, and water below (Figure 5.4). The illustrator adapts the usual T-O format to show its elemental creation, as described both in Book VII of the *Confessio* and Book 1 of Ovid's *Metamorphoses*. T-O shaped elements also appear in other historical manuscripts, such as the *Historia Gothica* by Rodrigo Jiménez de Rada in San Marino, Huntington Library, MS HM 1034 (Figure 5.5). The Spanish chronicle's elemental diagram forms a decorated initial that introduces a description of the continents assigned to each of Noah's three sons. The fifteenth-century *Vox Clamantis* in San Marino, Huntington Library, MS HM 150 almost exactly duplicates the Hunter manuscript's elemental image, yet it produces a different collection of elements (Figure 5.6). The Huntington diagram replaces the red fire with a quadrant of blue sky, including stars and the moon. The minor exchange of one element for another demonstrates a modicum of independence for the illustrator, a sense of independence enhanced by the additional insertion of the red crosses on top of the T-O sphere and in the insignia of the fluttering

---

21; M. B. Parkes, "Patterns of Scribal Activity and Revisions of the Text in Early Copies of Works by John Gower," in *New Science Out of Old Books: Studies in Manuscripts and Early Printed Books in Honour of A. I. Doyle*, ed. Richard Beadle and A. J. Piper (Aldershot: Scolar Press, 1995), 81–121.

Ad mundum mitto mea iacula, dumque sagitto;
At ubi iustus erit, nulla sagitta ferit.
Sed male viuentes hos vulnero transgredientes,
Conscius ergo sibi se speculetur ibi.

FIGURE 5.6. *Vox Clamantis* and Other Latin Poems, San Marino, California, Huntington Library, MS HM 150, fol. 13v. This item is reproduced by permission of The Huntington Library, San Marino, California.

FIGURE 5.7. Oxford, Bodleian Library, MS Laud Misc. 719, fol. 21r.
By permission of The Bodleian Libraries, University of Oxford.

flag. The two red crosses present an earth conquered by Christianity, further narrowing Gower's earthly target to topics of Christian import.

The repetition and variation of the image might evince that *Vox Clamantis* illustrators considered the earth to be more than a backdrop for the archer's pointed critiques. As an image subject to revision, the earth diagrams, just like their aforementioned counterparts in historical traditions, gesture towards a malleable construction of the earth's designated boundaries. The flexibility of the format is perhaps nowhere more evident than in the crudest example of the archer image, that in the fifteenth-century manuscript Oxford, Bodleian Library, MS Laud Misc. 719 (Figure 5.7). The illustrator repeats the depiction of the archer perched on grassy terrain, but he aims at an earth divided into vertical bands instead of tripartite sections. The vertical strips present water at the top and bottom, with a collection of red and blue circles bordering the water and a crenellated castle in the middle. The divisions imitate the zonal format, much as the elemental diagram adapts the T-O design. The modified zonal diagram has precedents, such as London, British Library, Cotton MS Tiberius B. v, a miscellany produced in

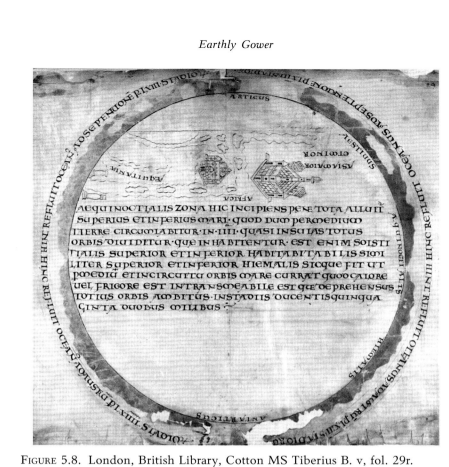

FIGURE 5.8. London, British Library, Cotton MS Tiberius B. v, fol. 29r. © The British Library Board.

England between the tenth and twelfth centuries (Figure 5.8). In the middle discursive note, the modified zonal diagram includes a description of zones, beginning with the equinoctial zone beneath the sea and separating the earth into uninhabitable and habitable areas with hot or cold climates. Above the discursive note, the illustrator integrates aspects of the T-O diagram by labeling Africa, Asia Major and Minor, and Aquitaine as a metonym for Europe. This depiction of the earth, like that in Bodley's Laud Misc. 719, suggests the existence of zones but emphasizes watery boundaries and fortifications more than the regions of the earth. The Gower example similarly foregrounds one building surrounded by water. The building likely represents the Tower of London described in Book I of the *Vox Clamantis* and discussed below, converting the archer's earth into a specific geographical target for his political criticism.[30]

---

[30] In some respects, this worldly scale used to frame one building relates the diagrammatic design more to Roman politicized maps than the Greco-Roman

These variations in the diagrammatic shape of the earth illustrate the fluidity of geographical topics in the Middle Ages. Rather than a collection of fixed boundaries, medieval audiences inherited a set of representational principles that could be adjusted to the contents of a text, such as the integration of Noah's sons or the elements, but not necessarily dictated by the world constructed by the text alone. In the case of the archer images, the representations of the earth recall elemental diagrams from chronicles and zonal diagrams from classical poems like Ovid's, yet they also pertain to the contents of the *Vox Clamantis* beside which they appeared. In these respects, the image of the terrestrial target introduces the *Vox Clamantis'* treatment of malleable geo-historical subjects.

THE *VOX CLAMANTIS'* EXPERIMENTS WITH GEOGRAPHICAL HISTORY

The *Vox Clamantis'* manipulations of geographical topics do not appear as frequently as the *Confessio*'s, despite using many of the same sources – especially Ovidian ones.[31] Those that do occur accumulate primarily within the first book's series of visions pertaining to the 1381 uprising, including a vision of the riotous masses transforming into animals and ravaging London, there renamed New Troy.[32] The dream of New Troy especially elaborates on Gower's geo-historical precedents. He appropriates the demolished ancient Troy because, according to Gower, the madness of London's people turning against their own city in 1381 surpasses the madness of the battles of Thebes, Carthage, and Rome (I.13). In one respect, these ancient locations function like standard classical allusions, whose mere mention adds layers of significance within the literal history; nevertheless, Gower also uses allusions to enfold the destruction of renowned classical sites within a contemporary local history and geography.

---

design of the zonal diagram. Roman maps were instead known for emphasizing the grandeur of the Empire instead of mapping the whole earth's terrain. Loredana Teresi, "Anglo-Saxon and Early Anglo-Norman *Mappaemundi*," in *Foundations of Learning: The Transfer of Encyclopaedic Knowledge in the Early Middle Ages*, edited by Rolf H. Bremmer Jr. and Kees Dekker (Leuven, Belgium: Peeters, 2007), 345. Conversely, David Woodward attributes zonal diagrams and the Macrobian tradition in particular to a pre-existing Greco-Roman mapping tradition. See his "Medieval *Mappaemundi*," in Harley and Woodward, eds, *History of Cartography*, 1, 299–318.

[31] For more about the *Vox*'s Ovidian citations, see especially Yoshiko Kobayashi, "Lament to Prophecy in Book I of John Gower's *Vox Clamantis*," in *Through a Classical Eye*, ed. Galloway and Yeager, 339–62; and Wickert, *Studies in John Gower*, 43 and 43 n. 61.

[32] For more about uses of New Troy, see especially Sylvia Federico, *New Troy: Fantasies of Empire in the Late Middle Ages* (Minneapolis: University of Minnesota Press, 2003).

Gower particularly exploits a parallel New Troy to set the dreamer's experiences in a historical tragedy, but one which, as Gower states, lacks corresponding epic heroes like Hector for Troy or Achilles for Argos (I.13). Without heroes, the so-called Beast Vision, in which the rebelling peasants transform into various animals, is left with bestial Ovidian anti-heroes. The metamorphoses of these anti-heroes still rely on geographical history to reveal their meaning, regardless of their mythic natures. For instance, the third group of metamorphosizing peasants, or rabble, become swine, with one wild boar produced in Kent and another hailing from the North[33] (*VC* I.5). In this instance, the Kent reference helps establish the dream allegory's historical subject as Robert Cave, a baker who led a mob of rebels from Kent.[34] The dream proceeds to discuss the localized and mythologized commoners as producing a more savage boar than even the Tegean wood (*VC* I.5). Gower emphasizes geographical locations even as he transforms the historical Cave into an allegorical animal, re-establishing the historical level of meaning. The vision superimposes a contemporary reading of classical imagery, placing the Kentish and Northern boars in a classical realm that also houses the Erymanthian boar that destroyed the lands of Arcadia or Tegea until Hercules killed it as one of his twelve labors. The similarly characterized boars supply a link between the almost historical present and the mythologized past, with the locations being used for differentiation. These geographical variants for the bestial destruction of land thus become part of a shared historical narrative whose only distinguishing features are the names of ancient, not medieval, heroes and the places, not periods, of destruction. In so doing, these references also contextualize the mob's destruction as a heinous act of epic proportions.

The use of place to connect histories becomes increasingly pronounced in the first book's third vision, or Ship Vision, which depicts the dreamer's concluding distress and salvation in terms of a shipwreck and the sudden calm that precedes a storm at sea. The dreamer presents himself as one of the nobles who sought refuge from the uprising in the Tower of London, which, in the dream, resembles a ship about to encounter a storm and Scylla. As rain pours upon them, Gower characterizes the tower in ancient terms:

---

[33] Eric W. Stockton suggests that the Northern boar might refer to John Wraw, who led the rebels in Suffolk, and Geoffrey Litster in Norfolk. Even though neither Wraw nor Litster met up with Wat Tyler or Robert Cave, the allegorical dream vision states that the North boar joined the Kentish boar, a misconstrued event also presented in the *Chronicon Angliae*. Eric W. Stockton, trans., *The Major Latin Works of John Gower: The Voice of One Crying and the Tripartite Chronicle* (Seattle: University of Washington Press, 1962), 349 n. 7.

[34] Stockton, *The Major Latin Works of John Gower*, 349 n. 1, in reference to Charles Oman, *The Great Revolt of 1381* (Oxford: Clarendon Press, 1906), 34 ff.

> Nuncia Iunonis varios tumefacta colores
> Induit, et vario more refudit aquas:
> Nulla set est gutta dulcis quam fuderat, immo
> Turpis, amara, rudis, vilis, acerba, grauis;
> Nil valet ad gustum liquor hic, qui corda bibentum
> Perforat, et quassat viscera tota simul.
> O felix, tales qui tunc euaserat ymbres,
> Qui sunt Stige magis et Flegetonte graues! (*VC* I.xvii.1637–44)[35]

[Juno's swelling messenger put on her varied colors and poured the waters back a different way. But no drop which she poured was sweet; instead it was foul, bitter, sharp, vile, harsh, heavy [1640]. This flowing water, which penetrated to the hearts of those drinking it and at the same time shattered their viscera, was worthless to the taste. O happy was the man who escaped such cloudbursts, which were more grievous than Styx or Phlegethon!][36]

The passage begins with a homage to Ovid in the shape of a quotation about Juno's messenger and the personification of rainbows, namely, Iris (*VC* I.21).[37] Rather than finishing the Ovidian allusion, however, Gower identifies the problematic nature of a rainbow that portends no cessation of the downpour, unlike the rainbow after Noah's Flood that God offers as a covenant not to obliterate creation again by flood. The vision further undercuts both pagan Ovid's and biblical Noah's rainbow significations when the ensuing lines intermingle different species, such as an owl swimming with larks, a wolf with sheep, and the wicked with the upright (1640–50). Unlike Noah's ark, in which all animals are paired and only the virtuous are saved, this tower-turned-ship upends creation in an anti-ark. As a result, those in the tower trying to escape the rebellious peasants are the ones who find no refuge and instead encounter cloudbursts more burdensome (or *graves*) than Styx and Phlegethon.

Understandably, Robert Meindl relates Gower's underworld allusions in the *Vox Clamantis* and the *Cronica Tripertita* to Dante's *Inferno*.[38] Gower's knowledge of Dante's works is difficult to establish with certainty, yet the comparison remains apt: Gower and Dante both combine modern politics

---

[35] Macaulay, ed., *Complete Works*, IV.
[36] Stockton, *The Major Latin Works*, 85.
[37] For more about the *Vox Clamantis*' allusions, see Pamela Longo, "Gower's Public Outcry," *Philological Quarterly* 92.3 (2013): 357–87; and Nolan, "The Poetics of Catastrophe."
[38] Meindl claims that Gower, like Dante, divides the *Cronica Tripertita* into three parts that move from an earthly purgatory to hellish territory and then to heavenly salvation. Meindl argues that the first part refers to earthly purgatory with a Lancastrian account of the Appellant Lords, the second represents a devilish king manipulating Parliament, and the third depicts heavenly intervention in the form of Henry Bolingbroke. Meindl, "The Latin Works," 348.

with classical cosmography and both poets integrate this combination into a topography shared by the Judeo-Christian and Greco-Roman traditions. Yet there are also purposeful differences that bear directly on Gower's intended message. Dante inserts his contemporaries like Brunetto Latini into an established classical topography,[39] whereas Gower depicts these mythic realms to demonstrate their dissimilarity from the world around him. Judeo-Christian anagogy and Greco-Roman allegory, traditionally separate forms of interpretation, become one in Gower's interpretive experiment. The literal meaning of the dream presents a deluge without a Christian consolation, that is, without the promise to Noah at the end. Gower then enfolds within it an anagogical meaning pertaining to the Christian afterlife, including Hell. The blended literal and anagogical meaning here suggests a greater hell on earth than Noah's Flood because this hell lacks the Judeo-Christian consolation of God's covenant and turns instead to pagan allegories. The resulting dream interweaves historical, anagogical, and allegorical meanings by interrelating Judeo-Christian and Greco-Roman allusions to rewrite the terror of the nobles striving to survive the revolt. The literal Tower of London comes to signify Greco-Roman and Judeo-Christian towers as well as Greco-Roman and Judeo-Christian hells. Thus, unlike conventional euhemerism, which uses locations to historicize narratives, Gower layers narratives and meanings onto one location. Many of the same geographical, mythological, and historical details also appear in the *Confessio*, including allusions to Iris and to the aforementioned infernal rivers.[40] In the *Visio*, however, these are presented simultaneously, to suggest that explaining the significance of the Tower of London requires multiple interpretive levels and historical precedents.

Maura Nolan has already addressed the *Vox Clamantis*' allusive, layered readings that complicate Ovid's poetry at the same time as Gower quotes it,[41] yet in the *Vox* the geo-historical layers cannot entirely be divorced from the rest of the text as they can in the *Confessio*.[42] Rather than ascribe to the

---

[39] Dante places Latini among sodomites in the seventh circle of Hell. Dante, *Inferno*, 15.

[40] For example, the *Confessio* mentions Iris, the messenger of Juno, who appears as a rainbow in V.1184–88.

[41] Nolan, "The Poetics of Catastrophe," 114–15.

[42] Medieval Ovidian scholarship, such as the so-called Vulgate commentary, tends to place allegorical comments in the top and bottom margins, whereas literal explications tend toward the right and left margins. Additionally, Arnulf of Orléans' allegorical and literal commentaries ended up circulating independently from each other, with the latter offering an introductory philological guide to the *Metamorphoses*. See David Gura, "A Critical Edition and Study of Arnulf of Orléans' philological commentary on Ovid's *Metamorphoses*," Ph.D. dissertation, The Ohio State University (THE:CLA2010PHD873), 19–24. Not all allegorical readings are physically separated in this manner, but, as in the *Confessio*, annotators did tend to demarcate interpretive distinctions by using labels such as "allegorice" or "allegoria talis est."

divided interpretive formats or even to Ovid's poetic lines, the *Visio* models a paradigm in which interpretive and allusive layers as well as inherited and original Latin lines become part of Gower's account of his own era. For example, Gower accumulates these interpretive layers in his ship-as-tower vision that characterizes people from different classes, especially the nobility, praying for divine aid:

> O quam tunc similis huic naui Londoniarum
> [...]
> Turris diuisa linguis Babilonis ad instar,
> Turris, vt est nauis Tharshis in ore maris.
> Sic patitur pressa vicii sub gurgite turris,
> Nescia qua morum parte parare viam.
> Quisque dolet, set non vt ego, dum talis amarum
> Spectat ad interitum naufraga Cilla meum.
> Hec ita sompnifero vigilans quasi lumine signa
> Vidi, quo timui dampna futura rei. (*VC* I.xviii.1743 and 1763–70)

[O, how like this ship was the Tower of London then, [...] a Tower divided like Babel with its tongues; a Tower like a ship of Tarshish on the face of the sea. Thus did the Tower suffer, overwhelmed in a whirlpool of vice, and not knowing which way to find the path of righteousness. Everyone suffered, but not as I did, for this shipwrecking Scylla was on the lookout for my bitter destruction. With my eyes almost asleep, I remained awake and witnessed these portents, for I was afraid of the disasters to come from the whole affair.][43]

Gower links the Tower of London to the biblical Tower of Babel and biblical Tarshish, a ship that David Carlson identifies as the Old Testament's Tharsus, a figure of excessive wealth to be overturned by the vengeful God.[44] The dreaming narrator then mentions his own suffering in relation to Scylla, a classical monster who, in some Ovidian manuscripts such as Vatican City, Biblioteca Apostolica Vaticana, MS Urb. Lat 341, is located in Italy.[45] Gower's passage also integrates classical geography to convert the monstrous events surrounding the Tower of London into a geo-historical symbol modelled after the ancient histories of both Greco-Roman Scylla and Judeo-Christian Tharsus in precisely this way. The Tower of London thus simultaneously becomes a figure of one moment in English historical time and of biblical, classical, and contemporary moments combined. The Bodleian Laud manuscript's presentation of an earth with nothing on it but

---

[43] Stockton, *Major Latin Works*, 87–88.
[44] David Carlson, ed., *John Gower: Poems on Contemporary Events: The Visio Anglie (1381) and Cronica tripertita (1400)*, trans. A. G. Rigg (Toronto: Pontifical Institute of Mediaeval Studies, 2011), 232.
[45] Vatican City, Biblioteca Apostolica Vaticana, MS Urb. Lat. 341, fol. 155r.

a singular fortified structure (Figure 7), that is, a singular edifice betokening one London location as well as similarly turbulent historical locations (such as Babylon, Troy, Noah's earth, and Hell) would seem to represent this type of combined moment. By constructing an edifice that signifies multiple locations, historical periods, and religious traditions simultaneously, the *Vox Clamantis* uses the tower and its biblical and classical counterparts to signify a universally relevant place, not just one historical location, period, or narrative context. The same claim could be extended to all of the Gower-as-archer images, which present the entire earth as Gower's target. The result expands euhemeristic meaning, compiling locations whose significations cross regional, textual, and historical divides.

Conclusion

The *Confessio* and Book I of the *Vox Clamantis* accumulate geo-historical readings into layered presentations of biblical, classical, and contemporary locations. With the same sources and the same polyvalent interpretation, the *Vox Clamantis*' *Visio* and the *Confessio* demonstrate Gower's pointedly flexible approach to geographical details. Both texts exhibit how accumulated layers can change meaning when juxtaposed with others. The *Confessio* follows more traditional exegetical guidelines to separate layers of exegesis from each other, especially the historical from the moral exegesis that reframes each tale. Diachronic narratives thus emerge from allusions (e.g. the inferable youth for Pluto), blurring the line between history and mythology. Conversely, the *Visio* opts for a comparative synchrony for the locations it mentions (e.g. the Tower of London's relationship to Babylon and Troy), focusing on them as symbols from specific moments rather than as developments over time. The *Confessio* and *Visio* provide dissimilar treatments of geographical information because of their divergent applications of worldly knowledge. However, despite their disparities, both texts present a geographical landscape that intentionally integrates meanings beyond the basic narrative backgrounds they provide for individual tales. As the manuscripts' verbal and visual images establish, geography in Gower's hands is not only a backdrop for his political targets but also a discourse that reflects a pervasive curiosity about the earth's material composition and the geographical foundation for historical readings.

Particularly in the *Visio*, these textual practices initially proffer a lived experience for which his audience would not need additional context. It is this, his own historical moment, that Gower mythologizes, rather than historicizing his mythological sources. In a sense, Gower's *Visio* converts contemporaneous events into allusions, whereas the *Confessio* follows established methods for converting ancient allusions into history. These allusions presume a certain level of knowledge from their audience, for which reason the *Confessio* provides verbal context and the *Vox* manuscripts a visual one, including explanations of geographical references such as the tripartite earth and the rivers of Hell. Much like the deceptive simplicity of geo-historical readings, the juxtaposition of these explanatory impulses of the *Confessio* and the allusive impulses of the *Visio* reveals a rich literary culture whose exegesis offers more creative license than initially appears. Gower repeatedly recites geographical details from his textual sources within their historical, rather than moral, context. Nevertheless, this traditional textual layering of geo-historical terrains offered Gower possibilities for flexible interpretations. Thus, although he might not create the geographical landscapes that have fascinated many Chaucerians, Gower demonstrates that the most basic of educational exercises can become a tool to convert mythology into history and history into mythology.

CHAPTER 6

PARATEXTUAL DEVIATIONS: THE TRANSMISSION AND TRANSLATION OF GOWER'S *CONFESSIO AMANTIS* IN THE IBERIAN PENINSULA*

Tamara Pérez-Fernández

ONE OF THE MOST widespread perceptions regarding John Gower's *Confessio Amantis* is the relative regularity shown by text and *mise-en-page* across all recensions and manuscript groups. Scholars, of course, have noted the differences between the extant witnesses of the poem, but so far the efforts to engage in a comprehensive study of what makes them distinct from each other – and what this means for our idea of the author, the text, and the scribe – are still scant. In part, Gowerians might have been disinclined to undertake the collation of all the extant copies of the poem because of the existence of several excellent editions based on Oxford, Bodleian Library, MS Fairfax 3,[1] a manuscript that embodies the long-held idea that the text of the *Confessio* "exhibited a steady tendency to rid itself of error."[2] But

---

* I would like to thank Ana Sáez-Hidalgo for her insightful comments and her help during the preparation of this chapter. Research for this essay is part of the research project "Exilio, diplomacia y transmisión textual: Redes de intercambios entre la Península Ibérica y las Islas Británicas en la Edad moderna," funded by the Agencia Española para la Investigación, Ministerio de Economía (MINECO, Spain), ref. FF12015-66847-P.
[1] G. C. Macaulay, ed., *The English Works of John Gower*, 2 vols. (London, New York, Toronto: Oxford University Press for the Early English Text Society, 1900); and John Gower, *Confessio Amantis*, ed. Russell A. Peck, transl. Andrew Galloway, 2nd ed., 3 vols. TEAMS Middle English Texts Series (Kalamazoo, MI: Medieval Institute Publications, 2004–13), http://d.lib.rochester.edu/teams/text-online, accessed 12 February 2018.
[2] Macaulay, "English Works" I, cxxxi. Although Macaulay's edition of the *Confessio* includes a list of variants, it does not take into account all the manuscripts.

there is value in divergence, in the variants, scribal or otherwise, found in the poem and in the Latin apparatus that accompanies it.[3]

Divergence can be especially useful to study the Iberian translations of the *Confessio*: the rendering of a text into another language inevitably brings forward modifications that range from lexical variation, to content adaptation, or changes in the layout introduced to conform to a new geographical and cultural context. One of the most radical adaptations undergone by the English *Confessio* in its new life in the Iberian Peninsula was the loss of its Latin apparatus, which was either translated into Portuguese and Castilian or eliminated completely.[4] The manuscript Madrid, Real Biblioteca MS II-3088 (henceforth MS Real Biblioteca) contains the Portuguese translation of the *Confessio*, the *Livro do Amante*:[5] it was copied in Ceuta in 1430 by the scribe Joham Barroso at the behest of a Portuguese nobleman called Fernando de Castro, "o Moço" [the younger]. The original Latin apparatus that features in the majority of the extant English manuscripts of the poem was translated into Portuguese and greatly reduced, both in size and content: the Latin verses and most of the marginal glosses common in the English manuscripts are omitted in the Portuguese copy, and of the roughly five hundred Latin prose summaries that precede the tales in the *Confessio*, only three hundred and fifty are kept in the *Livro do Amante*, written in red and inserted in the text column before the tales. These rubrics are shorter than their Latin counterparts, and they usually contain the initial reference to the main topic of the tale and a succinct summary of the story. The rubrics in MS Real

---

[3] Siân Echard laments the regularity of the extant manuscripts of the *Confessio* and the apparent lack of interest in those differentiating features that, though minor, could be fundamental in the study of the reception of the poem. Siân Echard, "Pre-Texts: Tables of Contents and the Reading of John Gower's *Confessio Amantis*," *Medium Aevum* 66 (1997): 270.

[4] This fact changed the face of the poem not only in regard to its layout, but also concerning how it portrayed the author and the different frameworks he created. For more information about this topic, see my articles "The Margins in the Iberian Manuscripts of John Gower's *Confessio Amantis*: Language, Authority and Readership," in *Gower in Context(s). Scribal, Linguistic, Literary and Socio-historical Readings* (Special issue of *ES. Revista de Filología Inglesa* 33.1), ed. Laura Filardo-Llamas, Brian Gastle, and Marta Gutiérrez Rodríguez (Valladolid: Publicaciones Universidad de Valladolid, 2012), 29–44; and "From England to Iberia: The Transmission of Marginal Elements in the Iberian Translations of Gower's *Confessio Amantis*," in *Text and Transmission in the European Middle Ages, 1000–1500. Cursor Mundi 28*, ed. Carrie Griffin and Emer Purcell (Turnhout: Brepols, 2018): 119–40.

[5] For a full codicological description of the Iberian manuscripts, see Manuela Faccon, *La Fortuna de la Confessio Amantis en la Península Ibérica: el testimonio portugués* (Zaragoza: Prensas Universitarias de Zaragoza, 2010); and Mauricio Herrero Jiménez, with Tamara Pérez-Fernández and Marta Gutiérrez Rodríguez, "Castilian Script in the Iberian Manuscripts of the *Confessio Amantis*," in *John Gower in Iberia: Manuscripts, Influences, Reception*, ed. Ana Sáez-Hidalgo and R. F. Yeager (Cambridge: D. S. Brewer, 2014).

Paratextual Deviations

Biblioteca are almost always accompanied by decorated initials, which were not always executed, leaving blank spaces in several parts of the manuscript. Closely linked to the prose summaries is a table of contents written in Castilian that takes up the first seven folios of MS Real Biblioteca and which was added to the *Livro do Amante* at some point after the manuscript's arrival in Castile.[6] The entries in this table are based on the Portuguese rubrics, but they are even more concise, and frequently state only the subject of the tale. The anonymous Castilian tabulator had a tendency to skip the rubrics that point out subsections within larger tales, so the entries in the table of contents do not always coincide with the Portuguese rubrics.

The *Confisyon del Amante*, the Castilian translation of the *Confessio*, is found in one surviving copy, Madrid, Biblioteca del Escorial g-II-19 (henceforth MS Escorial). This manuscript has been dated to the late fifteenth century, but the scribe and the place of production are unknown.[7] The brief introduction to the book found in fol. 1r right before the table of contents identifies Juan de Cuenca as the Castilian translator and mentions how Robert Payn, a canon in Lisbon, translated the English poem into Portuguese. Like the *Livro do Amante*, its Portuguese counterpart, the *Confisyon del Amante* also features two different sets of paratexts: on the one hand, a series of prose summaries in Castilian that precede each chapter, inserted within the text column and written in the same ink as the text. These summaries have an almost unbroken correspondence with the Portuguese rubrics. There are, however, notable differences: the translations are often not word-for-word; a number of the Portuguese rubrics are omitted; and original material has been added. MS Escorial also opens with a table of contents written by the same hand who copied the rest of the manuscript. The entries in this table are the lengthiest of all the Iberian paratexts and include more comprehensive recapitulations of the tales than those provided in the Portuguese and Castilian summaries. The entries are intended to work in conjunction with the Castilian summaries, but the chapter and folio numbers provided do not always correspond with those in the summaries, rendering this table largely ineffectual.

Even though there is a clear correlation between the paratexts in MSS Real Biblioteca and Escorial, there are numerous deviations that set them apart and that pose challenges to the way we understand these texts and the translators and scribes who shaped them. Needless to say, the loss of

---

[6] The first eight folios do not belong to the original manuscript of the *Livro de Amante*: they comprise the table of contents, a zodiac, a soap recipe, and several scribbles. They were inserted in the mid-fifteenth century, which suggests that the manuscript was in Castile at that point. See Herrero, "Castilian Script," 22–23.

[7] Herrero Jiménez has proved that the Castilian codex was in fact two manuscripts copied by the same scribe that were joined in the early sixteenth century. "Castilian Script," 27.

the original English manuscript used by Robert Payn as well as the absence of other Portuguese and Castilian copies result in gaps in the textual transmission that limit our approach to the paratextual material; with the textual witnesses available to us, we cannot, in full confidence, ascribe the particularities of the paratexts in the Iberian manuscripts either to the Portuguese or the Castilian translators, since Robert Payn's and Juan de Cuenca's holographs have not survived. Therefore, in most cases we can only trace the origin of the deviations in the paratextual material back to MS Real Biblioteca, the earlier manuscript, or to MS Escorial.

However, on occasion the divergences in the paratexts allow us glimpses of the lost English exemplar used for the Portuguese translation. One such example is the summary before the tale of Amphitrion and Geta: in the English manuscripts, the Latin summary briefly recounts how Amphitrion supplanted his friend Geta in order to get to his wife Almena, whom he loved:

> Qualiter Amphitrion socium suum Gentam, qui Almeenam peramavit, seipsum loco alterius cautelosa supplantacione substituit. (*CA*, II.2459)[8]

> [How Amphitrion substituted himself for his companion Geta by a deceptive supplantation in another's place.]

This summary is translated almost word for word in the Portuguese rubric:

> De como anphetriom enganosamente soplantou seu sogro ieta do amor dalmena que elle muyto amaua. (*LA*, fol. 57v)[9]

> [About how Amphitrion deceptively supplanted his father-in-law Geta for the love of Almena, whom he loved dearly.]

However, there is one important deviation: whereas in the original Latin summary Geta is Amphitrion's "socium" – from *socius*, "companion, comrade, partner"[10] – in the Portuguese translation he is described as his "sogro," or father-in-law. Because the Castilian version derives from the Portuguese

---

[8] All the quotations from the English text are taken from Russell A. Peck's edition, and the translations of the Latin summaries are Andrew Galloway's. John Gower, *Confessio Amantis*, ed. Russell A. Peck, transl. Andrew Galloway, 2nd ed., 3 vols. TEAMS Middle English Texts Series (Kalamazoo, MI: Medieval Institute Publications, 2004–13), http://d.lib.rochester.edu/teams/text-online, accessed 12 February 2018. I have used the following abbreviations in the quotations: *CA* stands for *Confessio Amantis*, *LA* for *Livro do Amante*, and *Confisyon* for *Confisyon del Amante*.

[9] All the translations from Portuguese and Castilian into English are my own.

[10] *Dictionary of Medieval Latin from British Sources*, s. v. #5, http://logeion.uchicago.edu/index.html, accessed 12 February 2018.

translation, and not directly from an English manuscript, to find "suegro" in MS Real Biblioteca is predictable. Gower describes the relationship between both men with the terms "friendschipe" and "compaignie" (*CA*, II.2461); this suggests that Amphitrion and Geta were indeed friends and not relatives. In this context, the abovementioned change in their relation, from friend to "father-in-law," could be considered as something merely anecdotal, perhaps a misreading on the part of the Portuguese translator that would eventually be passed onto the Castilian. And yet, this deviation reveals a wider implication for the textual transmission of Gower's poem. Macaulay's collation of the variants in other manuscripts of the *Confessio* reveals that there is a group of manuscripts that contain the variant "socrum" instead of "socium."[11] It is possible that at some point in the textual transmission of the English *Confessio* a scribe miscopied the original "socium," which was then kept in the subsequent copies derived from that manuscript. Although the English manuscript that was translated by Robert Payn is now lost, the Portuguese translation of this term in the *Livro do Amante* suggests that it also contained the variant "socrum." This example shows that the Iberian manuscripts contain deviations whose origins can be connected with the textual transmission of the English copy used for the translation. As a result, the analysis of the deviations can help us narrow down not only its textual family, but also the textual characteristics and the transmission of that lost English manuscript into the Iberian Peninsula. A more comprehensive collation of the variants in the Latin apparatus of the English manuscripts of the *Confessio* would allow us to identify more deviations originated in the copy that was translated into Portuguese.

As I already noted, most of the divergences between the English, Portuguese, and Castilian copies can only be tracked back to the Portuguese manuscript. It is the Portuguese prose summaries in particular that seem to have determined the characteristics of the other paratexts, both in the table of contents of MS Real Biblioteca and in MS Escorial. As I said before, the rubrics throughout the *Livro do Amante* provide the main subject of the tales and forego most of the plot details, and the other paratexts generally follow them. But sometimes the work of rewriting is more complex, as in the case of the summary before the tale of Robert Grosseteste and the consequences of his tarrying:

> Nota de grosteta ogrande astronomo e como ell por atardança dhūu momento perdeo oacabamiento dhūa sotil obra que auya sete anos que auya começada. (*LA*, fol. 88r)

---

[11] The manuscripts in this group are H1, X, G, E, R, C, L, and B2. Macaulay, "English Works" I, clxxxi.

[Note about Grosseteste the great astronomer, and how by a momentary tardiness he could not finish a subtle work that he had started seven years before.]

This prose summary is the Portuguese rendition of the following Latin summary:

> Nota adhuc super eodem de quodam Astrologo, qui quoddam opus ingeniosum quasi ad complementum septennio perducens, vnius momenti tardacione omnem sui operis diligenciam penitus frustrauit. (*CA*, IV.234)

[Note moreover about the same matter, concerning a certain astrologer who, pursuing for seven years a certain most cunning labor almost to its completion, totally negated all the diligence of his work by the delay of a single moment.]

In the English *Confessio*, the prose summary mentions an astrologer without disclosing his name, whereas in the *Livro do Amante* the Portuguese rubric identifies Grosseteste right from the start. The same happens in the *Confisyon*, where the paratexts follow the rubric in the *Livro* almost word for word.

Similar rewritings can help us draw a thought-provoking picture of the political and cultural interests of the person – translator, adaptor, scribe – behind the Portuguese rubrics. One such example is the summary before the "Tale of the Three Questions." In the English poem, this tale is preceded by a long Latin summary that describes in depth the story of King Alphonse and Petro, his knight, and the three questions that Alphonse asks him:

> Hic narrat Confessor exemplum simpliciter contra Superbiam; et dicit quod nuper quidam Rex famose prudencie cuidam militi suo super tribus questionibus, vt inde certitudinis responsionem daret, sub pena capitalis sentencie terminum prefixit. Primo, quid minoris indigencie ab inhabitantibus orbem auxilium maius obtinuit. Secundo, quid maioris valencie meritum continens minoris expense reprisas exiguit. Tercio, quid omnia bona diminuens ex sui proprietate nichil penitus valuit […]. (*CA*, I.3068)

[Here the Confessor narrates an instructive example against pride in general; and he says that in recent times a certain king, famous for his prudence, presented to a certain one of his knights a logical challenge comprising three questions, whence he might give a correct response under pain of capital punishment: first, what having less need has obtained greater help from inhabitants on earth; second, what having merit of greater value demands less expense; third, what diminishes all good things but is worth utterly nothing in itself...]

The Portuguese summary is notably shorter, as usual:

> Aqui tracta oconfesor por enxenplo · em sollido · contra a soberua e conta sobrello hũa storia que aconteçeo antre hũu onrrado Rey que foi naspanha muy famoso em sabedoria por nome chamado · dom afonsso e hũu seu cauallero que auja nome dom pero e sua filha a petronylla. (*LA*, fol. 40r)

> [Here the Confessor treats *in solidum* against pride and tells about it a story that happened between an honorable king that was very famous in Spain because of his wisdom, whose name was Dom Affonso, and his knight whose name was Dom Petro and his daughter Petronylla.]

The differences regarding the Latin original are evident: the Portuguese summary states the main subject of the tale, pride, but instead of recounting the three questions, as the Latin paratext does, the Portuguese summary focuses on the three main characters and acknowledges their names and identities, locating the story in Spain. Upon first examination this rewriting is similar to that of the abovementioned Grosseteste rubric. However, whereas in the former the supplementary material can be found in the first lines after the rubric, in this case the names of Alphonse, Petro, and Peronelle are introduced three hundred lines after the beginning of the tale:

> And over this good is to wite,
> In the cronique as it is write,
> This noble king of whom I tolde
> Of Spaine be tho daies olde
> The kingdom hadde in governance,
> And as the bok makth remembrance,
> Alphonse was his propre name:
> The knyht also, if I schal name,
> Danz Petro hihte, and as men telle,
> His dowhter wyse Peronelle
> Was cleped, which was full of grace. (*CA*, I.3387–97)

This indicates that Robert Payn, or some later editor or scribe, read the whole tale and then created a new version of the original Latin annotation. The modified Portuguese summary, therefore, was not merely an attempt to simplify the original paratext but a conscientious effort to bring forward specific elements within the tale that were not included in the Latin paratext found in the English exemplar. The allusion to Spain – or, properly speaking, Castile – places the tale in a Peninsular setting from the start; using the term "dom" to refer to King Alphonse underscores that Iberian context, as it is a title that was given to kings and noblemen in Portugal and Castile. Both deviations can be understood as a desire to cater to the concerns of the new

Iberian audience, and especially the Castilian one, who might have been interested in reading a story about some of their countrymen.

But in the modification of the original paratext there seems to be other interests at work: the Portuguese summary translates "Rex famose prudentie" as "Rey que foi naspanha muy famoso em sabedoria" [King that was well known in Spain on account of his wisdom]. *Prudentia* was a Latin term with different meanings in the Middle Ages, among them "prudence" or "ability, skill, proficiency."[12] It was also related to *wisdom*, as in the Aristotelian notion of "practical wisdom,"[13] but the most common Latin equivalent to *wisdom* was *sapientia*. That is why the decision to translate "prudentie" as "sabedoria" – "wisdom" – instead of the more accurate Portuguese term *prudência* is crucial to understand this paratext: the reference to a wise Spanish king named "Afonso" seems to me a deliberate effort to identify the Alphonse in Gower's tale with King Alphonse X of Castile and León, commonly known as Alphonse the Wise.[14] An Iberian reader of the fifteenth century reading the Portuguese summary would probably establish the same connection, including Fernando de Castro "o Moço," who commissioned MS Real Biblioteca and whose ancestors had a close relationship with some of the most notable descendants of Alphonse X. The royal house of Avis, thought to be at the heart of the arrival into Portugal and subsequent translation of Gower's *Confessio Amantis*,[15] could also have appreciated the reference. Dom Duarte himself possessed copies of several Alphonsine

---

[12] DMLBS, *prudentia*, s. v. #1 and #3.

[13] For a discussion of the influence of the Aristotelian *prudentia* in the works of John Gower, see Matthew W. Irvin, *The Poetic Voices of John Gower: Politics and Personae in the* Confessio Amantis (Cambridge: D. S. Brewer, 2014).

[14] R. F. Yeager has suggested that the King Alphonse of Gower's tale could be a reference to Pedro Alfonso, whose *Disciplina Clericalis* might have been the source of this story. My argument here only pertains to the "dom Afonso" of the Portuguese translation, not to Gower's original intentions or sources. See Yeager, "Spanish Literary Influence in England: John Gower and Pedro Alfonso," in *John Gower in England and Iberia: Manuscripts, Influences, Reception*, ed. Ana Sáez-Hidalgo and R. F. Yeager (Cambridge: D. S. Brewer, 2014), 119–29.

[15] See R. F. Yeager, "Gower's Lancastrian Affinity: The Iberian Connection," *Viator* 35, No. 1 (2004): 483–515; Joyce Coleman, "Philippa of Lancaster, Queen of Portugal – and Patron of the Gower Translations?," in *England and Iberia in the Middle Ages, 12th-15th Century: Cultural, Literary, and Political Exchanges*, ed. María Bullón-Fernández (New York: Palgrave Macmillan, 2007), 135–65; Tiago Viúla de Faria, "From Norwich to Lisbon: Factionalism, Personal Association, and Conveying the *Confessio Amantis*," in *John Gower in England and Iberia: Manuscripts, Influences, Reception*, ed. Ana Sáez-Hidalgo and R. F. Yeager (Cambridge: D. S. Brewer, 2014), 131–38; Clara Pascual-Argente, "Iberian Gower," in *The Routledge Research Companion to John Gower*, ed. Ana Sáez-Hidalgo, Brian Gastle, and R. F. Yeager (London and New York: Routledge, 2017), 210–21.

works in his personal library,[16] and he was influenced by the figure of Alphonse X and his ideas of state and nation, which became popular in the historiographic works written in Duarte's court.[17]

But while the reference to the wisdom of the king in the Portuguese prose summary suggests an allusion to Alphonse X, the Castilian table of contents in MS Real Biblioteca does not include it:

> aqui tracta el confessor in solidum contra la soberuja e pone por enxenplo lo que conteçio a vn rrey don alffon en espanna. (*LA*, fol. 1v)

> [Here the Confessor deals *in solidum* against pride and puts as an example what happened to a king Don Alfon in Spain.]

The entry does retain the emphasis on the Iberian context of the tale that was already present in the Portuguese prose summary, but as a result of the omission of his wisdom the "rrey don alfonso de espanna" of the table of contents no longer intimates a specific historical figure. This is surprising inasmuch as the table of contents in MS Real Biblioteca was presumably made by a Castilian person for a Castilian audience, who would probably have found the presence of the Castilian king Alphonse X an alluring feature in the tale. The reasons that led the tabulator to introduce this change are unknown: he might have considered the king's wisdom a superfluous piece of information that could be cut in order to create a more condensed entry for the table of contents. But he might also have had ulterior political or cultural reasons to omit the allusion to Alphonse X, perhaps related to the complicated relationship between the Trastamara rulers and Alphonse's legitimate and illegitimate heirs.[18] More details about the tabulator could

---

[16] Dom Duarte's vernacular books are listed as "livros in lingoajem" in the *Livro dos Conselhos*, and they include the Alphonsine *General Estoria*. See João José Alves Dias, ed., *Livro dos Conselhos de El-Rei D. Duarte (Livro da Cartuxa)* (Lisboa: Estampa, 1982).

[17] For more information on the influence of Alphonse X on Dom Duarte's historiographic efforts, see Filipe Alves Moreira, "Notas sobre a convivência de línguas em Portugal no século XV e a tradução da Crónica de Alfonso X," *e-Spania* 13 (2012), http://journals.openedition.org/e-spania/21113, accessed 12 February 2018; Rosa M. Rodríguez Porto, "La *Crónica Geral de Espanha de 1344* (ms. 1 A de la Academia das Ciências) y la tradición alfonsí," *e-Spania* 25 (2016), http://journals.openedition.org/e-spania/25911, accessed 12 February 2018; and Teresa Amado, "O projecto histórico de um Infante," in *Lindley Cintra. Homenagem ao homem, ao mestre a ao cidadão*, ed. Isabel Hub Faria (Lisboa: Cosmos, 1999), 303–09.

[18] See José-Luis Martín, "Defensa y justificación de la dinastía Trastámara. Las Crónicas de Pedro López de Ayala," *Espacio, Tiempo y Forma, Serie III, H.ª Medieval* 3 (1990): 157–80; and Fernando Arias Guillén, "El linaje maldito de Alfonso X. Conflictos en torno a la legitimidad regia en Castilla (*c.* 1275–1390)," *Vínculos de Historia* 1 (2012): 147–63.

prove instrumental in the study of the reception of Gower's work in Castile and Portugal, the *Confisyon* and its readership, especially in their relation to the *Livro do Amante* and the context where it was produced.[19]

The paratexts in MS Escorial follow the entry in the *tabula* of MS Real Biblioteca:

Table of contents

que trata delos vanagloriosos e cuenta vn enxenplo delo que conteçio al rrey don alfonso en espanna con un cavallero suyo çerca de algunas preguntas que el rrey le fasya y de commo vna fija suya lo libro de muerte e caso con el rrey. (*Confisyon*, fol. 3r)

[Which deals with vainglorious people and tells an example of what happened to king Don Alphonse in Spain with a knight of his, about some questions that the King asked him and how his daughter freed him from death and married the king.]

Prose summary

que trata contra aquellos que son vanagloriosos e cuenta lo que conteçio al Rey don alfon en espanna. (*Confisyon*, fol. 73v)

[Which talks against those who are vainglorious and tells what happened to a king Don Alphonse in Spain.]

Neither paratext contains allusions to the king's wisdom but they do retain the fact that he was the king of Spain, which suggests that they were shaped not by the Portuguese prose summary in MS Real Biblioteca, but by the entry in its Castilian table of contents.

In this framework, the table of contents in MS Real Biblioteca is an invaluable resource due to its position, both linguistically and geographically, halfway between Portugal and Castile, between the *Livro do Amante* and the *Confisyon*. This *tabula*, written in Castilian and inserted in the Portuguese manuscript while it was in Castile, has been primarily analyzed as evidence of the peregrinations of Gower's poem in the Iberian Peninsula of the fifteenth century.[20] Beyond that, scholars have noted its reliance on the Portuguese prose summaries, as well as its inconsistencies and mistakes.[21] However, there are deviations in it that could provide more details regarding

---

[19] In future publications I intend to track and analyze other examples of deliberate departures from the original Latin apparatus to draw a more detailed picture of the historical and cultural circumstances that resulted in the *Livro do Amante* and the *Confisyon* as we know them.

[20] See Herrero, "Castilian Script," 22–26.

[21] Faccon, "Fortuna de la *Confessio*," 29–30.

the textual relationship of the Iberian translations. The prose summary that opens Book II in the *Livro do Amante* is an amalgamation of the first two Latin captions in the English manuscripts of the *Confessio*:

> Hic in secundo libro tractat de Inuidia et eius speciebus, quarum dolor alterius gaudii prima nuncupatur, cuius condicionem secundum vicium Confessor primitus describens, Amanti, quatenus amorem concernit, super eodem consequenter opponit. (*CA*, II.9)

> [Here in the second book he discourses about Envy and its species, the first of which is called Sorrow for Another's Joy; and the Confessor, initially describing to the Lover its condition as a vice as far as love is concerned, subsequently interrogates him about this.]

> Hic ponit Confessor exemplum saltem contra istos qui in amoris causa aliorum gaudiis inuidentes nequaquam per hoc sibi ipsis proficiunt. Et narrat, qualiter quidam iuuenis miles nomine Acis, quem Galathea Nimpha pulcherrima toto corde peramauit [...]. (*CA*, II.101)

> [Here the Confessor presents an illustrative example at least against those who, while in the cause of love being envious of the joys of others, do not at all profit themselves by this. And he tells about a certain young knight named Acis, whom the most beautiful nymph Galatea deeply loved with her whole heart...]

> Este liuro segundo tracta do uiçio da enueia e dos seus rramos dos quaaess auer pesar do prazer doutrem he oprimeiro e conta sobrello hũa fabulla de hũu caualero nouo pero nome chamado açys e de gallathea que das nymphas he amais fremosa. (*LA*, fol. 39r)

> [This second book deals with the sin of envy and its types, of which having sorrow for another man's pleasure is the first. And it recounts the fable of a new [young] knight called Acis and Galatea, who was the fairest of the nymphs.]

Instead of following it, the table of contents opens Book II with two different entries:

> Aqui comiença el libro segundo e trata dlos rramos del inujdia delos quales auer pessar del plaçer de otro es el primero viçio. (*LA*, fol. 1v)

> [Here begins the second book, concerning the types of envy, of which having sorrow of another man's pleasure is the first sin.]

delo que dixo ouj[*overline* dio] que conteçio a polifemos enel amor de Galatea. (*LA*, fol. 1v)

[Concerning what Ovid said that happened to Polyphemos in the love for Galatea.]

Without the original English copy, or a different rendition of the Portuguese translation, the tabulator could not have known that there was a brief introduction to the sin of Envy before the "Tale of Acis and Galatea." How, then, could the tabulator restore the two-gloss arrangement of the English text otherwise? The answer is in the Portuguese text itself: the prose summary that should have introduced the "Tale of Acis and Galatea" is not there, but the decorated initial that usually accompanies the rubrics remains, filling the space that had been left blank for the introduction of the summary. The tabulator, understanding that there was a missing summary there, turned to the first three lines of the text – "Ouuydio da testemunho em seu liuro doque aconteçeo a pollifemus em amando gallthea"[22] – and adapted them to create a new entry for the table of contents, one that includes a reference to Ovid absent from the original Latin summary.

But the most significant fact is that the Castilian manuscript keeps the two entries established in the Portuguese table of contents almost unchanged, both in its table of contents and in its prose summary:

Table of contents

comjença el libro segundo que trata de los rramos de la ynbidia de los quales vno es aver pesar del plaser de otro e cuenta sus condiçiones. (*Confisyon*, fol. 3r)

[Here begins the second book, concerning the types of envy, one of which is having sorrow of another man's pleasure, and it tells its conditions.]

que trata de lo que dixo Oujdio a Poljfemus en el amor Galitea porque ella amava de todo su coraçon a Açis e no qujso amar a el et por enbidya se fiso su açechador. (*Confisyon*, fol. 3r–v)

[Concerning what Ovid said to Polyphemos in his love for Galatea, because she loved Acis with all her heart and did not want to love him, and he, because of his anger, became her stalker.]

---

[22] This is a relatively faithful translation of the English "As Ovide in his bok recordeth, / How Poliphemus whilom wroghte, / Whan that he Galathee besoghte" (*CA*, II.106–08).

Prose summaries

> que trata el libro segundo y dise de los rramos dela ynbidia delos quales vno es aver pesar del plaser de otro. (*Confisyon*, fol. 78v)
>
> [The second book talks about the types of envy, one of which is having sorrow of another man's pleasure.]
>
> delo que dixou oujdio a poljfemus en el amor de galatea. (*Confisyon*, fol. 78v)
>
> [concerning what Ovid said to Polyphemos in the love of Galatea.]

As we shall see later, this invites us to reconsider the relation of the Portuguese and Castilian manuscripts both from a textual and translatological point of view.

This is not the only instance of how the tabulator reinterpreted the gaps in the layout of the manuscript by supplying his own paratexts. In the Prologue, the Portuguese text omits the original Latin summary referring to Albert and Berengar:

> De seculo nouissimis iam temporibus ad similitudinem pedum in discordiam lapso et diuiso, quod post decessum ipsius Karoli, cum imperium Romanorum in manus Longobardorum peruenerat, tempore Alberti et Berengarii incepit [...]. (*CA*, Pro.779)
>
> [Concerning the age of the most recent times, in the likeness of the feet, fallen and divided in discord, which began after the passing of that Charles, when the Roman Empire fell to the hands of the Lombards, in the time of Albert and Berengar...]

Once again, the blank space left for the inclusion of the summary is filled just with decorative elements from the capital letter – but no summary at all. As in the example above, the table of contents adds an entry – "de commo duro el inperio en poder dlos lonbardos fasta el tiempo de alberto berringario" [Which addresses the duration of the empire under the Lombards until the time of Albert Berengar] (*LA*, fol. 1r) – based on the first lines of text "Assy durou o emperio en poder dos lonbardos ataa o tenpo dalberto e beringario" (*LA*, fol. 12v). But the tabulator introduced a slight mistake: in the new entry in the table of contents, the figures of Albert and Berengar, distinguished correctly in the Portuguese translation, become a single person – "alberto berringario" – by dropping the Tironian note. This variant was kept in the Castilian paratexts, which are an almost word-for-word rendition of the Portuguese entry:

Table of contents

de commo duro el ynperio en poder delos lonbardos fasta en tiempo de alberto beringario. (*Confisyon*, fol. 1v)

[Concerning the duration of the empire under the Lombards until the time of Albert Berengar.]

Prose summary

Que trata en commo duro el ynperio en poder de los lonbardos fasta en tiempo de Aluerto Beringarjo. (*Confisyon*, fol. 30v)

[Which addresses the duration of the empire under the Lombards until the time of Albert Berengar.]

It is relevant to note that the tabulator of the Portuguese manuscript did not always identify those occasions where the Portuguese copy omits prose summaries: for instance, there is no Portuguese prose summary translating the Latin paratext at I.98, and the table of contents does not provide a new one.[23] In this case, tellingly, there is no decorated initial in the Portuguese text indicating the beginning of a new chapter. All of this is clear evidence of the tabulator's reliance on the manuscript's capital letters to establish textual divisions akin to those pointed out by the prose summaries, and therefore it shows he used the Portuguese text itself to create the new entries where there was no summary available.

These divergences between the table of contents and the prose summaries in the Portuguese manuscript indicate that the tabulator was not as careless or as hasty as it has been previously argued, and that there was a conscientious labor of adaptation and improvement behind this seemingly straightforward list of chapters. Some of the additions and modifications that he introduced to the table of contents surface in the paratexts of the *Confisyion*, which suggests that the table of contents in the Portuguese manuscript was recopied later on, and probably used as the basis for other tables of contents in manuscripts that are now lost. This questions Cortijo Ocaña's view that neither table of contents was derived from the other.[24] Moreover, the traces of the Portuguese table of contents in the Castilian paratexts suggest that the tables of contents were not *ad hoc* arrangements, but that they were copied

---

[23] The paratexts in the *Confisyon* do not register this summary either.
[24] Antonio Cortijo Ocaña, "La *Confessio Amantis* en el debate del origen del sentimentalismo ibérico: un posible contexto de recepción" in *Actas del VIII Congreso Internacional de la Asociación Hispánica de Literatura Medieval (Santander, 22–26 septiembre, 1999)* (Santander: Asociación Hispánica de Literatura Medieval, 2000), 586, n. 16.

as an integral part of the poem, regardless of the modifications introduced to accommodate the demands of the Iberian readership.[25]

So far, this analysis has focused on paratextual deviations that could be traced back either to the lost English copy of the *Confessio* or to MS Real Biblioteca. Some divergences in the paratexts of MS Escorial appear to have been introduced at some point after the copy of the Portuguese manuscript and possibly at the time of the translation of the *Livro do Amante* into Castilian. Scholars have pointed out the careful work of translation executed by Juan de Cuenca in the *Confisyon del Amante*. Robert Wayne Hamm, Bernardo Santano Moreno, and Manuel Alvar have highlighted de Cuenca's faithful approach to Gower's English text, which at the same time abandons the constraints of a word-for-word translation in favor of a more relaxed rendition of the original.[26] Some modifications introduced in the Castilian translation have been identified and analyzed, including a notable work of amplification and omission that affects several parts of the Castilian text. Clara Pascual-Argente has recently identified the *Sumas de Historia Troyana* as one of the sources of the additional material unique to the *Confisyon*. Several borrowings from the *Sumas* can be found in several tales that recount episodes from the classical matter, like the "Tale of Jason and Medea" (*CA*, V.4248–4361), the "Tale of Thereus, Procne, and Philomena" (*CA*, V.5551–6052), or the "Tale of Ulises and Telegonus" (*CA*, VI.1392–1788).[27] In the same vein, the Castilian rendition of the "Tale of Deianira, Hercules, and Nessus" (*CA*, II.2148–2326) contains several additions and modifications, including the character of Nessus, who is a giant in the English and Portuguese versions and a "sagitario" or centaur in the Castilian text.[28] The paratexts in MS Escorial reflect this change: whereas the Latin and Portuguese summaries describe Nessus as "gigas" (*CA*, II.2148) and "ogigante" (*LA*, fols. 2r, 55v) respectively, the Castilian paratexts follow the text of the *Confisyon* and characterize him as "nesus el sagitario:"

---

[25] In this regard, an in-depth analysis of the (in)equivalences between the chapter and folio numbers in the table of contents and summaries of MS Escorial could reveal more about the circumstances in which they were produced.

[26] Robert Wayne Hamm, "A Critical Evaluation of the *Confisyon del Amante*, the Castilian Translation of Gower's *Confessio Amantis*," *Medium Aevum* 47, (1978): 91–106 (92); Bernardo Santano Moreno, *Estudio sobre Confessio Amantis de John Gower y su versión castellana, Confisyon del Amante de Juan de Cuenca* (Cáceres: Ediciones Universidad de Extremadura, 1990), 47–168; Manuel Alvar, "Prólogo," in *John Gower: Confesión del Amante. Traducción de Juan de Cuenca (S. XV). Edición Paleográfica. Anejos del Boletín de la Real Academia Española (45)*, ed. Elena Alvar (Madrid: Real Academia Española, 1990), 126.

[27] Clara Pascual-Argente, "La huella de las *Sumas de historia troyana* en la *Confessio Amantis* castellana," *Revista de Filología Española* XCV, 1 (2015): 127–52.

[28] Pascual-Argente, "Huella de las *Sumas*," 139.

Table of contents

> que trata de aquellos que en amor so color de bien querençias engannan a otros et cuenta sobre ello vn enxenplo de hercoles e nesus el sagitario quando le lleuo a daynyra. (*Confisyon*, fols. 3v–4r)

> [Which addresses those who, in love, under the cover of benevolence deceive others, and tells about it an example of Hercules and Nessus the centaur, when he took Deianira.]

Prose summary

> que trata contra aquellos que en amor so color de bien querença engannan a otros e cuenta lo que conteçio a hercoles e anesus el sagitario commo lleuo a daynyra. (*Confisyon*, fol. 105v)

> [Which talks against those who, in love, under the cover of benevolence deceive others, and recounts what happened to Hercules and Nessus the centaur, how he took Deianira.]

This deviation shows that the modifications in the text of the *Confisyon* had an echo in the paratexts and provides further evidence that the table of contents and the prose summaries were considered an integral part of the *Confisyon*.

I have found a similar, albeit subtler, example of an external source in the "Tale of Tristram and Isolde:" in Book VI.467–84, Gower introduces a brief account of how Tristram fell in love with Fair Isolde. Both the English text and the Latin summary that precedes this tale name the lady as "Belle Isolde," and this is translated as "fermosa Ysollda" in the Portuguese text and as "fermosa yseo" in the Castilian. As such she is also known in the Portuguese prose summary:

> Aqui por enxenplo da beuediçe damor conta em como Tristam por hũu beuer quelhe foy dado se enbeuedou por amor da fermosa ysollda. (*LA*, fol. 178r)[29]

However, the paratexts in MS Escorial use a different epithet for Isolde:

Table of contents and prose summary

> que trata dela bebdes en amor et pone enxenplo de tristan de leonjs commo por vn beuer que le fue dado se enbeudo en el amor dela fermosa yseo la brunda. (*Confisyon*, fol. 12v; 266v)

---

[29] The entry in the Portuguese table of contents is significantly shorter, and it mentions neither Tristram nor Isolde.

[Which addresses the drunkenness in love and gives the examples of Tristram of Leonis, how because of a drink that was given to him he became drunk in love of the fair Isolde the Blonde.]

Here Tristram is "Tristan de leonjs," an epithet that specifies the origin of the character but that is absent in the English and Portuguese manuscripts. Isolde is also characterized by a new epithet, in this case "la brunda," which is added on top of the "fermosa" that was present in the English, Portuguese, and Castilian versions of the *Confessio*. The versions of the story of Tristram that are known to have circulated in the Iberian Peninsula in the fifteenth century use two different epithets to refer to Isolde: the Castilian-Aragonese *Cuento de Tristán de Leonís* (Vatican Library, MS 6428) names her "Yseo la Baça" [Isolde, the dark-haired], whereas the Castilian *Códice de Tristán* (Biblioteca Nacional de Madrid, MS 20262/19 and 22644) calls her the same "Yseo la brunda" found in the *Confisyon*.[30] This fact suggests that Juan the Cuenca or an unknown adapter or scribe who introduced this deviation in the Castilian paratexts was familiar with the Castilian version of the story, and not with the Castilian-Aragonese.

It is difficult to ascertain now the exact chronological point where these deviations were introduced in the paratexts of the *Confisyon*: they do not have marks of rewriting or erasure, which suggests that the modifications could have been done at some point during the translation of the *Livro de Amante* into Castilian or shortly afterwards, before the production of MS Escorial. The borrowings from external sources and their impact on the paratexts of the *Confisyon* can help us draw a more defined portrait of the scribes and translators that adapted the *Livro do Amante* for a Castilian readership, because they are proof of the literary texts that they read and that could have influenced their own adaptation of Gower's poem.

In this essay I have put forward some of the most notable examples of deviations in the paratexts of the Iberian manuscripts of Gower's *Confessio Amantis* in order to illustrate how the changes introduced in the translated text reveal the processes of textual transmission and reception of the literary work. The divergences analyzed here show new clues regarding the lost English manuscript that was translated into Portuguese, allowing us to position it more clearly within the textual tradition of the *Confessio*. At the same time, the examples of deviations found in the Castilian and Portuguese manuscripts establish links between the *Livro do Amante* and the *Confisyon*

---

[30] Isolde is also known as "la Brunda" in the later sixteenth-century printed versions of the story. For more information on the dissemination of the story of Tristram in the Iberian Peninsula, see David Hook, ed., *The Arthur of the Iberians: The Arthurian Legends in the Spanish and Portuguese Worlds* (Cardiff: University of Wales Press, 2015).

del Amante that had so far been overlooked, probably because they affect the paratextual materials and not the text itself. Lastly, some of the divergences that are unique to the *Confisyon* hint at the cultural background of the Castilian readers of Gower's work at the end of the fifteenth century, and how that background places it amid a specific literary scene.

CHAPTER 7

"MESCREANTZ," SCHISM, AND THE PLIGHT OF CONSTANTINOPLE: EVIDENCE FOR DATING AND READING LONDON, BRITISH LIBRARY, ADDITIONAL MS 59495

David Watt

LONDON, BRITISH LIBRARY, ADDITIONAL MS 59495 (previously known as the Trentham manuscript) is a trilingual manuscript of Gower's verse that has long been associated with the earliest years of Henry IV's reign. An inscription on the manuscript's first leaf suggests that Gower had the book made for Henry "att <or before> his Coronation."[1] The laudatory Latin poems addressed to the new king in the manuscript would have been appropriate for such an event, but the manuscript was definitely completed after October 1399. Additional MS 59495 certainly includes verse that was written earlier: R. F. Yeager dates the *Cinkante balades* to the 1390s and the *Traitié selonc les auctours pour essampler les amantz marietz* before 1390.[2] Critics now tend to agree that the manuscript's only English poem provides the best evidence about the date of the manuscript as a whole, and Sebastian Sobecki makes a compelling case that "In Praise of Peace" and Additional MS 59495 were completed "between Henry IV's coronation in October 1399 and his confirmation of the truce with France on 18 May 1400. The occasion for this poem and for the compilation of the Trentham manuscript was the prospect of imminent war with France in early 1400."[3] Once the

---

[1] London, British Library, Additional MS 59495, fol. 1r. For a discussion of the coronation, see Siân Echard, *Printing the Middle Ages* (Philadelphia: University of Pennsylvania Press, 2008), 110 and 124.

[2] For their dates of composition, see R. F. Yeager, "John Gower's Audience: The Ballades," *The Chaucer Review* 40 (2005): 81–105.

[3] Sebastian Sobecki, "*Ecce patet tensus*: The Trentham Manuscript, *In Praise of Peace*, and John Gower's Autograph Hand," *Speculum* 90 (2015): 925–59 (935). For a different account of the manuscript's verse in a French context, see Ardis Butterfield, *The Familiar Enemy* (Oxford: Oxford University Press, 2009), 235–65.

truce with France had been signed, Sobecki argues, the manuscript was no longer relevant, and it remained with Gower at St Mary Overys. Although I agree with most of Sobecki's argument, I nonetheless propose to reconsider his assertion that the truce "remov[ed] the need for Gower's manuscript."[4] "In Praise of Peace" certainly expresses Gower's concern about the war in France, but it also reveals his concern about division in the Church, which Gower identifies as the cause of the war, and the appearance of "mescreantz," which he sees as a consequence of war and schism. The diction Gower uses when articulating these concerns suggests that he knew of the diplomacy that culminated in the Greek Emperor, Manuel II Palaeologus, arriving in England at the end of 1400 and staying until early 1401 in order to seek help for the defense of Constantinople against the Ottoman Turks.

This essay connects Gower's discussion of "mescreantz" and schism to the plight of Constantinople and, ultimately, the Greek Emperor's visit. I contend that Gower had Manuel II in mind when writing the final stanza of "In Praise of Peace," which calls for all other Christian princes to set the rightful pope upon his stall – and that he may have been writing it while the Emperor was in England. I therefore agree with Yoshiko Kobayashi and Zachary E. Stone that this poem is deeply concerned with schism,[5] but I argue that Gower was just as concerned with the Great Schism (from 1054) as he was with the Western Schism (1378–1417). When read in this context, Gower's selection of Constantine, the founder of Constantinople, as his final *exemplum* in "In Praise of Peace" takes on new significance. By emphasizing the importance of "pite" – presented as both mercy and piety – in his version of Constantine's conversion, Gower counters Philippe de Mézières' arguments for a crusade, adumbrates the conciliar movement's call for reform in head and members, and invites readers to refine their conception of the king's "pite" through MS Additional 59495 as a whole.

"Mescreantz" and the Plight of Constantinople

Gower's use of the word "mescreantz" in his discussion of the schism indicates that he had the Greek Emperor's visit in mind when writing "In Praise of Peace." Gower prepares readers for the appearance of "mescreantz"

---

[4] Sobecki, "*Ecce patet tensus*," 951.
[5] Yoshiko Kobayashi, "Letters of Old Age: The Advocacy of Peace in the Works of John Gower and Philippe de Mézières," in *John Gower: Others and the Self*, ed. R. F. Yeager and Russell A. Peck (Cambridge: D. S. Brewer, 2017), 204–22; Zachary E. Stone, "'Between tuo stoles': The Western Schism and the English Poetry of John Gower (1378–1415)," *New Medieval Literatures* 19 (2019): 205–43 (240–43).

by claiming that "Uppon thre points stant Christes pes oppressed" (253).[6] "First," he writes, "holy churche is in hirsilf divided" (254). Kobayashi contends that Gower's concern with the Western Schism here echoes Philippe de Mézières *Epistre au Roi Richard II* (1395), connecting them both to "a cross-Channel literary movement committed to the promotion of peace in Europe."[7] Both de Mézières and Gower link division in the Church to a second problem: war between Christian nations. As Sobecki shows, the war between England and France was certainly an urgent matter in 1400, yet "In Praise of Peace" fairly quickly moves on to consider a third point, a consequence of the first two:

> The two defaltes bringen in the thridde,
> Of *mescreantz*, that sen how we debate,
> Betwen the two thei fallen in amidde,
> Wher now aldai thei finde an open gate.
> Lo, thus the dedly werre stant algate. (*IPP* 267–71, my emphasis)

Seeing the schism and the war between Christian nations as an opportunity, people whom Gower calls "mescreantz" have found their way in and threaten perpetual war. This stanza's final couplet takes an optimistic turn: "Bot evere Y hope of Kyng Henries grace, / That he it is which schal the pes embrace" (*IPP* 272–73). This stanza raises two important questions: Who are the "mescreantz?" And why does King Henry's grace offer hope in this context?

Gower's definition of the word "mescreantz" deserves special attention because the *Middle English Dictionary* identifies it as one of the first – if not the first – written instances of the noun in English.[8] It can be translated as misbelievers, which connotes non-Christians as well as heretics or possibly schismatics.[9] I will return to these connotations below. For now, I will consider Gower's use of "mescreantz" to be a transliteration of the French word "mescreans," which seems to have denoted a very specific group of people in the late fourteenth century. Philippe de Mézières uses this word in *Le Songe du vieil pelerin* (1389) to contrast the behavior of the Ottoman Turks with that of the crusading knights: "en la guerre des mescreans encontre les Crestiens, les mescreants ne sont pas si cruelx envers les Crestiens, et de

---

[6] All references to "In Praise of Peace" are from *John Gower: The Minor Latin Works* (with *In Praise of Peace*, ed. Michael Livingstone), ed. and trans. R. F. Yeager (Kalamazoo, MI: Medieval Institute Publications, 2005).
[7] Kobayashi, "Letters of Old Age," 203.
[8] *MED*, s.v. miscrēaunt (n.).
[9] The *MED* defines mescraunt (n.) as "an infidel, a pagan; a non-Christian," but Gower's coinage of its homonym, "mescreaunce" (*CA* V.1444 and VI.2366), as a synonym for "misbelieve" (*CA* V.1456) indicates that the word "mescreantz" could also apply to those who hold beliefs he considered false. All references to the *Confessio Amantis* are from *The Complete Works of John Gower*, ed. G. C. Macaulay, 4 vols. (Oxford: Clarendon Press, 1899–1902).

l'eglise, des nobles, et du peuple, comme sont les dessudiz pillars" [in the war between the miscreants and Christians, the miscreants are not as cruel to the Christians, and the Church, and the nobles, and the people, as the thieves mentioned below].[10] This word was important for de Mézières since, according to Kiril Petkov, he distinguished between the Ottoman Turks and "the Saracens" (i.e. the Arabs of Egypt), whom he believed "were the main adversary, since they were the oppressors of Christendom" in Jerusalem.[11] The word "miscreans" does not appear in de Mézières' *Epistre au Roi Richart* (1395) because its purpose was to exhort the English king to go on crusade to the Holy Land against the Saracens. After Christian forces were defeated at Nicopolis in 1396, however, the threat posed to Constantinople by the Turks seemed imminent, and Greek ambassadors renewed their efforts to seek help from western nations.

Whoever wrote the Privy Seal letter responding to the Greek request for help from the English in 1398 used the word "mescréants" in the same way that de Mézières uses it in the *Songe*: to denote Ottoman Turks. This letter reveals that even if Gower was the first to use the word "mescreantz" as a noun in English, he was not the first to use it as a noun in England. According to the letter-writer, Richard was in Coventry for the Hereford-Norfolk duel when Greek ambassadors requested money from him to "relevre la dite citee de Constan-[tinople] et maintenir et comforter les cristienes encontre la malice et envasioun de les *mescréants*" [relieve the said city of Constantinople and maintain and comfort the Christians against the malice and invasion of the miscreants].[12] The Privy Seal letter acknowledges the "grandes perils" [great perils] and "meschiefs verisemblables" [true mischiefs] that have come "parmy les guerres par les *mescréants* a la citee de Constantinople et par consequens a toute cristianitee" [throughout the wars by the miscrants to the city of Constantinople and consequently all of Christianity].[13] Framing the plight of Constantinople as an affront to the whole Christian body, Richard promised to provide "un somme notable en relevement de les guerres" [a notable sum in the relief of the wars] by the Octave of Candlemas (2 February) 1399.[14] Things did not go as Richard planned in 1399. The collection of this particular sum of money was "maladministered in various ways," according to David Carlson, and it eventually disappeared into the hands of "Reginald Grillo, who was to have

---

[10] Philippe de Mézières, *Le Songe du Vieil Pèlerin,* 2 vols, ed. G. W. Coopland (Cambridge: Cambridge University Press, 1969), I.531.

[11] Kiril Petkov, "The Rotten apple and the good apples: Orthodox, Catholics, and Turks in Philippe de Mézières' crusading propaganda," *Journal of Medieval History* 23 (1997): 255–70 (265).

[12] M. Dominica Legge, ed., *Anglo-Norman Letters and Petitions from All Souls MS. 182*, Anglo-Norman Texts III (Oxford: Blackwell, 1941), 152, my emphasis.

[13] Legge, ed., *Anglo-Norman Letters*, 152.

[14] Legge, ed., *Anglo-Norman Letters*, 152.

delivered cash to the Greek emperor."[15] When Richard was deposed, there may have been some doubt about whether the funds would ever be paid.

Not long after Richard's deposition, however, Henry IV gave the Greeks reason to place their hope in him. In September of 1400, Henry's treasurer "summoned all the collectors of customs in the ports to come to the exchequer in mid-October with all their records in the hope that money could be found for the wars in Scotland and Wales and for the Emperor of Constantinople, who was appealing for funds."[16] In October, Henry met with the Emperor's ambassadors and told them that "a final reply would be given to them by the council."[17] Meanwhile, the Greek Emperor himself arrived in Calais, where he stayed at the English king's expense until there was a break in the campaign against Welsh rebels and the Scots. Three Greek emperors visited Western Europe between 1369 and 1423, but only Manuel II made it to England. In December 1400, he crossed from Calais to Dover, on to Canterbury, and eventually to London. Adam Usk provides this contemporary account of his visit:

> Imperator Grecorum, pro subsidio contra Sarazenos habendo, regem Angl', ab eo honorifice receptus, in festo sancti Thome apostolic London' uisitat, cum eodem rege, maximis sui expensis, per duos menses continue existens, et eciam in recess maximis donariis releuatus.[18]

> [On the feast of St Thomas, the apostle [21 December], the emperor of the Greeks visited the king of England in London to seek help against the Saracens, and was honorably received by him, staying with him for two whole months at enormous expense to the king, and being showered with gifts at his departure.]

It seems clear that Usk did not limit the word "Sarazenos" [Saracens] to a description of people in the Holy Land in the same way that de Mézières did. Usk's diction here suggests that Gower's concession that men might be armed to fight "The Sarazins, whiche unto Crist be lothe" (*IPP* 250) can be read as an expression of sympathy for the plight of Constantinople and English plans to offer limited support, especially since it appears just before "In Praise of Peace" itemizes the three points upon which the Church was

---

[15] David R. Carlson, "Greeks in England, 1400," in *Interstices: Studies in Late Middle English and Anglo-Latin Texts in Honour of A. G. Rigg*, ed. Richard Firth Green and Linne Mooney (Toronto, University of Toronto Press, 2004), 74–98 (79).

[16] J. L. Kirby, *Henry IV of England* (London: Constable, 1970), 106. Cf. *Anglo-Norman Letters*, 418–19.

[17] Kirby, *Henry IV*, 108.

[18] Adam Usk, *The Chronicle of Adam Usk, 1377–1421*, ed. and trans. Chris Given Wilson (Oxford: Clarendon Press, 1997), 118–19.

oppressed.[19] This is not to suggest that there is a lack of clarity about why the Greeks were in England: as Thomas Walsingham writes, "the emperor of Constantinople visited England to ask for help against the Turks."[20] Rather, Gower's use of these two terms indicates that he drew both on the French associated with diplomacy (especially in the Privy Seal) and the Latin associated with legal and historical discourses (both manifest in Usk's chronicle) in order to frame his thinking in this section of "In Praise of Peace."

The chroniclers all agree that Manuel II was right to place his hope in Henry's grace. Walsingham concurs with Usk that the English king paid "the expenses of the emperor's stay," and that his departure was marked "by grand presents showing respect for a person of such eminence."[21] John Capgrave also notes that the Greek Emperor enjoyed a "good hostel at þe kyngis cost" and departed with "large giftis."[22] One of these gifts was money promised by Richard II for the relief of Constantinople, delivered two years and a day after it was initially expected (3 February 1401). "In Praise of Peace" may not refer to this gift explicitly because it was composed before the Greek Emperor left England. It seems just as likely, though, that Gower wanted both Henry and other readers to remain focused on the hope that his grace offered rather than its partial fulfilment in the form of aid for the defense of Constantinople.

THE GREAT SCHISM AND THE PRICE OF WESTERN AID

"In Praise of Peace" reveals that Gower is less concerned with temporary measures for the relief of Constantinople than he is with the circumstances that have led to the emerging threat of "mescreantz" as diverse as Ottoman Turks in Constantinople and heretics in England. The final stanza widens its appeal beyond Henry in order to make an explicit appeal for an end to war between Christian nations and schism in the Church:

> Noght only to my king of pes y write,
> Bot *to these othre princes cristene alle*,
> That ech of hem his oghne herte endite,
> And see the werre er more meschief falle:

---

[19] On the range of connotations that the word "Saracen" could have in English, see Siobhain Bly Calkin, *Saracens and the Making of English Identity: The Auchinleck Manuscript* (New York: Routledge, 2005).

[20] Thomas Walsingham, *The Chronica Maiora of Thomas Walsingham, 1376–1422*, trans. David Preest; notes and intro. James G. Clark (Woodbridge: Boydell Press, 2005), 319.

[21] Walsingham, *Chronica Maiora,* 319.

[22] John Capgrave, *John Capgrave's Abbreuiation of Cronicles,* ed. Peter J. Lucas, EETS, o.s. 285 (Oxford: Oxford University Press, 1983), 217.

> Sette ek the rightful Pope uppon his stalle,
> Kep charite and draugh pite to honde,
> Maintene lawe, and so the pes schal stonde. (*IPP* 379–85, my emphasis)

My argument here is that Gower includes Manuel II among "other princes cristene alle" and that "In Praise of Peace" is therefore an appeal to end the Great Schism as well as the Western Schism. Not every writer would have extended this offer so graciously. While those in the Western Church recognized the plight of Constantinople, many blamed the Greeks for their circumstances. According to Kiril Petkov, de Mézières believed that "the Orthodox Greeks were schismatics and heretics and had committed offences, because of which all of Christendom suffered."[23] So long as the schism persisted, the Greeks were unlikely to receive military support. As Christopher Tyerman writes, "the price of a substantial western crusade, from the papacy's point of view, was Greek obedience to Rome."[24] This problem would have been especially difficult for Manuel II to manage in 1400–01 since obedience to Rome would have alienated him from nations that supported the pope in Avignon.

Adam Usk's chronicle reveals that English attitudes about the plight of the Greeks may have differed from those expressed by de Mézières, though he also implies that Manuel II might resolve his problems by showing obedience to Rome. Reflecting on the plight of the Greek delegation, Usk writes, "Cogitaui intra me quam esset dolendum quod iste maior et ulterior Christianus uersus orientem princeps, qui per infidels compulsus, ulteriores occidentis insulas pro subsidio contra eosdem uisitare cogebatur" [I thought to myself how sad it was that this great Christian leader from the remote east had been driven by the power of the infidels to visit distant islands in the west in order to seek help against them].[25] Instead of condemning them as schismatic or heretical, Usk praises their Christian piety in terms that align them with Henry IV rather than Richard II:

> Iste imperator semper uniformiter et sub uno colore, scilicet albo, in longis robis ad modum tabardorum formatis semper cum suis incedere solebat, multum uarietatem et disparitatem Anglicorum in uestibus reprehendendo, asserens per eas animarum inconstanciam et uarietatem significari. Capita neque barbas capellanorum ipsius non tetigit nouacula.[26]
>
> [This emperor and his men always went about dressed uniformly in long robes cut like tabards which were all of one color, namely white,

---

[23] Petkov, "Rotten apple," 264.
[24] Christopher Tyerman, *God's War: A New History of the Crusades* (London: Allen Lane, 2006), 849.
[25] Usk, *Chronicle*, 119–21.
[26] Usk, *Chronicle*, 119–21.

and disapproved greatly of the fashions and varieties of dress worn by the English, declaring that they signified inconstancy and fickleness of heart. No razor ever touched the heads or beards of his priests.]

The Greek disapproval of English fashions on moral grounds echoes Lancastrian critiques of the Ricardian regime;[27] Usk's emphasis on the Greeks' beards suggests that Henry's can be read as a sign that his piety surpasses that of Richard, whose own piety was regularly expressed through beardlessness.[28] Notwithstanding his admiration for their piety, Usk critiques the Greek practice of singing the office in their native language: "In diuinis seruiciis deuotissimi erant itsi Greci, ea tam per milites quam per clericos quia in eorum uulgari *indifferenter* cantando" [These Greeks were extremely devout in their religious services, having them chanted by knights or by clerics, for they were sung in their native tongue indistinctly].[29] Usk was writing this in early 1401, the period when *De Heretico Comburendo* was passed by Parliament and William Sawtre was executed.[30] Read in the context of Usk's own description of Sawtre's refusal to recognize the Roman Church's authority, this passage suggests that the Greeks ought to submit to Rome for the sake of Christian unity. Singing in Latin would not only be a sign of their obedience to Rome, but it would also allow someone like Usk to share fully in the experience of divine services with the Greeks. Writing at the time Manuel II was in England in 1401, Usk explicitly acknowledges his piety as a Christian prince and implicitly asks him to set the rightful pope upon his stall. It seems reasonable to think that Gower was writing the final stanza of "In Praise of Peace" around the same time, with the same prince and the same purpose in mind.

---

[27] For an account of Lancastrian critiques of fashion, see Jenni Nuttall, *The Creation of Lancastrian Kingship: Literature, Language, and Politics in Late Medieval England* (Cambridge: Cambridge University Press, 2007), 19–22. For an example of the kinds of dress being critiqued, see the opening miniature in de Mézières' *Epistre*, which depicts Richard's councilors in footwear that is so prodigiously pointy that it breaks the frame and in robes that are either so long that they trail underfoot or so short that they seem unfit for purpose.

[28] See the frontispiece of the *Epistre* and the Wylton Diptych, which J. N. N. Palmer has argued "should be associated with the crusade plans of 1395 in date and iconography" in *England, France, and Christendom 1377–99* (London: Routledge and Kegan Paul, 1972), 242–44.

[29] Usk, *Chronicle*, 120. The translation provided differs from Chris Given-Wilson's in that I translate *indifferenter* as *indistinctly* rather than *variously*. The phrase may be an allusion to the derisive Latin phrase "Graecum est; non legitur" [it is Greek; it cannot be read]. Shakespeare's Casca reports something similar when he tells Cassius "it was Greek to me" in *Julius Caesar* (1.2.286).

[30] Steven Justice argues that these sections were written in early 1401: *Adam Usk's Secret* (Philadelphia: University of Pennsylvania Press, 2015), 12–15.

The Founder of Constantinople and Gower's Rejection of Crusade

Although the final stanza of "In Praise of Peace" echoes Usk's suggestion that the Greek Emperor can act to bring about an end to the schism, Gower resists the idea that Greek obedience to Rome should trigger a crusade in defense of Constantinople. Gower's decision to use the conversion story about Constantine, founder of Constantinople, as the final *exemplum* in "In Praise of Peace" seems designed to reject this idea altogether. It is even possible that Gower chose this story in order to refute de Mézières directly. In his *Epistre,* de Mézières points out to Richard II that Constantine's mother, Helen, was a member of the English royal family:

> Constantin, empereur de Romme, pere du grant Constantin, prist a femme Helaine, lors une hosteliere, tres sage et aournee de grans vertus, laquele, selonc l'opinion de plusiurs, estoit fille du roy d'Angleterre, et toutefois pour sa vertu Constantin la prist, / non pas comme fille de roy, mais comme une povre femme; laquele sainte Helaine deserve par grace de trouver en Jherusalem la sainte vraie crois, a confirmacion de l'empire de Romme quie devint crestien.[31]

> [Constantin, Emperor of Rome and father of the great Constantine, took to wife Helen, at that time an inn-keeper, a very wise woman and of great virtue. Many thought that she was the daughter of the King of England, but Constantin married her for her goodness and as a poor woman, and not as a king's daughter. This same St Helen, through grace, was judged worthy to find in Jerusalem the true Cross, thus strengthening the Roman Empire, which became Christian].

De Mézières suggests that the English king can fulfil the typological role established by the daughter of the King of England: by going on crusade to the Holy Land, figuratively finding the true cross in Jerusalem, Richard would help restore a unified Christian Empire. Gower, on the other hand, uses Constantine's story to reject the idea of a crusade: in the version Gower tells about his conversion in "In Praise of Peace," Constantine chooses "pite" over a literal and figurative bloodbath.

My claim here is based on my assumption that readers of "In Praise of Peace" would likely know the version of Constantine's conversion story that Gower tells in Book II of the *Confessio* and the one he chooses not to tell at all. When Constantine is afflicted with leprosy (*CA* II.3191–94), his clerks tell him that the only cure is to bathe in the blood of children (*CA* II.3206–07). He orders that children should be sought out and brought to

---

[31] Philippe de Mézières, *Letter to King Richard II: A Plea made in 1395 for peace between England and France,* intro. and trans. G. W. Coopland (Liverpool: Liverpool University Press, 1975), 41–42.

the palace, but the noise they and their mothers make catches his attention (*CA* II.3283–85) and engenders "pite" within his heart (*CA* II.3290). "Pite" leads Constantine to forsake his doctors and put himself into God's care (*CA* II.3395–98). God sends Saints Peter and Paul to Constantine in a dream (*CA* II.3333–36), where they tell him that Sylvester will come to teach him about salvation, and assure him, "The nedeth of non other leche" (*CA* II.3364) in order to cure his leprosy. Sylvester arrives, and teaches the king the "holi writ" (*CA* II.3386) necessary for his salvation. Constantine is ultimately baptized by water in the vessel that had initially been made for him to bathe in the blood of the children (*CA* II.3445–50), and all signs of his "grete maladie" (*CA* II.3459) are washed away: his "pite" (mercy) for the children leads to "pite" (piety) in his conversion. As Frank Grady points out, Gower borrows from the *Confessio* when he tells this story in "In Praise of Peace," suppressing certain elements "in order to clean the tale up for the king's consumption."[32] Gower also suppresses the other version of Constantine's conversion, told by Eusebius, which describes how a vision on the eve of battle taught the pagan emperor to put an image of the cross at the head of his troops and thus guaranteed his victory over Maxentius at the Milvian Bridge in 312, after which he became a Christian and began to promote Christianity in the empire.[33]

Grady points out that Gower's selective telling in this instance draws attention to the paradox that lies at the heart of this poem: in order to write "In Praise of Peace," Gower must not write about the violence that often secures peace. I contend that Gower selected and suppressed certain elements of this story in order to assert that mercy and piety are better than a bloodbath – both literally, in the case of the bath full of children's blood, and figuratively, in the form of the carnage sure to result from leading an army into battle under the sign of the cross. This would have been a particularly urgent argument at a time when the emperor himself had come to England to seek help in the wake of Nicopolis, especially if Greek obedience to Rome actually held out the promise for a crusade.[34]

---

[32] Frank Grady, "The Lancastrian Gower and the Limits of Exemplarity," *Speculum* 70 (1995): 552–75 (569).
[33] Grady, "Lancastrian Gower," 569.
[34] There is widespread agreement that Nicopolis was perceived as a bloodbath from the perspective of Western Europe almost immediately after the battle took place. Kelly DeVries observes that the execution of most of the prisoners – including members of the nobility – gave rise to many stories about the sultan's atrocities, and the perception of Nicopolis as a disaster had implications for the next two centuries; see Kelly DeVries, "The Lack of a Western European Military Response to the Ottoman Invasions of Eastern Europe from Nicopolis (1396) to Mohács (1526)," *The Journal of Military History* 63 (1999): 539–59 and "The Effect of Killing the Christian Prisoners at the Battle of Nicopolis," in *Crusaders, Condottieri, and Cannon: Medieval Warfare in Societies Around the Mediterranean*, ed. Donald J. Kagay and Andrew Villalon (Leiden: Brill, 2003), 157–72.

The story of Constantine's conversion allowed Gower both to agree with de Mézières' contention that the schism was a serious affliction for the Christian body, and to suggest alternative forms of healing. Both authors agreed that the Church was suffering and, as Kobayashi notes, "the prevalence of metaphors of wounds and illness" connects "In Praise of Peace" to the *Epistre*.[35] De Mézières asserts that the injury to the corporate Christian body affects all of its members: "Ceste plaie principalment est destruction de la foy et touche a l'ame sanz moien, voire tous les crestiens, et catholiques et sismatiques, et par consequent as roys" [This injury lies chiefly in the destruction of the Faith and reaches directly to the soul of all Christians, both Catholic and schismatic, and so to all kings].[36] Constantine's leprosy provides an exceptional allegory for this situation insofar as its association with erroneous, heretical, or schismatic beliefs was deeply entrenched by the time Gower was writing. According to Saul Nathaniel Brody, Isidore of Seville's commentary on Leviticus 13 "allegorizes leprosy as false doctrine and lepers as heretics, men who profess doctrines of error and confuse true and false."[37] Isidore's interpretation rapidly became conventional and is cited "in the *Glossa Ordinaria* and abstracted in the commentary on the Pentateuch by Bede (c. 673–735)."[38] De Mézières argues that the solution to the problem afflicting the corporate Christian body is obvious. Claiming that "naturalement chascun malade, qui longuement a languy, desire de trouver un bon fusicien" [it is natural that every sick man who has suffered long should wish to find a good doctor],[39] de Mézières tells the story of Malavisé and Vigilant in order to insist a crusade is the only medicine powerful enough to heal this affliction:

> Dont il est assevoir, parlant moralment, que par la grande medicine sustoucie puet estre entendu le saint passage d'oultremer, qui par la bonte de Dieu a mon voloir se fera par la haulte pouesse de vostre frere et de vous, a la gloire de Dieu et exaltacion de la foy catholique.[40]
>
> [Speaking figuratively, by the greater medicine is meant the holy passage *d'outremer*, which I hope, by God's grace, will be undertaken by the lofty courage of your brother and yourself, to the glory of God and the exaltation of the Catholic Faith].

He turns to a different historical example in his appeal to Richard: "Mais quant a magnificence royale et imperial, l'un de vous ii. Soit par imitacion

---

[35] Kobayashi, "Letters of Old Age," 212.
[36] De Mézières, *Letter,* 103 and 30.
[37] Saul Nathaniel Brody, *The Disease of the Soul: Leprosy in Medieval Literature* (Ithaca, NY: Cornell University Press, 1974), 126.
[38] Brody, *Disease*, 126.
[39] De Mézières, *Letter,* 79–80 and 7.
[40] De Mézières, *Letter*, 104 and 31.

les tres Vaillant et tres preux Charlemaine, et l'autre soit le tres excellent et tres preux roy Artus, c'est assavoir contre les anemis de la foy, contre *les scismatiques et hereges*" [And in the matter of royal and imperial splendor, one of you may imitate the very valiant and knightly Charlemagne and the other that very bold and excellent King Arthur, when you fight against the enemies of the Faith, against *schismatics and heretics*.][41] Gower calls the war between England and France an "old sor" (*IPP* 122) and depicts the schism as an illness, yet he invites Henry to imitate Constantine rather than Arthur. Gower had good reason to believe that the idea of a crusade would appeal to Henry, who had "actually taken the cross in a formal ceremony" before going to Prussia in 1390.[42] John Capgrave later wrote in praise of Henry for fighting the "inimicis Crucis Christi" [enemies of Christ's Cross] there in order to "vendicare Crucifixi" [avenge the crucified].[43] Gower, writing at a time when crusade may have seemed to be a real possibility, calls Henry's attention to "pite" instead.

"Pite" and the Need for Reform in Head and Members

Whereas de Mézières exhorts Richard to heal the Christian body's affliction by going on crusade, Gower calls Henry to consider alternative solutions suggested by the story he tells about Constantine's conversion. At the climax of this story in "In Praise of Peace," Gower repeats the word "pite" twice in one line as he recounts Constantine's decision to suffer rather than bathing in the blood of children:

> Whan him was levere his oghne deth desire
> Than do the younge children to martire,
> Of crualte he lafte the querele,
> *Pite* he wroughte and *pite* was his hele. (*IPP* 340–43, my emphasis).

Gower plays with the two different senses of the word "pite" in order to assert that Constantine's act of mercy healed him, transforming his leprous body into a pious Christian one. Andrew Galloway has shown that Gower exploits the connection between the primary meanings of "pite" in English and "pietas" in Latin with the concept of "piety" in both the *Cronica* and the *Confessio* in order to reveal "the higher plan of true piety in purging and

---

[41] De Mézières, *Letter*, 70 and 144.
[42] Tyerman, *God's War*, 708. See also F. R. H. du Boulay, "Henry of Derby's expeditions to Prussia 1390–1391 and 1392," in *The Reign of Richard II: essays in honour of May McKisack,* ed. F. R. H. du Boulay and Caroline M. Barron (London: Athlone Press, 1971).
[43] John Capgrave, *Liber de Illustribus Henricis,* ed. F. C. Hingeston, Rolls Series (London, 1858), 99.

reforming the entire body politic."[44] From this story to the end of "In Praise of Peace," the word "pite" is so prevalent that R. Balfour Daniels identifies it as an example of the rhetorical figure *traductio*.[45] Galloway suggests that "the theme of pity nearly overtakes the narrative of "In Praise of Peace," written for Henry IV, turning the short poem midway (from line 330) into little else but a praise of pity."[46] I will discuss the way the manuscript as a whole refines the concept of "pite" in the following section. In this section, however, I will dwell on the fact that mercy is not sufficient on its own: Constantine's conversion to Christianity, and thus the conversion of the empire as a whole, rests on an acceptance of the doctrine that Sylvester has to teach.

Here, as elsewhere in "In Praise of Peace," Gower insists that Christians are called to convert others through the teaching of doctrine rather than through acts of violence. Earlier in the poem, Gower acknowledges that "It is to wondre above a mannys wit / Withoute werre how Cristes feith was wonne" (*IPP* 211–12), yet he insists that Christ called his followers to preach the good news of the gospel:

> To every creature undir the sonne
> Crist bad himself how that we schulden preche,
> And to the folk his evangile teche. (*IPP* 215–17)

Thus "In Praise of Peace" reiterates principles set forth in the *Confessio*, where the apostles converted through evangelism rather than war:

> Bot if thei wolde in other wise
> Be werre have broght in the creance,
> It hadde yit stonde in balance. (*CA* III.2497–2506)

Harry J. Brown suggests that these lines mark a moment where "'Moral Gower' warns against pursuing an ideology that at the close of the fourteenth century was not only obsolete, but potentially suicidal."[47] However suicidal crusading may have been, I hope to have shown in this essay that it was not obsolete; on the contrary, it may have seemed a very real possibility in

---

[44] Andrew Galloway, "The Literature of 1388 and the Politics of Pity in Gower's *Confessio Amantis*," in *The Letter of the Law: Legal Practice and Literary Production in Medieval England*, ed. Emily Steiner and Candace Barrington (Ithaca, NY: Cornell University Press, 2002), 67–104 (90).

[45] R. Balfour Daniels, "Rhetoric in Gower's 'To King Henry the Fourth, in Praise of Peace'," *Studies in Philology* 32 (1935): 62–73 (67–68).

[46] Galloway, "Literature of 1388," 95.

[47] Harry J. Brown, "For Worldes Good" in *The Crusades: Other Experiences, Alternate Perspectives: Selected Proceedings from the 32nd Annual CEMERS Conference*, ed. Khalil I. Semaan (Binghamton, NY: Global Academic Publishing, 2003), 179–91 (188).

1400–01. It is precisely in this context that Gower turns to Constantine's conversion in order to suggest that secular leaders might more effectively bring about "creaunce" by fighting "mescreance" peacefully – through reform in head and members – in themselves, their realms, and the corporate Christian body.[48]

Constantine not only embodies the idea that reform in the head can heal the members, but he was also responsible for calling a Church council to distinguish between "creaunce" and "mescreaunce." The Council of Nicaea renounced the Arian heresy and agreed upon a common creed, providing a model of reform in head and members to which later supporters of the conciliar movement returned in their attempt to establish the right of Church councils to act authoritatively. Coming shortly after the story of Constantine's conversion, Gower's insistence that "these othre princes cristene alle" (*IPP* 380) bear the responsibility to set "the rightful Pope upon his stalle" (*IPP* 383) echoes arguments in the 1390s by authors like Jean Gerson for a Church council that could bring about an end to the Schism. Zachary Stone has recently suggested that these lines link "In Praise of Peace" to Nicholas Fakenham's *Determinatio de schismate*, which he was asked to develop in November 1395 and which "reflected the shift in English attitudes towards the Schism in favour of a negotiated, conciliar, solution."[49] Growing in force, these arguments led to the Councils of Pisa (1409) and Constance (1414–18), and eventually the Council of Florence (1431–49). By bringing together concerns about reform in head and members, proper belief, and unity in the Church, "In Praise of Peace" certainly adumbrates concerns held by later writers. As Alexander Russell has noted, Jean Picard claimed, in a speech made in November 1425, that "the king, clergy and people of England, in particular, wished to purge the Church of its corrupt manners, refute the heretics and unify the Greek and Latin Churches."[50] Like Gower, Picard looked to Constantine for his authority, claiming that "the Arian and Manicheaean heretics and those rebelling against the authority of the pope had all been brought back to the path of reason by the authority of the general council."[51] Thus "In Praise of Peace" suggests that Gower was thinking about conciliar authority in the

---

[48] Gower also seems to have coined the word "mescreance" in *CA*. The confessor uses it to critique the faith of early Greeks (V.1444) and later to describe the "nigromance" employed by Nectanabus (VI.2365–66). It functions here as a synonym for "misbelieve" (V.1456), and it came to connote "unbelief," "heresy," and "treachery." *MED*, s.v., *miscrēaunce* (n.).

[49] Stone, "Western Schism," 241.

[50] Alexander Russell, *Conciliarism and Heresy in Fifteenth-Century England: Collective Authority in the Age of the General Councils*, Cambridge Studies in Medieval Life and Thought, Fourth Series (Cambridge: Cambridge University Press, 2017), Chap 1.

[51] Russell, *Conciliarism*, Chap 1.

late fourteenth century; it therefore seems likely that his work would have resonated with later conciliarists.

"In Praise of Peace" places special emphasis on the need for reform in the head as a necessary condition for peace in the realm. Having described the schism as an affliction of the head that affects the entire Christian body, "Of that the heved is sick, the limes aken" (260), Gower suggests that it is Henry's embodiment of "pite," not the pope's, that will establish peace:

> My worthi liege lord, Henri be name
> Which Engelond hast to governe and righte,
> Men oghten wel thi *pite* to proclame
> Which openliche in al the worldes sighte
> Is shewed with the help of god almighte,
> To yive ous pes, which longe hath be debated,
> Wherof thi pris shal nevere ben abated. (*IPP* 358–64, my emphasis)

Just in case the reader misses the key word here, Gower repeats it in the following lines:

> My lord, in whom hath evere yit be founde
> *Pite* withoute spot of violence,
> Kep thilke pes alwei withinne bounde,
> Which god hath planted in thi conscience (*IPP* 365–68, my emphasis)

Just as God sent the Saints to Constantine in a dream, God has "planted" the ability to keep peace in Henry's "conscience." Gower implies that Henry's right to govern England arises from his "pite."

More specifically, Henry's "pite" offers England a chance to achieve the peace it could not attain under Richard II. In a poem that does not appear in BL Additional MS 59495, the "Carmen super multiplici viciorum pestilencia" [A Poem on the Manifold Plague of Vices], Gower uses the same imagery to describe the state of England in the twentieth year of Richard's reign (22 June 1396–21 June 1397) that de Mézières was using in 1395 to describe the state of Christendom as a whole. Like de Mézières, Gower does this in the hope that "medicos" [doctors] will cure them (Prose 6–7).[52] Gower devotes the first major division of "Carmen" to the Lollards, who disturb both the Church and the faith (23). He asserts that "vetus insurgit heresis" [the old heresy arises] (32) in the Lollards and that "Scismata Lollardi de novitiate serunt" [The Lollards sow schisms of novelty] (91). The "Carmen" depicts Lollards as the embodiment of "mescreance," especially when Gower contrasts their false belief with "Recta fides" [Correct

---

[52] All references to Gower's Latin poems are from R. F. Yeager, ed. and trans., *John Gower: The Minor Latin Works* (Kalamazoo, MI: Medieval Institute Publications, 2005).

faith], which "quicquid rectum petit" [seeks whatever is correct] (50). This poem's characterization of Lollards confirms that when Gower uses the word "mescreantz" he expects it to connote heretics as well as Turks as other people who have seen division in the Church as their opportunity. Both here and in the *Vox Clamantis*, Gower blames the schism for the emergence of the Lollards.[53] In the "Carmen," he applies this argument to the realm, implying that misrule in head and members has caused England to be afflicted by Lollardy, along with pride, lust, perjury, and greed. Its closing couplet tells members of the realm that they can do their part for peace even if the head does not:

> Vir qui vult ideo pacem componere mundo:
> Pacificet primo iura tenenda Deo. ("Carmen" 320–21)
>
> [Let the man who wants to, have peace in the world in this way:
> First make peace by keeping God's laws].

The final couplet of "In Praise of Peace" reprises these lines, addressing Henry directly in order to insist upon the importance of the king's piety:

> Kep charite and draugh pite to honde
> Maintene lawe, and so the pes schal stond. (*IPP* 384–85)

Together, these poems imply that there is a need for constant vigilance to ensure both head and members, king and commons, maintain laws dutifully and piously.

The King's "Pite" in BL Additional MS 59495

Gower's emphasis on "pite" through the final lines of "In Praise of Peace" primes readers to look for it throughout the rest of BL Additional MS 59495, which regularly uses the vocative and imperative to focus attention on the king's obligation to behave piously and mercifully. The manuscript opens by addressing the king as "Electus Christi, pie Rex Henrice fuisti" [Dutiful King Henry, who was chosen by Christ]. "Rex celi Deus" also employs the vocative "O pie Rex" [O pious king] (21) and its variant "Rex pie" [pious king] (10) in the same poem and twice in "O recolende" (1, 15). Yeager's decision to translate "pie" as "dutiful" in one instance and "pious" in the other reminds readers of the linguistic connection between duty and piety that the words "pie" and "pietas" connote. Galloway points out that "the word *pietas* is invariably translated by Gower in the *Confessio amantis* (as the Latin glosses show) as 'pity' rather than 'piousness' or 'dutiful

---

[53] I am grateful to R. F. Yeager for pointing this out.

respect', the classical and earlier medieval senses," but Gower invites readers to identify the connection between these two meanings when he uses "pie" or "pietas" in Latin.[54] "O recolende" insists on the king's duty to act piously by using other words: "Rex confirmatus, licet undique magnificatus, / Sub Cristo gratus viva stamen immaculatus" [Although you are confirmed king and glorified on all sides, / Still you must live pleasing to Christ without blemish] (8–9). Gower adds yet another layer of nuance to this cluster of terms by insisting that mercy offers a kind of protection that cannot be undone:

> Sic qui transibit opus et *pietatis* adibit
> Hunc Deus ascribit: quod ab hoste perire nequibit;
> Et sic finibit qui pia vota bibit. (19–21, my emphasis)

> [Thus, one who passes through his life and approaches the work of
>   *mercy*
> God marks him; which can be undone by no enemy;
> Thus will he end who drinks in the deeds of mercy.]

In "Rex celi Deus," Gower suggests that evil dissipates in the face of a king who avoids bad council:

> Omne quod est turpe vacuum discedat, et omne
>   Est quod honorificum det Deus esse tuum.
> Consilium nullum *pie rex* te tangat iniquum,
>   In quibus occultum scit Deus esse dolum. (31–34, my emphasis)

> [May all that is evil disperse harmlessly, and all
> That is honorable may God grant to be yours.
> Let no iniquitous counsel touch you, *dutiful king*,
> In things where God knows evil is hidden.]

While Yeager's translation of "pie Rex" as "dutiful king" is convincing here, "pious" and "merciful" are equally reasonable. Indeed, Gower's use of Latin allows him to imply that a particularly effective king is one who is "pie" in every one of these senses.

Additional MS 59495 offers an even more nuanced understanding of the concept of "pite" through its incorporation of French verse that had been written before "In Praise of Peace." The *Cinkante balades* opens by listing "pité" as the king's primary attribute (*CB* I.1).[55] The word appears six more times in the *balades,* where it describes the pity conventionally sought by the lover from the beloved (*CB* X.6, *CB* XII.20, *CB* XVII.26, *CB* XX.27, *CB*

---

[54] Galloway, "Literature of 1388," 86.
[55] All references to the French poems are to John Gower, *The French Balades,* ed. and trans. R. F. Yeager (Kalamazoo, MI: Medieval Institute Publications, 2011).

XXXVI.22) or in a personified form who might speak on behalf of the lover (*CB* XIV.15). Each of these scenes acknowledges the power that the beloved who is asked for "pité" holds over the lover. This is sometimes figured as a matter of life and death: in *CB* XIII.15–21, the lover claims that if pity does not compel the lady to offer him mercy, he will fall sick or die. This is a conventional claim in love poetry, as is the depiction of the beloved's "danger" [standoffishness] (*CB* XXX.15) as "cruel" [cruel] (*CB* XXX.17). Nonetheless, the connection between love and pity connects the *balades* to the Ricardian epilogue of Gower's *Confessio,* where "the rub in the emphasis on royal pity is that it is predicated on a suspension of cruelty. As such, it is an expression of power, good or evil, and it therefore demands a careful if tenuous distinction between its good and bad forms."[56] Both the *Confessio* and the *Cinkante balades* call their readers to exercise their moral judgment about how and when pity should be offered. The *Cinkante balades* also provide a model for thinking about how the addressee ought to respond to pleas for pity: the lover aims to elicit pity by sending a "balade" (*CB* XVII25, XXXVI.23) or "ceo lettre" [this letter] (*CB* XX.27). Gower, of course, has written the *balades* and "In Praise of Peace," which he describes as "this letter" (*IPP* 375), to move Henry to "pite:" it is for the king to decide whether to withhold his cruelty or not.

The *Traitié selonc les auctours pour essampler les amantz marietz* further enhances this manuscript's focus on "pite" through its representation of the dutiful, merciful, and pious lover. Gower twice uses the word "pité" in the *Traitié* in a sense modern readers would recognize, saying "ceo fuist grant pité" [that was a great pity] (*Tr* VIII.16) and "ceo fuist pité" [that was a pity] (*Tr* X.13). The third time the word appears, in the *exemplum* of David's adultery with Bathsheba and murder of Uriah, it offers readers yet another way of thinking about the concept. Gower omits the part of the story where Nathan makes David recognize both the lack of pity he has shown Bathsheba and Uriah and his need to ask God for mercy by telling him a story about a rich man who has taken a poor man's lamb to feed a traveller. David tells Nathan a man who has done such a thing would need to "restore the ewe fourfold, because he did this thing, and had no pity."[57] Nathan tells David he is the man, and David recognizes his sinfulness. The *Traitié* expands this scene:

> Mais cil, qui dieus de sa pité remeine,
> David, se prist si fort a repetir,
> Q'unqes null homme en ceste vie humeine
> Ne receust tant de pleindre et de ghemir:
> Merci prioit, merci fuist son desire,
> Merci troevoit, merci son point ne tarde.
> N'ert pas segeur de soi qui dieus ne garde. (*Tr* XIV.15–21)

---

[56] Galloway, "Literature of 1388," 93.
[57] 2 Samuel 12.6.

[But he whom God in His pity restored,
David, himself very forthrightly acted to repent,
So that – as no man ever in this human life –
He welcomed such mourning and groaning:
He prayed for mercy, mercy was his desire,
Mercy he found, mercy his point did not delay.
He has no security, whom God does not protect.]

God shows pity by granting the mercy to David, who has sought "pité" as Nathan advised. Nonetheless, others pay with their lives for the king's lack of pity: Uriah is already dead and God then takes the son born to Bathsheba even though David has fasted. Thus David learns that his power is limited in comparison to God's and that his failure to show pity has consequences, even if he does not bear the full cost himself.

This *exemplum* insists that the king's capacity to show pity depends on God. It begins by indicating that "Trop est humaine char frele et vileine; / Sans grace nulls se poet contretenir" [Human flesh is exceedingly frail and base; / Without grace no one is able to defend himself] (*Tr* XIV.1–2). This view of human desire echoes the account of love given in "Ecce Patet Tensus," which comes between the *Cinkante balades* and the *Traitié* in the manuscript, which insists that love is omnipotent:

Sic amor omne domat, quicquid natura creavit,
Et tamen indomitus ipse per omne manet
Carcerat et redimit, ligat atque ligata resoluit,
Vulnerat omne genus, nec sibi vulnus habet. (15–18)

[Thus Love subdues everything that Nature has created
While he himself remains unsubdued by all.
He imprisons and sets free, binds and releases the bound,
He wounds every nation, but receives no wound himself.]

In lines that resonate with the *Traitié*, this poem insists that "Nullus ab innato valet hoc euadere morbo sit nisi quod sola gracia curet eum" [No one is strong enough to evade this inborn malady / Unless grace provides a cure] (35–36). Pity is to be sought, then, because God's grace is more powerful than all else. Throughout BL Additional MS 59495, Gower acts as Nathan to Henry's David, exhorting the king to seek God's help to enact pity as mercy, piety, and devotion. In "Rex celi deus," which comes between "In Praise of Peace" and the *balades,* Gower insists that Henry's embodiment of "pite" creates the condition for healing: "Sic tua sors sortem mediante Deo renovatam / Sanat et emendat, que prius egra fuit" [Thus your fortune renews and heals ours, with God's help, / Making whole what was ailing] ("Rex" 19–20). "In Praise of Peace" suggests to Henry that his personal "pite" has the capacity to bring about an end to the "mescreance" engendered by "mescreantz" who come in many forms, from Ottoman Turks to schismatics to Lollard heretics.

Even the appearance of BL Additional MS 59495 contributes to the sense that it records a wise counselor's intimate and personal appeal to the king's "pite." This becomes especially clear when it is compared to the copy of de Mézières' *Epistre* that Robert the Hermit delivered to Richard II in 1395. Although de Mézières claims to be writing a "poure et simple epistre" [poor and simple letter], London, British Library, Royal MS B.20. vi is a lavish French manuscript with an elaborate frontispiece and written in a formal hand. In contrast, Additional MS 59495 is an austere book that contains texts in three languages addressed to Richard's successor.[58] R. F. Yeager has suggested that Henry IV likely had access to the contents of this manuscript at some point early in his reign in "a fancier version of London, British Library Additional MS 59495."[59] Nonetheless, the manuscript that survives invites readers to imagine the king reading this book as an intimate and personal appeal to his pity and piety. In contrast to Royal MS B.20. vi, which argues that divisions in the faith can only be cured through grandiose gestures, Additional MS 59495 encourages readers to imagine a king wondering how he might respond to "mescreantz" and, implicitly, "mescreance" with "pite." Read in the context of de Mézières' call for a crusade and Manuel II's visit to England in 1400–01, Gower's compilation offers a meditation on the king's responsibility to address schism and heresy without excessive violence.

Conclusion

The final poem in Additional MS 59495 confirms that Gower was working on the manuscript around or after the time of Manuel II's visit. "Quicquid homo scribat" describes how "Henrici quarti primus regni fuit annus / Quo michi defecit visus acta mea" [it was in the first year of the reign of King Henry IV / that my sight failed for my deeds] (1–2). The reference in the past tense to the first year of Henry's reign reveals that the earliest this poem could have been copied into the manuscript was September 1400. This evidence is tenuous for the dating of the manuscript as a whole if one accepts Sobecki's argument that Additional MS 59495 remained with Gower at St Mary Overys and that he copied this poem in his own hand.[60] Whoever copied it, the poem was certainly added to BL Additional MS

---

[58] John Fisher contends this manuscript is similar to other high-quality Gower manuscripts in *John Gower: Moral Philosopher and Friend of Chaucer* (New York: New York University Press, 1964), 72.

[59] Yeager, "Ballades," 88.

[60] Sobecki refers to this poem by its opening line, *Henrici Quarti Primus,* in "*Ecce patet tensus*" (951).

59495 at a late stage.[61] Nonetheless, it indicates that the earliest point at which BL Additional MS 59495 could have been completed was the same month that Henry's treasurer summoned records to find money for the wars and for the defense of Constantinople. This manuscript may not have left St Mary Overys, but this was not because it was deemed irrelevant after Henry confirmed the truce with France in May of 1400. At least one poem was added after this date and, as I hope to have shown here, "In Praise of Peace" and the manuscript as a whole speak directly to issues that became increasingly relevant after the French truce had been sealed. It seems reasonable to conclude, then, that BL MS Additional 59495 was still in process until at least late 1400 if not 1401, and that its subject matter remained highly relevant beyond the moment of its completion.

---

[61] Arthur Bahr argues that this poem formed part of Gower's initial plan for the manuscript, contributing to its chiastic structure by mirroring the Latin lines that precede "In Praise of Peace" to open the manuscript: "Reading Codicological Form in John Gower's Trentham Manuscript," *Studies in the Age of Chaucer* 33 (2011): 219-62 (213).

CHAPTER 8

JOHN SHIRLEY AND JOHN GOWER

Margaret Connolly

THE FIFTEENTH-CENTURY SCRIBE JOHN Shirley (c.1366–1456) presents the following poem as a moral balade written by John Gower:

    Passe forþe þou pilgryme / and bridel wele þy beeste
    Loke not ageine / for thing þat may betyde
    Thenke what þou wilt / but speke ay with þe leeste
    Avyse þee weele / who stondeþe þee besyde
    Let not þyne herte / beo with þy tonge bewryde   5
    Trust not to muche / in fayre visayginge
    For peynted cheere / shapeþe efft to stynge.

    Byholde þy selff / or þat þou oþer deme
    Ne beo not gladde / whane oþer done amysse /
    Sey never al þat / which wolde þee soþe seme /   10
    þou maist not wit / what þy fortune is
    For þere is / no wight on lyve ewysse /
    þat stondeþe sure / þerfore I rede beware
    And looke aboute / for stumbling in þe snare.

    Reporte not muche / on oþer mens sawe   15
    Be ay adradde / to here a wicked fame
    For man shal dye / by dome of goddes lawe
    þat here enpeyreþe / any mans name
    Avyse þee wele / þerfore / or þowe attame
    [fol. 18r] Suche as þou mayst never revoke ageyne   20
    A gode name loste is loste for ay certaine

    Pley not with pecus ne Fawvel to þy feere
    Chese þou hem never yif þou do affter me
    þe hande is hurte þat bourdeþe with þe bere
    Fawvel fareþe even / right as doþe a bee   25
    Honymowþed right ful of swetnesse is she
    But loke behinde and ware þee frome hir stonge
    þowe shalt kache hareme to pley with þeos beestis longe

> Dispreyse no wight but if effte þou may him foreyse
> Ne preyse no firre / but þou may discomende   30
> Weyghe þy wordes / and hem by mesure peyse
> Thenke þat þe gilty may by grace amende
> And eke þe gode may happen to offende
> Remembre eke / þat what man doþe amisse
> þou haste or arte / or may be suche as he is.[1]   35

Shirley furnished the poem with the title "Balade moral of gode counseyle," and a running header which repeats the same information: "Balade of moralite," in both instances then concluding with the clear attribution of authorship: "made by Gower." He copied the poem into the latest of his three extant manuscript anthologies, Oxford, Bodleian Library, MS Ashmole 59, where it sits amidst a cluster of items that are otherwise all by Lydgate: three extracts from the *Fall of Princes* precede it, and five short poems follow, two of which are verse prayers.[2] Most of this material has a moralizing intent and "Passe forþe þou pilgryme," with its counsel against hasty or unguarded speech, fits easily into a selection of short admonitory items which Shirley describes, slightly opaquely, as "þe abstracte brevyayre" (fol. 13ʳ). In this context, were the poem not so clearly labelled as Gower's it could pass for one of Lydgate's. Its sentiments are in tune with those expressed in Lydgate's proverbial pieces such as "A wikked tong wol alway deme amis" (*NIMEV* 653), and it accords with the advisory nature of much of his work. Another selection from the *Fall of Princes* that occurs later in this same manuscript is given the almost identical title "Balade of Good Counseyl."[3] In Shirley's earlier anthology, Cambridge, Trinity College, MS R.3.20, a copy of Lydgate's "Thoroughfare of Woe" (*NIMEV* 1872) is also introduced as "a balade of goode counseyle" (p. 25), and equivalent titles, in French not English, are attached to other short poems: "Balade de bone counseyle" is used as the title of two poems, one English, one French, and another French poem is entitled "Balade moral et de bone conseylle."[4] Chaucer's poem "Truth" is also sometimes titled "Balade de bon conseyl" (and with the equivalent terms in English and Latin), though not by Shirley, who copied it twice in the Trinity manuscript.[5] Similarly, in Bodley

---

[1] *NIMEV* 2737, transcribed here from Oxford, Bodleian Library, MS Ashmole 59, fols. 17ᵛ–18ʳ. I have silently expanded the few abbreviated forms and followed modern conventions of word division, but I have retained Shirley's capitalization and punctuation, particularly his extensive use of the virgule.

[2] For details of the surrounding texts, see Margaret Connolly, *John Shirley: Book Production and the Noble Household in Fifteenth-Century England* (Aldershot: Ashgate, 1998), 146–47.

[3] Bodley Ashmole 59, fol. 28ᵛ, *NIMEV* 1168.

[4] Trinity R.3.20, 48, "If it befalle that god the lyst visyte," *NIMEV* 1419; 89, "Tant de perilz sont a fuir la court," 103, "Que vault tresor qui na joye ne leesse."

[5] For details see *A Variorum Edition of The Works of Geoffrey Chaucer, Volume V: The Minor Poems, Part One*, ed. George B. Pace and Alfred David (Norman: University of Oklahoma Press, 1982), 59.

Ashmole 59, Shirley introduces Henry Scogan's poem, "My noble sones and eke my lordis dere," as "A moral balade."[6] The frequency with which this type of title appears in manuscript copies of later medieval short poems suggests that its use had little significance beyond marking approval of texts that offered wholesome advice; the very widespread occurrence of such texts might also indicate that their origins lay in composition exercises on moral topics, or as translations. At the very least this reveals a long history of poetic composition on admonitory themes, and audience interest in the same, that stretches from Chaucer's (and Gower's) lifetimes through Lydgate's and beyond.

Despite Shirley's clear direction the modern editor of Gower's works, George Campbell Macaulay, rejected the authenticity of "Passe forþe þou pilgryme." He afforded the poem scant attention in the Clarendon edition of *The Complete Works of John Gower*, including only a brief note about it in Volume II at the end of his long introduction to Gower's English works.[7] The introduction to this second volume is 175 pages long, and is largely focussed on the *Confessio*, which was Macaulay's main interest;[8] the introduction concludes with a sub-section devoted to the "Other English Works," but this comprises merely two pages and only two "other English" items are mentioned.[9] For the first of these, the poem "In Praise of Peace," the reader is referred elsewhere: its single manuscript witness, the Trentham MS (now BL Additional MS 59495), had already been fully described in Volume I in connection with Gower's French poems, and the poem itself, securely admitted to the canon of Gower's works, appears in Volume III after the text of the *Confessio*, accompanied by four and a half pages of textual notes.[10] By contrast, the text of the *other* "other English" poem, "Passe forþe þou pilgryme," is placed in the *introduction* rather than the main part of Volume II, and no proper description of its witnesses is offered at all. Instead Macaulay merely notes its three manuscripts and the various titles and ascriptions that they contain before printing its text from one manuscript and providing the substantive variant readings of a second as footnotes beneath the text. He also surrounds the text of the poem with judgments about its authenticity. He introduces it with the assertion that: "It is almost impossible that these verses can have been written by Gower;" and immediately after the text concludes he comments: "This is full of lines that Gower would not have written."[11] A

---

[6] Bodley Ashmole 59, fol. 25r, *NIMEV* 2264.
[7] G. C. Macaulay, ed., *The Complete Works of John Gower, edited from the manuscripts with introductions, notes, and glossaries*, 4 vols (Oxford: Clarendon, 1899–1902). Volume I covers Gower's French works, volumes II and III his English works (principally *Confessio Amantis*), and volume IV his Latin works.
[8] "[...] to publish a correct text of the *Confessio Amantis* has been throughout the main object," I, vi.
[9] II, clxxiii–clxxiv.
[10] *NIMEV* 2587; I, lxxix–lxxxiii, and III, 481–94 and 550–54.
[11] II, clxxiii and clxxiv respectively. Further quotations in this paragraph are taken from these same pages.

short paragraph (just three sentences) offers a brief commentary on meter and style that justifies Macaulay's point of view: he complains that there are superfluous syllables in the meter; there is accent on weak syllables; there is defective rhyme; a particular form is not found "in any respectable Gower MS;" and finally, "the style is not that of Gower, but evidently imitated from Chaucer's poem 'Fle from the pres'." Still, Macaulay printed the text in order, he said, "that the reader may judge."

Critical editions of medieval texts are of fundamental importance in establishing modern scholarly access to the works of medieval authors. In this sense editors of medieval texts play a crucial role in opening up subject areas for other researchers. Yet as well as providing the raw materials for scholarly enquiries of a literary, linguistic, and critical nature, editions of medieval texts may influence modern responses to those works and shape understanding of them in subtle ways. Even the very best editions both present and hide material from public view according to judgments made by their editors: such judgments relate to the selection of manuscript witnesses, the acceptance and rejection of individual readings, the choice of glosses, and the provision of annotation. Essentially an edition allows researchers to bypass the task of consulting original sources, because someone else has already done so. When that work has been done comprehensively and to high standards of scholarship the subject becomes effectively closed: no one will seek to re-edit the material for a long time, if at all, especially if the task would be a large one due to the length of a text, or a high number of surviving witnesses, or a complex textual tradition, or a combination of these factors. Despite its age Macaulay's work has generally stood the test of time and few modern scholars have been tempted to approach the task of editing Gower's *oeuvre* anew.[12]

Yet this single short poem, "Passe forþe þou pilgryme," is not well-served by Macaulay's monumental achievement. His editorial decisions about its presentation and placement mean that readers may *not* judge very easily, or very open-mindedly, whether the poem's exclusion from the Gower canon is truly justified. Macaulay leads us to follow and concur with his own conclusions about its unworthiness by placing the poem in the introduction to the volumes that deal with Gower's English works rather than in the main section of those volumes where the texts of those works are presented. Not only is this "other English" work not admitted to the main part of the edition, it is placed at the very end of the introduction as well, where

---

[12] Exceptions are Russell Peck, whose edition of *Confessio Amantis* is ongoing, with three volumes in print (Kalamazoo: Medieval Institute Publications, 2003–13), and R. F. Yeager, who has produced editions of Gower's French and Latin poems: *The French Balades* (Kalamazoo: Medieval Institute Publications, 2011), and *The Minor Latin Works* (Kalamazoo: Medieval Institute Publications, 2005); the latter, it might be noted, also includes the English poem "In Praise of Peace," edited by Michael Livingston.

it is easily overlooked. Its inclusion seems almost an afterthought, and its assigned position is clearly one of low importance. Even the typeface that presents its text suggests a lack of significance: the font used is very small, no larger than that used for the *bas-de-page* variant readings, and tellingly the same as that used for the list of corrigenda and addenda on the facing page.[13] The semiotics of this editorial *mise-en-page* are inescapable: this is a text that is associated with error which does not really deserve to be included in the volume at all. In this way Macaulay reinforces the stylistic judgments that he openly articulates about "Passe forþe þou pilgryme" with more subtle strategies that influence the reader's responses when using the edition.[14]

This marginalizing treatment of the poem was appropriate given that Macaulay had reached the conclusion that "Passe forþe þou pilgryme" was not an authentic work. As Gower's editor, Macaulay had a responsibility to present the poet's work to best advantage, and to guide modern readers towards its appreciation. Part of that task entailed firmly establishing the canon of Gower's writing, winnowing out any pieces that had accidentally come to be regarded as his. In this regard the publication of the Clarendon Chaucer in the 1890s must have offered a model for Macaulay's own edition: the canon of Chaucer's works had been swelled by the interventions of various sixteenth- and seventeenth-century printers and early editors, but was slimmed down at the end of the nineteenth century through the efforts of various Victorian scholars, and above all by Walter Skeat.[15] The process of sifting true from spurious involved much consultation of surviving copies. Macaulay is at pains to describe his extensive research in libraries and private houses and he certainly appreciated the value of the manuscript witnesses of Gower's works.[16] But this attitude makes it all the more difficult to understand why he reached the conclusion he did about "Passe forþe þou pilgryme" since the earliest surviving manuscript copy of that poem gives it a very clear ascription to Gower. Such a circumstance (an early manuscript witness, of known provenance, with a clear authorial attribution) would normally carry significant weight with an editor, but Macaulay seems to have been happy to disregard these factors.

The poem "Passe forþe þou pilgryme" survives in only three manuscripts. John Shirley's copy, Bodley Ashmole 59, already discussed above, is

---

[13] Unnumbered leaf following II, clxxiv.
[14] For a recent discussion of how the form of an edition may influence perceptions about the text it presents see Margaret Connolly, "The Edited Text and the Selected Text and the Problem of Critical Editions," in *Editing and Interpretation of Middle English Texts: Essays in Honour of William Marx*, ed. Margaret Connolly and Raluca Radulescu (Turnhout: Brepols, 2018), 229–47.
[15] Walter W. Skeat, ed., *The Complete Works of Geoffrey Chaucer: Edited from Numerous Manuscripts*, 7 vols. (Oxford: Clarendon Press, 1894–97). Macaulay acknowledged that work done on Chaucer by Skeat, Furnivall, and ten Brink had proved helpful to his editing of Gower, I, vii.
[16] See below.

the earliest, and was probably written in the 1440s when Shirley was resident in the precincts of St Bartholomew's Hospital in London.[17] The text of the poem in a second manuscript, Oxford, Bodleian Library, MS Rawlinson C. 86, closely resembles that of Bodley Ashmole 59, suggesting a direct relationship of copy and exemplar. This is chronologically and geographically possible: the Rawlinson manuscript is a composite of four booklets that seems to have been compiled in the late fifteenth or early sixteenth century in London or at least in a metropolitan context.[18] It shares five texts in total with Bodley Ashmole 59, all of which are located in its second booklet, indicating that the scribe responsible for this section had access to Shirley's last anthology. Although that scribe is unidentified, Rawlinson C. 86 shares a number of other texts with British Library, MS Harley 2251, a manuscript copied by the Hammond scribe who was active in the 1460s–80s, and who clearly worked from exemplars written by John Shirley.[19] This gives the impression that Shirley's manuscripts remained available to other London copyists in the decades after his death, allowing repeated transmission of texts that he had preserved. The Rawlinson text of "Passe forþe þou pilgryme" is less complete than its predecessor: it has no title or running header, and consists of only four stanzas. The absence of the fifth stanza was presumably accidental and post-medieval (the text continues to the bottom of the leaf on fol. 89^v, after which the following leaf has been lost from the volume), but the omission of the title and running header seems a more deliberate scribal choice, and one which means that no ascription of authorship is offered either.

A completely different title accompanies the poem in its third and latest manuscript copy, British Library, MS Additional 29729. This manuscript was written in the 1550s by the historian and antiquary John Stow. He gave the poem the title: "A leson to kepe well ye tonge," and ended with an explicit in the same vein: "to kepe thy tonge well." More significantly he also furnished it with an entirely different statement of authorship: "per magistrum benedictum burgh" (fols. 6^v–7^r), and the preceding poem is also attributed to Burgh.[20] Stow compiled his collection by drawing on various different exemplars, one of which was Shirley's earlier anthology, Trinity R.3.20. He also handled Bodley Ashmole 59, which he used as an

---

[17] On this manuscript see Connolly, *John Shirley*, 145–69.

[18] See Julia Boffey and Carol Meale, "Selecting the Text: Rawlinson C. 86 and Some Other Books for London Readers," in *Regionalism in Late Medieval Manuscripts and Texts*, ed. Felicity Riddy (Cambridge: D. S. Brewer, 1991), 143–69.

[19] For a list of the manuscripts attributed to this scribe see Linne R. Mooney, "A New Manuscript by the Hammond Scribe Discovered by Jeremy Griffiths," in *The English Medieval Book*, ed. A. S. G. Edwards, Vincent Gillespie, and Ralph Hanna (London: British Library, 2000), 113–23.

[20] "Nat dremyd I in ye mount of pernaso," *NIMEV* 2284, the unique copy of this poem in praise of Lydgate.

exemplar for part of what is now British Library, MS Harley 367.[21] Shirley's copy of "Passe forþe þou pilgryme" and its attribution caught his attention: Stow wrote "gowre / [...] Chaucer" in his characteristically cramped hand in the left margin alongside the poem's decorative opening capital "P".[22] Nevertheless he found his own copy-text for the poem elsewhere, in "mister hanlays booke."[23] Both Mr Hanlay and his book are as yet unidentified, but it is possible that the latter was Rawlinson C. 86. Textually Stow's copy of the poem shares a number of variant readings with Rawlinson that do not occur in Shirley's version (7 efft] her; 17 dome] deathe; 20 mayst never] nevar mayst; 26 right] *om*.). Most significantly, the two manuscripts share what seem to be erroneous readings in the fourth stanza where in line 24 the "bere" (bear) of Shirley's version becomes a "brere" (briar), creating a lack of concord with "þeos beestis" (line 28) and thus necessitating further modifications in that line.[24] But whether Rawlinson C. 86 was or was not Mr Hanlay's book, its imperfect state makes it impossible to establish whether Stow found the attribution to Burgh there or whether he added this on his own authority. His disregard for Shirley's information is uncharacteristic, but may be more apparent than real since we do not know the relative chronology of Stow's handling of Bodley Ashmole 59 and his compilation of BL Additional 29729.

In the case of this poem all textual roads eventually lead back to John Shirley. Of the three manuscript witnesses available to him, Macaulay chose to use the earliest, Bodley Ashmole 59, "out of deference to Shirley's authority," though he immediately qualified this comment by continuing "(which is not very weighty however)."[25] It is worth considering what influences, at the very end of the nineteenth century, could have led Macaulay to this conclusion. Current critical opinion about Shirley's reliability in matters of authorship is divided between those who think that he is, by and large, a credible witness, and those who do not.[26] But in Macaulay's day Shirley was held to be the "greatest authority for the authorship of the minor poems of his time" (a pronouncement made by Frederick Furnivall in 1871), and Walter Skeat had accepted many of Shirley's attributions when defining the canon of Chaucer's shorter poems in 1894, a reliance that Macaulay must surely

---

[21] The annotations are on fol. i[r] and fol. 17[v]; in BL Harley 367 the texts are on fols. 80–87, see Connolly, *John Shirley*, 182–85.
[22] I cannot read the second word of the annotation.
[23] BL Additional 29729, fol. 6[v].
[24] "Thow shalt haue hurt yf þou play with her ~~lond~~ longe," Bodley Rawlinson C. 86; "Thow shalt have harme, & thow play with hir longe," BL Additional 29729.
[25] II, clxxiii.
[26] For a recent summary of different views on this topic see Margaret Connolly, "What John Shirley Said About Adam: Authorship and Attribution in Trinity College Cambridge MS R.3.20," in *The Dynamics of the Medieval Manuscript: Text Collections from a European Perspective*, ed. Karen Pratt, Bart Besamusca, Matthias Meyer, and Ad Putter (Göttingen: V&R Unipress, 2017), 81–100.

have observed.[27] The earliest recorded negative view of Shirley's ascriptional reliability seems to be that of John Manly, who commented: "Is there any instance in which information given by Shirley has, when tested, proved to be correct?" But this was in 1913, more than a decade after Macaulay's edition had appeared.[28] That there was a generally enduring sense of Shirley's authority may be deduced from Aage Brusendorff's comment in 1925 (a decade after Macaulay had died) that "Shirley practically never wavers in his ascriptions of certain poems to certain writers, and accordingly he becomes an exceptionally important witness in the matter of authorship."[29] In the final decades of the nineteenth century there is no evidence of a negative attitude towards Shirley's trustworthiness, such as might have naturally prompted a disregard of his testimony. It seems therefore that Macaulay must have decided for himself that "Passe forþe þou pilgryme" was not an authentic work of Gower's.

In reaching this conclusion Macaulay was probably influenced above all by his familiarity with the manuscripts of Gower's works. His knowledge was extensive: he had examined all but two of the witnesses of Gower's French and Latin writings, and forty-two of the forty-nine complete copies of the *Confessio*, five manuscripts of extracts, and two sets of fragments.[30] In particular he praised the "excellence" of those copies of the *Confessio* that were available to him in Oxford. When Macaulay refers to "excellence" it is ostensibly in relation to text ("I was struck by the excellence of the authorities for its text"), but in attributing excellence he was certainly influenced by physical aspects such as material, script, layout, and decoration.[31] The physical regularity of many of the manuscripts of the *Confessio* (well-written, spaciously laid out in double-column format with a regular decorative hierarchy, on parchment),[32] may have been the model that Macaulay had in mind when he spoke of "respectable" Gower manuscripts.[33] Certainly the manuscript that he chose as the base text for his edition, Oxford, Bodleian Library, Fairfax 3, was of this caliber, as were

---

[27] Frederick J. Furnivall, [untitled] *The Athenaeum*, (18 February 1871), 210; Skeat, *Complete Works of Chaucer*, I: *The Romaunt of the Rose and Minor Poems* (1894), 25.

[28] John M. Manly, "Note on the Envoy of 'Truth'," *Modern Philology*, 11 (1913): 226; the comment was occasioned by Edith Rickert's discovery of the identity of Sir Philip (de) la Vache, subject of the "Envoy of 'Truth'."

[29] Aage Brusendorff, *The Chaucer Tradition* (Oxford: Clarendon, 1925), 234.

[30] For details see Derek Pearsall, "The Manuscripts and Illustrations of Gower's Works," in *A Companion to Gower*, ed. Siân Echard (Cambridge: D. S. Brewer, 2004), 73 n. 2; Macaulay records his own handling of manuscripts of the *Confessio* at II, cxxxviii.

[31] I, v.

[32] For the characteristics of the "standard" manuscripts of the *Confessio* see Pearsall, "The Manuscripts," 80.

[33] II, clxxiv.

the three manuscripts against which its text was collated: Macaulay describes these approvingly as, respectively, "an excellent copy, the best of its class" (Bodley 902), "a carefully written MS" (Oxford, Corpus Christi College 67), and "a good copy" (Bodley 294).[34] Alongside such manuscripts Bodley Ashmole 59, a paper anthology written by an aged scribe, would have appeared unimpressive. It would also have seemed very distant from Gower's time, which was at odds with the value Macaulay placed on contemporary witnesses: Fairfax 3 was written "in a very good hand of the end of the fourteenth cent.", and, in respect of the *Traitié* Macaulay judged it "at least as good as any of the three other copies which I have called contemporary."[35] His inherent distrust of later witnesses may be inferred from his dismissal of Oxford, Wadham College MS 13, whose text of the *Traitié* he judged "late and full of blunders," to be "set down as worthless," and whose text of the *Confessio* was "late and full of mistakes, and the spelling bad," its scribal hand "cramped and ugly."[36]

Macaulay's statements justifying his rejection of "Passe forþe þou pilgryme" indicate that he was primarily guided by his sense of the characteristics of Gower's poetry. It is worth considering these points in greater detail. One of his objections is concerned with lexis. He noted that "the form 'mayst' (maist) for 'miht' is not found in any respectable Gower MS." By respectable I think, as mentioned above, that Macaulay probably had in mind those "standard" manuscripts of the *Confessio*, all of which had been produced considerably closer to Gower's lifetime than Shirley's copy had been. Nonetheless, this is a big claim, and one that is hard to verify even with the convenient resources available to the modern scholar. Pickles and Dawson excluded the commonest words from their *Concordance*, so mayst/maist/miht etc. does not feature in their lists.[37] However, selective checking of the vocabulary of "Passe forþe þou pilgryme" reveals words that occur in the *Confessio* only with different meanings, such as "feere" (22) "companion," not *fere* "fear" as in the *Confessio*, or with quite different spellings, for example "pilgryme" (1: cf. *pilegrin*), "ewysse" (12: *iwiss*), "stumbling" (14: *stomble*), "kache" (28: *cacche*), "hareme" (28: *harm*). There are also words that are not evidenced in the *Confessio* at all: "visayginge" (6); "snare" (14); "reporte" (15); "attame" (19); "revoke" (20); "pecus" (22); "bourdeþe" (24); "bee" (25); "honymowþed" (26); "stonge" (27); "beestis" (28); "dispreyse" (29); "foreyse"

---

[34] These comments occur under the subheading "The Present Edition," II, clxx.
[35] Respectively II, clvii and I, lxxxvi.
[36] Respectively I, lxxxvii and II, clxiv.
[37] See J. D. Pickles and J. L. Dawson, *A Concordance to John Gower's* Confessio Amantis, Publications of the John Gower Society, 1 (Cambridge: D. S. Brewer, 1987); this may now be consulted electronically at https://middleenglish.library.jhu.edu/search/.

(29); "firre" (30); "discomende" (30).[38] Yet this total of fifteen words – rather less than five per cent of the poem, which comprises *circa* 314 words – does not constitute the dense accumulation of unique or uniquely-used forms that might, collectively, suggest a different authorship.

Only one of Macaulay's objections is based on lexis: most relate to meter. He states that there are superfluous syllables in the meter (citing lines 1, 5, 10, 17, 29, 33, and 35), and indicates that more might be found because he is "omitting those that might pass with amended spelling." Further, he finds that there is accent on weak syllables (citing lines 20, 25, 26, and 31). Thirdly, there is defective rhyme: the two instances singled out are in lines 4 and 5: "beside"/"bewryde," and in lines 22 and 24: "feere"/"bere." And fourthly, there is the suppression of a syllable at the beginning of the line in line 12. It is hard to argue with these points. Macaulay understood the laws of meter thoroughly, and was deeply familiar with the versification of the *Confessio*: what he observed in "Passe forþe þou pilgryme" clearly did not measure up to that standard. Some disruption may have been caused by miscopying and errors in transmission, but disturbance to regular scansion is also partly caused by Shirley's eccentric spelling practices. Although Macaulay claims to have allowed for this, Shirley's idiosyncratic doubling of some consonants, evidenced here in "efft" (7) and "selff" (8), and tolerance of "eo" spellings in words such as "beo" (5) and "þeos" (28), would have been visually offensive to a reader who was accustomed to what Derek Pearsall has described as the "extreme regularity of the spelling-system" in Gower's manuscripts.[39] Beneath this veneer of visual discomfort lies a more fundamental linguistic difference. Jeremy Smith has shown that the origins of Gower's language were in Suffolk, in the East Midlands, rather than Kent, as Macaulay believed. But the jarring note that Macaulay would hear in the register of "Passe forþe þou pilgryme" stemmed from the influence of Shirley's language which, though overlaid with London usage, was rooted in the dialect of the South West Midlands.[40]

Macaulay's last stated objection is a more diffuse one. Finally, and more generally, he states that "the style is not that of Gower, but evidently imitated from Chaucer's poem 'Fle from the pres'." There is of course a circularity in this type of stylistic analysis, namely that the poem is judged not to be Gower's because it does not resemble Gower's other work, whilst Gower's other work is defined more narrowly because this piece is not admitted to be his. This problem has also plagued studies of Chaucer, especially in relation to the minor poems and, to a lesser extent, Lydgate, and is endemic in attempts to define the authenticity of any writer's works where

---

[38] This may not be an exhaustive list. "Fawvel" (lines 22 and 25), also not in the *Confessio*, seems to derive from Langland's figure Favel (Flattery).

[39] Pearsall, "The Manuscripts," 95.

[40] Jeremy J. Smith, "John Gower and London English," in *A Companion to Gower*, ed. Echard, 61–72. On Shirley's language see Connolly, *John Shirley*, 196–203.

the circumstances of composition are not recorded. There are also some other considerations that ought to be taken into account. What if a short piece like "Passe forþe þou pilgryme" were apprentice work, undertaken by an aspiring poet, perhaps following a set theme, or imitating the work of another poet (either a recognized authority or a contemporary), or as a translation? Characteristics of mature style would not be present in a piece of such origins, and its uniqueness might be the product of an accidental survival, other similar apprentice work having perished. A very late piece of writing, prone to the vicissitudes of age and senility, might be similarly unreflective of a poet's perceived style.

Editors of texts are also inescapably affected by their own environment. As well as influences such as the availability of witnesses and convenient access to them, and prevalent trends in textual criticism, other considerations such as the many practicalities of seeing complex academic work through the press, and personal and financial pressures, are likely to have a bearing on any academic enterprise. With this in mind it is worth considering how and when Macaulay might have come by his knowledge of "Passe forþe þou pilgryme." Its inclusion in the introduction but not the text section of his edition of Gower's English works bespeaks a deliberate marginalization, but its placement there, at the very end of the introduction, might also indicate more accidental factors such as a late acquisition of information. It seems significant, for example, that information about John Stow's copy of the poem had come to light only very recently, when Macaulay's edition (the relevant volume was published in 1901) must have been at an advanced stage. In 1898 the German scholar Max Förster included the full text of "Passe forþe þou pilgryme" from BL Additional 29729 in a study of the life and work of Benedict Burgh, presenting the poem as hitherto unprinted ("die Verse bisher nirgendwo gedruckt sind").[41] His article appeared in the periodical *Archiv für das Studium der neueren Sprachen und Literaturen*, but in the very next issue of the journal Förster published a short notice thanking a colleague for the information that two other copies of the same poem had in fact already been published in an 1889 doctoral dissertation at the University of Bonn. Förster immediately struck the poem from the canon of Burgh's works on the grounds, it should be noted, of Shirley's greater authority: "Schon des zeitlichen Abstandes wegen verdient natürlich Shirley mehr Glauben in diesem Punkte als Stowe" ("Because of the distance in time Shirley of course deserves more faith in this point than Stow"). Of the three versions of the poem Förster now rejected the one he had published (Stow's) as the worst, judging the "purest" to be the Rawlinson copy which was, however, unfortunately imperfect, since it lacked the final verse.[42]

---

[41] Max Förster, "Über Benedict Burghs Leben und Werke," *Archiv für das Studium de neueren Sprache und Literaturen*, 101 (1898), 29–64 (50–51).

[42] Max Förster, "Kleine Mitteilungen," *Archiv für Studium de neueren Sprache und Literaturen*, 102 (1899), 213–14.

Macaulay certainly knew of Förster's work, and he knew of the Bonn dissertation as well, referencing both in his brief discussion of "Passe forþe þou pilgryme." Karl Meyer, the writer of the Bonn dissertation, had visited Oxford in 1888, and there had been time for Macaulay to have become aware of his research and to make use of his accounts of Gower's manuscripts. Meyer's dissertation laid out full transcriptions of the poem from both Bodley Ashmole 59 and Bodley Rawlinson C. 86, though Macaulay complained that these were printed "not quite correctly."[43] What Meyer did not do was to make a judgment about authorship, though he seems to raise the question by stating that he was presenting the texts of the poem "ohne an dieser stelle zu untersuchen, ob die ballade wirklich Gower zuzuschreiben ist oder nicht" [without at this point examining whether the ballade is really attributable to Gower or not]. And he further remarks that he had seen a note in the manuscripts' catalogue at Oxford stating that the poem seemed to have been borrowed from Chaucer's "Balade of Good Counsel."[44]

It is interesting to consider how far Macaulay may have been influenced by these German scholars. Meyer's dissertation would certainly have offered a useful starting point for someone who was embarking on an edition of Gower's works: its lists of manuscripts and summaries of their contents would at the very least have saved a great deal of time and effort in the preliminary business of tracking down all the witnesses to Gower's writings. Considering the speed with which Macaulay accomplished the task of editing Gower's works, apparently single-handedly, it seems more than likely that he would have used Meyer's dissertation as a source of information about manuscripts, and about the texts of this poem in particular. Specifically, it seems possible that Meyer's comment that he *was not* going to tackle the question of the poem's attribution, and his mention of the notice in the Oxford manuscripts' catalogue that suggested a Chaucerian influence, may have encouraged Macaulay towards the conclusion that the poem was not a genuine work of Gower's. Macaulay must also have seen that comment in the Oxford catalogue for himself, and its inference that this poem (if it were Gower's) showed that the poet was influenced by Chaucer would probably not have pleased him. In fact he repeats the comment in his edition in saying that the poem's style evidently imitated Chaucer's "Fle from the pres" (that is, Chaucer's "Balade of Good Counsel," better known by the title "Truth").[45] Then, sometime after Förster's 1898 article appeared (it seems impossible to quantify how long it might have taken for the article to reach him), Macaulay would have seen the poem attributed to an entirely different author, Benedict Burgh. How much did this undermine the poem's clear

---

[43] Karl Meyer, "John Gower's Beziehungen zu Chaucer und könig Richard II," Ph.D. dissertation, University of Bonn, 1889; Macaulay, *Complete Works*, II, clxxiii.

[44] Meyer, 71; the transcriptions are on 72–73.

[45] II, clxxiv.

attribution in an early witness, information that should have carried weight and inspired trust?

Macaulay's conclusion that Shirley's authority was "not very weighty" is at odds with Förster's judgment that Shirley's voice was a more credible one than Stow's, but Förster made that comment in the short addendum that he published in the next volume of *Archiv*, where he also retracted the ascription of the poem to Burgh. It is not entirely clear that Macaulay saw this corrective note: it goes uncited in his edition of Gower, although his citation of Förster's work is somewhat confused in that he gives the volume number of the second piece (102) when citing the first.[46] The tight chronology certainly makes it possible that Förster's second piece may not have reached Macaulay before his edition went to press. And the fact that Macaulay did not incorporate the readings of Stow's copy of "Passe forþe þou pilgryme" into his edition of the poem gives the sense that he may only have become aware of Förster's first article at the eleventh hour, in time to reference this material, but not to do much with it.

Macaulay offers descriptions of forty-six manuscripts of Gower's English works in his edition.[47] He describes his archival research in this way: "The following account of the MSS. is given on my own authority in every detail. I have been able to see them all [...] Except in the case of one or two, to which my access was limited, I have examined every one carefully."[48] He does not describe Bodley Ashmole 59, Bodley Rawlinson C. 86, or BL Additional 29729, probably because these manuscripts held no interest for him since they did not contain the *Confessio*, and publishing a correct text of that poem was his stated objective. "Passe forþe þou pilgryme" is an orphan in these manuscripts, unlike "In Praise of Peace" which in its manuscript context survives in conjunction with the *Cinkante Ballades* and the *Traitié*. "In Praise of Peace" had also been printed and ascribed to Gower by Thynne in 1532 in his collection of Chaucer's works, and subsequent editions by Wright and Skeat had endorsed that ascription; its authorship was already therefore well-established and there was little need for Macaulay to make a fresh assessment. Conversely, in the case of the orphaned "Passe forþe þou pilgryme," there was little on which he could rely. The poem was hitherto unprinted, the three manuscripts in which it survived contained no other texts by Gower, and only one of those manuscripts attributed the poem to him. That attribution is very clear and is voiced by a scribe whose lifetime

---

[46] II, clxxiii.
[47] He mentions five manuscripts which contain extracts and some fragments in addition to describing forty-two manuscripts of the complete text, for which see the essay by A. S. G. Edwards elsewhere in this volume (n. 29). I am grateful to have had the opportunity to read this essay before publication.
[48] II, cxxxviii. Derek Pearsall comments: "For the manuscripts that were known to him, *and that he had inspected*, Macaulay provides descriptions that are remarkably full and accurate for their day," "The Manuscripts," 73 (my emphases).

overlapped with Gower's, and who was regarded as a great authority by other late Victorian editors. But John Shirley's status as an important copyist may not have cut much ice with Macaulay precisely because he was so thoroughly associated with the works of Chaucer and Lydgate, and not with Gower. Amongst the extant manuscripts written by Shirley's own hand are only two ascriptions of texts to Gower, and one of these is clearly wrong: this is the stanza, "A whetstone is no karving instrument," actually from *Troilus and Criseyde*, but given the heading "Gower" by Shirley when he copied it into a gathering that now prefaces San Marino, Huntington Library, MS Ellesmere 26.A.13.[49] It is just possible that Macaulay might have seen this misattribution when that manuscript was still in the possession of the Earl of Ellesmere, and if he had it would not have improved his opinion of Shirley's reliability.[50] Even so, by far the greater majority of Shirley's ascriptions continue to find acceptance.[51]

Editors sometimes have the opportunity to return to their published works with the benefit of further knowledge, and can make adjustments or even edit texts anew: such opportunities did not present themselves to Macaulay, but the question of the authenticity of "Passe forþe þou pilgryme" deserves renewed and urgent attention. No editor can be correct in every decision, and all who edit texts are necessarily influenced by historical circumstance. Macaulay's reasons for excluding this poem from the canon of Gower's works are not, when scrutinized, wholly compelling. As a consequence of his judgment this short poem has languished for more than a century in a backwater of the *Complete Works*. Excellent as that edition is in other respects, in the case of this poem its impact has been catastrophic.

---

[49] *Troilus and Criseyde*, Book I, lines 631–37, copied on fols. ii^v–iii^r; for further discussion see Connolly, *John Shirley*, 104–06.

[50] Macaulay thanked the Earl of Ellesmere for allowing him to make use of the Stafford manuscript of the *Confessio* (now San Marino, Huntington Library, MS Ellesmere 26.A.17) but does not mention how or where he consulted it; in several instances owners deposited their manuscripts for his use at the Bodleian, but he also seems to have visited private libraries to consult manuscripts *in situ*.

[51] See Connolly, "What John Shirley Said About Adam," 88.

Part II

IN PRINT

CHAPTER 9

GOWER BETWEEN MANUSCRIPT AND PRINT

Siân Echard

> In tyme paste whanne this warke was prynted, I can not very well
> coniecte, what was the cause therof, the prologue before was cleane
> altered. And by that mene it wold seme, that Gower dydde compyle it
> at the requeste of the noble duke Henry of Lancastre. And all though
> the bokes that be wrytten, be contrary, yet I haue folowed therin the
> prynt copie, for as moche as it may serue both weyes, and bycause
> most copies of the same warke are in printe: but yet I thought it good
> to warne the reder, that the writen copies do not agre with the prynted.
> Therfore syr I haue prynted here those same lynes, that I fynde in the
> wrytten copies. The whiche alteration ye shall perceyue beganne at the
> .xxiii. lyne in the prologue, and goth forth on, as ye se here folowynge.[1]

IN THE PREFACE TO his 1532 printing of the *Confessio Amantis*, Thomas Berthelette alerts his audience to the textual discrepancies he has found between the written books – the manuscript copies – and the printed ones, by which he means William Caxton's edition of 1483. He is referring specifically to the differences in the Prologue that distinguish the Ricardian version from the Henrician text presented by Caxton, and he prints lines 24* to 92* in his Preface, to illustrate that difference. Accustomed as we are to Macaulay's below-the-line, asterisked representation of the Ricardian commission story, Berthelette's choice may seem at first to align with Macaulay's editorial preference for the Henrician version. Examining Berthelette's language, however, gives us rather a different story. Macaulay's choice was based on an assessment of the manuscript record and on the critical assumptions of his day about how to represent an author's final intentions, when dealing with a revised work. Berthelette's decision, on the other hand, is based on attitudes towards the material witnesses and their status.

---

[1] *Jo. Gower de confessione Amantis, Imprinted at London in Fletestrete by Thomas Berthelette Printer to the kingis grace* (London, 1532), aa iii r. The preface is also found in the 1554 printing, with some alterations in spelling.

Berthelette presents his decision as a pragmatic one, saying that he has chosen to follow print for his own edition, rather than the manuscript record, as there are more printed books than there are manuscripts. By Berthelette's day it doubtless was easier for Gower's would-be readers to access print rather than manuscript copies.[2] But in the end Berthelette draws on print, not just because there is more of it, but also because of his views of its status and utility, views which we can tease out from the language he uses in his Preface. In the Ricardian manuscripts, the Prologue is, in his telling, "cleane altered." The adjective, which is not necessary to convey the sense, carries an air of disapproving astonishment. The written copies are "contrarye," a phrasing which certainly means that they disagree with the print, but which also frames the written record as recalcitrant or wayward. After printing the Ricardian lines, Berthelette reiterates that "there be as many other printed, that be cleane contrarye vnto these bothe in sentence and in meanyng," and goes on to characterize other variations that he has noted as a "blemysshe vnto a noble auctour," resulting from "chaungynge" and "misordrynge" of the text.[3] Berthelette's phrasing could implicate Caxton's print in his charge of blemishing a noble author; that is, it is not entirely clear whether at this juncture he is criticizing the print copies, or the written ones, or both. What is clear is that in this framing, the variation that manuscript culture has transmitted to print becomes an active and even harmful agent whose meddling risks obscuring the value of an ancient text. And that variation, whether in earlier print or in manuscript, must now be tamed by Berthelette's editorial and technological interventions, so that Gower may appear "in his owne shappe and lykenes."[4] Furthermore, Berthelette tells us that he has chosen to follow the print rather than the manuscript record as it may "serue both weyes." It is not clear what he means by this phrase. His own print serves "both weyes," if by that we mean that it serves to represent the variety of the tradition, because he prints some of the alternate version of the Prologue. The grammar suggests, however, that "it" must be Caxton's print, and so perhaps the "weyes" that it serves are those of different kinds of readers, readers of both manuscript and print. Print, in

---

[2] The *Short Title Catalogue* records twenty copies of Caxton's printing of the *Confessio Amantis*; about thirty of the 1532 printing by Berthelette; and forty-six of the 1554 printing. We can assume there were many more copies printed: Eric White's database of print runs of fifteenth-century incunables (https://www.cerl.org/resources/links_to_other_resources/bibliographical_data#researching_print_runs) shows runs from a low of forty-five to a high of five thousand, with a common range being two hundred and fifty to four hundred; while there is little available English data of this sort, even a cautious extrapolation would suggest quite a few copies. There are almost fifty surviving manuscript copies, and most, by the time of the early prints, would have been in private hands. It is reasonable to suppose, then, that print was more readily available than the manuscript copies.

[3] Berthelette 1532, aa iii v.

[4] Berthelette 1532, aa iii v.

any case, is imagined as more serviceable in some way, performing the same function as manuscript, but perhaps more reliably or capaciously.

Print also has the capacity to fix, in both senses of the word; that is, as Berthelette imagines it, print becomes that which corrects, restores, and preserves. It is perhaps not accidental that Berthelette moves on from an account of the labors that have produced his textual monument, to a description of Gower's tomb in Southwark. The design of Berthelette's handsome edition has itself been called monumental,[5] and there is no question that it is a beautiful book. Nevertheless, fixing a varied and variable text in place, as Berthelette has done, can have unintended consequences.

In printing some of the manuscript variations in his Preface, Berthelette makes part of the manuscript record available to his readers, but it is inevitably much more varied than he could represent (or even know). There are some eighty surviving manuscripts and manuscript extracts of Gower's work.[6] Almost fifty are manuscripts of the *Confessio Amantis*. These are often deluxe copies, made for, and owned by, people in the higher ranks of society. Many of the extracts appear in domestic miscellanies and commonplace books, including the book of Richard Hill and the Findern manuscript, speaking to the spread of Gower's work into the gentry and urban merchant classes through the fifteenth and sixteenth centuries. It is not surprising, then, that Caxton printed the *Confessio Amantis,* nor that Berthelette followed his 1532 printing with another, in 1554. This early print record suggests a solid reputation, even popularity, in the fifteenth and sixteenth centuries, and while the 1554 Berthelette was the last printing of the *Confessio* until 1810, many medieval writers met similar, or worse, fates.[7]

Nevertheless, in this essay I want to focus on loss and insufficiency. While Gower's presence in early print may not be bad, it is partial, because Gower clearly understood himself, and his own *auctoritee*, in terms of the totality of his work, and yet, these early printings represent only the *Confessio*. Furthermore, there are elements of Gower's poetics that did not easily transition to early print. Whether by conscious design or unconscious habit (I think a bit of both), Gower is a poet whose work relies on, and intersects in telling ways with, the practices of manuscript culture. In this essay I plan to explore how the unique features of Gower's *oeuvre* were often muted, redirected, or lost entirely, when the medieval poet's work encountered the strictures and expectations of early print.

---

[5] Joseph Dane, *Who is Buried in Chaucer's Tomb? Studies in the Reception of Chaucer's Book* (East Lansing: Michigan State University Press, 1998), 67–69.

[6] For a complete account, see Derek Pearsall, "The Manuscripts and Illustrations of Gower's Works," in *A Companion to Gower*, ed. Siân Echard (Cambridge: D. S. Brewer, 2004), 73–97.

[7] For an overview of Gower's print history, see my "Gower in Print," in *A Companion to Gower*, 115–35.

Language

I want first to deal with language. When Caxton and Berthelette printed the *Confessio Amantis*, they included the English poem's Latin frame. But Gower was, of course, a trilingual poet. His tomb in Southwark shows his head resting on three books, one in each language. He also wrote the "Quia unusquisque," a lengthy colophon describing these books and underlining their differing languages (*gallico sermone, sermone latina, anglico sermone*).[8] But even these monuments, physical and textual, do not give the full sense of Gower's linguistic range, nor how that range interacts with manuscript practice. In addition to the longer works that made it onto the tomb, he also wrote shorter pieces in each of his three languages. The manuscripts of his work often combine pieces from the different linguistic parts of his poetic repertoire. While it is quite true, as Derek Pearsall has persuasively argued, that the manuscripts of the *Confessio* display a high degree of sameness in their design, I think of that as a kind of macro-sameness.[9] On the micro level, one finds significant variation, and scribal interactions with Gower's languages are one of the places that variety manifests itself, both in *Confessio* manuscripts, and in manuscripts of the other works.

The most famous example of the intersection of Gower's trilinguality with manuscript practice is London, British Library, MS Additional 59495, the Trentham manuscript, which seems to have been a deliberate attempt to display and impress, commissioned or even written by Gower, and perhaps intended for Henry IV.[10] The manuscript showcases Gower's poetic skill in all three of his languages, and is clearly carefully constructed as well so as to sequence the texts in those languages in a meaningful way, though scholars

---

[8] The fact that Gower revised the colophon several times also suggests its importance to him. For a discussion of the significance of Gower's various gestures of closure, see my "Last Words: Latin at the End of the *Confessio Amantis*," in *Interstices: Studies in Middle English and Anglo-Latin in Honour of A. G. Rigg*, ed. Richard Firth Greene and Linne R. Mooney (Toronto: University of Toronto Press, 2004), 99–121.

[9] In "Manuscripts and Illustrations," in *A Companion to Gower*, Pearsall writes, "There is a type of manuscript of the *Confessio* which is so frequently found among the surviving copies that it can almost be characterized as 'standard'," 80.

[10] As early as the eighteenth century, it had been suggested that the manuscript was intended as a presentation copy for Henry, though G. C. Macaulay was not entirely convinced (*The Complete Works of John Gower*, I.lxxxi). John Fisher reviewed what was then the state of the argument in *John Gower: Moral Philosopher and Friend of Chaucer* (New York: New York University Press, 1964), 71–72. R. F. Yeager revisited the discussion in "John Gower's Audience: The Ballades," *Chaucer Review* 40 (2005): 81–105.

have not always agreed as to what that meaning might be.[11] Most recently, against the backdrop of Anglo-French tensions (and détentes) at the end of the fourteenth century, Sebastian Sobecki considers the intersection of the manuscript's structure with its texts, and in particular the balance between the English "In Praise of Peace" and the French poems included in the manuscript, to suggest we might "read the entire manuscript as an attempt to balance not only English and French, but also England and France."[12] The material and textual survival are in this reading significantly intertwined so as to create a potent political, as well as poetic, object.

As compelling and convincing as recent readings of Trentham might be, however, it is important to point out here that a manuscript need not be as purposefully designed at both the material and textual level as Trentham seems to be, in order to have effects similar to those critics have discerned in Trentham's sequence of texts. Routine production practice, along with the variation that is a marker of manuscript culture, means that many manuscripts could include a wide variety of Gowerian material, and that this material might be arranged in sequences that serve to make meaning, even if they were not intended to do so. Consider, for example, the following table, which compares the contents of three Gower manuscripts chosen more or less at random:[13]

---

[11] The manuscript's structure and purpose are discussed in Candace Barrington, "The Trentham Manuscript as Broken Prosthesis: Wholeness and Disability in Lancastrian England," *Accessus* 1 (2013): 1–33; Arthur W. Bahr, "Reading Codicological Form in John Gower's Trentham Manuscript," *Studies in the Age of Chaucer* 33 (2011): 219–62; and Siân Echard, *Printing the Middle Ages* (Philadelphia: University of Pennsylvania Press, 2008). For a recent argument that the manuscript in fact contains Gower's hand, see Sebastian Sobecki, "*Ecce patet tensus*: The Trentham Manuscript, *In Praise of Peace*, and John Gower's Autograph Hand," *Speculum* 90 (2015): 925–59. Sobecki also establishes a provenance for the manuscript that supports his view that it was "never presented to Henry IV," 931; that conclusion does not affect the broad consensus that the manuscript was intended to highlight Gower's trilingual poetics.
[12] Sobecki, "*Ecce patet tensus*," 947.
[13] Oxford, Bodleian Library, MS Bodley 294, is a second-recension copy of the *Confessio*, dating to the first quarter of the fifteenth century, one of Scribe D (John Marchaunt's) copies; Glasgow, Glasgow University Library, MS Hunter 59, is a manuscript of Gower's Latin and French works, dating to around 1400; and London, British Library, MS Harley 3869, is a third-recension copy of the *Confessio*, dating to the second quarter of the fifteenth century.

Confessio Amantis	*Vox clamantis*	Verses on Queen Margaret
Explicit	*Cronica tripertita*	*Confessio Amantis*
Quam cinxere freta	*H. aquile pullus*	*Explicit*
Traitié	*O recolende bone*	*Quam cinxere freta*
Quis sit vel qualis	*Quia unusquisque*	*Traitié*
Est amor in glosa	*Eneidos Bucolis*	*Quis sit vel qualis*
Lex docet auctorum	*Carmen*	*Est amor in glosa*
Quia unusquisque	*De lucis scrutinio*	*Lex docet auctorum*
Carmen	*Quis sit vel qualis*	*Carmen*
Bodley 294	*Est amor in glosa*	*Quia unusquisque*
	Rex celi deus	*Eneidos Bucolis*
	O Deus immense	*O flos pulcherrime*
	Nota hic in fine	*Ave virgo virginum*
	Vnanimes esse	*Deus omnipotens creator*
	Presul ouile Regis	Harley 3869
	Dicunt scripture	
	Traitié	
	Hunter 59	

Two of these are manuscripts built around the *Confessio Amantis*. The third, Hunter 59, is a manuscript of French and Latin works. Some thirty copies of the *Confessio* include the farewell sequence of the *Explicit* and "Quam cinxere," but only a handful of these also contain the "Carmen" and a selection of the short Latin poems.[14] In general, the majority-Latin manuscripts, such as Oxford, MS All Souls College 98, or London, British Library, Cotton MS Tiberius A.iv, include the highest number of the shorter Latin pieces, while the *Confessio* manuscripts may have only one or two pieces, beyond the closing sequence of Latin matter. The sequence of texts in the sample manuscripts in the table may be original to these manuscripts, or it might have been suggested by what was in their exemplars. In either case the sequences, some shared and some unique, have the potential to affect the reading experience. For example, we commonly describe "Quia unusquisque" as a colophon, a term suggested not only by its summary of the author's works – content, that is, that suggests some kind of final, or finalizing, stance – but also by its frequent appearance at the end of Gower manuscripts. This is the piece's most common manuscript location.[15] Furthermore, in other manuscripts, while the "Quia unusquisque" might not be the very last item,

---

[14] See my "Last Words" for a table of the Latin end matter in *Confessio* manuscripts.
[15] It appears in this position in, for example, Oxford, Bodleian Library, MS Arch Selden B.11; Cambridge, Pembroke College, MS 307; Cambridge, St Catharine's College, MS 7 (though misbound); Cambridge, St John's College, MS B 12; Chicago, Newberry Library, MS f 33 5; London, British Library, MS Egerton 1991; London, British Library, MS Royal 18 C xxii; London, Society of Antiquaries, MS 134; New York, Morgan Library, MS M 125; Oxford, Bodleian Library, MS Bodley 693; Oxford, Bodleian Library, MS Bodley 902; Oxford, Bodleian Library, MS Laud Misc 609; Oxford, Christ Church, MS 148; and Oxford, Corpus Christi College, MS 67.

it appears as part of what we might think of as an emphatically conclusive package, closing not merely the manuscript, but also Gower's life work. In these cases, the colophon is followed by the praise of the author in the (perhaps self-authored) "Eneidos, Bucolis,"[16] as well as, sometimes, by prayers and markers of the poet's mortality, as for example in All Souls College 98, where the final sequence is "Quia unusquisque," "Eneidos, Bucolis," "O deus immense," and the elegiac "Quicquid homo scribat."

In Bodley 294, however, the colophon is not the final word, with, instead, the "Carmen super multiplici vitiorum" closing the manuscript.[17] More dramatically, in Hunter 59, the "Quia unusquisque" is nowhere near the end, appearing instead as a kind of transition point between the longer Latin poems and the shorter ones. Furthermore, in Hunter 59, this description of books in three languages occurs in a manuscript that features only two of them; the manuscript consists entirely of Latin works, before closing with the French *Traitié*.[18] The text remains purposeful as a display of Gower's learning, perhaps particularly important in a manuscript whose contents emphasize the political, but its location in some sense also repurposes it. The political may drive the sequence in Hunter 59, or it may arise from it; certainly the arrangement of poems about kingship after two long Latin accounts of the demands, and failures, of political systems is pointed, whether or not it was intended to be.

In Harley 3869, there is another potentially meaningful end sequence, as the colophon is followed by the praise of Gower, in "Eneidos, Bucolis," as a writer who surpassed Virgil, in part because he wrote in three languages (all of which are represented in this manuscript). The opening and final poems in this codex, however, are not Gower's. They are written in a separate hand, and the verses on Margaret's entry into London are written on a separate quire. They are not, in other words, integral to the manuscript's design, but at some point in its history, they became part of the codex, and while a Gower-inclined reader might well simply skip over them, the manuscript is no longer the same object it was when it was first created, and the very lack of obvious fit between the parts could provoke readerly confusion, however briefly. Both the decisions and the chance occurrences of manuscript production mean that each copy – any copy – of work by Gower has the potential to frame his trilinguality in different ways. Macaulay's division of his edition into French, English, and Latin volumes performs a neat linguistic sorting we do not find in the manuscripts. Instead, that separation began when England's first printer made the first edition of Gower's work.

---

[16] As in Oxford, Bodleian Library, MS Fairfax 3, for example.
[17] The "Carmen super" also follows the "Quia unusquisque" in Cambridge, Trinity College, MS R.3.2.
[18] The *Traitié* also appears in final position in Oxford, Wadham College, MS 13, a manuscript of the *Confessio*.

As he often did for the texts he printed, Caxton provided front matter to his edition of Gower's *Confessio*. In the case of the *Confessio*, there was a short paragraph introducing the text, and then quite a long table of contents. I will return to the table below, but first, I want to focus on the opening of the brief preface. Caxton says that the book is called *Confessio Amantis*, and then gives the English translation of the title ("This book is intituled confessio amantis/ that is to saye in englysshe the confession of the louer").[19] This is an innocuous gesture on the face of it, but it rapidly becomes meaningful when placed against Gower's own description of what it is that he is doing in his poem. Gower opens in Latin, not English, with a complex hexameter verse that declares his intention to write in English with the help of Carmenta (that is, Latin).[20] Latin ushers a reader into Gower's English poem, and Latin remains central to the project, through both the Latin verses and the Latin glosses.

Caxton does include the Latin apparatus of the *Confessio*. His edition prints the verses and glosses, with all this Latin appearing in the text column. Figure 9.1 shows a typical layout, with Latin verse set as prose; followed by a Latin gloss; followed by the start of the English text, which in its turn gives way again to another Latin gloss. In some copies, red display capitals have been added by hand over the printed guide letters, so that the division between the parts of the text is clear enough. The division between languages, however, is not: Latin and English receive superficially identical treatment, appearing in the same color, the same type, the same location, and with the same initials. By comparison, a brief survey of different approaches to the bilingual aspect of the *Confessio* in a range of typical manuscripts gives a sense of the essential flatness and unhelpfulness of print. Quite a few of the early manuscripts, like Fairfax 3 (Figure 9.2), Macaulay's base text, render English and Latin in the same color, but although all these elements are in black, they are clearly distinguished in this manuscript, both by display capitals and by layout, as the Latin glosses appear in the margins, while the verse appears in the text column.

---

[19] *This book is intituled confession amantis, that is to saye in englysshe the confession of the louer* [Emprynted at westmestre: By me willyam Caxton, 1483], ii r.

[20] The role of Latin in the *Confessio* has been discussed by many critics; for a particular focus on the deployment of the Latin apparatus in manuscript and/or print, see Joyce Coleman, "Lay Readers and Hard Latin: How Gower May Have Intended the *Confessio Amantis* to Be Read," *Studies in the Age of Chaucer* 24 (2002): 209–35; Siân Echard, "With Carmen's Help: Latin Authorities in the *Confessio Amantis*," *Studies in Philology* 95 (1998): 1–40; Tim William Machan, "Thomas Berthelette and Gower's *Confessio*," *Studies in the Age of Chaucer* 18 (1996): 143–66; Winthrop Wetherbee, "Latin Structure and Vernacular Space: Gower, Chaucer, and the Boethian Tradition," in *Chaucer and Gower: Difference, Mutuality, Exchange*, ed. R. F. Yeager (Victoria, BC: University of Victoria Press, 1991), 7–35; R. F. Yeager, "English, Latin, and the Text as 'Other': The Page as Sign in the Work of John Gower," *Text* 3 (1987): 251–67.

Gower between Manuscript and Print

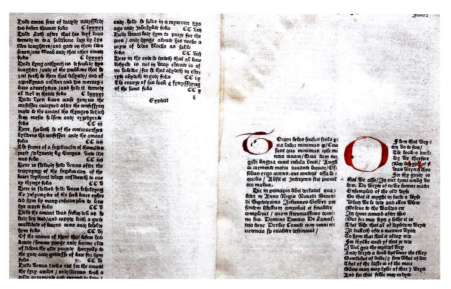

FIGURE 9.1. The end of the table of contents, and the opening of the *Confessio Amantis*, in William Caxton's 1483 printing. By permission of the Chapter of Worcester Cathedral.

The Fairfax layout is not the most common, however. The majority of *Confessio* manuscripts write the Latin, both verse and prose, in red, and move the glosses from the margins into the text column.[21] The color, along with the enlarged capitals or the markers that section divisions tend to attract, makes the Latin framing easily visible, and easily distinguishable from the English text. One manuscript, London, British Library, MS Stowe 950, displays an additional strategy, copying the Latin verse in black, underlined in red, while the prose is copied in red (Figure 9.3). The use of red for the prose in this and other copies – a relatively common feature

---

[21] Most *Confessio* manuscripts place the glosses in the text columns. The exceptions are London, British Library, MS Additional 12043; London, British Library, MS Egerton 913; Manchester, Chetham's Library, MS A 7 38 (in this copy, most of the Latin glosses are replaced by abbreviated English versions); Oxford, Bodleian Library, MS Bodley 902; Cambridge, Trinity College, MS R 3 2; Princeton, Firestone Library, MS Taylor 5; San Marino, Huntington Library, MS EL 26 A 17; Geneva, Fondation Bodmer, MS Bodmer 178; London, British Library, MS Harley 3869; Oxford, Bodleian Library, MS Fairfax 3; Oxford, New College, MS 266; and Oxford, Wadham College, MS 13 (some glosses are omitted or cut short in this copy). There are also some copies with a mixed layout: Cambridge, St John's College, MS B 12; Cambridge, Cambridge University Library, MS Mm 2 21 (mixed); Cambridge, Sidney Sussex College, MS 63 (mixed); and Nottingham, Nottingham University Library, MS WLC LM 8 (mixed).

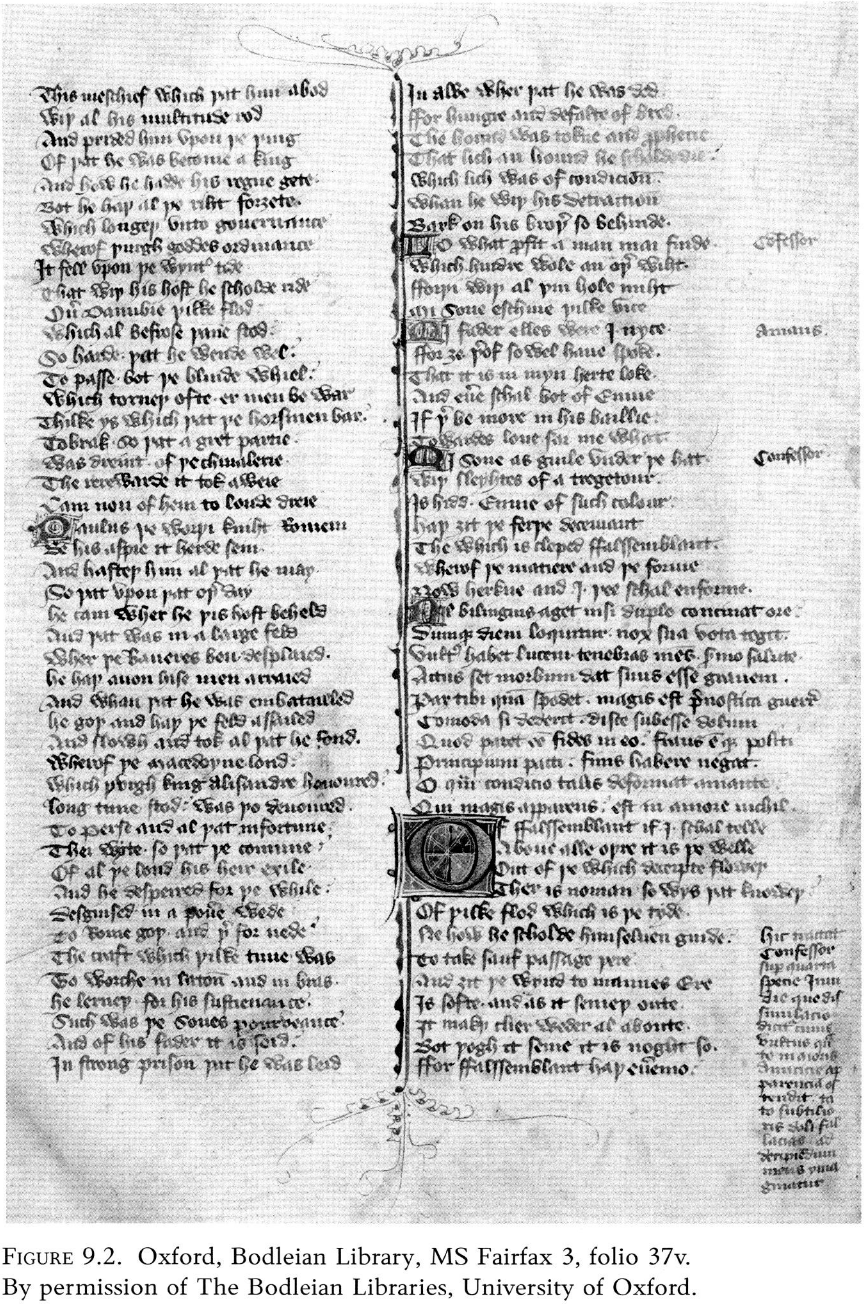

FIGURE 9.2. Oxford, Bodleian Library, MS Fairfax 3, folio 37v.
By permission of The Bodleian Libraries, University of Oxford.

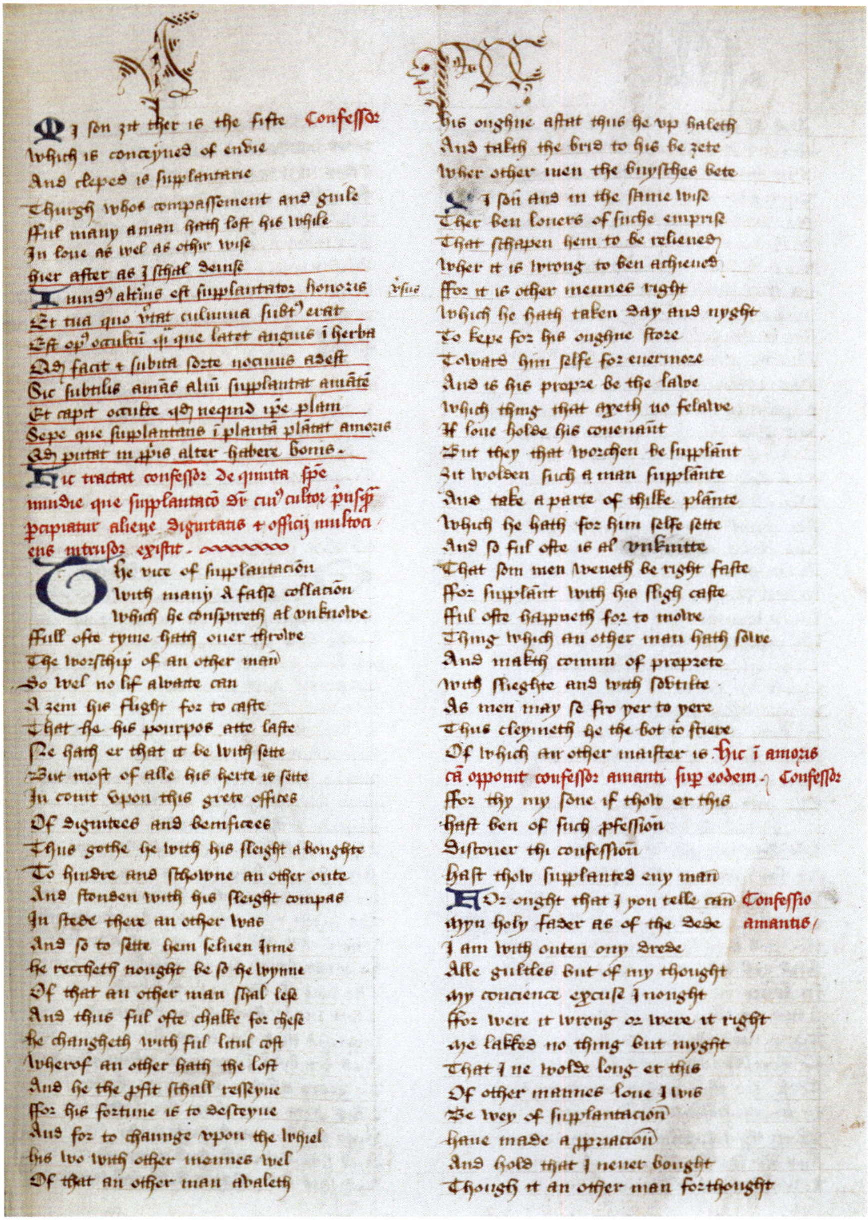

FIGURE 9.3. London, British Library, MS Stowe 950, folio 35r.
© The British Library Board.

of *Confessio* manuscripts, once the glosses have moved from the margins into the text columns – is in part a pragmatic choice, allowing a reader to distinguish between the parts of the text. It also, however, carries potential meaning, as a bibliographic code that signals rubrics and chapter divisions in medieval manuscript production more broadly. The language of those paratextual elements may well be Latin, and it is possible to read red as a marker of the prestige language. At the same time, however, rubrics can be mundane and, in the information they convey, stripped of much significance beyond "and here is the next chapter." In the *Confessio* manuscripts, then, the Latin apparatus might, depending on design choices and how a reader is accustomed to navigating such choices, be read primarily as commentary or some other kind of engagement with the text, or simply be reduced to handy section-divisions.

Furthermore, while some manuscript approaches serve to distinguish not only Latin from English, but also different kinds of Latin from each other, such careful distinctions are not universal. In a recently-discovered manuscript of extracts, still in private hands, the Latin verses and glosses are run together.[22] In London, British Library, MS Harley 3490, both the Latin prose and the Latin verse are treated in the same way, as black text underlined in red, in the text column. And the movement of the glosses into the prose columns brings its own problems, even when the Latin prose is visually distinguished from the Latin and English verse, as the Latin prose sometimes intrudes into the middle of an English sentence. A typical instance is found in the story of Constance, in this instance as it appears in Washington, DC, Folger Shakespeare Library, MS v b 29, where one reads, sequentially, "Dame hermengild, which was the wif/ Of Elda lich hir ougne lif/ Qualiter constancia cum vxore sua hermengilda.../ Constance loueth." This kind of disruption occurs in quite a few *Confessio* manuscripts.[23]

While many of the manuscripts I have just discussed are superficially attractive, the visually pleasing features of red ink or underlining, or balanced columns of red and black text, do not necessarily signal an *ordinatio* that aligns with Gower's poetic practices.[24] Manuscripts may exhibit bad, as well

---

[22] Jane Griffiths, "Gower's *Confessio Amantis*: A 'New' Manuscript," *Medium Aevum* 82 (2013): 244–59, at 248. I have not seen this manuscript myself, and so am relying on the description in this article.

[23] I have found instances of awkward, intrusive gloss placement in at least eighteen copies, and there may well be more, as I have performed test soundings, rather than reading every single copy for any possible instance of disruption.

[24] For example, Gower's desire to make Latinity an integral part of his English poem does not necessarily always survive in manuscript. There are three *Confessio* manuscripts that omit the Latin framing: Manchester, Chetham's Library, MS A 7 38; Oxford, Bodleian Library, MS Ashmole 35; and Princeton, Firestone Library, MS Garrett 136. There are also some *Confessio* manuscripts that omit some of the Latin apparatus. Nevertheless, most manuscripts retain the routine bi- and trilingualism of which Gower was so evidently proud in his own *oeuvre*.

as good, design, and that is the point. If the general, macro-appearance of *Confessio* manuscripts is remarkably uniform (and pleasing), once out in the wild, there can be a productive chaos at the micro level. In this case, there is something potentially wonderful about the Latin gloss elbowing its way into the Hermengild/Constance relationship. This example also shows an aspect of Gower's multilinguality that I have not yet discussed. The Latin is typically abbreviated in the manuscripts, sometimes highly so. When the glosses move into the text column, as in the Folger manuscript, then two different language practices, suggesting two different readerly as well as writerly *habitus*, struggle for possession of the narrative and the text column. The variety – and that includes the happy variety of error and ineptitude – in manuscript production means that Gower's multilingual enterprise is signaled on the medieval manuscript page in a whole range of ways. Gower's original audience, immersed in manuscript culture, was primed to navigate these meaningful *ordinationes,* and perhaps also to notice when an orderly layout framed clashes that arose from less skillful, or more rote/routine production.

There is a practical reason for Caxton's decision to print all aspects of the poem in the verse column, and in black. Early print was limited in its resources, and layout was difficult and time-consuming. Printing in more than one color was rare, and early printers typically left finishing to scribes. So much is true for all early print, and for the fate of all medieval poets in those prints. But I have been suggesting that Gower was particularly ill-served by these strictures, because the difficulty of visually distinguishing the Latin apparatus from the English poem mutes the effect of his multilingualism. A particularly interesting case is Oxford, Bodleian Library, MS Hatton 51. This manuscript was copied directly from Caxton's printed edition. Figure 9.4 shows how the copyist has made routine use of the features of manuscript culture to enhance the print design, rendering the Latin in red, and bracketing many of the couplets. Caxton's printed edition gave this reader a text, but he also clearly felt, and corrected for, a lack.

Like many manuscript copies of Gower's works, Caxton's edition of the *Confessio* concludes with a range of Latin matter, including the colophon "Quia unusquisque"; the praise of Gower in the "Eneidos, Bucolis;" the short Latin poem "Est amor in glosa;" and the prose appeal for prayers, "Orate pro anima." Thus, while the volume's design, constrained by the limits of early print, has no visual cues to suggest linguistic distinction between the parts and texts it contains, the book remains a bilingual package, and one that conveys not only Gower's long English poem, but also some of his other, Latin pieces, in prose and verse, serving a range of functions (closure, praise, prayer). The visual-linguistic flattening in Caxton's design might have contributed, however, to what happened in the next early printing of the *Confessio*, Thomas Berthelette's, of 1532.

The fifty years or so that passed between Caxton's and Berthelette's printings of the *Confessio* brought considerable sophistication to print. Caxton printed in a single font throughout. Berthelette, on the other hand,

Siân Echard

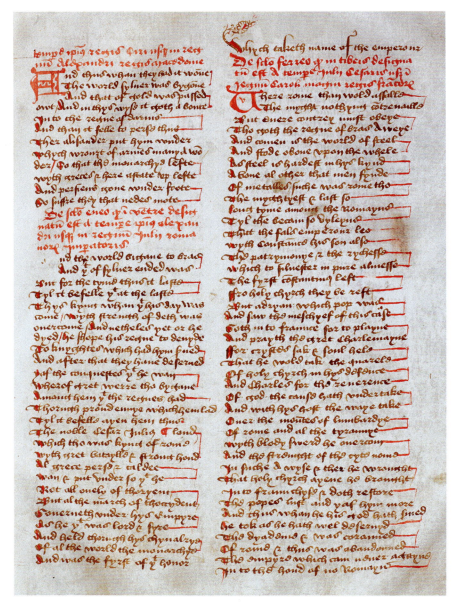

Figure 9.4. Oxford, Bodleian Library, MS Hatton 51, folio 7r.
By permission of The Bodleian Libraries, University of Oxford.

PRIMVS.

For as me thinketh by thy speche,
Thy wittes be right far to seche,
As of thyn eare, and of thine eie
I woll no more specifie:
But I woll asken ouer this
Of other thynge howe that it is.

Celsior est aquila, leone forcior ille,
   Quem tumor elati cordis ad alta mouet.
Sunt species quinq; quib' est superbia ductrix
   Clamat & in multis mundus adheret eis.
Laruando faciem ficto pallore subornat
   Fraudibus hypocrisis mellea verba suis.
Sicq; pios animos q̃ sæpe ruit muliebres
   Ex humili verbo sublatitante dolo.

¶Hic loquitur, quod septem sunt peccata mortalia, quorum caput superbia varias species habet, & earū prima hypocrisis dicitur, cuius proprietatē secundum Vitium Confessor amanti declarat.

¶My sonne, as I shall the informe,
There ben yet of an other forme
Of dedly vices seuen applied,
wherof the herte is often plied
To thyng, whiche after shall hym greeue:
The first of them thou shalt beleeue
Is pryde, whiche is principall,
And hath with hym in speciall,
Mynistres fyue full dyuerse:
Of whiche as I shall the reherce,
The firste is saide hypocrisie,
If thou arte of his companie
Tell forth my sonne, and shriue the cleane
    Amans
¶I wote not fader what ye meane.
But this I wolde you beseche,
That ye me by some wey teche,
what is to ben an hypocrite,
And than if I be for to wite
I woll beknowen, as it is
    Confessor
¶My sonne, an hypocrite is this:
A man, whiche feigneth conscience,
As though it were all innocence
without, and is not so within:
And doth so for he wolde winne
Of his despyte the vaine astate:
And whan he cometh anone there at,
He sheweth than, what he was,
The corne is torned in to grasse.

That was a Rose, is than a thorne,
And he that was a lambe beforne
Is than a wolfe: and thus malice
Under the colour of iustice
Is hid, and as the people telleth,
These ordres witen where he dwelleth,
As he that of her counsell is,
And thilke worde, whiche thei er this
Forsoken, he draweth in apene.
He clotheth riches (as men seyne)
Under the simplest of pouerte,
And doth to seme of great deserte
Thynge, whiche is littell worthe within.
He seith in open, phy, to sinne,
And in secrete there is no vice,
Of whiche that he nys a nouice:
And euer his chere is sobre and softe,
And where he goth he blesseth ofte,
wherof the blynde worlde he dretcheth.
But yet all onely he ne stretcheth
His rewle vpon religion,
But nert to that condicion,
In suche as clepe them holy churche.
It sheweth eke how he can worche
Amonge the wide furred hoodes
To gete them the worldes goodes,
And them selfe ben thilke same,
That setten moste the worlde in blame.
But yet in contrarie of their lore
There is nothyng thei louen more,
So that feignyng of light thet werke
The dedes, whiche are inwarde derke,
And thus this double hypocrisie,
With his deuoute apparancie
A vyser set vpon his face
wherof towarde the worldes grace
He semeth to be right well shewed:
And yet his herte is all beshrewed.
But netheles he stant beleued,
And hath his purpos ofte acheued
Of worship, and of worldes welthe,
And taketh it, as who saith by stelthe
Through couerture of his fallas:
And right so in semblable cas
This vice hath eke his officers
Amonge these other seculers
Of great men, for of the smale
As for to accompte he set no tale.

              But

FIGURE 9.5. Thomas Berthelette's printing of the *Confessio Amantis*, in the second (1554) edition. By permission of Rare Books and Special Collections, the University of British Columbia.

uses Roman type for the Latin verses, and two different sizes of black letter, a larger one for the English text, and a smaller one for the Latin glosses (Figure 5). He has the ability to print display capitals and section markers, rather than leaving them to be filled in by hand. This is a design that does allow one to see all the different linguistic parts on the page. But at the end of Berthelette's edition, there is no Latin colophon, no shorter Latin poems, no poem in praise of Gower, no prayer; instead, there is only a half-*English* explicit, "Thus endeth De confessione Amantis." Technological limitations do not explain this shift in the closing moves of Berthelette's book. Instead, the end of the volume is of a piece with a reimagining of Gower's poem, a reimagining that simultaneously moves the medieval work forward in time, into the world of print – I am thinking here of the remarks in Berthelette's preface, with which this essay opened – and freezes it in a particular moment, one that has its own ideas, its own judgments, about what matters, which is Gower's role as a laureate English poet. We can see these ideas materializing on Berthelette's pages from the very start of the book.

Gower began the *Confessio* with a Latin poem expressing the significance of Latin for his English poetic enterprise. Berthelette pulls the *Carmenta iuvante* poem away from the English text that follows it, in the manuscript tradition and in Caxton, and instead sets it on a flyleaf, a relocation that, intentionally or not, diffuses its bilingual claims. It is a standard gesture in humanist printing to have Latin at the start of a book, whether as a tag on a title page or in an epigraph, as in Berthelette's *Confessio*. Berthelette's design, then, hooks the book's contents into particular reading practices and assumptions, but these are far more general than Gower's specific claims for his own poetics, and for Latin's role in "aiding" the English poem. The humanist habit signals a debt to classical Latinity and is a display of learning and filiation, with other humanists, and with the models of the past. Gower, too, frequently signals his classical sources, and (particularly if he is the author of "Eneidos, Bucolis"), his claims to auctorial status. But while the fondness for classical tags at the start of humanist books may well accord with Gower's own frequently-stated recourse to old books, his invocation of Carmen does a different kind of poetic work, making a case for a very particular combination of form and language. Gower asserts that he needs Latin to write for England, not simply because he is presenting himself as a conduit for or translator of Latinity, but rather because (as his other works also show) multilingualism is baked into the politics and culture of fourteenth-century Britain. To occupy the public, poetic sphere, Gower must write across his languages. In moving the first Latin verse, then, Berthelette relocates the poem that could be understood as the key to the bilingual work to follow.

Furthermore, the epigraph introduces not Gower's poem, but rather Berthelette's discussion of Gower's language – his *English* language – as Berthelette offers Gower as an excellent example of "englysshe wordes and vulgars" that represent a venerably antique contrast to the fashionable "newe termes" of modern writers.[25] Gower is here a poet of English "antiquitie," and the *Confessio*, a word-hoard from that ancient place. And because the Latin poem Gower placed at the start of his work has moved, in this design, to the flyleaf, when the *Confessio* begins, the first poetic words Berthelette prints are in English, not Latin, and they speak "Of them, that wryten vs to fore": that is, of Gower's compiling and collecting activities, also praised in Berthelette's preface. In other words, what is unique in Gower, his insistence on the integral role of Latin to his English project, risks being elided as Berthelette's admittedly beautiful design slots the *Confessio* into a new presentation. Berthelette's preface indicates that for him, Gower is a source of English style. His design marches in tandem with that vision of the poet.

Dialogue by Design

I have been suggesting that early print could not represent Gower's multilingual design for his English poem adequately, and that more generally, Gower's sense of himself as a poet of many tongues did not translate well to the early printed page, in part because of technological limitations, and in part because of a preference for his English poem, and a growing laureate identification of Gower as a founder of the English poetic tradition. I close this essay by looking at another kind of linguistic interaction and its representation in manuscript and print. I mean here the dialogic structure of the *Confessio*. Much of the poem is a conversation, and the manuscripts clearly mark that aspect. While some manuscripts omit the markers altogether, most have at least some version of markers for the parts of Confessor and Amans, often in the margins, sometimes decorated, making the page look rather like a script for a play. Both deluxe and plain copies witness this aspect of Gower's poem.[26] In some manuscripts, the speaker markers are, visually, part of the Latin glossing program, appearing in the same marginal placement as full glosses. Often they consist simply of the (Latin) names Amans and Genius, sometimes highly abbreviated, and sometimes in the longer forms "Opponit Confessor" and "Respondet Amans," using Latin phrases to introduce the conversation. Similarly brief Latin glosses – and these can occur in marginal placement even in copies where the longer Latin prose passages have moved to the text column – are often references to the *auctores* on whom Genius (and Gower) is drawing. Two levels of design thus coincide: Gower's own dialogic design for his

---

[25] *Jo. Gower de confessione Amantis*, aa ii v.
[26] I discuss the treatment of the speaker markers in the manuscript tradition in "Dialogues and Monologues: Manuscript Representations of the Conversation of the *Confessio Amantis*," in *Middle English Poetry: Texts and Tradition: Essays in Honour of Derek Pearsall*, ed. Alastair Minnis (York: York Medieval Press, 2001), 57–75.

work, which imagines not only the interaction of two speakers, but also the interaction of languages and traditions; and the design of the physical, bilingual page itself.

What happens to the dialogic design of the *Confessio* in early print? Caxton's design centers the speaker markers in the text column, thus making them quite prominent. Berthelette does the same, and in addition, he prints them in Roman type, the type he also uses for the Latin verses, separating them from the English poem both typographically and literally (see Figure 5). Such a layout highlights the structural markers of dialogue, to be sure, but other elements of the early printings end up working against Gower's dialogic design. The *Confessio* is a very long poem, and Caxton provided his edition with a table of contents. He explains that "by cause there been comprysed therin dyuers hystoryes and fables towchyng euery matere/ I haue ordeyned a table here folowyng of al suche hystoryes and fables where and in what book and leef they stande in as here after foloweth."[27] Caxton's table runs to twelve pages in print, and it is certainly useful. It also serves to frame the *Confessio* as a collection of stories, rather than as a dialogue. The table does introduce Genius and Amans, but Gower's sly burial of Amans' identity in the gloss that announces how the "auctor" "fingens se esse amantem"[28] is given away at the outset when Caxton announces that "cupydo smote Johan Gower With a fyry arowe and wounded hym so that Venus commysed to hym genyus hyr preest for to here hys confession."[29] As a result, an aspect of the poem's complexity that would have been available only to a Latinate reader (at least until the end of the poem) is revealed in the vernacular before the poem even begins. The conversation between languages and traditions, such as (Latinate) Boethian dialogue and (vernacular) exemplary narrative, is thus muted. What is more, the vast majority of Caxton's table entries are brief summaries of the stories Genius tells. After two entries detailing Genius and Amans' entry into the confession structure, references to dialogue between the two vanish almost entirely, buried in an avalanche of "How" entries introducing the stories Genius tells. That is, Caxton's table presents the *Confessio* as a compendium of narratives "touching every matter,"[30] while burying its various conversations.

---

[27] *This book is intituled confession amantis*, iir.
[28] The gloss appears next to the section of Book I of the *Confessio* that begins, "And forto proven it is so,/ I am miselven on of tho,/ Which to this Scole am underfonge" (I.61–63). The gloss is entirely clear that the speaker is not presenting himself truthfully: "Hic quasi in persona aliorum, quos amor alligat, finges se auctor esse Amantem."
[29] *This book is intituled confession amantis*, iir.
[30] For a discussion of tables of contents in manuscript and print copies of the *Confessio*, see my "Pretexts: Tables of Contents and the Reading of John Gower's *Confessio Amantis*," *Medium Aevum* 66 (1997): 270–87.

In his preface, Berthelette similarly presents Gower as a goldmine of old stories:

> And who so euer in redynge of this warke/ dothe consyder it well/ shal fynde/ that it is plentifully stuffed and fournysshed with manyfolde eloquent reasons/ sharpe and quicke argumentes/ and examples of great auctorite/ perswadynge vnto vertue/ not onely taken out of the poetes/ oratours/ history wryters/ and philosophers/ but also out of the holy scripture.[31]

Like Caxton, he then provides a table of contents for easy access to all of this material; in fact, he provides Caxton's table of contents, with some expansions of his own. These additions include extra entries for much of the scientific material in Book VII, offering one hundred and ten entries to Caxton's eighty-seven. As a result, Berthelette's readers are presented, not just with a collection of stories, but also with an encyclopedia.

Gower himself describes the *Confessio* in part in terms of the stories it tells, and so these printers are not so much misrepresenting the poet's project, as choosing to emphasize a particular aspect of it. And there is some continuity between manuscript and print practice: manuscripts often include finding-aids, such as the *capituli* typical of histories, and there are two manuscript copies of the *Confessio* with tables of contents of their own.[32] In other words, collection and compilation matter in the manuscript, as well as the print, context, and they matter to Gower's understanding of what he was doing. Gower frames the poem in references to his own writing practice, telling us at the start how he came to write the book, and, in the "Quia unusquisque" at the end, he tells us, at some length, what *other* books he has also written. I have already noted that Caxton, unlike Berthelette, prints the colophon at the end of the book, but his representation of that colophon in the table of contents is telling, as Gower's careful curation of his poetic reputation in the colophon is reduced in the table to a brief and unspecific acknowledgement that the book ends: "The enuoye of his book & fynysshyng of the same. Explicit."[33] A reader would not, at this stage, know that the English poem is followed by Latin prose and poetry that speaks to the author's larger *oeuvre* and poetic reputation.

Berthelette's table reflects his print's more radical reshaping of Gower's end matter. He expands Caxton's entry on Gower's final English lines: "Here in the ende he maketh a recapitulation on that, that he promysed, touchynge loues cause, in the begynnynge of the boke: for he concludeth, that all delectation of loue out of Charite, is nothynge," and then removes

---

[31] *Jo. Gower de confessione Amantis*, aa ii r–aa ii v.
[32] These are Oxford, Magdalen College, MS 213, and Princeton, MS Taylor 5. Both of these tables were added at or near the point of production.
[33] *This book is intituled confession amantis*, vii v.

Caxton's brief entry for the author's "enuoye," substituting a reference to the printed paratext, "Thus endeth the table of this warke entitled Gower de Confessione Amantis.[34]

The title given here echoes the explicit Berthelette provides at the end of the work, where, as discussed above, he does *not* print Gower's authorial colophon. Printerly gestures thus overwrite Gower's anxious curation of his *auctorite* here at the beginning, a move paralleled by the excision of the Latin matter from the end of the book. Gower's presentation of his larger poetic project as a conversation in many languages, with many books, is bounded and muted by the gestures – routine, deliberate, or some combination of both – of print.

Gower clearly made efforts to have an impact on the production and circulation of his works. He understood and promoted himself as a writer of books in English, French, and Latin. He was also, I think, deeply conscious of the materiality of the poetic word and of the fundamental slipperiness of language. He knew how manuscript culture could change the contents and appearance, and thus the reception, of a book. Manuscripts could underline his bi- and trilingual practice, whether by including the colophon even when placing it somewhere other than at the manuscript's end or by slotting in (or removing) shorter pieces from the manuscripts of the longer works; or by constructing a manuscript like Trentham. They could also problematize his poetics, as in the designs that mangled or misplaced his apparatus. They could hitch him to companions he might, or might not, have chosen for himself. And for all the admittedly rather anxious promotion of his reputation in the "Quia unusquisque," I suspect that this kind of variety and multiplicity was nevertheless central to Gower's understanding of his project. The opening line of the *Confessio* is "Of hem that writen ous tofore/ The bokes duelle." In John Gower, we have a poet whose work "dwells" in many (manuscript) books, and in a few (printed) ones. The early printed books had an outsized effect. Other medieval poets experienced the same drop in visibility and popularity after the sixteenth century that Gower did, and even a constantly reprinted poet like Chaucer appeared on black and white pages that could not compete with the complexity and beauty of a medieval manuscript page. But Gower understood himself as a writer of books in English, French, and Latin, and as a writer who often combined these languages, needing more than one of them in any given work, in order to achieve his goals. He showed himself to be deeply conscious of the materiality of the poetic word. In his 1630 poem *In Praise of Hemp-Seed*, John Taylor lauded paper, a metonymy for printing, for preserving "Old Chaucer [and] Gower." Taylor is quite right that paper had a lot to do with Gower's survival, but parchment, to my mind, is the better realization of his achievement.

---

[34] *Jo. Gower de confessione Amantis*, aa viii v [? Not marked].

CHAPTER 10

GOWER FROM PRINT TO MANUSCRIPT: COPYING CAXTON IN OXFORD, BODLEIAN LIBRARY, MS HATTON 51

Aditi Nafde

OXFORD, BODLEIAN LIBRARY, MS Hatton 51, a copy of the *Confessio Amantis*, most likely produced c.1500, contains a mistake.[1] The penultimate line of fol. 181r reads "Or otherwkse yf it stode," with the word "otherwise" misspelt with a "k." This is not a scribal error but a printing error: Caxton's 1483 edition of the *Confessio* (STC 12142) contains an identical mistake, the result of the "i" and "k" compartments in the type case being adjacent to one another and the compositor reaching for the wrong one while setting the forme.[2] Hatton 51 is copied from the print and the scribe reproduces the mistake. Tasked with the lengthy job of copying the *Confessio*, the scribe of Hatton 51 would have had training enough to recognize and correct a misspelling in his exemplar. In choosing to copy it verbatim, the scribe preserves a mistake that could only have been made through the mechanical processes of print production. This odd moment reveals a scribe thinking carefully about what it meant to copy an exemplar that is printed. Copying a manuscript from a printed book was not unusual. As the number of printed books in circulation grew, it became increasingly typical for scribes to use them as exemplars. Indeed, as Curt F. Bühler puts it, "every manuscript ascribed to the second half of the fifteenth century

---

[1] The *Summary Catalogue of Western Manuscripts at the Bodleian Library* states the manuscript was "written about 1500," *Summary Catalogue* (Oxford: Clarendon Press, 1895–1953) vol. 2, Part 2, 840. N. F. Blake dates the manuscript to "c.1500," "Manuscript to Print," in *Book Production and Publishing in Britain 1375–1475*, ed. Jeremy Griffiths and Derek Pearsall (Cambridge: Cambridge University Press, 1989), 403–32, 420. Derek Pearsall dates the manuscript to "s.xvi first half," "The Manuscripts and Illustrations of Gower's Works," in *A Companion to Gower*, ed. Siân Echard (Cambridge: D. S. Brewer, 2004) 73–97, 76.
[2] This printing error was first noted by Blake, "Manuscript to Print," 416–17.

is potentially (and often without question) a copy of some incunable."[3] Bibliographers such as Bühler, N. F. Blake, David McKitterick, and Julia Boffey have demonstrated the happy co-existence of manuscript and print, the ongoing production of manuscripts after the introduction of print, and the prevalence of manuscript-print hybrid books.[4] They call into question Elizabeth Eisenstein's notion that print supplemented and then supplanted manuscripts.[5] Books such as Hatton 51 go further still to suggest that scribal practices were not just co-existing with print but being altered by it. As part of a larger project which examines how scribes were actively responding to a book market changed by the introduction of print, this essay demonstrates the multiple ways in which the Hatton scribe reproduced the look of the printed page, including its errors, in order to bring the styles and practices of print to his manuscript. In doing so, it demonstrates how the scribe was rethinking and redefining his role, and the role of the manuscript, in a shifting post-print book market.

Manuscripts of the *Confessio* are highly uniform in appearance. A. I. Doyle and M. B. Parkes suggested that the reason for the "standardized" presentation is the circulation of "initial copies issued earlier by the author himself" which were then possibly retained by stationers for further reproduction in the fifth and sixth decades of the fifteenth century.[6] These

---

[3] Curt F. Bühler, *The Fifteenth-Century Book: The Scribes, the Printers, the Decorators* (Philadelphia: University of Pennsylvania Press, 1960), 16.

[4] Bühler, *The Fifteenth-Century Book*, 16, 34–35; Blake, "Manuscript to Print," 403–32; David McKitterick, *Print, Manuscript and the Search for Order 1450-1830* (Cambridge: Cambridge University Press, 2003) i; Julia Boffey, *Manuscript and Print in London c. 1475-1530* (London: The British Library, 2012), especially 45–80, and "From Manuscripts to Print: Continuity and Change," in *A Companion to the Early Printed Book in Britain 1476-1558*, ed. Vincent Gillespie and Susan Powell (Cambridge: D. S. Brewer, 2014), 13–26. See also J. K. Moore, "Manuscripts Copied from Books Printed Before 1640," *Primary Materials Relating to Copy and Print in English Books of the Sixteenth and Seventeenth Centuries* (Oxford: Oxford Bibliographical Society, 1992), 1–9; M. D. Reeve, "Manuscripts Copied from Printed Books," in *Manuscripts in the Fifty Years after the Invention of Printing: some papers read at a colloquium at the Warburg Institute on 12-13 March 1982*, ed. J. B. Trapp (London: Warburg Institute, 1983), 12–20; A. S. G. Edwards, "The Circulation of English Verse in Manuscript after the Advent of Print in England," *Studia Neophilologica* 83, no. 1 (2011): 67–77; Cora E. Lutz, "Manuscripts Copied from Printed Books," *Yale University Library Gazette* 49, no. 3 (1975): 261–67; Ann Blair, "Reflections on Technological Continuities: Manuscripts Copied from Printed Books," *Bulletin of the John Rylands Library* 91, no. 1 (2015): 7–33.

[5] Elizabeth L. Eisenstein, *The Printing Press as an Agent of Change: Communications and Cultural Transformations in Early-Modern Europe* (Complete in One Volume) (Cambridge: Cambridge University Press, 1979), especially 3–159.

[6] A. I. Doyle and M. B. Parkes, "The Production of Copies of the *Canterbury Tales* and the *Confessio Amantis* in the Early Fifteenth Century," in *Medieval Scribes, Manuscripts, and Libraries: Essays Presented to N. R. Ker*, ed. M. B. Parkes and Andrew Watson (London: Scolar Press, 1978), 163–210, quote at 200.

later copies were likely produced by independent scribes copying individual quires of the larger work that were then brought together. The highly standardized format of the text and its presentation would have facilitated co-ordination between them and further "cross-imitation and cross-copying" between these scribes resulted in considerable similarity between different manuscripts.[7]

It is in this context of *Confessio* manuscript production that Caxton produced his edition.[8] He strove to imitate the standard layout of early copies: his edition has double columns with c.46 lines per column (there are fewer in the Table of Contents, 43–44 lines per column), spaces for large and small initials, and follows the hierarchy of decoration typically found in *Confessio* manuscripts.[9] However, Caxton was sometimes required to deviate from the "standard" presentation of *Confessio* manuscripts because of the practical requirements of print production. The mechanics of the printing press necessitated changes to the look of the printed page. In particular, as books were printed out of sequence, quire signatures were necessary for the binder to understand the order in which quires were to be gathered and bound.[10] Caxton included quire signatures and folio numbers in the paratextual material that surrounds the two central text columns, meaning that his edition appears distinct from the *Confessio* manuscript tradition. McKitterick describes the printing of quire signatures and catchwords in the main text block as a "major aesthetic concession to the demands of the press" that made print look less like the manuscripts on which it was modelled.[11]

---

[7] Doyle and Parkes, "The Production of Copies," 200, quote at 203.
[8] For further discussion of Caxton's processes, and of MS Hatton 51, see the preceding essay in this volume, by Siân Echard, "Gower between Manuscript and Print."
[9] There is some disagreement over Caxton's exemplar for his edition. G. C. Macaulay suggested that the text is a composite taken from "at least three MSS", one of which is Oxford, Magdalen College, MS 213, which has a similar Table of Contents: G. C. Macaulay, *The Complete Works of John Gower: The English Works* (Oxford: Clarendon Press, 1901), II, clxviii. Gavin Bone finds "only the minutest differences" between the manuscript and the print, which shows that the marks in MS 213 correspond to the beginnings of columns in Caxton's edition, though he states that it "cannot have been Caxton's only source": Gavin Bone, "Extant Manuscripts Printed from by W. De Worde with Notes on the Owner, Roger Thorney," *The Library*, 4th ser. 12 (1932): 284–306, 285–86. Blake doubts the validity of this claim: N. F. Blake, "Caxton's Copy-Text of Gower's *Confessio Amantis*," in *William Caxton and English Literary Culture* (London: Hambledon Press, 1991), 187–98.
[10] See McKitterick, *Print, Manuscript and the Search for Order*, 38, and Philip Gaskell, *A New Introduction to Bibliography* (Delaware: Oak Knoll Press, 1972), 51–53. Although quire signatures were frequently used in fifteenth-century manuscripts, they are more prominent in printed books.
[11] McKitterick, *Print, Manuscript and the Search for Order*, 38.

It is the imitation of these printing concessions in Hatton 51 that makes it clear that the Hatton scribe did not accidentally copy Caxton's printing error but aimed to imitate the exact look of the printed book. While there is a single quire signature in the manuscript, "d i" on fol. 15r, and others may have been cropped, more perceivably, the scribe copied folio numbers where he found them in the print and omitted them where they were omitted in the print. He copied the full word, "folio," followed by a numeral.[12] Though repeating the foliation on every recto would have been a simple job for the printer, who only needed to reset the numeral and not the whole forme, it would have been time-consuming for the scribe, who would have needed to change ink colors and write out the word in full throughout the book. The efforts of the scribe make it clear that he did not see these features as an "aesthetic concession," as the printer might have, but as an aesthetic necessity in order to make his manuscript look like print.

Copying folio numbers is functional and practical as well as aesthetic. Foliation was not common in early printed books. As Martha Driver observes, Caxton was experimenting with arabic and roman numerals in his edition of the *Confessio*.[13] He used arabic numerals in the prologue, indicating fols. 2 to 4, then after a gap in foliation, switched to roman numerals on fol. 17r, printed as "folio xvii" (sig.c1r). The Hatton scribe copied these identically, using arabic numerals in the same place as the print and switching to roman numerals when the print does. The scribe understood Caxton's purpose in foliating his edition, which was to relate the contents of each folio to the Table of Contents, and he strove to replicate this. Both tables, that in the manuscript and that in the print exemplar, are very similar in presentation. Both are in two columns with rubrics and both have almost exactly the same text on each page. The rubricated opening of the table in the manuscript is more spread out than it is in the print, but the scribe tried to follow the line spacing of the print with the same words on each line. He did so in particular where he started to run out of space and he then used the print exemplar as he would a manuscript exemplar, to calculate how much space he needed for the rubricated text and how best to organize the rest of the text in the space he had available.

Tables of Contents were unusual both in vernacular printing and in *Confessio* manuscripts.[14] They were one of Caxton's major innovations,

---

[12] There is a discrepancy between the scribe's red-ink foliation and the modern pencil foliation in the manuscript. Where this essay indicates folios it refers to the scribe's foliation.

[13] Martha W. Driver, "Printing the *Confessio Amantis*: Caxton's Edition in Context," in *Re-Visioning Gower*, ed. R. F. Yeager (Asheville, NC: Pegasus Press, 1998), 269–303, 270.

[14] On tables of contents in the *Confessio*, see Siân Echard, "Pre-Texts: Table of Contents and the Reading of John Gower's 'Confessio Amantis'," *Medium Ævum* 66, no. 2 (1997): 270–87. Echard argues that it is unlikely that Caxton copied

enabling him to better market the contents of his editions and the ease of navigating through the text.[15] The scribe copied the table partly because he replicated all the features of his print exemplar, including its errors, and partly because he recognized the rarity of the table. While his efforts to keep the table demonstrate his desire to imitate the aesthetic of his exemplar, his efforts to ensure that it functions correctly demonstrate his recognition of Caxton's innovation. The print is unclear in its use of folio numbers. In the first two gatherings, folio numbers are more often omitted than included even if they are required by the table and numerated within it. It took the compositors until the third gathering they printed to recognize that they needed to provide folio numbers in addition to quire signatures in order to relate the folios to the table.[16] Here too, the scribe did not correct the compositors' error but imitated the print so that there are no folio numbers where they are missing in the print exemplar. Reproducing the table was particularly difficult because the printed table lists the tales of the *Confessio* and the folio numbers on which they are found, which then corresponds to the folio numbers at the top of each recto throughout the book. The scribe tried his best to ensure he had the same text on each folio as the print exemplar so that his foliation matched the table of contents. However, because his writing often takes up less space than the print he imitated, and because he forgot to copy a large c.20-line gap left in his print exemplar before the opening of the Prologue (fol. 2v) and a c.14-line gap before the opening of Book I (fol. 9v), the folio numbers listed in the manuscript's table do not correlate with the contents of those folios. In order to make up for this, the scribe took the rather unusual step of providing folio numbers on the versos. When the roman numeral folio numbers start in the print exemplar at "folio xvii" after a series of non-foliated folios (sig.c1r), the scribe replicated this by also numbering his folio "folio xvii." However, the contents of that folio do not correspond exactly with the contents of "folio xvii" in the print exemplar. The scribe is off by one page and his "folio xvii" (fol. 17r) contains the text that is on the verso in the print (sig.c1v). To rectify this slip, the scribe labelled his fol. 17v as "folio xviii," where the text more or less matches that of the print exemplar (sig.c2r). He then had to label fol. 19v "folio xix." His text finally almost corresponds with the print exemplar on fol. 21r and he writes the folio number on the recto in imitation of the print. The folio numbers on the versos, while aesthetically unusual, were also a practical solution to the tricky process of reproducing

    his table from any of the tables in the surviving manuscripts of the *Confessio* and suggests that Caxton used the Latin glosses to produce his table (276–79).

[15] On marketing printed tables of contents, see Alex da Costa, "'That ye mowe redely fynde...what ye desyre': Printed Tables of Contents and Indices 1476-1540," *Huntington Library Quarterly* 81, no. 3 (2018): 291–313.

[16] The third gathering is the current fourth gathering because the table was printed later but added as the first gathering.

a copy of the *Confessio* with a table of contents, allowing the scribe to copy the table without having to revise it. The result is that the manuscript looks overloaded with print features, preserving aspects of the print that make it distinct from the manuscript tradition. The manuscript seems to outdo its print exemplar, providing more of the print features than Caxton's version has itself.

As well as the changes required by the printing process, Caxton's edition also deliberately deviates from the "standard" presentation of *Confessio* manuscripts. The scribe closely followed Caxton's layout in these deviations. For instance, speaker markers that indicate the parts of the dialogue between Amans and the Confessor are frequently placed in the margins alongside the opening of their respective speeches in *Confessio* manuscripts.[17] Placing the speaker markers in a similar place in the printed edition would have required the additional labor of setting text in the margins, so instead the speaker markers are incorporated into the main text column where they precede the speeches of Amans and the Confessor. The speaker markers in Hatton 51 are also in the main text column, centered and, further imitating the print exemplar, they are unabbreviated and appear in full as "Confessor," "Amans," "Opponit Confessor," despite the extra labor this would have caused the scribe.

More noticeably, there is a series of gaps in the print exemplar which are atypical in "standard" *Confessio* manuscripts.[18] The placement of the gaps in the print exemplar is inconsistent. The gaps are either before the Latin verse and the Latin prose summaries that precede the main text (Prologue, Books I, VI, and VII), between the Latin (verse and prose) and the main text (Books IV and VIII), after the end of the previous book and the Latin verse at the bottom of a column followed by another gap before the main text (Book V), or before the main text where the opening Latin verse and prose are not printed (Book II). There are two gaps at the opening of Book III, which starts at the top of the second column of the page, because the compositor left the gap at the end of Book II which ends half-way down the first column of the page, and a gap between the Latin (verse and prose) and the main text. The Hatton scribe failed to copy the gaps at the opening of the Prologue and Book I, continuing the text immediately after the end of the preceding book. He would have found it much easier simply to start each new book this way, ignoring the gaps; instead, although at the start of Books III, VII, and VIII his Latin verse and prose starts to encroach on

---

[17] On the tradition of speaker markers in *Confessio* manuscripts, see Siân Echard, "Dialogues and Monologues: Manuscript Representations of the Conversation of the *Confessio Amantis*," in *Middle English Poetry: Texts and Traditions: Essays in Honour of Derek Pearsall*, ed. Alastair Minnis (York: York Medieval Press, 2001), 57–75.

[18] For a fuller description of these gaps, see Driver, "Printing the *Confessio Amantis*," 271–80.

the gap he had previously left, he imitated the presentation of the print as carefully as he could.

As the *Confessio Amantis* was Caxton's first large book to be set in two columns, these gaps may have been an accident of the complicated layout; equally they may have been left deliberately for illustrations, painted or woodcut, to be added at a later stage of production. N. F. Blake suggests both possibilities.[19] Only in Books II and V is there any missing text which might account for the gaps: the Latin verse and prose are both missing from Book II and the Latin prose alone is missing from Book V, though there is an additional gap left for the prose in both the print and the manuscript. However, the Latin verse and prose summaries are not missing from the openings of any other book where there are also gaps, suggesting that instead they were left for illustrations. There are only two manuscripts which have an extensive series of illustrations such as would account for the gaps: New York, Morgan Library and Museum, MS M 126 and Oxford, New College, MS 266. Neither is linked directly to Caxton's edition. Driver finds no connection between Caxton's edition and MS 266, which has miniatures at different places in the text, to the gaps left by Caxton; she also finds little evidence for the connection between Caxton's edition and MS M 126, which has miniatures at the same points as Caxton's edition and may have been circulating in the same aristocratic circles as Caxton.[20] More typically, there are only two "standard" illustrations (or spaces left for illustrations) in *Confessio* manuscripts: of Nebuchadnezzar and his dream, usually located in the Prologue, and of Amans and the Confessor, usually located in Book I before 1.203.[21] The imitation in the manuscript of the gaps left in the print edition therefore suggests that the scribe was not following the tradition of the presentation of *Confessio* manuscripts, but rather following Caxton's deviations from that tradition. In fact, Caxton brought to the presentation of the *Confessio* a tradition more usual in print production. It was highly common to leave a series of gaps in print for illustrations to be added at a later date. William Blades compares the gaps in Caxton's *Confessio* to "several of the Bruges books printed by Colard Mansion"; Driver compares the gaps more broadly to "printers like Jan Veldener, Arendt de Keiser, and Colard Mansion, Caxton's early colleagues in Bruges, to name a few, [who] produced

---

[19] See N. F. Blake, "Early Printed Editions of the *Confessio Amantis*," *Mediaevalia* 16 (1990): 289–306, especially 294–95, and Blake "Manuscript to Print," 405. On woodcuts or painted images added later to manuscripts more generally, see McKitterick, *Print, Manuscript and the Search for Order*, 53–96.

[20] Driver, "Printing the *Confessio Amantis*," 279–83.

[21] On the tradition of the two illustrations in the *Confessio*, see Jeremy Griffiths, "*Confessio Amantis*: The Poem and its Pictures," in *Gower's* Confessio Amantis: *Responses and Reassessments*, ed. A. J. Minnis (Cambridge: D. S. Brewer, 1983), 163–78, and Pearsall, "The Manuscripts and Illustrations of Gower's Works," 86–88.

a number of books with spaces left for pictures never completed."[22] Mansion produced an edition of Boethius and an edition of Boccaccio, both of which have gaps at the openings of their constituent books, and Lotte Hellinga posits that the similarity in technique between the engravings found in Caxton's and Mansion's books "would not exclude the possibility that they shared the same engraver."[23] In imitating the presentation of the print, the Hatton scribe brings to his manuscript copy the contexts of the printing press: its style of presentation, tradition of illustration, the relationships between printers, and the networks within which they were working.

The scribe's intention is more overt when he copies Caxton's short printer's prologue to the *Confessio*. As A. S. G. Edwards and Carole Meale describe, one of Caxton's primary marketing techniques was to assume "a distinctive identity as producer."[24] Caxton did this in his prologue to the *Confessio*, stressing that the Table of Contents was his own innovation: "I haue ordeyned a table here folowyng of al suche hystoryes and fables where and in what book and leef they stande in as here after foloweth" (sig. ii r). Written in first person, the prologue advertises the unique aspect of the edition and the originality of the printer who produced it. The Hatton scribe copied the prologue word for word, including the reference to Caxton in the first person. Reproduced in Hatton 51, it is ambiguous as to whom the "I" of the printer's prologue is meant to refer: the printer of the exemplar or the scribe himself, taking on the role of the innovative producer in replicating his table and making it function in the manuscript. Copying the prologue suggests that the print is imitable, meaning that Caxton no longer has a "distinctive identity as producer" but shares that identity with the scribe. Caxton's well-known epilogue to his *Recuyell of the Historyes of Troye* makes a similar marketing claim regarding the identity of the printer, separating it from that of the scribe: "all the bookes of this storye named the recule of the historyes of troyes thus enpryntid as ye here see were begonne in oon day and also fynysshid in oon day" (STC 15375, 1473 or 1474, unsigned leaf). E. Gordon Duff finds the wording of the epilogue to be "slightly ambiguous" but understands it to mean that Caxton was distinguishing his printed books, in which multiple identical sheets for multiple copies were produced simultaneously "in oon day" by a single printer, from manuscripts

---

[22] William Blades, *The Life and Typography of William Caxton* (London: Joseph Lilly, 1863), Vol II, 140–41. Driver, "Printing the *Confessio Amantis*," 273 and n. 11. See also Blake, "Early Printed Editions of *Confessio Amantis*," 295.

[23] Driver, "Printing the *Confessio Amantis*," 275–76; Lotte Hellinga-Querido, "Reading an Engraving: William Caxton's Dedication to Margaret of York," in *Across the Narrow Seas: Studies in the History and Bibliography of Britain and the Low Countries Presented to Anna E. C. Simoni*, ed. Susan Roach (London: The British Library, 1991), 1–15, quote at 2.

[24] A. S. G. Edwards and Carol M. Meale, "The Marketing of Printed Books in Late Medieval England," *The Library* 6th ser. 15 (1993): 95–124, quote at 95.

which were produced separately one after the other.[25] Caxton indicated that his editions were different from scribal editions because his were the work of a single printer producing copies of an entire text, rather than quires copied separately by individual scribes, as Doyle and Parkes describe of the Trinity Gower.[26] The Hatton scribe's imitation of Caxton's prologue suggests that his identity as producer is more akin to the printer's than the printer claims.

Edwards and Meale explain further that the producer of a printed book is "signalled most obviously by the use of colophons and devices, which appear only infrequently in manuscripts."[27] Caxton certainly did this at the end of his printed edition of the *Confessio*: his colophon reads, "Emprynted at Westmestre by me Willyam Caxton and fynysshed the ii day of Septembre the fyrst yere of the regne of kyng Richard the thyrd the yere of our lord a thousand CCCC lxxxxiii" (sig. C5v). The colophons in printed books invariably indicate the method of production and may also indicate the specific date or place of production or the printer who produced it, and so serve to remind readers that the text they are reading is produced by new and innovative mechanical means. The scribes of a number of manuscripts copied from printed books copy the colophons exactly, also adopting the first person of the printer.[28] The colophon in Hatton 51 is, unfortunately, missing because the manuscript ends imperfectly but, as the scribe adopted a number of aspects of the print that "appear only infrequently in manuscripts" elsewhere, it is likely that he also copied the colophon word for word.[29] In including these statements in their manuscript copies of the printed books, they remind potential purchasers that scribes can also produce the new types of books now available. The selling points of printed books are extended to those manuscripts copied from print.

Printed books changed as a result of these tactics and another marketable aspect of print was its completeness. An obvious instance of this is seen in Caxton's edition of *Dicts and Sayings*, in which he recalls a fabricated but jovial conversation with Earl Rivers who asks him to "oversee" and complete the edition, giving him cause to add an entire chapter to Rivers' translation that was "left out" (STC 6826, 1477, unsigned leaf). This marketing of completeness is also found in Caxton's edition of the *Confessio*. Caxton included ten lines at the end of the prologue that are missing from all manuscripts except Cambridge, Sidney Sussex, MS 63. G. C. Macaulay believes they were also included in San Marino, Huntington Library, MS

[25] E. Gordon Duff, *William Caxton* (Chicago: The Caxton Club, 1905), 28.
[26] Doyle and Parkes, "The Production of Copies," 200.
[27] Edwards and Meale, "The Marketing of Printed Books," 95–96.
[28] A few examples can be found in the colophons copied into: Oxford, Bodleian Library, MS Arch Selden B.11; London, British Library Additional, MS 22718; New Haven, Yale University, Beinecke Rare Books and Manuscript Library, Mellon 25, though there are several more on which I have an article forthcoming.
[29] Edwards and Meale, "The Marketing of Printed Books," 96.

EL 26 A 17 (the Stafford MS), which has a missing leaf at this point, and suggests that there is a high probability that the lines are "such as Gower might have written."[30] If Caxton had recognized that the lines are likely to be Gower's own, he may have sought out either the Sidney Sussex manuscript or the Stafford manuscript as his source for the *Confessio* or to supplement his source in the interests of completeness. Caxton claimed to have done just this in the proheyme to the second edition of *The Canterbury Tales* (STC 5083, 1483), writing that because other "wryters haue abrydgyd it [the *Tales*] and many thyngs left out / and in somme place haue sette certain versys / that he [Chaucer] neuer made," he has supplemented his first edition with a copy that is "very trewe / and accordyng unto hys owen first book by hym made" (sig. a ii r–v) in his second. While this statement cannot necessarily be taken at face value – indicating the errors in the first edition is a way of marketing the second edition – Caxton's emphasis on creating a copy of the text that is most complete and closest to the author's own was a key selling point for this edition. Berthelette later attempted to produce an edition of the *Confessio* that was even more complete, filling in Caxton's omissions of "lynes and columnes, ye, and sometyme holle padges" (STC 12143 sig. aa iii v).[31] The Hatton scribe had a similar concern to Gower's two earliest printers in producing the most complete copy of the text. He copied the final ten lines of the prologue that Caxton preserved, ensuring that Caxton's completeness is reflected in his own. This, along with his inclusion of the Table of Contents and the painstaking alignment of folio numbers to content, indicates the scribe's intentions to produce a manuscript that can boast the merits of his printed exemplar.

While laying claims to the qualities of Caxton's printed edition, the scribe also took advantage of the possibilities afforded by manuscript production. Printed books were usually created unfinished with gaps for colored initials, for instance, which were intended to be finished by hand. Printing in two colors was difficult and expensive and so comparatively rare in England.[32] Caxton's editions of *The Canterbury Tales*, for instance, were printed with gaps awaiting the colored initials that were later filled in by rubricators and decorators. The Hatton scribe's copy of the printed text provides such hand-finishing, and he supplied most of the initials in his copy, following the hierarchy of initials that Caxton imitated from standard *Confessio* manuscript presentation. The Hatton scribe has therefore worked hard to make his manuscript look like a copy of the printed book that has then been carefully hand-finished. However, he also used different colors of ink and sizes of script to distinguish between the Latin and English texts, disregarding the single color and size of type in his print exemplar. There is

---

[30] Macaulay, *The Complete Works*, II, 466.
[31] On Berthelette's additions to the text, see Macaulay, *The Complete Works*, II, clxix.
[32] McKitterick, *Print, Manuscript and the Search for Order*, 38.

evidence that the red ink text was both written at the same time as the black ink text, opening by opening, and added after the black ink text was fully copied. In the prologue, the red ink text fits neatly up to the black ink text, suggesting that the scribe was switching ink as he filled the page; from fol. 26r onwards, there is more space around the red ink text, suggesting that the scribe left spaces for it that were slightly too large as he was writing in black ink and returned to them later with red ink. Both techniques required efforts that were customary in manuscript production, either in switching ink or calculating how much space would be required for missing red ink text. The scribe provided red ink braces, common in manuscripts of the fifteenth century, to indicate rhyming couplets and to clarify the ends of lines where the layout causes them to spill over two lines. The compositor of the print exemplar left an indented space for an initial at the opening of the prologue, for instance, which meant that he only had space for half-lines adjacent to the initial. He accidentally ran two lines together following it. The scribe copied the indented space for the initial, leaving him with half-lines of text, but he used red ink to mark where the lines end and indicated the following couplet with a red brace (fol. 2v). As a result, his copy signals the lines of the text more clearly than the print. Unlike the printer who needed the scribe to finish his text, the Hatton scribe was able to produce his edition of the *Confessio* single-handedly and created a more complete and more accurate copy (in terms of indicating its lines and rhyme) than the printing press could offer.

In combining features of manuscript production with those of print, the scribe blurs the distinction between the two. His manuscript reveals a knowing exploitation of both manuscript and print forms to create a volume which is better than its exemplar. Quoting Foucault, Alexandra Gillespie argues that there was "a willingness, on the part of producers and consumers, to let books 'shift shapes, one into the other'."[33] Her discussion is of *Sammelbände* which, as she demonstrates, display a "remarkable openness on the part of printers and owners to the malleable, multiple forms of books."[34] *Sammelbände* or hybrid books in which print material was combined with manuscripts do demonstrate a flexibility towards the material form in which books were available. Manuscripts such as Hatton 51 suggest that another category of books – manuscripts produced in imitation of print – were also taking advantage of the flexible attitudes of buyers and readers towards book forms.

In offering a book which outdoes its printed exemplar, the Hatton scribe attempted to lay a claim to the buyers' purse. Book purchasers before print were

---

[33] Alexandra Gillespie, "Poets, Printers, and Early English Sammelbände," *Huntington Library Quarterly* 67, no. 2 (June 2004): 189–214, quote at 204.
[34] Gillespie, "Poets, Printers," 205.

accustomed to the book trade being "almost entirely bespoke."[35] Although the manuscript market was starting to make ready-made anthologies on a speculative basis, Edwards and Meale show that the "potential for an element of self-reflectiveness on the part of the purchaser" is what really "gives the manuscript its distinctiveness."[36] Print, though not produced bespoke in the way manuscripts were, could still attract patrons, such as those that recognized the potential "power of print as a propaganda weapon."[37] Both the patron and the printer saw the merits of their relationship. Scribes saw the merits of the relationship too. They continued to produce books after print and so continued the bespoke trade; but they also created for themselves another market, offering manuscripts which were both bespoke and, in being copied from print, imitated the styles of mass-produced books. They catered to the tastes of the patrons of print while offering a text that was distinctive enough from print to compete with print's offerings. Hatton 51 may itself have been commissioned: there are ownership marks in the margins of fol. 189v in an early sixteenth-century hand, "Thys ys Harry Fawkener boke [&] Andria Fawkner," as well as other names in later hands. The blurring of book categories allows the scribe to make the most of his situation as a producer of manuscripts after print, creating a book that imitates the desirable styles of print with the benefits of his craft.

Caxton attempted to distinguish between print and manuscript in order to market his books, stating that his "book [is] in prynte after the maner & forme as ye may here see and is not wreton with penne and ynke as other bokes ben" (*Recuyell*, STC 15375). Berthelette's edition of the *Confessio* does the same: his prologue carefully points out that he consulted both the "wrytten copies" and "the prynte copie," creating an edition that is based on the authority of both forms. In doing so, he separates manuscript from print and boasts his innovation in combining them in his edition. While the process of producing print and producing a manuscript "with penne and ynke" may differ, the Hatton scribe demonstrates that an amalgamation of manuscript and print practices was happening earlier than Berthelette's edition suggests, soon after the invention of print. The Hatton scribe blurs the distinctions between the two forms of books, taking advantage of the shifting market for books and suggesting that he still has a place within it.[38]

---

[35] Graham Pollard, "The English Market for Printed Books (The Sanders Lectures, 1959)," *Publishing History* 4 (1978): 7–48, 10.
[36] Edwards and Meale, "The Marketing of Printed Books," 96.
[37] Edwards and Meale, "The Marketing of Printed Books," 99.
[38] I am grateful to Alex da Costa, Ruth Connolly, and the editors of this volume for commenting on an earlier draft of this essay.

CHAPTER 11

A CAXTON *CONFESSIO*: READERS AND USERS FROM WESTMINSTER TO CHAPEL HILL

Brian W. Gastle

ON WEDNESDAY 12 OCTOBER 1960, the University of North Carolina at Chapel Hill celebrated the 167th anniversary of its foundation with "pomp and splendor," capped by an address from Nathan Pusey, then-president of Harvard University. A special gift to the university library, to serve as its one-millionth acquisition, also marked the occasion: William Caxton's 1483 edition of John Gower's *Confessio Amantis* (UNC-CH Incunabula 532.5).[1] The volume was donated to the library by the Hanes Foundation, a private philanthropic organization devoted to supporting education, arts, and sciences in North Carolina.[2] But this symbolic moment was only the latest in the history of this particular copy of Caxton's edition of the poem. While much of the history of this volume has been lost in the five centuries since its printing, there are tantalizing witnesses to and hints of its readers and users since it emerged from Caxton's print shop in Westminster. The binding of this particular copy – one of only a handful of extant copies by Caxton's original binder – included a papal indulgence consigned by a contemporary of Caxton's with literary ties. And there are several marginal notations from later readers and users, including the opening lines of a popular sixteenth-century lyric, a number of signatures both partial and

---

[1] "Pusey Speech, Book are Highlight of University Day Celebration," *The Daily Tar Heel*, 13 October 1960, 1, and *One Million Books: Proceedings of a Convocation Honoring the Acquisition of the One Millionth Volume by the Library of the University of North Carolina* (Chapel Hill, NC: The University of North Carolina Library, 12 October 1960). I am extremely grateful to the staff of the Rare Book Collection, Wilson Special Collections Library, UNC-Chapel Hill, especially Emily Kader, Rare Book Research Librarian, for generous assistance in providing me with access to the volume, helping to secure permissions for me to photograph the volume and to allow those photographs to be posted online. While select images from the volume are reproduced in this essay, the entire volume may be viewed online at the John Gower Society website (www.JohnGower.org).

[2] The Hanes Foundation for the Study of the Origin and Development of the Book was established at UNC-CH in 1929.

complete, and a Spanish notation that potentially situates the volume (and Gower's poem) in a wider conversation about Gower's Iberian connections and literary afterlife. The UNC-CH copy of Caxton's edition of Gower's *Confessio Amantis* illuminates the relationship between the printer and the poem, as well as the ways in which later users of the volume profited from the peculiar material and symbolic prestige that the volume (and its associated author and printer) represents.

England – Westminster

Shortly after establishing himself at Westminster in 1476, Caxton, in his *Book of Curtesye* (1477), echoed Chaucer's assessment of Gower by referring to Gower's "writing morale" and encouraged reading Gower since he is "full of sentence and langage."[3] It would be six more years, however, before Caxton published his edition of the *Confessio*, the work to which his prior encomium referred. By 1483, the publication date of his edition of the *Confessio Amantis*, Caxton had already published a number of works at Westminster, including Chaucer's *Canterbury Tales* (1478) and his translation of Boethius' *Consolation of Philosophy* (1478), *The Chronicles of England* (1480), Trevisa's translation of Higden's *Polycronicon* (1482), and a number of Lydgate's works. In 1483, alongside the *Confessio*, Caxton issued a second edition of *The Canterbury Tales* as well as an edition of *Troilus and Criseyde*.[4]

Caxton's edition of Gower's *Confessio* "seems to have been one of the most popular productions of his press."[5] As N. F. Blake puts it, Caxton "was uniquely placed to chart literary developments in England and abroad," and his work was not merely responsive to the demands of his clients and patrons but preemptive, creating a demand for texts as well as responding to one.[6] While his decision to print the *Confessio* reflects Caxton's editorial work to establish a canon, the production of Caxton's edition of the *Confessio* is also an interesting witness to Caxton's career as a printer. Caxton's *Confessio* is the first large work that he printed in two-column format. Its two hundred and twenty-two leaves are "quired in eights, with

---

[3] F. J. Furnivall, ed., *Caxton's Book of Curtesye*, EETS, e.s., 3 (London, 1868), 32.
[4] Seymour de Ricci, *A Census of Caxtons*, Bibliographical Society Illustrated Monographs 15 (Oxford, 1909), see especially "Books Printed at Westminster," 9–107.
[5] G. C. Macaulay, ed., *The English Works of John Gower*, 2 vols., EETS, e.s., 81–82 (London: Kegan Paul, Trench, Trübner, 1900–01; Oxford: Oxford University Press, 1969), I. ix.
[6] N. F. Blake, *William Caxton and English Literary Culture* (London: Hambledon Press, 1991), 17, cf. 1–18.

four blanks."[7] It is printed in Caxton's Type 4. Gower's Latin commentary appears interlineally rather than in the margins, where it often appears in *Confessio* manuscripts. Space was left before a number of major sections, apparently to allow for the inclusion of woodcuts, drawings or possibly engravings at some later date; spaces were left for initials throughout the volume; and the UNC-CH copy contains the red lettering in these sections throughout the volume. The edition also includes an extensive table of contents, probably drawn from the Latin glosses appearing in the manuscript tradition of the *Confessio*.

As a witness, the UNC-CH copy is flawed in some aspects, while remaining remarkable in others.[8] Foremost among its distinctive features is the rare example it constitutes of an original Caxton binding, one of only a handful extant. The binding of this volume is "brown calf over oak boards, ornamented with geometrical patterns of double-ruled lines and stamped fleurs-de-lis in blind, that is, without gilding."[9] The ruled decoration and the form of the fleur-de-lis impressions mark the UNC-CH volume as the work "of the craftsman known as the first Caxton binder who is thought

---

[7] Martha W. Driver notes further: "the blanks are leaves 1, 8, 9, and 222, though almost all surviving copies lack the blanks or blanks may occur elsewhere in the volume." See "Printing the *Confessio Amantis*: Caxton's Edition in Context," in *Re-visioning Gower*, ed. R. F. Yeager (Asheville, NC: Pegasus Press, 1998), 271. E. Gordon Duff, *William Caxton* (Chicago: Caxton Club, 1905; repr. New York: Burt Franklin, 1970), 94.

[8] The UNC-CH copy is missing some twenty leaves (seventeen printed and three blanks). While it contains the first printed leaf, missing in other copies, this copy nonetheless lacks the final six leaves (comprising the end of Book VIII and Caxton's colophon). Furthermore, one quire (u 8) is mis-bound so that: 136v ends with line 7080 of Book V; 137r begins with line 58 of Book VI; 146v ends with line 1931 of Book VI; 147r begins with line 902 of Book VII; 147v ends with line 1041 of Book VII; 148r begins with line 1932 of Book VI. Throughout this essay, folio numbers given for UNC-CH Incunabula 532.5 represent the folios as they appear in that volume, not the foliation of a complete copy. To allow for easier cross-examination with other copies, "numbered leaf" references refer to the printed leaf numbers as they appear in the volume.

[9] William Wells, "Gower and Caxton," *South Atlantic Bulletin* 27, no. 1 (1961): 10. None of the descriptions provided in de Ricci, either of copies with known owners or copies with unknown owner, match this binding. De Ricci, *Census*, 56–59. Frederick R. Goff, ed., *Incunabula in American Libraries; a Third Census of Fifteenth-Century Books Recorded in North American Collections* (New York: Bibliographical Society of America, 1964), G-329. Wells points out that of the five hundred and seventy-eight copies of Caxton's books listed in de Ricci, only eight retain bindings original to Caxton.

to have followed Caxton to England from Bruges in 1476."[10] Additionally, when the book was recently restored, other Caxton materials were found to have been used as filler or reinforcement inside the original binding, further establishing the volume's production at Caxton's workshop.

ENGLAND – THE INDULGENCE

Important as it is as an example of Caxton's production process, UNC-CH Incunabula 532.5 also offers a unique window into fifteenth-century politics and culture. When the volume was restored by UNC-CH, four filler pieces were removed from the binding. Together they constitute almost the entirety of a papal indulgence, printed by Caxton in 1481, two years before he printed his *Confessio* edition in 1483; Giovanni dei Gigli, a papal nuncio, appears to have commissioned the printing of this indulgence in order to collect revenue for a war against the Turks who had attacked Otranto.[11] The copy found in this binding is one of only four extant, all recovered from other bindings, and this copy is the only one with its opening lines intact.[12]

---

[10] Wells, "Gower and Caxton," 10. For further discussion of the chronology of binding and rubrication in this volume, see also Vaughn Stewart, "Reading Nobility: Authority and Early English Print" (Ph.D. diss., University of North Carolina at Chapel Hill, 2016), 136–44. George D. Painter lists this volume as one of thirteen known bindings by the Caxton binder on Caxton editions: see "Caxton Through the Looking Glass: An Enquiry into the Offsets on a Fragment of Caxton's Fifteen OES, with a Census of Caxton Bindings," in *Studies in Fifteenth-Century Printing* (London: Pindar, 1984), 130–37 (131). Painter posits that this volume may be one attributed as "ownership unknown" by Oldham (viii), but I see no evidence of that, other than the unknown attribution; on this, see J. B. Oldham, *English Blind-stamped Bindings* (Cambridge: Cambridge University Press, 1952), 27 n .5. For a discussion of Caxton bindings, and details on the tools used in this particular volume, see Howard M. Nixon, "William Caxton and Bookbinding," *Journal of the Printing Historical Society* 11 (1976–77), esp. 95 and 108 n. 12.

[11] A. W. Pollard and G. R. Redgrave, *A Short-Title Catalogue of Books Printed in England, Scotland, & Ireland and of English Books Printed Abroad, 1475-1640 2nd ed., Revised & Enlarged*. Completed by Katharine F. Pantzer (London: Bibliographical Society, 1976–91), henceforth STC. STC 14077c.112. "IOhannes de giglis iuris vtriusqe doctor sanctissimi [...] [Indulgence, singular issue, for contributors to the defence of Rhodes.] s.sh.*obl*.4°. [*Westminster, W. Caxton*, 1481.] L(IA.55052).c⁴(frag.).; PML.Ncu(imp.). Duff 209. (Formerly 22586)." See also Paul Needham, *The Printer and the Pardoner: An Unrecorded Indulgence Printed by William Caxton for the Hospital St. Mary Rounceval, Charing Cross* (Washington: Library of Congress, 1986), Cx49. Plural issue, STC 14077c.112, Duff 210, and Needham Cx 50.

[12] Apart from the UNC-CH copy, copies (all with partial or missing opening lines) are owned by the Pierpont Morgan, the British Museum, and King's College, Cambridge. Goff, in his 1964 edition, notes the presence of this indulgence at

A *Caxton* Confessio

The indulgence was first discovered in this volume in 1932 when it was examined by Belle de Costa Green and Seymour de Ricci for then-owner James F. Bell.[13] The four pieces of the indulgence had been used to reinforce the binding of the book, with two pieces pasted to the front board and two to the back board.[14] The indulgence was finally removed from the binding in 1975 during the restoration of the book.[15]

Use of scrap material for such binding filler was, of course, common practice. Indulgences had long been a notable source of revenue for early printers both on the Continent and in England, and while these documents were ephemeral, and often destroyed or discarded after the death of the owner, "probably about six hundred printed editions of indulgence instruments from the fifteenth century survive, more than any other class of early job printing."[16] Many, like the indulgence discovered in this book, appear not to have been distributed or sold, and the copies survive with no names attached to them (plural issue). Given the size and routineness of these print jobs, it is no wonder spare copies were available in print shops and binderies for auxiliary uses like filler for binding.[17] No rationale other than convenience can be assumed for the choice of the indulgence, but its use suggests a possible connection between the Caxton *Confessio* and the commissioner of this indulgence: Giovanni dei Gigli.

Giovanni dei Gigli was born in Bruges in 1434. Educated in Oxford, by 1476 he was living in England and working as a papal collector and nuncio, or ambassador; later he administered the see of Worcester in

---

Chapel Hill, but Stillwell, in her prior 1940 edition, only documents the Pierpont Morgan copy of the indulgence. "S-565 (S511) – 1481. [Westminster: William Caxton, 1481.] Bdsde (4°). *N.B*: Johannes de Gigliis, *Commissary*. For promoting the war against the Turks. *Ref*: C 5507; Duff 209; DeR (C) 58; GW (Einbl) 796. *Cop*: PML (vell) (DeR 58.1); UNCaL." Goff, 564. "S511 – 1481. [Westminster: William Caxton, 1481.] [...] *Ref*: C 5707 [...] *Cop*: PML (vell) (DeR 58.1)." Margaret Bingham Stillwell, ed., *Incunabula in American Libraries: A Second Census of Fifteenth-Century Books Owned in the United States, Mexico, and Canada* (New York: The Bibliographical Society of America, 1940), 463.

[13] "In lifting up a portion of the paper lining of the covers, Mr. de Ricci and I found pieces of the Caxton Indulgence of 1481. If you bought the book, as I understand – from Rosenbach, he will doubtless gnash his teeth when he hears this!" Belle de Costa Greene to James F. Bell, 21 December 1932, UNC-CH Incunabula 532.5 Curatorial File, Wilson Library, University of North Carolina – Chapel Hill. The indulgence was first revealed in print in 1934, by John W. Clark, "A New Copy of Caxton's Indulgence," *Speculum* 9 (1934): 301–03.

[14] Clark, "New Copy of Caxton's Indulgence," 301.

[15] For a discussion of the restoration process for this volume, see S. E. Zach, "The One-Millionth Volume: Restored," *The Bookmark* 45 (1975): 9–12.

[16] Needham, *Printer and the Pardoner*, 30.

[17] Needham, *Printer and the Pardoner*, 26–28, details the use of one such indulgence, cut into strips and applied as reinforcement strips in the folds of quires in bound volumes.

absentia from Rome (1497–98).[18] Caxton printed two indulgences for Gigli: this, in 1481, and a second in 1489 "for the crusade that Henry VII ordered to be proclaimed in England in 1488–9."[19] Caxton was printing such indulgences, a common revenue source for printers along with other ecclesiastical documents, "as early as 1476, and the trade continued until the crisis of Church and State under Henry VIII." By 1481, "it seems to have been routine for the papal collectors such as Giovanni de Gigli to have indulgences printed."[20] While Gigli may have employed Caxton merely as a periodic printer of his documents, the two indulgences some eight years apart suggest the possibility of an ongoing relationship, either in person or via an intermediary, between nuncio and printer. Michael Wyatt states that, "In addition to his ecclesiastical responsibilities in England, Gigli was involved in promoting the revival of English literary culture after the conclusion of the Wars of the Roses. He wrote an epithalamium in celebration of the engagement of Henry VII to Elizabeth of York and subsequently obtained the papal dispensation necessary for the marriage to take place."[21] All of Gigli's extant writings, including his epithalamium for Henry VII and Elizabeth, are in Latin and most appear to have been composed while he was in England. Whatever Gigli's literary interests were in England, they seem to have focused on Latin writings rather than English. Caxton's indulgence-printing business with Gigli occurs at the same time

---

[18] E. B. Fryde et al., ed., *Handbook of British Chronology*, 3rd ed. (Cambridge: Cambridge University Press, 1996), 280.

[19] J. B. Trapp, "Gigli, Giovanni (1434-1498)," *Oxford Dictionary of National Biography*. www.oxforddnb.com. https://doi.org/10.1093/ref:odnb/10670. Two editions: STC 14077c.114 "JOhannes De Gigliis alias de Iiliis [...]" [Indulgence, with blank terminations to suit either singular or plural grantees, to contributors to crusade.] s.sh.*obl*.4°. [*Westminster, W. Caxton*, before 24 Apr. 1489.] L(3 copies, IA.55126-8).c[16].; PML. Duff 211. (Formerly 14100) and "[Anr. ed.] IOhānes de Gigliis [...] s.sh.*obl*.4°. [*Westminster, W. Caxton*, 1489.] D. Duff 212. (Formerly 14101)." Needham, *Printer and the Pardoner*, 89, Cx 88 (common issue) and Cx 89 (single issue).

[20] Felicity Heal, "The Bishops and the Printers: Henry VII to Elizabeth," in *The Prelate in England and Europe, 1300-1560*, ed. Martin Heale (Woodbridge: Boydell Press, 2014), 148. See also Gervase Rosser, "A Note on the Caxton Indulgence of 1476," *The Library*, 6th ser., 7, no. 3 (1985): 256–58.

[21] Michael Wyatt, *The Italian Encounter with Tudor England: A Cultural Politics of Translation* (Cambridge: Cambridge University Press, 2005), 54. Gigli's epithalamium survives in one copy: British Library, Harley 336. On Gigli's participation in literary culture in England, see especially Gilbert and Godelieve Tournoy-Thoen, "Giovanni Gigli and the Renaissance of the Classical Epithalamium in England," in *Myricae: Essays on Neo-Latin Literature in Memory of Jozef IJsewijn, Supplementa Humanistica Lovaniensia*, 16 (Leuven: Leuven University Press, 2000), 141–45, and Greg Walker, *John Skelton and the Politics of the 1520s* (Cambridge: Cambridge University Press, 2002), 37–38.

that Caxton himself was establishing an English literary canon by means of his selection and production of texts.[22]

However, the indulgence is concrete evidence of a business relationship between Caxton and Giovanni – two men who, in their different ways, shared a desire to promote literary history in England. And it is only a short time after the printing of the indulgence in 1481 that UNC-CH Incunabula 532.5 emerged from Caxton's press, with a scrap copy of the indulgence as filler as it was bound. While the indulgence is not proof of a relationship between printer and nuncio, nor of any influence over the *Confessio* copy by Gigli, its presence in the *Confessio* binding, and its timing, opens the possibility of such a relationship and such influence as ground for further study.

Westminster – The Cutouts

Not all such fragments in this volume are as identifiable as the indulgence. Materials relating to the restoration of this volume are archived with the volume at UNC-CH, and these materials include a set of unidentified fragments, mostly scraps, but also one damaged and worn leaf (Figure 11.1a) removed from the volume during restoration. Readily observable on this leaf are two figures, either partially or completely drawn or cut into the leaf. The image on the upper left corner (Figure 11.1b) is a poorly drawn but complete human figure, apparently male, wearing what would seem to be a tunic and leggings, with one hand raised. There appear the beginnings of two lines of faint and damaged text to the right of its upheld hand, perhaps a capital "I" on the upper line and an "e" on the lower.

Apart from the figure on the upper left of the leaf is another, less obvious, figure on the opposite, lower right, corner, less detailed but still clearly a human figure. Rather than being drawn on the page, this figure is cut into the page, with part of the figure cut through the entire leaf but part only partially impressed or carved into the page. While the figure is

---

[22] In 1477, a year after we have evidence of Gigli in England, Caxton printed his first edition of *The Canterbury Tales*. Within two years of this indulgence printing, Caxton printed his *Confessio*. There is evidence that Caxton was working with the *Confessio* prior to printing the first indulgence for Gigli. J. A. W. Bennett, Derek Pearsall, and Norman Blake have all discussed the striking similarities in language between Caxton's *Confessio* and his translation, in 1480, of Ovid's *Metamorphoses*. Caxton's translation of Ovid's Ceix and Alcione story includes specific lines from the *Confessio*. J. A. W. Bennett, "Caxton and Gower," *Modern Language Review* 45 (1950): 215–16; Derek Pearsall, "The Gower Tradition," in *Gower's Confessio Amantis: Responses and Reassessments*, ed. A. J. Minnis (Cambridge: D. S. Brewer, 1983), 188; N. F. Blake, "Caxton's Copytext of Gower's *Confessio Amantis*," *Anglia* 85 (1967): 282, 292. See also Driver, "Printing," 277.

FIGURE 11.1a. Unidentified Leaf. University of North Carolina at Chapel Hill, Wilson Library Incunabula 532.5.

FIGURE 11.1b. Detail 1 (Human Figure 1) – Unidentified Leaf. University of North Carolina at Chapel Hill, Wilson Library Incunabula 532.5.

FIGURE 11.1c. Detail 3 (Cutout of Human Figure 2) – Unidentified Leaf. University of North Carolina at Chapel Hill, Wilson Library Incunabula 532.5.

even less sophisticated than its neighbor on the leaf, the cutting is precise and careful, as if performed meticulously with a very sharp implement (Figure 11.1c).[23]

Given that the Caxton *Confessio* left spaces for woodcuts or later drawing insertions, these crude figures may have been initial draft or scratchpad images, later abandoned or never incorporated. The one clear aspect of the most complete figure on this scrap is that it is standing in a posture that clearly suggests – with its raised hand and pointed finger – that it is lecturing or stating something declaratively. If the figure was meant to represent a character in the *Confessio*, Genius, as the figure who regularly speaks declaratively throughout the *Confessio*, would be a likely candidate, but the figure is not in the garb of a priest.

Unfortunately, the documentation of preservation work for the volume, which contains a photographic record of the removal of the indulgence, does not record from where in the volume these fragments were removed, and the conservator's notes do not mention the images or the fragments at all.[24] The binding had been repaired twice before this restoration, but there is no indication that those repairs extended into the boards. Wherever they were originally located in this volume, the fragments, along with their intriguing cutouts, seem to have originated in Caxton's shop.

---

[23] I am rather at a loss as to what to make of these images. They are not wholly unlike the drawings added to the Pierpont Morgan copy of the *Confessio* that Martha Driver discusses; the figures in the UNC-CH volume have some similar characteristics – such as the lined tunic, foot shape, and foot placement. PML 689 The Pierpont Morgan Library, New York. Driver, "Printing," 289, Fig. 1. For further discussion of the illustration in the Pierpont Morgan copy of Caxton's *Confessio*, see also Nicola F. McDonald, "'Lusti Tresor': Avarice and the Economics of the Erotic in Gower's *Confessio Amantis*," in *Treasure in the Medieval West*, ed. Elizabeth M. Tyler (York: York Medieval Press, 2000), 136–54. The UNC-CH copy figures are nowhere near fine or precise enough to be a basis or template for woodcut. Neither do they appear to reflect any of the woodcuts Caxton employed in the second edition printing of *The Canterbury* Tales, which he produced the same year as the *Confessio*. All figures from that edition of *The Canterbury Tales* are either on horseback or seated and the *Confessio* fragment figures are standing. For a discussion of woodcuts in Caxton's 1483 *Canterbury Tales*, see David R. Carlson, "Woodcut Illustrations of the *Canterbury Tales*, 1483-1602," *The Library*, 6th ser., 19 (1997): 25–67. Fully digitized versions of both Caxton's first and second (with woodcuts) editions of *The Canterbury Tales* are available online, "Caxton's Chaucer," *British Library*, https://www.bl.uk/treasures/caxton/homepage.html.

[24] Zack, "Restored," 11.

England – Owners Reading and Using the *Confessio*

As one might expect given its age and history, this volume contains a number of marginal notations, doodles, and other marks added to the volume over the centuries. The first printed leaf, with Caxton's introduction prior to the table of contents, contains the signature of an unknown user, John Crofton. At the end of the table of contents, prior to the beginning of the Prologue to the *Confessio*, on the top of a blank leaf (numbered leaf 9), there appears a couplet:

> John a Kynaston wrote this
> to you sweet hart & cossen ywis.

The name, "John a Kynaston," appears again in the blank space before the opening of the Prologue. The identity of John Kynaston is still unknown, though he may be a distant relation of early seventeenth-century writer Sir Francis Kynaston (1586–1642) who, among other literary accomplishments, published a facing-page Latin translation of Chaucer's *Troilus and Criseyde*. The Kynaston heritage leads back several generations; though there are no "John" names recorded prior to Edward, a number appear later from the eighteenth century onward.[25]

Apart from John Crofton and John Kynaston, the volume includes two further names. The first is a partial and damaged signature in the top margin of folio 063v. In his note on this volume, Howard Nixon lists this former owner as "Thomas Genway (?) of Endlam," though the signature is so corrupt that, absent other evidence or further mention, this reading seems speculative.[26] The second name, "John Leche," appears on folio 86v (numbered folio 80v) in a much clearer ink. Nixon records this name as "J. H. Leche," but the signature itself is clearly "John Leche." The name of John Leche appears in a number of other manuscripts and early books.[27]

---

[25] R. Malcolm Smuts, "Kynaston, Sir Francis (1586/7-1642)," *Oxford Dictionary of National Biography*. John Burke, *A Genealogical and Heraldic Dictionary of the Peerage and Baronetage of the British Empire*. 6th. ed. (London: Henry Colburn, 1839), 607.

[26] Nixon, "William Caxton and Bookbinding," *Journal of the Printing Historical Society* 11 (1976–77): 92–113 (108, n. 12).

[27] The Huntington's description of HM 136, a *Brut Chronicle*, states: "Twice the name of John Leche, s. XV^{ex} or s. XVI^{in} appears, possibly by the same person who copied arts. 1 and 4: on front flyleaf iii, Liber Johannis Leche; on back flyleaf i, Liber Johannis Leche de Wico Malbano in Com. Cestr. (Nantwich, Cheshire). Other books owned by this and later John Leches are: Oxford, Trinity College 13, 14, 16a and 49; Sotheby's, 12 December 1966, lot 216; London, Brit. Lib. Add. 41321; Sotheby's, 6 December 1971, lot 14." HM 136, *Guide to Medieval and Renaissance Manuscripts in the Huntington Library*, http://bancroft.berkeley.edu/digitalscriptorium/huntington/HM136.html.

Jeremy Griffiths identified the Leche signature in Oxford, Trinity College, MS E 14 (fol. 69r) as the same signature as others found in a number of Trinity College, Oxford manuscripts.[28] Unfortunately, the Leche signature in UNC-CH Incunabula 532.5 does not appear to match the signature in any of these; the hand appears to date from the seventeenth century or later as opposed to the early Leche of the Trinity College manuscripts and others.[29] Identification beyond that is complicated by the fact that there appears to have been "a John Leche in every generation."[30]

It is not surprising, given the focus of the *Confessio*, to see notes about love from readers and users. Further along in the volume, at folio 44r (numbered leaf 37), there appear in the bottom margin some seven lines of verse interrupted by cropping of the bottom of the page, in a hand distinct from the signatures in the book (Figure 11.2).

These lines lament the inability of men to rule women in love, and they represent the opening lines of the early Tudor poem, "The Nutbrown Maid," which appeared around the turn of the sixteenth century and was popular enough to elicit a parody, "The New Notborune Mayd Upon the Passion of Cryste."[31] The entirety of "The Nutbrown Maid" runs some 180

---

[28] Jeremy Griffiths, "Book Production Terms in Nicholas Munshull's *Nominale*," in *Ashgate Critical Essays on Early English Lexicographers*, vol. 2: Middle English, ed. Christine Franzen (Farnham: Ashgate, 2012), 338–39, 345 n. 14, 346 n. 16. For further discussion of the various Leche signatures in these manuscripts, and the identification of these signatures, see Masako Takagi, "Caxton's Exemplar and a Copy from Caxton's Edition of the *Chronicles of England*: MS HM136 and BL Additional 10099," *Arthuriana* 22 (2012): 120–39 (132–34), as well as John M. Manly's and Edith Rickert's discussion of the Leche signatures in the Trinity College, Oxford MS ARCH.49 (TO) copy of *The Canterbury Tales* in *The Text of the Canterbury Tales* (Chicago: University of Chicago Press, 1940), I.540–44.

[29] Leche names appear well into the nineteenth century. See W. D. Parish, *List of Carthusians, 1800-1879* (Lewes: Farncombe and Co., 1879), 143, and Samuel Bagshaw, *History Gazetteer, and Directory of the County Palantine of Chester* (Sheffield: George Ridge, 1850), 8, 36, 121–62 *passim*.

[30] Jeremy Griffiths, "The Manuscripts," in *Lollard Sermons*, ed. Gloria Cigman, EETS o.s. 294 (Oxford: Oxford University Press, 1989), xv. The signature may be identifiable as one of the many found in the Leche of Carden MSS collection at the Cheshire Archives of the Cheshire Record Office, which contains a number of Leche documents.

[31] The earliest extant copy of "The Nutbrown Maid" may be found in Richard Arnold's *Customs of London* (*STC* 782), dating from about 1503. For a discussion of the various sixteenth- and seventeenth-century witnesses, see William A. Ringler Jr., "The Nutbrown Maid (a Reconstructed Text)," *English Literary Renaissance* 1, no. 1 (1971): 27–36. On the parody, and subsequent popularity of the poem in the sixteenth through eighteenth centuries, see Emily A. Ransom, "*The New Notborune Mayd Vpon the Passion of Cryste*: The Nutbrown Maid Converted [with text]," *English Literary Renaissance* 45, no. 1 (2015): 3–31. I am grateful to the attendees of my presentation concerning this volume at the joint IV International Congress of the John Gower Society and Fifteenth Biennial

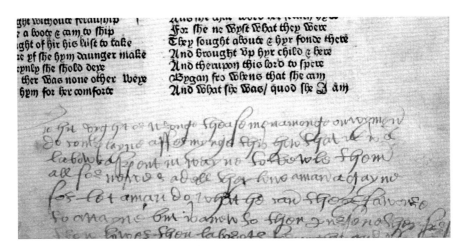

FIGURE 11.2. Opening lines of "Nutbrown Maid" added to bottom margin of fol. 043r. Incunabula 532.5. Rare Book Collection, Wilson Special Collections Library, UNC-Chapel Hill. By permission of Wilson Special Collections Library, UNC-Chapel Hill.

lines (in later versions, 360 lines in thirty 12-line stanzas) and takes the form of a debate between a man and a woman concerning the constancy of women. The opening voice, presumably male, laments the fickleness of women's affections. The subsequent, presumably female, voice counters with a story loosely in the vein of the Patient Griselda tradition, focusing upon a woman's fidelity in the face of adversity and cruel tests by her beloved. The subsequent story also features two voices: a supposedly banished knight and the Nutbrown Maid who loves him. The knight states that the maid will face great adversity if she follows him into banishment, including slander and discomfort, but she repeatedly states that she remains with him because of her love for him. When all these protestations fail, in a final test, he says to her that he loves another, more beautiful, woman. Her remarkable reply is that his threatened paramour "shall me fynd softe and kind and curteys euery owre, / glad to fulfill all that she will comaund me to my powere." The knight finally acknowledges her great fidelity, and the two narrative voices conclude that "Here may ye see that women be in love meke, kynd, and stable."[32]

Conference of the Early Book Society for their help in identifying this fragment, especially Julia Boffey of Queen Mary University, London, and Helen Phillips, Cardiff University, who serendipitously presented on "The Nutbrown Maid" in her paper "Debating the 'Nut Brown Maid': Questions about the Sources, Printing Contexts and Varied Afterlife of an Early Sixteenth-Century Ballad."

[32] Text from Ringler, "The Nutbrown Maid," ll.153–54, 175.

A Caxton Confessio

While the lines presented in UNC-CH Incunabula 532.5 focus upon the misogynistic opening stanza of the poem, considering that passage in isolation ignores the wider context of an apparently well-known poem that ultimately was intended to praise women. In addition, the tenor of the UNC-CH Incunabula 532.5 copy of the opening lines of the poem is affected by both an interesting variant in the passage and its placement in the *Confessio*. Some variants are minor, such as using the plural of "favor," but one variant in particular is striking. Rather than saying it is a labor spent in vain "to love them well," the lines in UNC-CH Incunabula 532.5 state it is a labor spent in vain "to rule them all."[33]

Though placement of these lines may be happenstance, the lines appear well into Gower's "Tale of Constance" (Book II.1075–1148). The "Tale of

---

[33] The following transcription is placed side-by-side with the text as reconstructed by Ringler, with line-breaks adjusted in Ringler to coincide with UNC-CH Incunabula 532.5:

UNC-CH Incunabula 532.5	*Ringler's Edition*
Be hit ryght or wronge thease men amonge on wymen do complayne affermynge this how that it is a labowre spent in vayne to rewle them all for never a dele they love a man agayne for let a man do what he can theyre favorse to attayne but if a new to them [...] trew lover then laboreth for noght and [...]	[1] Be it right or wrong, thes men amonge on wymen do complayn, [2] affermyng this, how that it is a labowre spent in vayn [3] to love them well, for neuer a dele they love a man agayn. [4] For late a man do what he can ther favowre to attayn, yet yf a newe to them pursue, ther ferste trew lover than [6] labowreth for nowght, for from her thowght he is a banysshed man.

Ringler argues that the copy text for the poem should be Balliol College Oxford MS. 354 (B). The lines in UNC-CH Incunabula 532.5 appear to follow B, or at least do not exhibit any of the variants from the other witnesses. Ringler notes the following variants for this opening stanza:

[1] Be it right or *B 21 03*; Right & noe *P*. on *B 21 03*; as *P*. wymen *B 03 P*; woman *21*.

[2] how that *B 21 03*; what a thing *P*. a *B 21 03*; of a *P*.

[3] *omit P*.

[4] late *B 21 03*; lett *P*. attayn *B 21 03*; obtaine *P*.

[5] yet *B 21 03*; & *P*. ther *B 21 03*; the *P*.

[6] labowreth *B 21 03*; he labours *P*. for from *B 21*; and from *03*; fur from *P*. he *B 21 03*; for he *P*.

Constance" (as well as Chaucer's "Man of Law's Tale," which may have been based upon Gower's version) is a secular saint's life in which Constance is betrayed repeatedly, remains true to her faith in the face of adversity, and is finally rewarded with prosperity and reintegration into her family. Unlike the Patient Griselda tradition, it is not a male lover who tests a woman's love in the "Tale of Constance"; rather, Constance's Christian faith is tested by physical trials and pagan antagonists. As María Bullón Fernández states, Constance's role is both "active and public": it speaks to the appropriate powers of both Church and State through her devotional acts.[34] Ultimately, Constance is found on the seas and rescued by a Roman senator. It is at this point – her wanderings across the sea, her survival of an attempted rape, and her rescue by the senator – that the UNC-CH Incunabula 532.5 "Nutbrown Maid" excerpt appears.

The story of Constance concerns religious faith – her faith in the love and protection of God – whereas "The Nutbrown Maid" presents the story of a secular love, yet both texts portray women who cannot be ruled by the figures of earthly authority. The Nutbrown Maid is threatened with the possibility of adversity, including the possibility of living her life in the greenwood, rather as Constance is buffeted by the seas as she is cast adrift and finds herself off the shores of northern Spain. It is possible that this connection was made by the anonymous annotator in writing the lines from the "Nutbrown" in the margins of the Chapel Hill Gower.

An Iberian Connection

Another annotation in UNC-CH Incunabula 532.5 hints at the book's possible movement (or at least reach) beyond England. Folio 183v includes the following two-line note, in brown ink, written in the top-left margin:

> En la villa de Vermeo, cabeça
> de Bisscaya, a qua días dell mes
>
> [In the town of Bermeo, at the head
> of the Province of Biscay, on the fourth day of the month]

The hand appears to be mid- to late-sixteenth century, perhaps copied between 1550 and 1575, and to be written either by a professional scribe or,

---

[34] María Bullón-Fernández, *Fathers and Daughters in Gower's* Confessio Amantis: *Authority, Family, State and Writing* (Cambridge: D. S. Brewer, 2000), 75–101. See also her "Engendering Authority: Father and Daughter, State and Church in Gower's 'Tale of Constance' and Chaucer's 'Man of Law's Tale'," in *Re-Visioning Gower*, ed. R. F. Yeager (Asheville: Pegasus Press, 1998), 129–46.

at the least, by someone accomplished in late cursive Gothic court hand.[35] While such a note alone cannot conclusively place the book in Bermeo, the implications of the possibility that it was in fact located there during the sixteenth century are provocative. Bermeo was an important port in the sixteenth century for trade between Spain and England (and also between Spain and Ireland, where Spanish fishing vessels were much maligned for intruding upon Irish fisheries). As Janet Hollinshead points out, lucrative import and export activities between England and the Basque region were maintained well into the end of the sixteenth century.[36] The Anglo-Spanish War (1585 to 1604) curtailed much of that trade, so that, for example, between five and ten ships per year left Bristol for northern Spain and Biscay from 1503 to 1566, but none are recorded from 1598 to 1601.[37] So approximate dating of the note as mid- to late-sixteenth century would coincide with a period of significant trade between England and northern Spain, prior to the curtailment of the war. We are left, however, with the question of why this particular book might have made such a journey or have been in the hands of a Spanish or Basque merchant either in England or abroad.

As far as is known, Gower's *Confessio Amantis* was the first English vernacular poem to be translated into a continental vernacular. In the early fifteenth century, possibly at the behest of Philippa of Lancaster, daughter of John of Gaunt and sister of Henry IV, and wife to João I of Portugal from 1387 until her death in 1415, the *Confessio* was translated into Portuguese as *Livro do Amante*.[38] Another translation, into Castilian, was completed shortly thereafter (probably no later than 1428) and the only copy we have of the Castilian version, *Confisyon del Amante* (Escorial, MS g-II-19), dates from

---

[35] The final clause would correctly read "a quatro dias del mes." "Qua" is not a regular abbreviation for "quatro" but appears to be the correct reading here. I am greatly indebted to Mauricio Herrero Jiménez and Ana Sáez-Hidalgo, both of the University of Valladolid, for their assistance in translating these lines and in identifying the hand of this note and its context.

[36] Janet E. Hollinshead, "Chester, Liverpool and the Basque Region in the Sixteenth Century," *The Mariner's Mirror* 85 (1999): 387–95. See also Michael M. Barkham, "The Spanish Basque Irish Fishery & Trade in the Sixteenth-Century," *History Ireland* 9 (2001): 12–15.

[37] Jean Vanes, ed., *Documents Illustrating the Overseas Trade of Bristol in the Sixteenth Century* (Bristol: Bristol Record Society, 1979), 170.

[38] For discussions of the possible commissioners of the poem, see Joyce Coleman, "Philippa of Lancaster, Queen of Portugal – and Patron of the Gower Translations?" in *England and Iberia in the Middle Ages, 12th-15th Century: Cultural, Literary, and Political Exchanges*, ed. María Bullón-Fernández (New York: Palgrave Macmillan, 2007), 135–65, and R. F. Yeager, "Gower's Lancastrian Affinity: The Iberian Connection," *Viator* 35 (2004): 483–515.

the end of the fifteenth century.[39] The Iberian translations appear to have emerged during a period when the Portuguese and Castilian courts were artistically interested in the very qualities that distinguish the *Confessio*: its encyclopedic nature, its focus on the education of kings, and its theological framework of confession.[40] The early history of the *Confessio*'s life in Iberia may explain a later interest in this book by a Spanish or Basque merchant or customer at that time.

UNITED STATES

How this volume made its way to the United States is still a mystery, but in 1932 the book was purchased for $13,500 from the famous turn-of-the-century antiquarian bookseller, A. S. W. Rosenbach, by James Ford Bell, founder of General Mills.[41] Bell's extensive collection of rare books later served as the foundation for the James Ford Bell Library at the University of Minnesota, and in the 1930s he was still actively procuring items, even throughout the Great Depression. The volume was listed for sale as item no. 16 in H. P. Kraus' Catalogue 90 from 1959.[42] According to documentation archived with the volume, UNC-CH acquired the book, for $40,000, in 1960 as its one millionth volume.[43] The purchase of the book was made possible by the John Wesley and Anna Hodgin Hanes Foundation for the Study of the Origin and Development of the Book, which was established in 1929 by Frederic M. Hanes and his seven siblings "in honor of their parents, John W. and Anna H. Hanes, to fund the purchase and the future acquisition of rare books and related materials at UNC-Chapel Hill."[44] The book's early

---

[39] For an overview of the dating and context for the Castilian manuscript, see Ana Sáez-Hidalgo, "Iberian Manuscripts of Gower's Works," in *The Routledge Research Companion to John Gower*, ed. Ana Sáez Hidalgo, Brian W. Gastle, and R. F. Yeager (New York: Routledge, 2017), 110–16.

[40] For a discussion of these artistic ties between the *Confessio* and these Iberian courts, see Clara Pascual-Argente, "Iberian Gower," in *The Routledge Research Companion to John Gower*, ed. Sáez Hidalgo, Gastle, and Yeager, 214–17. Ana Sáez Hidalgo notes that for Iberian readers the *Confessio* "was continually valued for its moral advice." "Gower in Early Modern Spanish Libraries: The Missing Link," in *John Gower: Others and the Self*, ed. Russell A. Peck and R. F. Yeager (Cambridge: D. S. Brewer, 2017), 344.

[41] James F. Bell, Notebook, *Book Prices 1925/1940*, James F. Bell Papers, James Ford Bell Library, University of Minnesota, Minneapolis, MN. I am grateful to Marguerite Ragnow, Curator, James Ford Bell Library, for finding this journal among Bell's papers. The approximate real price of $13,500 paid in 1932 is equivalent to $242,000 in 2017 dollars.

[42] H. P. Kraus Ltd., New York, Catalogue 90 (1959), no. 16.

[43] An approximate real price of $331,000 in 2017 USD, representing a substantial increase in worth of the volume from 1932 to 1960.

[44] https://library.unc.edu/wilson/rbc/history/

life appears to have been marked primarily by an interest in the religious and artistic cachet of the poem, with readers and users drawing upon the *Confessio*'s literary value and Gower's reputation as a moral, and especially Roman Catholic, medieval English poet, while the book's more recent worth has drawn increasingly upon its association with Caxton, and the prestige of the book itself. I venture to hope that future scholarship may explore the possibilities raised by the use of the indulgence and the mysterious cut-out images in the binding and the annotations in English and Spanish, and the light which these may cast upon the long and well-traveled history of the UNC-CH *Confessio Amantis*.

CHAPTER 12

ENGLISH POETS IN PRINT: ADVERTISING AUTHORSHIP FROM CAXTON TO BERTHELETTE*

Julia Boffey

THOMAS BERTHELETTE'S 1532 EDITION of the *Confessio Amantis* (STC 12143) is one of the important landmarks in the history of the printing of English literary authors, making available, in an impressive folio volume, the best-known work of one of the poets who, in Skelton's words, "first garnisshed our Englysshe rude."[1] Appearing in the same year as William Thynne's folio edition of *The workes of Geffray Chaucer* (printed by Thomas Godfray: STC 5068), Berthelette's *Confessio* took its place among a succession of printed titles whose publishers seem to have been especially concerned to construct and promote a history of poetry written in English, and (in Gower's words) "for Engelondes sake."[2] Such concern was manifest

---

* Throughout this discussion STC numbers refer to Alfred W. Pollard and G. R. Redgrave, *A Short-Title Catalogue of Books Printed in England, Scotland and Ireland and of English Books Printed Abroad 1475–1640*, 2nd edition revised and enlarged by W. A. Jackson, F. S. Ferguson and Katharine F. Pantzer, 3 vols (London: Bibliographical Society, 1986–1991). Titles of early printed books are mostly given in the forms listed in STC, unless for well-known works such as *The Canterbury Tales*, where familiar modern forms have been used. Dates given for early printed books follow the forms suggested in STC, in the case of books printed before 1501 taking account of any revisions in *Printing in England in the Fifteenth Century. E. Gordon Duff's Bibliography with supplementary descriptions, chronologies and a census of copies by Lotte Hellinga* (London: Bibliographical Society, 2009). Shelfmarks of specific copies of early printed books are given when relevant.
[1] From *The Garland of Laurel* (line 387), in *The Complete English Poems of John Skelton*, ed. John Scattergood, revised ed. (Liverpool: Liverpool University Press, 2015), 274–315.
[2] Gower, *Confessio Amantis*, prologue (line 24), in *The Complete Works of John Gower*, ed. G. C. Macaulay, 4 vols (Oxford: Clarendon Press, 1899–1902), II, 2. The British Library copy of Berthelette's edition, shelfmark 641.k.3, is available in digital facsimile at http://access.bl.uk/item/viewer/ark:/81055/vdc_100026167536.0x00 0001#ark:/81055/vdc_100026167556.0x00000a (accessed 10 January 2018).

not only in the publishers' choice of works to print but also in the varieties of paratextual apparatus with which the chosen works were set forth. Thynne opted for a preface addressed "To the kynges hyghnesse" as the primary means of establishing the credentials of his edition of Chaucer's works.[3] Berthelette, who was both editor and printer of the 1532 *Confessio Amantis*, followed suit with a dedication to Henry VIII (whose service he had joined as King's Printer early in 1530) and some other prefatory gestures.[4] These two dedications are instances of the kinds of printed paratextual material that has come to attract some attention, particularly in relation to Chaucer and Lydgate, and to the varieties of cultural capital to be claimed by making their works newly available in print.[5] Other forms of paratextual experiment have been highlighted in early printed editions of Skelton's works, where the significance of elements such as printed annotations and woodcuts to the construction of authorial presence has been noted.[6] Gower's early existence in print has not gone unmarked, but while Berthelette's 1532 edition of the *Confessio Amantis* has been the subject of valuable recent studies,[7] less has been said about the extent to which the construction of "Gower as author"

---

[3] STC 5068, sigs Aii-Aiii. The preface was written for Thynne, or in collaboration with him, by Sir Brian Tuke, treasurer of the chamber to the king. See further, most recently, Greg Walker, *Writing under Tyranny: English Literature and the Henrician Reformation* (Oxford: Oxford University Press, 2005), 29–99.

[4] Similar kinds of authorizing paratext had been used in another substantial work, Lord Berners' translation of Froissart's *Chronicles*, produced by Richard Pynson, Berthelette's predecessor as King's Printer, in a two-volume edition in 1523 and 1525 (STC 11396-7). Here the printer incorporated firstly a woodcut of the royal arms and then a translator's preface extolling the virtues of learning from history, and recounting Henry VIII's commissioning of the translation. See further Siân Echard, *Printing the Middle Ages* (Philadelphia: University of Pennsylvania Press, 2008), 162–72.

[5] For the fullest discussion, see Alexandra Gillespie, *Print Culture and the Medieval Author: Chaucer, Lydgate and their Books, 1473-1557* (Oxford: Oxford University Press, 2006). Also relevant are Joseph A. Dane, *Who is Buried in Chaucer's Tomb? Studies in the Reception of Chaucer's Book* (East Lansing, MI: Michigan State University Press, 1998); William Kuskin, *Symbolic Caxton: Literary Culture and Print Capitalism* (Notre Dame, IN: University of Notre Dame Press, 2008), and ed., *Caxton's Trace: Studies in the History of English Printing* (Notre Dame, IN: University of Notre Dame Press, 2006).

[6] Jane Griffiths, *Diverting Authorities: Experimental Glossing Practices in Manuscript and Print* (Oxford: Oxford University Press, 2014), and "What's In a Name? The Transmission of 'John Skelton, Laureate' in Manuscript and Print," *Huntington Library Quarterly* 67 (2004): 215–35.

[7] Derek Pearsall, "The Gower Tradition," in *Gower's 'Confessio Amantis': Responses and Reassessments,* ed. A. J. Minnis (Cambridge: D. S. Brewer, 1983), 179–97; N. F. Blake, "Caxton's Copytext of Gower's *Confessio Amantis*," *Anglia* 85 (1967): 282–93, and "Early Printed Editions of *Confessio Amantis*," *Mediaevalia* 16 (1993 for 1990): 289–306; Tim William Machan, "Thomas Berthelette and Gower's *Confessio*," *Studies in the Age of Chaucer* 18 (1996): 143–66; Siân Echard, "Gower in Print," in *A Companion to Gower*, ed. Siân Echard (Cambridge: D. S. Brewer, 2004), 115–35; Robert R. Edwards, "Gower's Reception," *The Routledge Research*

in this book might reflect the larger landscape of authorial promotion during the later fifteenth and early sixteenth centuries. The discussion that follows here will attempt to situate the 1532 *Confessio* in that landscape, outlining some of the forms of attention given to authorship in English books printed before 1532, and concentrating especially on discernible continuities and innovations in the printing of poetry in English.

In the years before 1532 Gower was not an especially visible author in printed form. Caxton's edition of *Gower de confessione amantis* appeared in 1483 (STC 12142)[8] and was not reprinted either by Caxton or by the successor to his business, Wynkyn de Worde. Between 1483 and 1532 the only one of Gower's works to appear in printed form was *The Praise of Peace*, in Thynne's 1532 collected edition of the works of Chaucer, the printing of which seems to have preceded Berthelette's printing of the *Confessio* by a matter of months.[9] Caxton's edition of the *Confessio*, as usual for Caxton's books, had no title page. His brief introductory discussion of the work, on the second folio of the first gathering of the book, provided some curious biographical details about the author, details sanctioned by no known manuscript source and not to be repeated in Berthelette's edition: "[t]his book is intituled confes=//sio amantis / that is to saye in englysshe the confessyon of // the louer maad and compyled by // Johan Gower squyer borne in Walys // in the tyme of kyng richard the second."[10] In this portion of the book Caxton supplied a table of contents, starting with a summary of Gower's prologue to Richard II, and beginning his account of the contents of the first book with the information that "fyrst the auctor nameth thys // book confessio amantis."[11] Rather surprisingly, in the light of the general sparseness of paratextual provision, he included at the end of the *Confessio* a number of the short Latin pieces found variously in manuscript copies of the *Confessio* and of the *Vox Clamantis* and *Traitié Selonc Les Auctours Pour Essampler Les Amantz Marietz*.[12] The decision to include these may have

---

Companion to John Gower, ed. Ana Sáez-Hidalgo, Brian Gastle, and R. F. Yeager (London and New York: Routledge, 2017), 197–209.

[8] The year is given in the colophon as 1493, but with the identification I Richard III, i.e. 1483.

[9] Peter W. M. Blayney, *The Stationers' Company and the Printers of London, 1501-1557*, 2 vols (Cambridge: Cambridge University Press, 2013), I, 279. The preface to STC 12143 mentions Chaucer's works "nowe of late put forthe to gether in a fayre volume" (sig. aaiij^v).

[10] STC 12142, sig. ij.

[11] STC 12142, sig. ij.

[12] Now most conveniently accessible, with translations, in *John Gower: The Minor Latin Works with "In Praise of Peace"*, ed. R. F. Yeager and Michael Livingston, Middle English Texts (Kalamazoo, MI: Medieval Institute Publications, 2005), http://d.lib.rochester.edu/teams/publication/yeager-gower-the-minor-latin-works-with-in-praise-of-peace (accessed 2 January 2018), these are (in the order in which they appear): *Quam cinxere freta*; *Quia unusquisque*; *Eneidos bucolis*; *Est amor*; *Orate pro anima*.

been prompted by the availability of some space in the book's final quire, a gathering of six, in which the English text ended on the verso of sig. [Civ]. Caxton's edition seems likely to have followed very closely the sequence of contents in the manuscript from which he worked. The detail he offered about Gower's Welsh birth has the rather vague air of hearsay; and he certainly went to no lengths at the start of the book to promote or advertise Gower as author in an elaborate way.

Berthelette's 1532 edition is quite different. He supplied a title page giving prominence to Gower's name, and set on the verso of this a Latin stanza found in many *Confessio* manuscripts, headed "Epigramma autoris in suum librum" (it begins "Torpor, hebes sensus").[13] He continued with his dedication to Henry VIII (a feature reflecting the introductory material to Thynne's Chaucer), following this with an address to the reader which spends some time on a discussion of Gower's text and the different states of the prologue. Next came a table of contents. At the end of the *Confessio* he rounded things off briskly with just a colophon, omitting the extra items that Caxton had used to mark his book's conclusion. For both Caxton and Berthelette, Gower was an old, dead author; but their sense of how to present one of these things was evidently rather different. Berthelette put his paratextual materials at the front of his book, for example, contributing more forcefully to the construction of an *auctor*, whose voice was represented in both Latin and English verse, and whose writings, as outlined in the address to the reader, were treated as a subject for textual analysis.

What options would have been open to an early printer who wanted to foreground an author as a distinctive presence? For Caxton, a printer's preface was the prime location for this. His prefaces offered biographical details about and assessment of a range of noble authors, including Boethius, Cato, Chaucer, Cicero, and Higden.[14] He was interested in noble translators too, and took care to supply information about John Trevisa, Benedict Burgh, and Anthony Woodville, for instance. But he does not seem to have seen reference to authorship as a necessary element of the prefatory material in a book, and information about authorship if present at all is sometimes reserved for the colophon or epilogue: reference to Christine de Pizan in his translation of *The book of fayttes of armes & of chyualrye* (1489, STC 7269), for example, is reserved until the epilogue. The variability of Caxton's practice (a feature which may of course relate to the availability of space in different parts of the books he printed) can be illustrated with his treatment of Lydgate's poems. Although Caxton invoked Lydgate's name at both the beginning and end of his edition of *The lyf of our lady* ([1483], STC 17023-4), he made no reference to him at all in his editions of *The temple of glas* ([1477], STC 17032), *The horse the ghoos & the sheep* ([1476],

---

[13] Macaulay, ed., *Complete Works*, II, 1.
[14] See the materials assembled in N. F. Blake, ed., *Caxton's Own Prose* (London: André Deutsch, 1973).

[1476–77], STC 17018-19), and *The chorle and the birde* ([1476], [1476–77], STC 17008-9). In some respects, Caxton seems to have been much more interested to draw attention to the kind of work he was printing (a history, a romance, a work of instruction) or to the circumstances in which it recommended itself to him.

For Caxton's immediate successors, opportunities to include information about authorship as an element of the prefatory or concluding matter in a book were multiplied by the possibilities opened up by new presentational developments. Title pages, although not provided by Caxton, gradually became regular parts of books printed in England in the final decades of the fifteenth century. First used by Machlinia about 1485 for a treatise on the pestilence translated from Canutus (STC 4591), and then by de Worde about 1493 for *The chastysing of goddes chyldern* (STC 5065), these offered inviting spaces for information about authors.[15] De Worde's 1498 edition of *The Canterbury Tales* (STC 5085), for example, unlike Caxton's two earlier editions, has a title page that includes the author's name. Woodcuts were also provided with more frequency in books from the 1480s onwards, and could be called into service to represent particular authors.[16] Martha Driver's work on the careful use of woodcuts and woodcut ornaments made by Wynkyn de Worde in title-page design has outlined the variety of ways in which authorial presence might be suggested. While some of de Worde's "author" woodcuts are simply generic representations of scholars, others have specific identifying features, with John Fisher and John Alcock, authors of sermons and treatises, depicted as mitered bishops, and Richard Rolle as a robed saint.[17] Such images seem to have been put to effective use as "branding" devices, probably mostly designed more with an eye to the marketing of the books than to any other consideration.

In relation to the design of books containing the works of English poets, however, these practices were employed somewhat sporadically. Although Lydgate might seem to have been a prime candidate for a branding exercise, to be easily represented in woodcuts as a Benedictine monk, many of the early printed editions of his works do not mention his name, and – if they employ woodcuts at all – use images related (sometimes only approximately) to the contents of the works in question. Among the many shorter works of Lydgate to appear in early printed editions only Pynson's 1520? edition of the *Testament* (STC 17035) and the spuriously Lydgatian collection known as *The prouerbes of Lydgate*, printed twice by de Worde (1510?, 1520?,

---

[15] See more generally Margaret M. Smith, *The Title-Page and its Early Development 1460-1510* (London and New Castle, DE: British Library and Oak Knoll Press, 2000).
[16] Caxton's c.1481 edition of his own translation of *The myrrour of the worlde* (STC 24762) introduced the use of woodcuts into English books.
[17] Martha W. Driver, *The Image in Print: Book Illustration in Late Medieval England and its Sources* (London: British Library, 2004), 77–114 (figs. 10, 11, 9).

STC 17026-7), illustrate an author on their title pages, and both of these use generic author images rather than anything with specific relevance to Lydgate. Early editions by Pynson of his much longer works, the *Troy Book* and *The Fall of Princes*, make some attempt to represent him but insist explicitly on his role as "translator" rather than author.

The woodcut that follows the table of contents to the 1513 *Troy Book* (STC 5579), beneath a heading introducing "The Prologue of the Translatoure," depicts a black-robed monk presenting the book. The two different images used by Pynson at the start of the 1494 and 1527 editions of *The Fall of Princes* (STC 3175, 3176) are however much less specific, and both were used by Pynson elsewhere to represent another author (the chronicler Robert Fabyan).[18] In *The Fall of Princes*, Lydgate is again billed as "translator" rather than author; and just as the *Fall* itself, a translation of Boccaccio's *De casibus virorum illustrium*, was often referred to as "Bochas" in wills and booklists, so this is also the identity it is given in the printed editions.

Long poems like the *Troy Book* and *The Fall of Princes* made for big books, whether in manuscript or printed form, and it may be that printers somehow felt that substantial, well-known works of this kind needed no introduction. In Pynson's 1526 three-volume edition of Chaucer's works, no mention is made of Chaucer as author in the individual volumes containing *The Canterbury Tales* and *Troilus and Criseyde* (STC 5086 and 5096): in each of these it may have been considered sufficient to announce the work by title alone, with Chaucer's authorship needing no special fanfare. Only the volume containing shorter poems (not all of which are by Chaucer, in point of fact) has an author attribution on its title page: "Here begynneth the boke of fame / made by Geffray Chaucer. With dyuers other of his works" (STC 5088). Chaucer is mentioned on the title page of de Worde's 1517 edition of *Troilus and Crisedye* (STC 5095), but any sense that this is evidence of real concern for recording authorship is somewhat complicated by the inclusion at the end of the poem of three patently non-Chaucerian stanzas, presumably composed by one of de Worde's staff writers but attributed to "the auctour."[19]

Chaucer and Lydgate, like Gower in 1532, were by this time long-dead authors, hardly likely to trouble printers with suggestions of their own about the design of the books in which their poems were transmitted. And it seems that their major works evidently had a reputation of their own in which authorship was somehow rolled up without needing to be made explicit. Living poets writing in the Chaucerian tradition, individuals who perhaps personally transmitted their works to printers, were by the 1520s

---

[18] Edward Hodnett, *English Woodcuts 1480-1535*, 2nd ed. (Oxford: Oxford University Press, 1973): both images (1945 and 1512 in Hodnett's list) were used for the 1516 edition of Fabyan's work (STC 10659).

[19] C. David Benson and David Rollman, "Wynkyn de Worde and the Ending of Chaucer's *Troilus and Criseyde*," *Modern Philology* 78 (1981): 275–79.

beginning to be treated rather differently. Skelton is a notable example here. The first of his works to appear in print, *The bowge of courte*, produced by de Worde in editions of about 1499 and about 1510 (STC 22597, 22598), bears no trace of Skelton's name. But *A goodly garlande or chapelet of laurell*, printed by Richard Faques in 1523 (STC 22610), looks very different. A work full of internal references to Skelton *auctor*, and featuring appearances by all of Gower, Chaucer, and Lydgate, it is introduced on the title page as the creation of "mayster Skelton Poete laureate," with a suitable author woodcut. The strengthening of Skelton's reputation, together with changes in title page conventions, seem to have made a real difference. As Julie Smith and Mary Erler have noted, some of the other 1520s printings of Skelton's works are "branded" with variations on a generic scholar woodcut in keeping with this reputation.[20]

The differences between Caxton's and Berthelette's presentations of Gower as author are thrown into relief when both are compared with early sixteenth-century printed editions of works by living English poets. Poems by Stephen Hawes, Alexander Barclay, and William Neville, whose works were transmitted almost entirely in printed form, are given interesting billing. In the case of Hawes, who seems to have had a close relationship with Wynkyn de Worde, it seems possible to detect a gradual foregrounding of the author's name as successive editions of his works were printed. In the edition of about 1504 of *The example of virtu* (STC 12945), the earliest of Hawes' works to be printed, his identity as author is noted not on the title page but at the end of the preliminary table of contents.[21] In the 1509 editions of *The conuercyon of swerers* and the *joyfull medytacyon* (STC 12943, 12953), his name is noted at the end of the works (in the case of the *conuercyon,* with a stanza attributed to "The Author"). But for the [1515] edition of *The comforte of louers* (STC 12942.5), de Worde put Hawes' name on the title page. And for the 1530 edition of *The exemple* (sic) *of vertu* (STC 12947), although his name is given at the end as in the 1504 edition, it is also there on the title page, in a rather elaborate introductory description of the book.

The printing of William Neville's single surviving work, *The castell of pleasure*, illustrates what seems to have been a growing taste for paratextual material relating to authorship, and underlines an interest in authorial

---

[20] Julie A. Smith, "The Poet Laureate as University Master: John Skelton's Woodcut Portrait," in *Renaissance Rereadings: Intertext and Context*, ed. Maryanne Cline Horowitz, Anne J. Cruz, and Wendy A. Furman (Urbana: University of Illinois Press, 1998), 159–83; Mary C. Erler, "Early Woodcuts of Skelton: The Uses of Convention," *Bulletin of Research in the Humanities* 87 (1986–87): 17–28.

[21] Since de Worde's 1509 edition of *The Pastime of Pleasure* (STC 12948) survives only in fragmentary form, it is not possible to know what was on its title page. The 1517 edition (STC 12949) follows the pattern of *The exemple of virtu*, with a reference to Hawes as author at the end of the preliminary table of contents.

identity and biography that would be apparent in the 1532 editions of both Chaucer and Gower. A dream vision somewhat in the mode of Hawes, the *castell* was first printed by Henry Pepwell in 1518 (STC 18476) and reprinted by de Worde in about 1530 (STC 18475). Nothing explicit is said about the author's identity on the title page of either of these two editions, but the poem is framed with a dialogue in which "Thauctour" discusses the topic of literary composition with an individual who names himself variously as "Copland" and "lymprimeur" (that is, Robert Copland, who was intermittently a printer himself, and also translated and edited a number of works for other printers).[22] In the dialogue Copland suggests that although the author has written a creditable poem, it will have no appeal for a reading public concerned only with profit and sensual appetite. The author's role is to defend his "boke of loue" as a work suitable for the pastime of "gentyll people": a form of pleasing flattery for anyone who has already purchased a copy, or might be persuaded into buying one. The author's identity is eventually revealed at the end of the book in an envoy in French, in which he is addressed as "Treshonoure filz du seigneur latimer / Surnomme Neuyl, de noble parentage, / O maistre guillaume." Although the framing dialogue invokes a "real" relationship between author and editor, Copland says rather comically in his envoy that he has had to edit the work without the benefit of input from its author, and he admits in his final (English) stanza that he presents it "Without your lycence."

Copland represents himself here and elsewhere as an energetic mediator between authors and readers, providing prefaces and envoys not only to his own translations but also to other works which came his way, or which he searched out for printing. The paratextual material he provides reveals an interest in the means by which texts come into being, and especially in the different agents (authors, translators, editors, printers) and processes responsible for their communication to an audience. Such a consciousness informs Berthelette's *Confessio*, and seems in general terms to have been on the rise during the early decades of the sixteenth century. It is perceptible in some of the writings of Alexander Barclay, primarily a translator, whose work (like that of Hawes and Neville) was transmitted almost entirely in printed form. In the preface to his handbook called *The introductory to wryte and to pronounce Frenche* (printed by Copland in 1521, STC 1386), Barclay carefully distinguishes between the different activities of men of letters: "some hath compyled, some translated, and some deuysed dyuers maters to dyuers purposes." When writing of his own endeavors he is careful to

---

[22] See *Robert Copland: Poems*, ed. Mary Carpenter Erler (Toronto: University of Toronto Press, 1993), 3–39 (information about Copland's life), and 58–63 (the dialogue from *The castell of pleasure*). Some of Copland's introductions and envoys are also discussed by Helen Phillips, "Aesthetic and Commercial Aspects of Framing Devices: Bradshaw, Roos and Copland," *Poetica, an International Journal of Linguistic-Literary Studies* 43 (1995): 37–42.

emphasize that he is a translator rather than an original author; a postscript to *The castell of laboure* (a translation from Pierre Gringore's French generally credited to Barclay; STC 12379-82) notes that "The cause why I folowe not these oratoures / Is for lack of intelligence / And that I haue not smelled of the floures / Spryngynge in the garden of parfyte eloquence." This apology is enshrined in a section of the work headed "Actoris excusatio," the *actor* being an agent of transmission distinct from the *auctor*.[23]

The distinctions made by Barclay between the various processes that bring a text into being seem to reflect a generally growing awareness of the body of agents concerned in the production of books – commodities that in printed form were coming to offer increasingly significant opportunities for financial profit. Details about the roles and identities of these various agents gradually settled into more or less conventional locations in the layout of printed books, with printers usually supplying details of their identities and places of residence at the end of a work, for example. But the identities of authors and translators are sometimes registered in curiously teasing ways. Perhaps because he was uncertain about the importance of naming the author, Copland's revelation of William Neville's identity at the end of *The castell of pleasure* is spread over three lines of French from which it has to be excavated as a series of nuggets. In other printed works from this period translators' identities are variously encrypted in acrostics and puzzles: the names of Henry Bradshaw, Thomas Feylde, Christopher Goodwin, and William Walter are all somehow made visible in printed editions of works they translated but in wittily covert ways.[24]

The interest in authorship and agency discernible in the writings of Barclay and Copland appears to have been part of a more general concern with textual matters, a concern evident in Berthelette's prefatory discussion of the differences between the printed and manuscript versions of the *Confessio* that were available to him. Barclay and Copland worried about the accuracy of the texts they mediated, and about the extent to which linguistic change might compromise the comprehensibility of the works they were transmitting. These anxieties surface in some of the framing material attached by Copland to works he prepared for print, taking forms rather more specific than conventional prayers that readers should amend

---

[23] See Cynthia J. Brown, *Poets, Patrons, and Printers: Crisis of Authority in Late Medieval France* (Ithaca, NY: Cornell University Press, 1995), 198–206, for a full discussion of these terms. Distinctions between *l'acteur* and *l'auteur* in a number of late medieval French works are also considered by Helen Phillips, "The Invisible Narrator of the *Chevalier des Dames*," in *Texts and their Contexts: Papers from the Early Book Society*, ed. John Scattergood and Julia Boffey (Dublin: Four Courts Press, 1997), 165–80.

[24] See Henry Bradshaw, *The lyfe of saynt Werburge* (Pynson, [1521]; STC 3506); Thomas Feylde, *The contrauerse bytwene a louer and a Iaye* (de Worde, [1527]; STC 10838.7); Christopher Goodwyn, *The maydens dreme* (Wyer, ?1542; STC 12047); William Walter, *Guystarde and Sygysmonde* (de Worde, 1532; STC 3183.5).

any faults they find. Copland's introduction to the romance *Ipomydon* (de Worde, c.1522, c.1527; STC 5732.5, 5733) laments that this is a "lytell Iest vndepured of speche" but stresses that the printer has to follow what is in front of him: "This is thy copy thou can it not refuse." The envoy he provided for an edition of Chaucer's *Parliament of Fowls* (de Worde, 1530; STC 5092) makes reference to the importance of preserving "thylke same langage that Chaucer to the gaue." Barclay was alert to similar anxieties, and wrote about them specifically in relation to Gower's poetry. At some point in or before 1518, Sir Giles Alyngton had evidently asked him to modernize and abridge the *Confessio Amantis*; although the task was never completed, Barclay wrote perspicaciously, in the prologue to another work, about the content and language of Gower's poem.[25] The official reason he gave for abandoning the commission was that a work about love was inappropriate to his age and vocation (Barclay was at this stage a Benedictine monk). But he stresses as well the challenges posed by Gower's "corrupte Englysshe":

> Right honourable mayster ye me requyred late
> A louers confession abrydgyng to amende
> And from corrupt Englysshe better to translate
> To your request wolde I ryght gladly condyscende
> Were nat that some reders my warke wolde reprehende
> As to my age and order moche inconuenient
> To wryte of thynge wanton nat sad but insolent ... (sig. Aiii).

To some extent Barclay's worries about the state of Gower's English were part of an established topos: Caxton, after all, had made similar comments in some of his prefaces, especially the remarks at the start of his 1483 second edition of *The Canterbury Tales* (STC 5083).[26] But these concerns not unnaturally seem to surface in the apparatus supplied with the works of older English poets as they were printed in the 1520s and onwards. When John Rastell printed Chaucer's *Parlyament of fowles* in 1525?, for example (STC 5091.5), he evidently used a text that had not been printed before, and drew attention to this fact in some stanzas he affixed to the poem:

> And be cause I am assuryd of this thyng
> That this lytyl treatese whiche is called
> The parlyament of fowles was of his [*i.e. Chaucer's*] doyng
> With oft inquisicyon I haue hyt achyuyd
> And hyt publisshide & made to be prentyd ... (sig. [ai]ᵛ).[27]

---

[25] *The myrrour of good maners* (Pynson, 1518?; STC 17242), translated from a Latin treatise by Dominicus Mancinus, apparently at the insistence of Richard Earl of Kent.
[26] Machan, "Berthelette and Gower's *Confessio*," 150–51.
[27] E. J. Devereux, "John Rastell's Text of *The Parliament of Fowls*," *Moreana* 27/28 (1970): 115–20.

When de Worde reprinted the *Parliament* separately again in 1530 as *The assemble of foules*, probably at Copland's urging, the copy was based not on Rastell's edition but on that in Pynson's 1526 *boke of fame* (part of his three-volume Chaucer; STC 5088). He also made use of a manuscript, identified by Mary Erler as Oxford, Bodleian Library MS Bodley 638.[28] These efforts to establish a text anticipate Berthelette's concern about the different available texts of the *Confessio*, and suggest a consciousness that an old author deserved respectful treatment: de Worde and Copland replaced Rastell's woodcut of a bird on a nest with a scholar woodcut, signaling Chaucer's "preclared" status in the words on the title page, and they supplied a preface which categorizes the *Parliament* among "olde morall bokes" from which profit can be derived.[29]

Once we start to map the landscape of printed English poetry in the first three decades of the sixteenth century, and to take note of the activities of individuals such as Copland and Barclay, the emergence of Thynne's Chaucer and Berthelette's Gower in 1532 seems less of a new departure. These are indeed large-scale testimonials to an interest in English verse; but this interest was not new, and its concerns were already marked in some of the features of earlier editions of the works of English poets. With their twin dedications to Henry VIII, Berthelette's Gower and Thynne's Chaucer do however draw to attention an interest in English poetry as a national project – a body of vernacular writing able to generate editions on a par with continental printings of the works of vernacular authors like François Villon, or Alain Chartier, even with *opera* of remoter classical authors. Some connection between the printers Berthelette and Godfray seems to be confirmed by the fact that a woodcut border and some ornamental initials used in the Chaucer edition were lent to Godfray by Berthelette, who had used them himself in a book printed in 1531.[30] And there is certainly evidence that the two editions emerged from the shared interests of a particular circle which saw the value of reproducing poems in printed form and enjoyed access to networks which could make this happen.

More extensive research into these networks, into the personnel involved in the printing of the works of English poets, the connections between them, and the manuscripts and printed books to which they had access, seems likely to be rewarding. Even the most cursory exploration turns up some suggestive indications of the kinds of reading matter available in the circles that have been discussed here. The patron who wanted Barclay to "translate" Gower, for example, Sir Giles Alyngton, married as his first

---

[28] Erler, *Robert Copland*, 137–43, and "Printer's Copy: MS Bodley 638 and *The Parliament of Fowls*," *Chaucer Review* 33 (1999): 221–29.

[29] Hodnett, *English Woodcuts*, numbers 2286 and 926.

[30] See Blayney, *Stationers' Company*, i, 279–80. Blayney notes: "It is therefore reasonable to suppose that Berthelette may have had a stake in the edition, though whether as a major or minor shareholder is a matter for guesswork alone."

wife Ursula Drury, daughter of the Sir Robert Drury who probably owned the Ellesmere manuscript of *The Canterbury Tales* in the early sixteenth century.[31] Berthelette, the printer of Gower, appears to have owned a copy of Pynson's 1494 printing of Lydgate's *Fall of Princes*.[32] The "William Poyntz" whose name appears in a copy of Caxton's 1483 edition of the *Confessio Amantis* was most likely the brother of the Francis Poyntz who translated a work for Berthelette to print, and of the John Poyntz addressed in Thomas Wyatt's first *Satire*, in which *The Canterbury Tales* are explicitly invoked.[33] The translators, editors, and printers who have featured in this essay seem to have had serious interests in the history of English poetry and in those considered most prominent in its shaping: Gower, Chaucer, and Lydgate. Their concern to make the works of these authors available in print necessarily involved them in considering the changing forms of the language and the different states in which texts had survived; and their reading and researches brought these poets to the fore as authors, to be prominently named, celebrated, and sometimes pictured in the printed forms in which their works were transmitted.

---

[31] Biographies of both Alyngton and Drury are available on the website of the History of Parliament online: http://www.historyofparliamentonline.org/. Drury's association with the Ellesmere manuscript (San Marino, Huntington Library, MS EL 26 C 9) is discussed by Ralph Hanna III and A. S. G. Edwards, "Rotheley, the De Vere Circle, and the Ellesmere Chaucer," *Huntington Library Quarterly* 58:1 (1996): 11–35.

[32] BL IB. 55497. See Lotte Hellinga, *A Catalogue of Books printed in the XVth Century now in the British Library. Part XI: England* ('t Goy-Houten, The Netherlands: Hes & De Graaf Publishers, 2007), 274–75.

[33] BL IB. 55077. See Hellinga, *BMC* XI, 142–43.

CHAPTER 13

IN PRAISE OF EUROPEAN PEACE: GOWER'S VERSE EPISTLE IN THYNNE'S 1532 EDITION OF CHAUCER'S *WORKES*

Yoshiko Kobayashi

Floruit Gouerus regnante in Anglia Richardo secundo, cui libros suos dedicauit, et cui de laude pacis cantionem, plenissimam consilii et uirtutis, etiam caecus obtulit. Vixit ad iustam usque senectutem, ut ex eius uersibus quos subscribam apparet.

Dum potui scripsi, sed nunc quia curua senectus
Turbauit sensus, scripta relinquo scholis.[1]

[Gower flourished during the reign of Richard II, to whom he dedicated his books; even when he had become blind he offered him his poem "In Praise of Peace," full of good counsel and virtue. He lived to a ripe old age, as is evident from his lines quoted here:

I wrote while I could, but now that stooped old age
Has muddled my senses, I leave writing to schools.]

THIS DESCRIPTION OF GOWER'S poetic achievement is taken from John Leland's *De uiris illustribus*, an unfinished bio-bibliography of British authors, written, according to its recent editor, James Carley, in two distinct phases, one before the dissolution of the monasteries, and one afterwards in the mid-1540s.[2] Although Leland's aim in this work was to rediscover a native tradition of Latin eloquence, dating back to Roman Britain and culminating in English humanists of his own time, he devoted one chapter

---

[1] John Leland, *De uiris illustribus: On Famous men*, ed. and trans. James P. Carley, with the assistance of Caroline Brett (Toronto: PIMS, 2010), 694–95. This and all subsequent citations from *De uiris illustribus* refer to this edition, which is based on Leland's autograph, Oxford, Bodleian Library, MS Top. gen. c. 4. Translations are also taken from this edition.
[2] Leland, *De uiris illustribus*, xi, clvii. *De uiris illustribus* derived from the extensive survey of monastic libraries that Leland conducted between 1533 and 1536 – a task which he claimed was commissioned by Henry VIII.

each to Gower and Chaucer to celebrate their accomplishments in refining the English language. Leland's account of Gower's poetic career, composed in 1535 or 1536, begins by describing his youth spent in the pursuit of *humaniores literae* and his fondness for Ovid as a model of Latin poetic style. Leland regards Gower's imitation of Ovid in his Latin verses as "studious" rather than "felicitous," but this is hardly surprising, Leland says, in view of the "semi-barbarous age" (*semibarbaro saeculo*) in which the poet lived. According to Leland, even in the present age of cultural efflorescence the "exuberant fruitfulness" (*redundantem felicitatem*) of Ovid's poetry can only be fittingly expressed by the likes of Giovanni Pontano, a distinguished humanist poet of Quattrocento Italy, whom Leland extols as equal to – or even surpassing – Catullus in one of the Latin encomia he wrote in the mid-to-late 1520s.[3] Having thus briefly remarked upon Gower's ambitious if not wholly successful attempts at Ovidian imitation, Leland goes on to praise him as the first to polish the native tongue, which was, before his time, "uncultivated and almost completely unformed" (*inculta et fere tota rudis*). Leland states that Gower's strenuous effort to elevate the vernacular produced work of such high quality that it merits serious attention from cultured readers. Although Leland mentions the *Confessio Amantis*, along with his two other major works – the *Speculum Meditantis* and the *Vox Clamantis* – as the fruit of fine literary endeavor, his particular praise is reserved for Gower's shorter English poem "To King Henry IV, In Praise of Peace." In the passage quoted above, Leland describes it as a poetic gift offered in the spirit of good counsel for the moral edification of the royal reader. Here that royal reader is inaccurately identified as Richard II – an error that resulted from the substitution of *Richardo secundo* for *Henrico quarto* in the first part of the sentence, which originally read *Floruit Gouerus regnante in Anglia Henrico quarto*.[4] The change was made by Leland himself, apparently prompted by his realization that Gower's literary career largely coincided with Richard's, rather than Henry's, reign. Notwithstanding the confusion caused by this rather hasty authorial revision, Leland's comment on "In Praise of Peace" provides important evidence of the fascination that the poem held for a Tudor humanist with close connections with the royal court.

[3] The poem I am referring to here is entitled *Ad Catullum* and included in the collection of Leland's epigrams, the *Principum ac illustrium aliquot & eruditorum in Anglia virorum, Encomia, Trophaea, Genethliaca, & Epithalamia*, edited by Thomas Newton and printed at London by Thomas Orwin in 1589, STC 15447, sig. B1v. This volume also contains three other poems which express Leland's admiration for Pontano's poetic gifts: *Ad Cygnum, Iouiani Pontani cultorem* (sig. A2r), *Ad Famam* (sigs. B1v–B2r), and *De quibusdam nostri saeculi poetis* (sigs. I4r–I4v). For a helpful discussion of these poems, see James P. Carley, "John Leland in Paris: The Evidence of his Poetry," *Studies in Philology* 83 (1986): 1–50, especially 2–3; Andrew Taylor, "John Leland's Communities of the Epigram," in *Neo-Latin Poetry in the British Isles*, ed. L. B. T. Houghton and Gesine Manuwald (London: Bristol Classical Press, 2012), 15–35.

[4] In Carley's edition, authorial revisions are recorded at the bottom of each page.

Leland's interest in Gower's short English poem is shared by other figures closely associated with Henry VIII's court. The first folio edition of Chaucer's "complete" *Workes*, compiled by William Thynne, chief clerk of the kitchen in Henry VIII's household, and printed at London by Thomas Godfray in 1532, assigns a privileged place to "In Praise of Peace" among Chaucerian and non-Chaucerian moral ballades.[5] In Thynne's volume, the poem is properly attributed to Gower and followed by a Latin *Explicit*, which describes the poet as the king's humble orator. It is also accompanied by Gower's other Latin pieces: verses addressed to Henry IV and a poem in elegiac distichs beginning "Henrici quarti primus," the same poem from which Leland quoted the two lines depicting Gower's old age and failing eyesight.[6] That Leland had an intimate knowledge of Thynne's volume is evident from the following passage included in his chapter on Chaucer in *De uiris illustribus*:

> Yet Caxton's edition has been superseded by Berthelet's through the exertions of William Thynne, who showed great labour, persistence, and care in seeking out old manuscripts, and has added a great deal to the first edition. Nor was my close friend Brian Tuke, a miracle of eloquence in the English tongue, without glory in this, since he composed a polished, sparkling, and elegant preface to the last edition.[7]

---

[5] *The Workes of Geffray Chaucer newly printed / with dyuers workes whiche were neuer in print before* (London, 1532), STC 5068. On Thynne's career in the years immediately preceding 1532, see Sidney Lee, "Thynne, William (d. 1546)," rev. A. S. G. Edwards, *ODNB*, online ed.; James E. Blodgett, "William Thynne (d. 1546)," in *Editing Chaucer: The Great Tradition*, ed. Paul G. Ruggiers (Norman, OK: Pilgrim Books, 1984), 35–52; Robert Costomiris, "Some New Light on the Early Career of William Thynne, Chief Clerk of the Kitchen of Henry VIII and Editor of Chaucer," *The Library*, 7th ser., 4 (2003): 3–15.

[6] Apart from Thynne's edition, this Latin poem only survives in London, British Library, Additional MS 59495 (*olim* Trentham), which is also a single manuscript witness to "In Praise of Peace." Although we cannot exclude the possibility that Leland consulted this particular manuscript or one related to it, his use of the Latin distich as a kind of gloss on the immediate circumstances surrounding the composition of "In Praise of Peace" seems to me to indicate that he used Thynne's edition in writing about Gower's poem in *De uiris illustribus*. On the relationship between "Henrici quarti primus" and two other versions of the poem, see *John Gower: The Minor Latin Works* (with "*In Praise of Peace*," edited by Michael Livingston), ed. and trans. R. F. Yeager (Kalamazoo: Medieval Institute Publications, 2005), 79; Arthur W. Bahr, "Reading Codicological Form in John Gower's Trentham Manuscript," *Studies in the Age of Chaucer* 33 (2011): 259–61.

[7] Leland, *De uiris illustribus*, 708–09: "Vicit tamen Caxodunicam aeditionem Bertholetus noster opera Gulielmi Thynni, qui multo labore, sedulitate, ac cura usus in perquirendis uetustis exemplaribus, multa primae adiecit aeditioni. Sed nec in hac parte caruit Brienus Tucca, mihi familiaritate coniunctissimus, et Anglicae linguae eloquentia mirificus, sua gloria, aedita in postremam impressionem praefatione elimata, luculenta, eleganti."

Readers of this passage have been puzzled by Leland's identification of Berthelette as the printer of Thynne's edition. Although it may well be that Leland confused the 1532 Chaucer with the edition of the *Confessio Amantis* printed by Thomas Berthelette, king's printer to Henry VIII, in the same year, we may take his words as reason to believe that Berthelette did have a stake in Thynne's edition, especially given the fact that he lent to Godfray the woodcut border used on the title page of Chaucer's *Workes*.[8] It is also worth noting in this connection that in his letter to the reader in the 1532 edition of the *Confessio*, Berthelette makes special mention of the recent publication of Thynne's volume after quoting Chaucer's address to "moral Gower" at the end of *Troilus and Criseyde*: "The whiche noble warke, and many other of the sayde Chausers, that neuer were before imprinted, & those that very fewe men knewe, and fewer hadde them, be nowe of late put forthe to gether in a fayre volume."[9] Peter Blayney conjectures that Berthelette's intention behind these words may have been to promote the Gower and Chaucer as companion volumes.[10]

The credibility of Leland's statement that the preface to the 1532 Chaucer was written by Brian Tuke has also sometimes been questioned, but recent criticism generally accepts his authorship of the opening paragraph of the preface, which discusses a continuous human endeavor to "beautify" and "better" one's native tongue.[11] Leland's praise for Tuke's

---

[8] Andrew N. Wawn, "Chaucer, *The Plowman's Tale* and Reformation Propaganda: The Testimonies of Thomas Godfray and *I Playne Piers*," *Bulletin of the John Rylands University Library of Manchester* 56 (1973): 177; Blodgett, "William Thynne (d. 1546)," 51. Alexandra Gillespie has shown that the title page border used in the 1532 Chaucer edition "was copied from one designed by Hans Holbein and used for the Johan Froben edition of Erasmus's *Epigrammata* that was printed with More's *Utopia* and some of More's own epigrams in 1518." See Gillespie, *Print Culture and the Medieval Author: Chaucer, Lydgate, and Their Books, 1473-1557* (Oxford: Oxford University Press, 2006), 135.

[9] *Io. Gower de confessione Amantis* (London, 1532), STC 12143, sig. aa.iii v.

[10] Peter W. M. Blayney, *The Stationers' Company and the Printers of London, 1501-1557*, 2 vols. (Cambridge: Cambridge University Press, 2013), 1: 279.

[11] In his "Appendix to the Preface" of the 1775 edition of *The Canterbury Tales*, Thomas Tyrwhitt blames Leland for inaccurately ascribing the preface, which stands in the name of William Thynne, to Brian Tuke, although he does not deny the possibility that it was composed for Thynne by Tuke. See Thomas Tyrwhitt, *The Canterbury Tales of Chaucer, to which are added an essay upon his language and versification, an introductory discourse, and notes*, 4 vols. (London, 1775), 1: xi–xii. More recently, Joseph Dane has argued that Leland's comment is at odds with the following words included in the preface: "I your most humble vassall / subiecte and seruaunt Wylliam Thynne." Dane also doubts the credibility of the handwritten comments in the Clare College copy of the *Workes*, which read: "This preface I sir Bryan Tuke knight wrot at the request of mister clarke of the kechyn then being / tarying for the tyd at Grenewiche." Gillespie, however, maintains that the preface is divided into two sections and that only the first section was written by Tuke. See Joseph A. Dane, *Who Is Buried in Chaucer's Tomb? Studies in the*

eloquence is redolent with affectionate respect for this court official, who, by the time of the publication of Chaucer's *Workes*, had become French secretary to the king and treasurer of the chamber.[12] Leland's close association with Tuke is also attested by the nine poems dedicated to him and published posthumously in Thomas Newton's 1589 collection of Leland's *epigrammata*. In one of these poems, entitled *Ad Briennum Tuccam, Equitem*, Leland compares Tuke to Plotius Tucca, a friend of Virgil, who, after the poet's death, took over the task of editing the *Aeneid* for publication.[13] This comparison of Tuke to the Roman editor of Virgil's epic, together with Leland's characterization elsewhere of Chaucer as "the English Virgil," has led Greg Walker to suggest in his *Writing Under Tyranny* that Tuke was not merely the author of the preface but a co-editor of the 1532 edition of Chaucer.[14]

If it is reasonable to assume, as Walker does, that Thynne and Tuke were both actively involved in decisions about the scope and structure of the Chaucer edition, then one wonders why they chose to print Gower's ballade, a poem which had never before appeared in any of the printed editions of Chaucer's works. Walker argues that an answer to this question may be found in the part of the poem in which Gower calls for Christian unity in the face of the threat from heathen forces:

> To yeue vs peace was cause why Christ dyde
> Without peace may nothing stonde auayled
> But nowe a man may se on euery syde
> Howe Christes faythe is euery day assayled
> With the paynems distroyed & so batayled
> That for defaute of helpe and of defence
> Unneth hath Christ his dewe reuerence.[15]

Walker argues that the poem's message must have had particular resonance for court officials and diplomats in the early 1530s because this was the time when "the backdrop to diplomatic activity in Europe was provided by fervent discussion of the possibility of an attack upon Christendom by

---

Reception of Chaucer's Book (East Lansing: Michigan State University Press, 1998), 39–43; Gillespie, *Print Culture and the Medieval Author*, 140.

[12] On Tuke's career, see P. R. N. Carter, "Tuke, Sir Brian (d. 1545)," *ODNB*, online ed.

[13] Leland, *Encomia*, sigs. C3v–C4r.

[14] Greg Walker, *Writing Under Tyranny: English Literature and the Henrician Reformation* (Oxford: Oxford University Press, 2005), 62–64. Leland praises Chaucer as an English follower of Virgil in his *In laudem Gallofridi Chauceri, Isiaci* (*Encomia*, sig. K4r). This epigram is also included in his entry on Chaucer in *De uiris illustribus*.

[15] *The Workes of Geffray Chaucer*, sig. 3T5v (ll. 190–96). All quotations from "In Praise of Peace" follow Thynne's 1532 edition, with line numbers given parenthetically in the text.

the 'paynem' Turks."[16] As J. Christopher Warner observes, with the capture of Belgrade and the island of Rhodes by the Ottoman Sultan, Suleiman the Magnificent, in 1521 and 1522, "Europe's conception of war against the Turk was transformed from a religious crusade for the recovery of Constantinople and Jerusalem to the preservation of western civilization."[17] During the rest of the decade, anxieties over the Ottoman threat to Christendom grew as the Turks invaded Hungary twice and laid siege to the city of Vienna for three weeks in 1529. Walker cites a speech made by Tuke in the Council chamber in October 1532, in which he tried to reassure the other members of the Council about the Holy Roman Emperor Charles V's commitment to the defense of Hungary against Turkish aggression.[18] Walker suggests that Tuke's speech is an indication of his pro-Imperial sympathies, which made him deeply concerned about England's strained relations with the Empire as a result of Henry VIII's divorce campaign. Walker maintains that even though Tuke was a favored official entrusted with the task of facilitating the king's case against his first marriage, this did not prevent him from advocating "moderation in the pursuit of the divorce campaign and the direction of foreign policy." In Walker's view, the inclusion of Gower's ballade in Chaucer's *Workes* is "designed to address a political agenda that was both very specifically pertinent to the circumstances of 1532, and rather more critical of the Crown than previous accounts have allowed."[19]

I find Walker's interpretation particularly insightful in that it highlights Gower's plea for Christian unity as the central theme of "In Praise of Peace." Although this poem has long been read in relation to the Lancastrian propaganda designed to justify Henry IV's seizure of the throne, critical attention has begun to shift in recent years to put more emphasis on its international context. This trend is best explained by Sebastian Sobecki, who demonstrates that the poem's meaning cannot be fully appreciated unless it is read against the background of the worsening Anglo-French

---

[16] Walker, *Writing Under Tyranny*, 95.
[17] J. Christopher Warner, *Henry VIII's Divorce: Literature and the Politics of the Printing Press* (Woodbridge: Boydell Press, 1998), 96.
[18] Walker, *Writing Under Tyranny*, 70.
[19] Walker, *Writing Under Tyranny*, 97. Kathleen Forni also stresses the contemporary relevance of "In Praise of Peace" as it was printed in Thynne's volume, but she sees it, rather, as "overtly nationalistic and monarchical." She writes: "Although Henry IV's usurpation and the Great Schism are the subjects of Gower's address, the royalist assumptions here would have clearly appealed to the Tudor Henry whose own ostensible sensitivity about the issue of legitimacy had led to direct conflict with the papacy." See Kathleen Forni, *The Chaucerian Apocrypha: A Counterfeit Canon* (Gainesville: University Press of Florida, 2001), 50–51.

relationship in the immediate aftermath of Henry's usurpation.[20] Early in the poem Gower reminds the reader that when Christ assumed manhood, "Peace was the firste thyng he lette do crye / Ayenst the worldes rancour and enuy" (174–75).[21] Despite this fundamental injunction against the use of violence, Christian nations are mired in internecine warfare, not for the sake of justice but merely in pursuit of "worldes good" (262).[22] At the heart of the poem is a critical assessment of the Anglo-French conflict, which emphasizes its devastating effects on the security of Europe and its interconnectedness with another form of division: the papal Schism. Employing pathological images of the body politic, Gower represents the Schism as a disease spreading from the head of Christendom to all its limbs.[23] Thus torn apart by inner discord, the Christian world grows vulnerable to the threat of Saracen invasion, as described in the stanza quoted above. Since the divided papacy is the ultimate cause of the ills besetting Christian Europe, it "ought of reason first to be redressed" (255),[24] but seeing the Church utterly incapable of overcoming its internal dissensions, let alone acting as a peacemaker between the warring nations, Gower insists that it is now the responsibility of secular princes, especially the kings of England and France, to restore Christian peace and unity:

> But though the heed of holy churche aboue
> Ne do nat al his hole busynesse
> Amonge the people to sette peace and loue
> These kinges oughten of her rightwysenesse
> Her owne cause among hem selfe redresse
> Tho Peters shyp as nowe hath lost his stere
> It lythe in hem the barge for to stere. (225–31)[25]

The same message is repeated at the end of the poem as Gower urges Henry and all the other Christian princes to achieve peace "or more myschefe fal" (382).[26]

---

[20] Sebastian Sobecki, "*Ecce patet tensus*: The Trentham Manuscript, *In Praise of Peace*, and John Gower's Autograph Hand," *Speculum* 90 (2015): 925–59. See also R. F. Yeager, "*Pax Poetica*: On the Pacifism of Chaucer and Gower," *Studies in the Age of Chaucer* 9 (1987): 97–121, and my "Letters of Old Age: The Advocacy of Peace in the Works of John Gower and Philippe de Mézières," in *John Gower: Others and the Self*, ed. Russell A. Peck and R. F. Yeager (Cambridge: D. S. Brewer, 2017), 204–22. On pages 935–37 of his article, Sobecki provides a helpful overview of the previous scholarship that focuses on the domestic dimension of the poem.
[21] *The Workes of Geffray Chaucer*, sig. 3T5v.
[22] *The Workes of Geffray Chaucer*, sig. 3T6r.
[23] Kobayashi, "Letters of Old Age," 208.
[24] *The Workes of Geffray Chaucer*, sig. 3T6r.
[25] *The Workes of Geffray Chaucer*, sig. 3T5v.
[26] *The Workes of Geffray Chaucer*, sig. 3T6v.

Greg Walker argues that when Gower's ballade was printed in the early 1530s, its message was thought to address real contemporary anxieties over the mounting tensions among European powers resulting from Henry VIII's pursuit of the annulment of his first marriage. That Thynne and Tuke's edition asserts the contemporary relevance of Gower's poem is the idea repeatedly emphasized by Walker's analysis, and this is the second point on which I fully agree with his interpretation. But it seems to me that the question of why this particular poem appealed to such people as Tuke and Leland demands further exploration. In the remainder of this essay, I will approach this question from a slightly different angle by bringing Gower's poem into conversation with the peace discourse developed among Henry VIII's humanist officials and their friends during the decades leading up to the publication of Thynne's volume.[27] In doing so, I will seek to offer fresh perspectives on the Tudor reception of Gower's poetry.

A fine illustration of such humanist discourse is provided by the Latin oration delivered by Richard Pace in October 1518 to celebrate the proclamation of the Treaty of London.[28] Also known as the Treaty of Universal Peace, this international peace agreement was signed by England and France, with the provision for the inclusion of other major and minor European sovereignties. Earlier that year, Pope Leo X had published his plan for a five-year truce among European powers to form a basis for a cooperative crusade against the Ottoman Turks. Legates were dispatched to England, France, Germany, and Spain to proclaim the papal truce. When Lorenzo Campeggio arrived in England as legate *a latere*, Cardinal Wolsey seized this occasion to "twist the papal truce into a shape of his own

---

[27] My understanding of the early modern peace discourse is indebted to the following studies: Robert P. Adams, *The Better Part of Valor: More, Erasmus, Colet, and Vives, on Humanism, War, and Peace, 1496-1535* (Seattle: University of Washington Press, 1962); Joycelyne G. Russell, *Peacemaking in the Renaissance* (Philadelphia: University of Pennsylvania Press, 1986); Philip C. Dust, *Three Renaissance Pacifists: Essays in the Theories of Erasmus, More, and Vives* (New York: Peter Lang, 1987); Ben Lowe, "Peace Discourse and Mid-Tudor Foreign Policy," in *Political Thought and the Tudor Commonwealth: Deep Structure, Discourse and Disguise*, ed. Paul A. Fideler and T. F. Mayer (Abingdon: Routledge, 1992), 108–39; Ben Lowe, *Imagining Peace: A History of Early English Pacifist Ideas, 1340-1560* (University Park: Pennsylvania State University Press, 1997); Catherine Curtis, "The Social and Political Thought of Juan Luis Vives: Concord and Counsel in the Christian Commonwealth," in *A Companion to Juan Luis Vives*, ed. Charles Fantazzi (Leiden: Brill, 2008), 113–76.

[28] Richard Pace, *Oratio Richardi Pacei in pace nuperime composita et foedere percusso inter inuictissimum Angliae regem et Francorum regem christianissimum in aede diui Pauli Londini habita* (London, 1518), STC 19081a. An English translation of the oration is included in Appendix A, "Richard Pace's oration," in Russell, *Peacemaking in the Renaissance*, 234–41.

planning."²⁹ What Wolsey proposed was a multilateral treaty of permanent duration under which all the signatories would undertake not to attack any other signatory and, in case of a threat to or breach of the peace, agree to submit the matter to the arbitration of Henry VIII. If no resolution could be reached, the signatories would be bound to declare war on the aggressor and to prosecute it until peace had been restored and reparation made.³⁰ As Catherine Curtis observes, "[t]he treaty was framed in such a way as to take the reins of the Christian empire from the hands of the pope alone, and place them partially in those of the princes."³¹ As ambassador and secretary to Henry VIII, Pace was one of the treaty's signatories, along with Thomas More and Cuthbert Tunstall.³² His oration was immediately printed in London by the king's printer, Richard Pynson, and Jean de Gourmont issued both the Latin text and an anonymous French translation (*Orayson en la louenge de la paix*) in Paris in the same year.³³

The oration opens with a eulogy on Henry VIII, whom Pace praises as a man of great learning, just as Gower posits the royal dedicatee of his ballade as a learned reader well conversant in "olde bokes" (96).³⁴ In other respects, too, Pace's oration recalls the themes addressed in Gower's poem. After citing Silius Italicus and the Greek orator Isocrates to demonstrate that peace is the best of nature's gifts to mankind, Pace asks himself why he turns to the pagan authors when Christ himself is a Prince of Peace "sent to reconcile the world to the Father and to instil into human hearts mutual love and indissoluble charity" (*missum ad mundum patri conciliandum et mutuum amorem indissolubilemque charitatem humanis animis instillandum*).³⁵ Similarly, as we have seen, Gower urges his reader to bear in mind that the first teaching Christ offered to the world was peace, "whiche is the foundement / Of charite" (179–80).³⁶ Pace then proceeds to highlight the advantages of "health-bearing peace" (*salutiferam pacem*) by setting them in contrast to the infinite evils of the "plague of war" (*pestem belli*),³⁷ in a

---

[29] Garrett Mattingly, "An Early Non-Aggression Pact," *Journal of Modern History* 10 (1938): 1–30 (6).
[30] Mattingly, "An Early Non-Aggression Pact," 7. See also Glenn Richardson, *The Field of Cloth of Gold* (New Haven: Yale University Press, 2013), 5–6.
[31] Curtis, "The Social and Political Thought of Juan Luis Vives," 117.
[32] Tunstall also gave an oration two days after Pace delivered his, on the occasion of the solemnizing of the betrothal of Princess Mary and the Dauphin of France. The marriage of the royal children was to cement the concord between the chief protagonists of the peace treaty. On Tunstall's oration, see Curtis, "The Social and Political Thought of Juan Luis Vives," 123.
[33] James Hutton, *Themes of Peace in Renaissance Poetry*, ed. Rita Guerlac (Ithaca, NY: Cornell University Press, 1984), 82, n. 5.
[34] *The Workes of Geffray Chaucer*, sig. 3T5r.
[35] *Oratio Richardi Pacei*, sig. A4r; Russell, *Peacemaking in the Renaissance*, 236.
[36] *The Workes of Geffray Chaucer*, sig. 3T5v.
[37] *Oratio Richardi Pacei*, sigs. B1r, A4v; Russell, *Peacemaking in the Renaissance*, 239, 237.

manner reminiscent of the imagery of sickness and medicine used by Gower to discuss war and peace. In speaking of the treaty, Pace invokes the image of the ship of Peter tossed on the seas, the same image employed by Gower to describe the problems arising from the divided papacy. Pace's use of the image is likewise designed to call attention to the correlation between internal discord and external threats, as is shown by the following passage:

> If it [peace] was needful at any other time, surely nothing can be so needful in these times of ours, when the whole Christian world is tossing and heaving like a ship at sea blown about by the wind, and a vast inexplicable danger to the Christian republic threatens from the external enemy of Christ's name. [...] Awake then ye Christian princes, holding – as the apostle says – the same wisdom, the same charity, the same unanimity![38]

For Pace, as for Gower, the Turkish threat creates the necessity for peace and union among all Christian princes, and such universal peace, according to Pace, can only be achieved when the kings of England and France "energetically and faithfully" (*strenue simul et fideliter*) commit themselves to this urgent task.[39] From here the oration shifts to an encomium on Henry VIII and Francis I, who are both presented as young monarchs endowed with personal prowess and abundant resources for war, and yet as having each "repressed by reason and counsel all that youthful spirit that is wont to be intent on gloriously extending frontiers" (*represso per rationem et consilium omni iuuenili spiritu: qui finibus per gloriam proferendis maxima parte intentus esse solet*).[40] The oration concludes with an expression of joy over the long-awaited restoration of peace and concord to the Christian world.

Glenn Richardson argues that Pace's oration is not as pacifist or pro-French as it may first appear. Drawing attention to its recurrent emphasis on Henry's military prowess and princely fidelity, Richardson maintains that the oration is at heart "a forceful assertion of Henry's personal and moral superiority over Francis" and "a warning to the French against discounting the significance of the treaty of Universal Peace and challenging the new status quo."[41] Yet even if, as Richardson suggests, Pace's primary concern is to make the French king acknowledge Henry's international prominence as the arbiter of Europe,

---

[38] *Oratio Richardi Pacei*, sigs. A5r–A5v; Russell, *Peacemaking in the Renaissance*, 237: "Quae si vnquam alias necessaria fuit: certe hac nostra tempestate / nihil potest esse aeque necessarium: vt pote quum totus orbis christianus ceu nauis in mari vento agitata vacillet et fluctuet: et ingens atque inexplicabile reipublicae Christianae periculum ab externo Christi nominis hoste immineat. [...] Expergiscimini igitur O principes christiani: idem secundum apostolum sapientes / eandem charitatem habentes / et id ipsum vnanimes sentientes."
[39] *Oratio Richardi Pacei*, sig. A5v; Russell, *Peacemaking in the Renaissance*, 238.
[40] *Oratio Richardi Pacei*, sig. B2r; Russell, *Peacemaking in the Renaissance*, 240.
[41] Richardson, *The Field of Cloth of Gold*, 29.

it cannot be denied that his oration is couched in the rhetoric of Christian humanist advocacy of peace. Pace interweaves his oration with echoes from the series of pacifist writings published by his friend Erasmus in the years immediately preceding the proclamation of the treaty. At the center of the oration is cited the Greek poet Pindar's proverb "Solis inexpertis bellum esse dulce" [War is sweet only to those who have not experienced it],[42] an obvious reference to Erasmus' famous essay *Dulce bellum inexpertis*, published in the 1515 edition of his *Adagia*.[43] In expanding on the contrast between pestilential war and health-giving peace, Pace draws on both this adage and *Querela pacis* [The Complaint of Peace], another of Erasmus' anti-war tracts that appeared in 1517. Also influenced by these two Erasmian texts is the passage in which Pace condemns the unnaturalness and irrationality of war by invoking the image of animals peaceful in their kinds: "But if not even tigers plot this manner of destruction against themselves, ought not men, who are endowed with reason, to do better than the beasts in any virtue?"[44] We may also find another source of inspiration for Pace's oration – or, for that matter, the whole concept of the treaty itself – in Erasmus' idea, succinctly articulated in his *Institutio principis christiani* [The Education of a Christian Prince] (1516), that "[t]he princes must set out to establish a perpetual peace among themselves and make common plans for it."[45]

It is thus no wonder that the successful conclusion of the treaty negotiations elicited an enthusiastic response from the Dutch humanist. In May 1519 Erasmus sent a letter to Henry VIII to celebrate his outstanding leadership in bringing about perpetual peace and thereby restoring "an age truly of gold" in which "the eternal Godhead is reconciled to us once more."[46] Presumably echoing Pace's eulogy on Henry, Erasmus praises the king for his firm determination to pursue peace despite his possession of "all the sinews of war."[47] The king is dedicated to promoting peace and the

---

[42] *Oratio Richardi Pacei*, sig. A4v; Russell, *Peacemaking in the Renaissance*, 237.
[43] This adage was published separately as *Bellum Erasmi* in 1517 and became an immediate success. See Ben Lowe, *Imagining Peace*, 163–64. Pace's indebtedness to Erasmus in his oration is discussed in James Hutton, *Themes of Peace in Renaissance Poetry*, 82, 225.
[44] *Oratio Richardi Pacei*, sig. A4v; Russell, *Peacemaking in the Renaissance*, 236: "Quod si ne tigrides quidem huiuscemodi in sese perniciem meditentur: nonne decet vt homines ratione præditi / quauis virtute feras superent beluas." This motif as it appears in Renaissance literature is analyzed in detail by Hutton, *Themes of Peace in Renaissance Poetry*, 220–64.
[45] Erasmus, *The Education of a Christian Prince*, trans. Neil M. Cheshire and Michael J. Heath, with the *Panegyric for Archduke Philip of Austria*, trans. and ed. Lisa Jardine (Cambridge: Cambridge University Press, 1997), 97.
[46] Erasmus, *The Correspondence of Erasmus: Letters 842 to 992, 1518 to 1519*, Vol. 6 of *Collected Works of Erasmus*, trans. R. A. B. Mynors and D. F. S. Thomson, annotated by Peter G. Bietenholz (Toronto: University of Toronto Press, 1982), 359, 357.
[47] Erasmus, *The Correspondence of Erasmus: Letters 842 to 992*, 358.

"well-being of the commonwealth" because, endowed with "a lofty mind worthy above all of a Christian monarch," he wisely perceives that nothing is more pernicious than warfare among Christian nations and "that nothing renders Christ's people so formidable to the enemies of our religion as concord between princes and between their peoples."[48] As these quotations show, Erasmus' praise of Henry is hyperbolic, but in a manner typical of his laudatory writings in general, this letter is a hybrid of panegyric and exhortation.[49] Having told Henry that a king's authority is an effective force when he issues orders, Erasmus asks him "how much greater the effect when he displays obedience to his own orders and holds the standard of his own laws before his eyes all his life long." Although Erasmus hastens to add that no one is "more strictly observant of his obligations" than Henry, this is not simple praise but a covert exhortation to the king to uphold the spirit of the treaty and to make the concord truly perpetual.[50] Likewise, under the guise of admiring the king's learning, Erasmus seeks to persuade him that the cultivation of *bonae literae* is essential for the proper execution of kingship and for the fulfillment of his role as the peacemaker of Europe: "it will be your Majesty's doing when in time to come, just as in old days it was the special glory of kings to excel in knowledge, so it will be again a most excellent thing for a prince to be well read."[51] Written as a "mirror for princes" with the specific intent to advocate peaceful settlement of conflicts, Erasmus' letter to Henry VIII provides another point of comparison with Gower's ballade, which takes the form of a verse epistle addressed to the ruling monarch with a similar intent.

Between the Treaty of London of 1518 and the Field of Cloth of Gold of 1520, "hopes for peace among Henry VIII's humanist counsellors and their friends remained high."[52] In the summer of 1520, in a narrow field in northern France, a tournament was held to inaugurate peace and alliance between England and France, and amidst a sumptuous display of amity between the two kings, Richard Pace again gave an oration in praise of peace, beseeching God "of all his infinite goodness, to be pleased to render this peace […] perpetual."[53] The peace so extravagantly celebrated on this

---

[48] Erasmus, *The Correspondence of Erasmus: Letters 842 to 992*, 357–58.
[49] Aysha Pollnitz, *Princely Education in Early Modern Britain* (Cambridge: Cambridge University Press, 2015), 76. For a discussion of Erasmus' laudatory writings as a hybrid of the two genres of panegyric and *speculum principis*, see also James D. Tracy, *The Politics of Erasmus: A Pacifist Intellectual and His Political Milieu* (Toronto: University of Toronto Press, 1978), 17–19, and Hanan Yoran, *Between Utopia and Dystopia: Erasmus, Thomas More, and the Humanist Republic of Letters* (Lanham, MD: Lexington Books, 2010), 50.
[50] Erasmus, *The Correspondence of Erasmus: Letters 842 to 992*, 359.
[51] Erasmus, *The Correspondence of Erasmus: Letters 842 to 992*, 360.
[52] Curtis, "The Social and Political Thought of Juan Luis Vives," 123.
[53] Adams, *The Better Part of Valor*, 185. For a recent comprehensive discussion of the Field of Cloth of Gold, see Richardson, *The Field of Cloth of Gold*.

occasion, however, unraveled in 1521, when, following a French attack on the Holy Roman Empire, England entered into alliance with the Emperor Charles V and subsequently invaded France in 1523. Thereafter, the political situation in Europe became volatile again, with England, France, and the Empire in constant struggle, but with ever-changing alliances, established through a complex series of diplomatic machinations in which people such as Pace, Tunstall, More, and Tuke were actively involved.[54] The details of these developments need not detain us here, but I would like to briefly mention the diplomatic missions carried out by Tuke and More in the late 1520s. In June 1528, Tuke joined Bishop Tunstall in negotiating a truce between England, France, and Margaret of Austria, Charles V's paternal aunt and regent of the Low Countries, which was signed at Hampton Court on 15 June.[55] Thomas More refers to this agreement in a letter sent to Frans van Cranevelt, a Dutch humanist and jurist, on 8 November, rejoicing over the conclusion of a general peace "which Christendom has been yearning for so long" (*cuius desiderio iam diu christianus orbis affligitur*).[56] In August 1529, More was part of a delegation charged with negotiating the Franco-Imperial Treaty of Cambrai, which halted French military efforts in Italy and brought a temporary peace to Europe. From England's perspective, this was hardly a diplomatic success. As Glenn Richardson describes it, "Henry was included in the treaty only at the last minute but left effectively isolated in Europe, or at least dependent upon French friendship."[57] Moreover, the treaty posed a serious obstacle to Henry's pursuit of his "great matter" because it led to a closer alliance between the Pope and the Emperor, who was the nephew of Henry's queen. Nevertheless, in the epitaph that More wrote for himself and enclosed in his letter to Erasmus in 1533, he referred to the Peace of Cambrai as "his culminating achievement in public office":[58]

---

[54] On England's foreign policy in this period, see, among others, David Potter, "Foreign Policy," in *The Reign of Henry VIII: Politics, Policy and Piety*, ed. Diarmaid MacCulloch (Houndmills: Macmillan, 1995), 101–33; Glenn Richardson, "Eternal Peace, Occasional War: Anglo-French Relations under Henry VIII," in *Tudor England and Its Neighbours*, ed. Susan Doran and Glenn Richardson (Houndmills: Palgrave Macmillan, 2005), 44–73.

[55] The treaty, no. 4376, is calendared in "Henry VIII: June 1528, 11–20," in *Letters and Papers, Foreign and Domestic, Henry VIII, Vol. 4, 1524-1530*, ed. J. S. Brewer (London: Her Majesty's Stationery Office, 1875), 1911–29. British History Online, accessed 25 April 2019, http://www.british-history.ac.uk/letters-papers-hen8/vol4/ pp1911-1929.

[56] Thomas More, *More to Cranevelt: New Baudouin Letters*, ed. Hubertus Schulte Herbrüggen, *Supplementa Humanistica Lovaniensia* XI (Leuven: Leuven University Press, 1997), 168, 172.

[57] Glenn Richardson, "The French Connection: Francis I and England's Break with Rome," in *The Contending Kingdoms: France and England 1420-1700*, ed. Glenn Richardson (Aldershot: Ashgate, 2008), 99.

[58] Cathy Curtis, "More's Public Life," in *The Cambridge Companion to Thomas More*, ed. George M. Logan (Cambridge: Cambridge University Press, 2011), 82.

[Thomas More] served as the King's ambassador at various times and in various places, last of all at Cambrai, as an associate and colleague of Cuthbert Tunstal [...]. In that place he witnessed, in the capacity of ambassador, to his great joy, the renewal of a peace treaty between the supreme monarchs of Christendom and the restoration of a long-desired peace to the world.

This account is followed by a fervent prayer that heaven will "confirm this peace and make it a lasting one."[59]

If More's words in his epitaph testify to the powerful influence that the ideal of universal peace continued to exert over him to the end of his public life, a vestige of that humanist ideal may be discerned in the poem composed by Leland more than a decade later to celebrate the Peace of Campe, the Anglo-French peace treaty concluded in June 1546.[60] Leland's *Laudatio pacis* is divided into two sections of almost equal length: the introductory section and the encomium proper. In the introduction, Leland modestly states that despite his wish to offer a praise of peace, he lacks the ability to do so adequately in verse as Ovid and Pontano might have done – a comparison reminiscent of the comment on Gower's Latin style that Leland made in *De uiris illustribus*.[61] The encomium that ensues is filled up by "the imitation of approved authors."[62] Among the Latin texts quoted or paraphrased as witnesses to the benefits of peace is Erasmus' *Dulce bellum inexpertis*, and James Hutton suggests that Leland may have been inspired by Richard Pace's *Oratio in pace* in the way he interprets and arranges quotations from ancient authorities.[63] Although no evidence survives to indicate the direct influence of Pace's oration on Leland's poem, he must almost certainly have known it, for his posthumously published collection of epigrams, the same volume that contains the verses addressed to Brian Tuke, includes a poem written on the occasion of Pace's return from his embassy in Venice.[64] Leland offers the highest praise for Pace's learning and his mastery of Greek and Latin, saying that "delighted to see his safe return, a crowd of men destined by nature for scholarly pursuits cheered him to the echo"(*Quem saluum ac reducem visere gestiens / Grex natus studijs, plausibus assonat*). Pace also figures in another occasional poem by Leland, which recounts how the study of *bonae literae*

---

[59] Thomas More, *St. Thomas More: Selected Letters*, ed. Elizabeth Frances Rogers (New Haven: Yale University Press, 1961), 181.
[60] *Laudatio pacis, Ioanne Lelando antiquario autore* (London, 1546), STC 15442. The following discussion of the *Laudatio pacis* is informed by James Hutton, "John Leland's *Laudatio Pacis*," *Studies in Philology* 58 (1961): 616–26.
[61] Leland, *Laudatio pacis*, sig. A4r.
[62] Hutton, "John Leland's *Laudatio Pacis*," 626.
[63] Hutton, "John Leland's *Laudatio Pacis*," 624.
[64] *In reditum Richardi Pacaei, vtriusque linguae ornamenti clariss*, in Leland, *Encomia*, sigs. D1r–D1v.

has spread across the European continent and taken root in Britain.[65] Here Pace is named among a group of eminent humanists, including Linacre, Tunstall, Colet, and Lily, who have brought back from their years of study in Italy the literary legacy of classical Greece. Thanks to "the happy industry of these learned men" (*doctorum faelix industria*), Leland proudly exclaims, his country has witnessed "the glory of revived learning" (*renascentis doctrinae gloria*) and the expanded "knowledge of three languages" (*Linguarum* [...] *cognitioque trium*).

As James Carley and Ágnes Juhász-Ormsby have pointed out, the third language mentioned here is most certainly Hebrew, not English, but Leland no doubt shared the conviction of Thynne and Tuke that English could be "bettered" and "beautified" in such a way as to match its classical models and their expressive capacities.[66] To this group of friends interested in demonstrating the potential of English to approximate the sophistication of the ancient languages, we can add Thomas Berthelette, who Leland claims asked him to write an encomium on Chaucer as a refiner of the native tongue.[67] In the prefatory material to his 1532 edition of the *Confessio Amantis*, Berthelette compares Gower to a "lanterne" which illuminates the path to vernacular eloquence:

> And who so euer in redynge of this warke dothe consyder it well shal fynde that it is plentifully stuffed and fournysshed with manyfolde eloquent reasons sharpe and quicke argumentes and examples of great auctorite perswadynge vnto vertue not onely taken out of the poetes oratours history wryters and philosophers but also out of the holy scripture. There is to my dome no man but that he may bi reding of this warke get right great knowlege as wel for the vnderstandyng of many & diuers autors whose resons sayenges & histories are translated in to this warke as for the plenty of englysshe wordes and vulgars [...].[68]

Berthelette introduces the *Confessio* as a vast compendium of classical texts, made accessible to a wide public through translation into the vernacular. For Berthelette, translation constitutes an important component of the humanist project of reviving *bonae literae* in that it contributes to a wider dissemination of ancient learning and to an enrichment of the vernacular as an apt medium for literary expression. Although his commitment to this enterprise is amply demonstrated by the English translations of Isocrates, Plutarch, and Xenophon that appeared from his press, what he sought to disseminate through vernacularization was not confined to the

---

[65] *Instauratio bonarum literarum*, in Leland, *Encomia*, sigs. K1v–K2r.
[66] James P. Carley and Ágnes Juhász-Ormsby, "Survey of Henrician Humanism," in *Oxford History of Classical Reception in English Literature*, Vol. 1: 800–1558, ed. Rita Copeland (Oxford: Oxford University Press, 2016), 529–30.
[67] Leland, *De uiris illustribus*, 706–07.
[68] *Io. Gower de confessione Amantis*, sigs. aa.ii r–aa.ii v.

ancient classics. In 1534 he printed an anonymous English translation of Erasmus' *Dulce bellum inexpertis*,[69] and his publication in 1531 of Thomas Elyot's *The boke named the Gouernour,* a work heavily indebted to Erasmus' *Institutio principis christiani*, may have also been motivated by his wish to promote the vernacular dissemination of Erasmian humanism.[70] Critics have frequently noted that the design features of the 1532 *Confessio*, including the same black-letter font used the year before to print Elyot's *Gouernour,* "mimic" humanist printings.[71] If the book's design has the effect of defining the *Confessio* as the work of "a pioneering humanist,"[72] Gower undergoes a similar metamorphosis in Thynne's volume, whose title page is framed by the border originally used in 1518 for Erasmus' *Epigrammata*.[73] As the author of an English *laudatio pacis*, Gower is here transformed into a humanist *orator*, offering a model for vernacular eloquence and upholding the ideal of universal peace cherished and promulgated by Erasmus and his English friends.

---

[69] *Bellum Erasmi translated into englyshe* (London, 1534), STC 10449.
[70] *The boke named the Gouernour, deuised by Thomas Elyot knight* (London, 1531), STC 7635.
[71] Siân Echard, *Printing the Middle Ages* (Philadelphia: University of Pennsylvania Press, 2008), 100–01. See also Tim William Machan, "Thomas Berthelette and Gower's *Confessio*," *Studies in the Age of Chaucer* 18 (1996): 143–66, esp. 145–47.
[72] Bart van Es, "Late Shakespeare and the Middle Ages," in *Medieval Shakespeare: Pasts and Presents*, ed. Ruth Morse, Helen Cooper, and Peter Holland (Cambridge: Cambridge University Press, 2013), 43.
[73] See n. 8 above.

CHAPTER 14

GEORGE CAMPBELL MACAULAY AND THE CLARENDON EDITION OF GOWER

A. S. G. Edwards

ON 6 JULY 1895 George Campbell Macaulay signed a contract with the Clarendon Press to produce an edition of *The Complete Works of John Gower*. The contract specified that it was to be "in not more than five volumes octavo" and of "not less than 2000 and not more than 2500 pages." It also stipulated that the work should be completed in less than four years, by 31 December 1898, although this was later modified to December of the following year for the bulk of the work.[1] The first volume did appear in 1899, the next two not until 1901, the last in 1902. In total the work just crept over the 2500-page limit, weighing in at 2519 pages of which 2178 were text, the rest prefatory matter or annotation.

For an individual to accomplish so much so speedily was in itself a notable achievement. It may seem the more so since it was undertaken by someone who had had no prior experience of editing medieval texts, who had never held an academic post, and who had had to support himself and a large family throughout this undertaking, and for some time before and after it, without regular employment. And more than a century after its completion Macaulay's edition of Gower remains the standard one. Indeed, in the current academic climate it is hard to see how it could be replaced.

To have completed such a massive edition in such circumstances suggests a figure whose intellectual and personal qualities invite some examination. George Macaulay remains elusive to posterity. His death was marked by a single obituary.[2] He does not appear in either the *Dictionary of National Biography* or the *Oxford Dictionary of National Biography*.[3] Such biographical

---

[1] The contract is in the Oxford University Press archives; I am indebted to Dr Martin Maw for permitting me access to materials relating to Macaulay's Gower edition there.
[2] In *Modern Language Review*, 10 (1915): 392.
[3] He did appear in *Who's Who* and *Who Was Who*.

material as I have been able to discover is fragmented, and fails to shed any light on crucial aspects of his career.[4] For the most part his life can only be seen obliquely, through his various publications and occasionally perhaps refracted through the writings of his second daughter, the poet, critic, and novelist, Rose Macaulay.

Hence, while what follows may make aspects of Macaulay's life slightly clearer in some aspects, the larger picture of his dealings with Gower continues to elude me and I am keenly aware of the inadequacies of my account. I can only hope to contribute a little to the appreciation of a remarkable scholar.

Some facts are readily established. Macaulay was born on 6 August 1852. His father, the Rev. S. H. Macaulay, rector of Hodnet, Shropshire, was a descendant of Thomas Babington Macaulay, the historian. George was educated at Eton (1863–72), where he was a King's Scholar.[5] From Eton he won a scholarship to Trinity College, Cambridge, in 1872; he was 4th Classic in the 1876 Tripos.[6] He became a Fellow of Trinity in October 1878, but had to resign later that year when he married. When any affiliation appears on the title pages of his publications it is invariably "formerly Fellow of Trinity College."

His wife Grace (1855–1925) was a daughter of William John Conybeare (1815–57), and came from a family with its own scholarly traditions; among her ancestors was John Josias Conybeare (1739–1834), one of the earliest Old English scholars. Macaulay evidently belonged to what Noel Annan has termed the "intellectual aristocracy" of the nineteenth century, particularly associated with Cambridge and continuing into modern times by a series of interlocking connections created by marriage between powerful academic families, like the Keynes's and the Trevelyans.[7]

Macaulay's marriage produced seven children: one daughter, Gertrude Mary (b. 1888), died in infancy in 1892, one son, Aulay (b. 1883), was

---

[4] Apart from such archival material as I cite elsewhere, I know only of correspondence from Macaulay to his parents from early childhood up to the end of his time at Eton (the last letter is dated 3 June 1872) that is now Trinity College Cambridge MS Add. 255, 17–56; I am grateful to Dr David McKitterick, former Librarian at Trinity, for drawing my attention to this material.

[5] His earliest publication seems to have been a letter, "Eton as it is," in the *Eton College Chronicle* (9 November 1871): 683.

[6] He was involved in an undergraduate scandal through writing verses imputing improper conduct to a proctor; see J. J. Hall, *Cambridge Act and Tripos Verses*, Cambridge Bibliographical Society Monograph no. 15 (Cambridge, 2009), no. 1875B.

[7] Noel Annan, "The Intellectual Aristocracy," reprinted in *The Dons* (London: Harper Perennial 1999), 304–41; the Macaulay family connections are discussed on 304–07.

murdered on the Northwest Frontier in 1909. None of the surviving children married. The last, Jean Babington (b. 1882), died in 1979.[8]

The responsibilities of marriage and family led Macaulay into school teaching. He became assistant master at Rugby in Easter 1878. It was there that he began a considerable, and considerably varied, career as critic, scholar, and editor. He produced two editions of parts of Livy, one of *The Hannibalian War* in 1880 and of Books XXIII–IV for MacMillan in 1885. Sandwiched between these is his first book on English literature, *Francis Beaumont, a Critical Study* (London: Kegan Paul & Co., 1883). If this book suggests a breadth to his interests not necessarily typical of one with his classical training, it may be seen in relation to a lengthy article he published in the previous year. Its subject was Walt Whitman and it is among the earliest critical assessments of the poet in England.[9]

Macaulay remained at Rugby until July 1887, when he resigned.[10] He removed his family to Italy, where he lived for the next seven years in a small fishing village, Varazze, near Genoa. The move was apparently undertaken in the belief that it would improve his wife's uncertain health; she had been diagnosed as tubercular.[11]

While in Italy Macaulay continued to write. Some of this was clearly hack work, like his *Graduated German Reading-Book* (London: Rivingtons, 1888). He also produced there a series of editions of Tennyson for MacMillan, a publisher for whom he had begun to work regularly: *The Marriage of Geraint* and *Geraint and Enid* (1892), *Gareth & Lynette* (1892), and *The Holy Grail* (1893). He also completed, in 1890, what seems to have been a quite widely popular translation of Herodotus' *Histories* and an edition of Book III from it, both again for MacMillan. He also published scholarly articles on Herodotus[12] and on historical topics while there.[13]

In July 1894 Macaulay returned to England and set up house in Oxford, initially at 3 Clarendon Villas, Park Town. What impulse or motive drew him

---

[8] The other children were Margaret Campbell (1880-1941); William John Conybeare (1884-1945); Eleanor Grace (1887-1952); Rose (1881- 1958). For information about Macaulay's children I have drawn on the Introduction to Martin Ferguson Smith, ed., *Dearest Jean: Rose Macaulay's letters to a cousin* (Manchester: Manchester University Press, 2011).

[9] "Walt Whitman," *The Nineteenth Century,* 70 (December 1882): 903–18. There is a letter from Macaulay to Whitman, on 9 January 1883, in The Charles E. Feinberg Collection of the Papers of Walt Whitman, 1839–1919, Library of Congress, Washington, DC.

[10] I am grateful to Dee Murphy, Temple Reading Room, Rugby School for information about Macaulay's time at Rugby.

[11] See Sarah LeFanu, *Rose Macaulay* (London: Virago, 2003), especially 80.

[12] "Notes on some MSS of Herodotus," *Transactions of the Cambridge Philological Society*, 3, part III (1890): 135–39.

[13] "The Capture of a General Council, 1241," *English Historical Review*, 6 (1891): 1–17; "A Local Historian [Agostino Giustiniani]," *MacMillan's Magazine* (April 1891): 464–73.

to Oxford is unclear. Nor is it possible to establish how he supported himself and his family. It appears that for most (and possibly all) of the period from his resignation from Rugby until 1901 he had no form of regular income and was dependent on what he earned by his writings and private resources. In Oxford he produced further editions for MacMillan of nineteenth-century verse, of Tennyson's *Guinevere* (1895) and of Arnold's poems in 1896. He also moved in different editorial directions; again for MacMillan he edited in 1895 *The Chronicles of Froissart* in Berners' translation.[14]

Shortly after settling in Oxford Macaulay made his first major Gower discovery. In April 1895 he announced in *The Academy* the identification of the unique manuscript of the *Mirour de l'Omme* in Cambridge University Library, and discussed it in more detail in two further articles in the same journal later in that year.[15] By July 1895 he had signed the contract for the Gower edition and was clearly at work on it. In one of the *Academy* articles, published in July, he has a note: "The quotations made in this paper from the *Confessio* are taken, not from Pauli's text, which is notoriously bad, but from the best MSS."[16] In this article, he makes stylistic and other comparisons between the *Mirour* and the *Confessio* and the *Vox Clamantis* that suggest that he already had a close knowledge of all of these works.

As the Gower edition moved towards completion, in 1901, Macaulay was appointed Professor of English Language and Literature at the University College of Wales, Aberystwyth. It was his first academic appointment; he was fifty. In December 1905 he was appointed lecturer in English at Cambridge and returned to the place of his youthful academic triumphs in April of the following year.[17] As he remarked to his publisher, MacMillan, "It is a poorly paid post, but offers the attraction of interesting work and of course the Cambridge libraries."[18] His last decade was one of unremitting industry. He was the only lecturer in English (then in the Faculty of Medieval and Modern Languages).[19] His lecture load was heavy in both

---

[14] He published two articles on Froissart at this time: "Froissart the Lover," *MacMillan's Magazine* (January 1895): 223–30; "Froissart the Historian," *MacMillan's Magazine* (March 1895): 384–92.

[15] "The Lost French Works of Gower," *Academy* (13 April 1895): 313–15; "The 'Speculum Meditantis' of John Gower," *Academy* (27 July 1895): 71–72; "The 'Speculum Meditantis' of John Gower II," *Academy* (3 August 1895): 91–92.

[16] *The Academy* (27 July 1895): 72.

[17] Cf. the gnomic comment of E. M. W. Tillyard, a Cambridge insider, on Macaulay's contribution to Cambridge English: "He was not important as a critic [...]. But not only was he one of those who helped to make English scholarship respectable academically, he also became the most important of all the agents of outside influence in Cambridge. Here was a reputable scholar – eager to introduce into Cambridge the kind of conditions that prevailed in a provincial university" (*The Muse Unchained* [London, 1958], 34).

[18] MacMillan Archive, University of Reading, 6 April 1906.

[19] Skeat had been Elrington and Bosworth Professor of Anglo-Saxon since 1878; he gave occasional courses of lectures in the Faculty.

volume and range. In 1910, for example, he lectured on English Literature Special Period 1815–30 and English Literature Special Period 1579–1603 in the Michaelmas and Lent terms; in the Easter term he lectured on Chaucer, Shakespeare, and Historical English Grammar. In 1914–15, his last year of teaching, he lectured on Special Period of English Literature 1700–40 in all three terms, gave two different lecture courses on Middle English subjects, an advanced course extending over all three terms and a beginning course in Michaelmas and Lent, and lectured on Chaucer and Shakespeare in the Easter term.[20] There were only occasional courses of lectures by others.

In addition to his teaching (his pupils included Rupert Brooke, whose parents had been friends from Rugby days), he wrote steadily. Gower completed, he published a life of James Thomson (MacMillan, 1907). In 1905 he had become the editor of the English section of the *Modern Language Review*. It was the chief outlet for his writings in his later years, but not the only one. His publications elsewhere in the period include articles on the English Bible[21] and on Horace[22] and chapters for the *Cambridge History of English Literature*.[23] His publications in *Modern Language Review* include over forty reviews in the last decade of his life, often lengthy, not just on medieval topics, but extending up to the nineteenth century. He also wrote several important articles for the journal, including one with M. R. James on Middle English carols[24] and his final, longest one (it runs to over fifty pages across four numbers) on the Corpus manuscript of the *Ancrene Riwle*, a study of eye-watering meticulousness.[25]

The general nature and quality of Macaulay's thinking about textual matters may be represented by a brief note on a line in *The Tempest* that appeared posthumously, which I reprint in its entirety:

"This blew ey'd hag, was hither brought with child."

The epithet "blew ey'd" has been variously explained, but it cannot be said to be appropriate in any sense. Shakespeare may probably have written "blere ey'd" or "blear ey'd," and "blew" is perhaps a misprint of the first folio, which is the only original authority for the text.[26]

---

[20] I take this information from the relevant volumes of the *Cambridge University Reporter*.
[21] "The English Bible," *Quarterly Review*, 215 (1911): 504–30.
[22] "On Horace *Ars Poetica*, ll. 128–30," *The Classical Review*, 26 (1912): 153–54.
[23] A. W. Ward and A. R. Waller, eds. Macaulay wrote articles on "The *Confessio Amantis*" (1908, II: 166–76) and "Beaumont and Fletcher" (1910, VI: 107–40).
[24] "Fifteenth Century Carols and Other Pieces," *Modern Language Review*, 8 (1913): 68–86.
[25] "The Ancren Riwle," *Modern Language Review*, 9 (1914): 63–78, 145–60, 324–31, 463–74.
[26] "Shakespeare's Tempest, Act I, sc. II, l. 29," *Modern Language Review*, 11 (1916): 75.

Macaulay died on 6 July 1915 at his home in Great Shelford, Cambridge, after a stroke. He was sixty-two. It was the twentieth anniversary to the day of his signing the Gower contract with the Clarendon Press.

Macaulay's life was not, even by Victorian standards, a long one. Very probably the burdens of maintaining a large family, often without regular employment, forced him to a range of editorial undertakings of a taxing kind, requiring the steady compliance with contractual deadlines and the weight of much that must have seemed hack work, however scrupulously executed. Such pressures must have served as necessary preparation for the Clarendon Gower, his central enduring scholarly achievement. This has some claim to be one of the most remarkable undertakings in the history of medieval English editing, both in its scale and in the expedition with which it was brought to completion. It involved the establishing of texts in three languages and, for most, in multiple manuscript forms and, in the case of the *Confessio*, of great length, together with introductions, manuscript descriptions, collations, and glossary, all in a period of less than six years, without institutional support of any kind. It is hard (for me) to conceive of the strength of purpose to sustain the necessary regime to do what Macaulay did.

If the Gower edition in its totality suggests much about character and intellect, it reveals little about motive and method. What led Macaulay to Gower and how did he develop his thinking about his works, particularly the *Confessio*? If these questions have some merit, my answers do not. Macaulay has this to say about his undertaking in the Preface to Volume I of his edition (dated 1899):

> While engaged some years ago in studying the Chaucer manuscripts in the Bodleian Library, I incidentally turned my attention also to those of the *Confessio Amantis*. The unsatisfactory character of the existing editions of that poem was sufficiently well known, and it was generally recognized that the printed text could not be referred to by philologists [...] I was struck by the excellence of the authorities for its text which existed in Oxford, and on further investigation I convinced myself that it was here that the much needed new edition could best be produced. Accordingly I submitted to the Delegates of the University Press a proposal to edit the *Confessio Amantis*, and this proposal they accepted on the condition that I would undertake to edit also the other works, chiefly in French and Latin, of the same author, expressly desiring that the *Speculum Meditantis*, which I had lately identified while searching the Cambridge libraries for copies of the *Confessio Amantis*, should be included in the publication. To this condition I assented with some hesitation [...].

Much of this cannot be explained. What, for example, had prompted Macaulay to examine the Chaucer manuscripts in Bodley? Did he initially contemplate an edition? He published very little on him; but most of it was either just before or just after he returned from Italy.[27] Skeat's great edition had appeared in 1894 and the collaborative Globe edition, which appeared in 1899, from Macaulay's main publisher, MacMillan, must have been in progress after Macaulay returned to England in 1894; there is nothing to suggest that Macaulay was ever involved with that. What "incidentally" deflected his interest into the study of the *Confessio*? And his account suggests that his discovery of the *Speculum Meditantis*, first announced in April 1895, was itself a consequence of an editorial plan for work on Gower that was already in progress some time before that date, even though the contract with the Clarendon Press was not signed until July 1895. I cannot clarify these matters. Macaulay's correspondence with the Clarendon Press is no more illuminating than his own prefatory comments in his edition. And the incomplete understanding we have of Macaulay the man in this respect leaves our understanding of the essential motives for his edition inevitably unclear.

What does seem clear is that the *Confessio* was always Macaulay's central concern in his edition. His own words show that it was the starting point for his thinking about editing Gower and it will provide the focus for my observations on the Clarendon edition.

The challenges that confronted Macaulay in his editing of the *Confessio* cannot be overemphasized. The only recent complete edition of the *Confessio* before Macaulay was that by Reinhold Pauli in 1857. This took Berthelette's 1532 printed edition as its base text, collating it with several Harley manuscripts and the "Stafford" manuscript, then in the library of Lord Ellesmere, now chiefly in the Huntington Library.[28] Macaulay's was the first edition since Caxton's in 1483 to be actually based on a manuscript and was the first to employ a full body of manuscript witnesses to establish his text.

This bibliographical aspect of Macaulay's achievement invites clearer acknowledgement in historical terms than it has received. Macaulay identified forty-two complete manuscripts of the *Confessio*, in both institutional and

---

[27] His earliest publication seems to have been his "note on Chaucer's borrowings from Benoit de Sainte Moire" in *Three More Parallel Texts of Chaucer's* Troilus and Criseyde *from MS. Li in St John's College, Cambridge; MS No. 61 in Corpus Christi College, Cambridge, and the Harleian MS. 1239 in the British Museum*. Put forth by F. J. Furnivall, Part I, Books I–III, Chaucer Society Publications, 1st series, LXXXVII (London, 1894). In the following year he published two letters, "'Troilus and Criseyde' in Professor Skeat's Edition," in *The Academy* (6 April 1895): 297–98, and (20 April 1895): 338–39.

[28] *Confessio Amantis: Confessions of a Lover*, ed. Reinhold Pauli, 3 vols (London: Bell & Daldy, 1857): "The present text [is] founded on Berthelette's edition" (I, xliii). Earlier, Pauli had claimed a propos of BL Harley 7184 that "this volume, on account of its antiquity and its judicious and consistent orthography, has been adopted as the basis for the spelling of this edition" (I, xxxix). It is not clear what this statement means. Harley 7184 lacks over fifty leaves.

private collections.[29] The previous census, by Karl Meyer, had identified thirty-two.[30] (Pauli had been aware of eighteen in his edition.) Modern scholarship has increased the number to forty-nine. Two of those that escaped Macaulay were in college libraries: M. R. James did not complete his catalogue of Pembroke until 1905;[31] a modern catalogue of Christ Church, including MS 148, only appeared in 2017.[32] The other five, at the time when Macaulay was editing Gower, were all in private collections;[33] none of these seems to be of great textual significance. Testimony to Macaulay's efforts at comprehensiveness may be seen in the fact that nine of the manuscripts he located were still in private hands.[34] To have been able to locate such a large number of manuscripts, so variously situated, with such speed was a remarkable feat of enumerative bibliography.

And also of descriptive bibliography. Macaulay's accounts of these manuscripts demonstrate considerable thought about descriptive method. They generally include systematic details of materials, foliation, size, layout, physical construction, and decoration as well as of other contents and of provenance; they also offer summary accounts of the textual characteristics of each. The succinct, comprehensive clarity of these descriptions is an aspect of Macaulay's achievement that it is easy to overlook. But his is the first edition of a major Middle English work to present such detailed information for such a large manuscript corpus and to understand that the material forms of a work needed to be both consistently described and placed in relationship to their textual forms. To understand, that is, that a description of a manuscript in an edition serves a different purpose from a catalogue description.

[29] Forty-one complete manuscripts are described in II, cxxxviii–clxv; a further one, now Pierpont Morgan Library M 126, sold at Sotheby's in June 1902, is described after II, 457.

[30] *John Gowers Beziehungen zu Chaucer und König Richard II* (Bonn, 1889), 47–71.

[31] M. R. James, *A Descriptive Catalogue of the Manuscripts in Pembroke College, Cambridge* (Cambridge: Cambridge University Press, 1905); MS 307 is described on 273–75.

[32] Ralph Hanna and David Rundle, *A Descriptive Catalogue of the Western Manuscripts in Christ Church, Oxford* (Oxford: Oxford University Press, 2017), 316–19.

[33] These were what are now Pierpont Morgan Library MS M 690; Columbia University MS Plimpton 265; New Haven, Beinecke Library MS Osborn fa 1; Oxford, Bodleian Library MS Lyell 31; Philadelphia, Rosenbach Museum and Library, MS 1083/29.

[34] These were *olim* Phillipps 2298 (now Princeton University Library, Garrett 136); *olim* Phillipps 8192 (now Princeton University Library, Taylor 5); *olim* Phillipps 8942 (Washington, DC, Folger Shakespeare Library Sm. 1 (V.b.29); *olim* Marquess of Bute (now in private hands on the Continent); *olim* Castle Howard (now Chicago, Newberry Library 33.5); the Stafford MS (now Huntington Library, EL 26.A.17); Keswick Hall (Gurney) MS (now Cologny-Geneva, Bodmer 178); and two now in the Morgan Library MSS M 125 and M 126.

It was, of course, in his assessment of the textual forms of the *Confessio* that Macaulay made his most significant contribution to the study of the poem. Whereas Pauli, his predecessor as Gower editor, has perceived the poem as existing in two versions, one dedicated to Richard II, the other to Henry of Lancaster, Macaulay understood the textual situation to be more complex. He argued that the *Confessio* "was put forth by the author in several different forms" (II, cxxvii) and distinguished "at least three" (II, cxxviii) broad textual groupings (he termed them "recensions") with a number of subcategories within the first of these groupings. The "at least" reflects his sense that the first recension exists in both "an earlier and a later text" (II, cxxix). These "recensions," as he termed them, he perceived as chronological, reflecting the modifications Gower made to the text particularly in the light of changing political circumstances, and the adjustment of associated references as a consequence of Henry IV's accession to the throne. The existence of an "intermediate version" (II, cxxix) he sees as evidenced in seven manuscripts. This version, Macaulay stresses, is not one that follows the preceding one by lineal descent "but existed and developed by its side, having its origin probably in the very same year, or at latest the next" (II, cxxxiii).

Macaulay's categorization was made he says, "for the sake of clearness" (II, cxxix). It is not easy to feel that he successfully imposes clarity on the textual state of affairs he perceives. His understanding of the manuscript evidence is shaped by his perception of the adjustment of some early copies by both erasure and addition to assume the form of subsequent versions (II, cxxx). His overall assessment of the evidence led him to place two manuscripts in a position of primary authority, the Stafford MS, then still in the possession of Lord Ellesmere, and Bodley Fairfax 3. He observes that:

> these are practically identical in orthography, and, except as regards the characteristic differences, which sufficiently guarantee their independence, exhibit essentially the same text, and one which bears the strongest marks of authenticity. Both are contemporary with the author, and it is perhaps difficult to say which best represents his final judgement as to the form of the work. (II, cxxxvii)

The Stafford manuscript is seen as "the earlier in time" (II, cxxxvii), and as possibly done for Henry of Lancaster. The process of the evolution of the text from Stafford to Fairfax can, in Macaulay's words, "hardly be satisfactorily understood" (II, cxxxvii) and probably, while begun around 1393, was not finally completed until after Richard's deposition in 1399.

What may seem strange to some is that while the importance of Stafford is asserted it seems to have no distinctive role in the text of the *Confessio* that Macaulay established. That text is based on the Fairfax manuscript collated in full against Bodley 902, Bodley 294, and Corpus Christi College Oxford "to represent respectively the first recension revised, the first recension unrevised and the second recension texts" (II, clxx). While the choice of Fairfax as base text seems defensible, it is hard to avoid a suspicion that pragmatic factors had some bearing on Macaulay's decisions about the other manuscripts that were fully collated. All these manuscripts were in Oxford, where he was. And Stafford, whatever its merits, was both in private hands and significantly imperfect, lacking seventeen leaves.

He goes on:

> In all cases where variation has been found [...] the readings of at least fourteen other selected copies have been ascertained, and by this procedure those variations which are merely individual have been distinguished from those which are shared by a class or group. (II, clxxi)

The result remains largely a text of the *Confessio* from Fairfax 3. Spot checking suggests that it is accurately transcribed apart from the elimination of thorn, the regularization of −u− and −v− and the introduction of modern punctuation.[35] There are only occasional attempts to represent any of the textual complexities that Macaulay discerned in the transmission of the poem. He does print variant forms of the Prologue (II, 2–6), and ending of Book VIII (III, 466ff), and variant passages chiefly from the "intermediate" version he identifies in Books V (II, 450–51, fn. 2; III, 121, 135, 139–44, 145), VI (III, 145, 198) and VII (III, 319–25). These are all based on Bodley 294 (see II, clv). It does not seem to be explained why these passages are singled out for representation.

Central to Macaulay's thinking is the assumption that Gower retained control over the text of the *Confessio* during the various reworkings he perceived it to have undergone. It is not, however, wholly clear how he saw this control as being exercised. The belief that he saw Gower as operating or directing some kind of scriptorium for the dissemination of the text of the *Confessio* is one that gained much modern currency. But in his discussion of the text Macaulay uses the word "scriptorium" only once and places it in quotation marks in his discussion of the changes to Fairfax 3, which he describes as "apparently made under the direction of the author" and hence "may be recognized as belonging to the 'scriptorium' of the poet" (II, cxxx). The grounds for his view about Gower's active role in production seem to have been the cancelled leaves and palimpsest passages in Fairfax 3, adjustments which were evidently done by a professional scribe, presumably felt to have been operating under some form of authorial direction. Quite how he envisioned such direction took place remains unclear. But the belief in the Gower scriptorium is the invention of later scholars, particularly John

---

[35] There are occasional unhelpful compounds: "noman," "forto," "forthferde."

Fisher, and cannot be laid at Macaulay's door.[36] He seems to use the term by default, to attempt to express, but define, a form of engagement between poet and copyist that he did not firmly grasp.

The question of Gower's "supervision" of the text of the *Confessio* has occasionally been based on other misunderstanding of Macaulay's arguments in general and about the status of the Stafford/Huntington manuscript in particular. Peter Nicholson, for example, asserts that "Macaulay concluded that [Stafford] was written, under Gower's supervision, between 1397 and 1399 for Henry of Bolingbroke, who is of course named in the dedication."[37] What Macaulay actually says is:

> It seems probable then that the book was prepared for presentation to a member of the house of Lancaster, probably either John of Gaunt or Henry. If it be the fact that the swan badge was not adopted by Henry until 1397, this would not be the actual copy sent on the occasion of the dedication to him in 1392-93. On the other hand, the absence of all royal emblems suggests that the book was prepared before Henry's accession to the throne. (II, clii–iii)

Macaulay does not claim this manuscript was produced "under Gower's supervision" and he also does not exclude the possibility of a dedicatee other than Henry.

Such misunderstandings about what Macaulay did say have led to some misrepresentation of aspects of his arguments. But while Macaulay did not postulate a scriptorium in the sense that the term has been understood by some later critics, he does seem to have assumed, as I have said, that the poet had an active role in shaping the actual transmission of the *Confessio* as his text evolved. This view has sometimes been challenged, notably by the most astute of Gower's textual critics, Peter Nicholson. But Nicholson has recently re-examined the evidence and concluded that Macaulay may have been right in his claims about Gower's involvement in the creation of Fairfax.[38]

Macaulay was evidently conscious of the circumstantial fluidity of the text of the *Confessio* as it was reshaped over time by Gower's sense of evolving political circumstances. Inevitably he found it necessary to give some account of the variant forms he perceived, if only for what he termed "practical purposes" and "for the sake of clearness" (II, cxxix). At the same time he clearly recognized that such an attempt had classificatory limits: "it must not be assumed that the manuscripts of each recension stand necessarily by themselves and that no connexion is traceable between one

---

[36] John Fisher, *John Gower, Moral Philosopher and Friend of Chaucer* (London: Methuen, 1965), especially 117, 124.

[37] Nicholson, "Poet and Scribe," 139.

[38] Peter Nicholson, "Gower's Manuscript of the *Confessio Amantis*," in *The Medieval Python: The Purposive and Provocative Work of Terry Jones*, ed. R. F. Yeager and T. Takamiya (Basingstoke: Palgrave Macmillan, 2012), 75–86.

class and another" (II, cccix). This may be an important observation, even if (not for the first time) its implications are not wholly clear. It suggests that Macaulay envisioned the possibility that versions were permeable, not invariably wholly distinct. This perception in its turn raises the possibility of contamination across versions. Such a possibility seems to suggest Macaulay's not fully realized awareness of the limitations of recension as an editorial method. If so, Macaulay seems close to anticipating the later pessimistic conclusions of Manly and Rickert and Kane about recension as a means of editing the texts of *The Canterbury Tales* and *Piers Plowman*.

This is not a conclusion that Macaulay actually reaches. One senses his struggle to find a formulation that would satisfactorily account for the variation between the different manuscript groupings of the *Confessio*. His inability to achieve such a resolution to the problems he identified should not be seen as an indication of his incapacity as editor. Even if he could not clearly resolve the complexity of the issues surrounding the text of Gower's poem Macaulay demonstrates his ability to identify and define crucial issues to do with the text.

And while some subsequent critics have sought to challenge his categorizations of the manuscripts and his general thinking about the poem's transmission, discussion has not yet led to any radical new assessment of the text of the poem.[39] Peter Nicholson has subjected Macaulay's arguments about the evidence of the manuscripts to detailed scrutiny in several predictably insightful articles. He has suggested that Macaulay's formal categorizations are of limited value and that instead we need to look at "the history of each manuscript." If by "history" he means the textual evidence of each manuscript, he is clearly right. A full collation of all *Confessio* manuscripts is the necessary preliminary to any sustained re-editing of the poem. Which is, of course, the chief reason why we still rely on Macaulay.

Derek Pearsall, another important textual critic of Gower, has been skeptical about aspects of Macaulay's editing on related grounds. He observes that:

> The variations in the forms of the *Confessio*, especially the changes clearly made for political reasons, clearly indicate authorial revision. But it is very doubtful whether the extant MSS will allow the recovery of detailed stages in this process of revision if there were any [...] Macaulay's division of the copies of the poem into recensions pre-empted his analysis of textual affiliations and prejudiced much of his description of them.[40]

---

[39] This is not the place to assess the extensive recent discussions of the text of the *Confessio*; for a judicious and lucid summary of the issues with further references see Joel Fredell, "John Gower's Manuscripts in Middle English," in *The Routledge Research Companion to John Gower*, ed. Ana Sáez-Hidalgo, Brian Gastle, and R. F. Yeager (London and New York: Routledge, 2017), 91–96.

[40] Derek Pearsall, "The Manuscripts and Illustrations of Gower's Works," in *A Companion to Gower*, ed. Siân Echard (Cambridge: D. S. Brewer, 2004), 73–97, quote at 94.

If by "recensions" is meant discernible distinct textual forms surviving in multiple manuscripts, then such forms clearly exist. Identifying such forms does not preclude analysis. At the very least they seem rather less of an impediment than the rather more arbitrary categorizations of the text of *Piers Plowman* into three versions, categorizations that have been largely uncritically adhered to for a hundred and fifty years.

Certainly, no subsequent edition has challenged his choice of base text.[41] Efforts in relation to the poem have been largely devoted to enlarging the necessarily brief annotation to the poem that Macaulay provided,[42] both in Bennett's 1968 selections and in Peter Nicholson's *Annotated Index* in 1989.

How good an editor was Macaulay? There are various ways of answering the question. The first, most obvious and perhaps most significant, is the historical situation in which Macaulay found himself. He was the first editor to attempt an edition of the *Confessio Amantis* that was based on an examination of the full range of the known textual resources, to seek to interpret the evidence of forty-odd manuscripts of a work in excess of 30000 lines. I do not think that any English textual critic before him had attempted to render intelligible such a large and complex body of evidence for any English text. And, more than a century on, his text has remained largely unchallenged. Peter Nicholson, one of the most searching of Macaulay's critics, has concluded that his identification of Fairfax as a base text "is still a defensible choice" and that any "new edition might not in the end be very different from his."[43]

In terms of establishing the specific readings of his text Macaulay was a conservative editor. His is not a critical edition as the term is now generally understood. He did not collate in full all the witnesses he knew or provide an exhaustive textual apparatus. This would have been both impossible, given his limited access to a number of the manuscripts, particularly those in private hands, and impracticable in view of the time, space, and expense it would have involved. And it is questionable whether such effort would, in any case, make significant difference to his text.

Macaulay does provide punctuation and capitalization to accord with modern usage, but otherwise the majority of his changes to his base text, Fairfax 3, are very minor, restricted to adjustments in spelling or word division or to the correction of obvious and readily explicable scribal

---

[41] J. A. W. Bennett in his *Selections from John Gower* (Oxford: Oxford University Press, 1968) is the only subsequent editor of the *Confessio* not to identify his base text; this may be because it is taken directly from Macaulay.

[42] Macaulay's notes are on II, 457–519, III, 495–550. He did not, of course, have any of the lexical, bibliographical, literary, or historical tools that are available to us. Nor did he have any obvious traditions or models of annotation on which he could draw.

[43] Peter Nicholson, "Poet and Scribe in the Manuscripts of Gower's *Confessio Amantis*," in *Manuscripts and Texts: Textual Problems in Middle English Editing*, ed. Derek Pearsall (Cambridge: D. S. Brewer, 1987), 130–42, quote at 142.

errors.[44] Throughout, no explanations are offered for such adjustments as Macaulay made to his base text. And the recording of variants seems selective and made on unclear principles, even given that only a limited number of manuscripts have been collated. Nor are the forms for noting variants always clear.[45] Macaulay's view of his editorial role does not seem to extend to conjectural emendation on the basis of either sense or meter. One scans his pages in vain for significant emendation on such grounds. This conservatism has perhaps been an important factor in the durability of his edition. It always remains very close to the form of his base text.

But while the textual authority of Macaulay's edition has remained largely unchallenged, it was neither a commercial nor a critical success. A glum note in the Oxford University files for 1959 reports that "no profits were ever realized" on either the Clarendon or Early English Text Society editions of Gower and that both "went out of print some years ago with debit balances still standing to their accounts."

Nor was the edition enthusiastically received by reviewers. Lucy Toulmin Smith was admiring: "We now know Gower as we never knew him before."[46] W. P. Ker used Macaulay's work as a point of departure for some general reflections on Gower.[47] And there were a few other respectful if rather tepid ones in scholarly journals.[48]

But two reviews stand apart from this generalization, both unsigned, both by the same person, both in the same rather improbable place, both previously unremarked by Gower scholarship. The *Daily Chronicle* (formerly *The Clerkenwell News and Daily Intelligencer*), on 18 June 1901, reviewed

---

[44] For example, Prologus, 370, where Fairfax's "argumeten" is changed to "argumenten"; I. 293, where Fairfax's "þer" is changed to "the"; I. 1378, where Fairfax's "Compleingte" is changed to "Compleignte."

[45] For example, VI. 10, where the reading in the text is "sette" and the recorded variants read "sette AJC, S, F   set BT"; the significance of the commas and spacing is not easy to grasp, or why the lemma is not set off by a half square bracket, as is the general, but not invariable, practice elsewhere. Nor is it clear why the variant form of BT is seen as significant. Such lack of clarity about form and substance in the recording of variants occurs throughout.

[46] In *Archiv für das Studium der neueren Sprachen und Literatur*, 110 (1903): 197–202, quote at 197.

[47] "John Gower, Poet," *Quarterly Review*, 197 (1903): 437–58; reprinted in his *Essays on Medieval Literature* (London, 1905), 101–34.

[48] I note the following reviews, not all of them included in R. F. Yeager's very valuable *John Gower Materials: A Bibliography through 1979* (New York, 1981) nor in John H. Fisher, R. Wayne Hamm, Peter G. Beidler, and R. F. Yeager, "Gower," in *A Manual of the Writings in Middle English*, ed. A. E. Hartung (New Haven, CT, 1986), 7: 2399–2418: Volume I was reviewed by G. L. Kittredge in *The Nation*, 71 (27 September 1900): 254–56 and anonymously in *The Athenaeum*, 7 (September 1901): 305–06; H. Spies has an extensive review in *Englische Studien*, 32 (1903): 251–75; Volume IV is reviewed by A. S. F. Gow in *The Classical Review*, 18 (1904): 62.

Macaulay's edition of the *Confessio*, and, even more remarkably, on 29 October 1902, the Latin works of volume IV. The first review, headed "Chaucer's Mate," contains careful analysis of Gower's narrative art in the *Confessio* before concluding that Gower "is now represented by a pure and delightful text which we hope will gain him justice." The second review acclaims at further length what is termed "the almost superfluously fine Oxford edition of Gower." The author of both these reviews was the poet, Edward Thomas.[49] His praise did not succeed in introducing Gower to a wider public. But that, nearly half a millennium on, Gower could earn the admiration of a fellow poet is testimony in important part to Macaulay's editorial achievement.

---

[49] Thomas's authorship of these reviews is established in Jeff Cooper, *Edward Thomas: Towards a Complete Checklist of his Writings* (Blackburn, 2004).

BIBLIOGRAPHY

Primary Sources

Manuscripts

olim Bute, Mount Stuart, Rothesay, Marquess of Bute MS 85 (now in private hands)
Cambridge, Cambridge University Library, MS Mm 2 21
Cambridge, Pembroke College, MS 307
Cambridge, St Catharine's College, MS 7
Cambridge, St John's College, MS B 12
Cambridge, Sidney Sussex College, MS 63
Cambridge, Trinity College, MS Add. 255
Cambridge, Trinity College, MS R.3.2
Cambridge, Trinity College, MS R.3.20
Chicago, Newberry Library, Case MS 33.5, Louis H. Silver Collection MS 3 (*olim* Castle Howard)
Collegeville, Minnesota, Hill Museum and Manuscript Library, MS Steiner 54
Frankfurt am Main, Stadt- und Universitätsbibliothek, MS Barth. 110
Geneva (Cologny), Fondation Bodmer, MS Bodmer 178
Glasgow, Glasgow University Library, MS Hunter 59
London, British Library, MS Additional 12043
London, British Library, MS Additional 22718
London, British Library, MS Additional 29729
London, British Library, MS Additional 59495 (*olim* Trentham)
London, British Library, MS Cotton Tiberius A. iv
London, British Library, MS Cotton Tiberius B. v
London, British Library, MS Egerton 913
London, British Library, MS Egerton 1991
London, British Library, MS Harley 367
London, British Library, MS Harley 2251
London, British Library, MS Harley 3490
London, British Library, MS Harley 3869
London, British Library, MS Royal 18 C xxii
London, British Library, MS Royal B.20.vi
London, British Library, MS Stowe 950
London, Society of Antiquaries, MS 134
Madrid, Biblioteca de El Escorial MS g-II-19
Madrid, Biblioteca Nacional MS 20262/19
Madrid, Biblioteca Nacional MS 22644
Madrid, Real Biblioteca MS II-3088
Manchester, Chetham's Library, MS A 7 38

New Haven, Yale University, Beinecke Rare Books and Manuscript Library, MS Takamiya 98
New Haven, Yale University, Beinecke Rare Books and Manuscript Library, MS Osborn fa 1
New Haven, Yale University, Beinecke Rare Books and Manuscript Library, Mellon 25
New York, Columbia University MS Plimpton 265
New York, Morgan Library, MS M 125
New York, Morgan Library, MS M 126
New York, Morgan Library, MS M 690
Nottingham, Nottingham University Library, MS WLC LM 8 (Middleton Collection MS Mi LM 8)
Oxford, All Souls College, MS 98
Oxford, Bodleian Library, MS Arch Selden B.11
Oxford, Bodleian Library, MS Ashmole 35
Oxford, Bodleian Library, MS Ashmole 59
Oxford, Bodleian Library, MS Bodley 294
Oxford, Bodleian Library, MS Bodley 638
Oxford, Bodleian Library, MS Bodley 693
Oxford, Bodleian Library, MS Bodley 902
Oxford, Bodleian Library, MS Eng. Poet.a.1
Oxford, Bodleian Library, MS Fairfax 3
Oxford, Bodleian Library, MS Hatton 51
Oxford, Bodleian Library, MS Hatton 92
Oxford, Bodleian Library, MS Laud 719
Oxford, Bodleian Library, MS Laud Misc.609
Oxford, Bodleian Library, MS Lyell 31
Oxford, Bodleian Library, MS Rawlinson C. 86
Oxford, Christ Church, MS 148
Oxford, Corpus Christi College, MS 67
Oxford, Magdalen College, MS 213
Oxford, New College, MS 266
Oxford, Wadham College, MS 13
Oxford, Oxford University Press Archives, Little Clarendon St.
Philadelphia, Rosenbach Museum and Library, MS 1083/29
Princeton University, Firestone Library, MS Garrett 136
Princeton University, Firestone Library, MS Taylor 5 (*olim* Phillipps 8192)
Reading, University of Reading, Macmillan Archive
San Marino, Huntington Library, MS Ellesmere 26 C 9
San Marino, CA, Huntington Library, MS EL 26.A.17 (*olim* Stafford ms)
San Marino, CA, Huntington Library, MS HM 150
San Marino, CA, Huntington Library, MS HM 1034
San Marino, CA, Huntington Library, MS HM 19960
Vatican City, Biblioteca Apostolica Vaticana, MS 6428
Vatican City, Biblioteca Apostolica Vaticana, MS Urb. Lat. 341
Washington, DC, Folger Shakespeare Library, MS V.b.29 MS (*olim* Phillipps 8942)

Bibliography

Printed Sources

Alves Dias, João José, ed., *Livro dos Conselhos de El-Rei D. Duarte (Livro da Cartuxa)* (Lisboa: Estampa, 1982).
Barclay, Alexander, *The introductory to wryte, and to pronounce Frenche* (London: Robert Copland, 1521), STC 1386.
Bell, James F., Notebook, *Book Prices 1925/1940* (James F. Bell Papers, James Ford Bell Library, University of Minnesota, Minneapolis, MN).
Biblia Sacra Vulgata, trans. *Douay-Rheims 1899 American Edition* (Bible Gateway, www.biblegateway.com/).
Blake, Norman Francis, ed., *Caxton's Own Prose* (London: André Deutsch, 1973).
Boccaccio, Giovanni, *Decameron*, ed. Vittore Branca (Torino: Einaudi, 1992).
——, *The Decameron*, trans. G. H. McWilliam (London: Penguin, 1972, rpt. 1995).
Bourchier, John, *Sir Johan Froyssart: of the cronycles of Englande, Fraunce*, [etc.], 2 vols, trans. Lord Berners (London: Richard Pynson, 1523 and 1525), STC 11396–7.
Bradshaw, Henry, *The lyfe of saynt Werburge* (London: Richard Pynson, 1521), STC 3506.
Canutus, *A ... litill boke aʒenst the pestilence* (London: William de Machlinia, c.1485), STC 4591.
Capgrave, John, *Liber de Illustribus Henricis*, ed. F. C. Hingeston, Rolls Series (London, 1858).
——, *John Capgrave's Abbreuiacion of Cronicles*. ed. Peter J. Lucas, EETS, o.s. 285 (Oxford: Oxford University Press, 1983).
Carlson, David R., ed., *The Deposition of Richard II: "The Record and Process of the Renunciation and Deposition of Richard II" (1399) and Related Writings* (Toronto: Pontifical Institute of Medieval Studies, 2007).
Caulibus, John D., *Meditaciones vite Christi*, ed. Mary Stallings-Taney (Turnhout: Brepols, 1997).
Caxton's Book of Curtesye, ed. Frederick J. Furnivall, EETS, e.s. 3 (London, 1868).
The chastysing of goddes chyldern (Westminster: Wynkyn de Worde, 1493), STC 5065.
Chaucer, Geoffrey, *The workes of Geffray Chaucer newly printed, with dyuers workes whiche were neuer in print before*, ed. William Thynne (London: Thomas Godfray, 1532), STC 5068.
——, *The book of fame* (London: Richard Pynson, 1526?), STC 5088.
——, [*The Canterbury Tales*] (Westminster: William Caxton, 1483), STC 5083.
——, *Caunterbury tales* (Westminster: Wynkyn de Worde, 1498), STC 5085.
——, *Caunterbury tales* (London: Richard Pynson, 1526), STC 5086.
——, *Troylus and Creseyde* (London: Wynkyn de Worde, 1517), STC 5095.
——, *Troylus and Creseyde* (London: Richard Pynson, 1526?), STC 5096.
——, *The parlyament of fowles* (London: John Rastell, 1525?), STC 5091.5.
——, [*The Parliament of Fowls*] (London: Wynkyn de Worde, 1530), STC 5092.
——, *The Canterbury Tales of Chaucer, to which are added an essay upon his language and versification, an introductory discourse, and notes*, ed. Thomas Tyrwhitt, 4 vols. (London: T. Payne, 1775).

——, *The Complete Works of Geoffrey Chaucer: Edited from Numerous Manuscripts*, ed. Walter W. Skeat, 7 vols. (Oxford: Clarendon Press, 1894–97).

——, *The Text of the Canterbury Tales, studied on the Basis of All Known Manuscripts*, eds John M. Manly and Edith M. Rickert, 8 vols. (Chicago: University of Chicago Press, 1940).

——, *The Riverside Chaucer*, ed. Larry D. Benson, *et al.*, 3rd edn. (Boston: Houghton Mifflin, 1986).

——, *A Variorum Edition of The Works of Geoffrey Chaucer, Volume V: The Minor Poems, Part One*, eds George B. Pace and Alfred David (Norman: University of Oklahoma Press, 1982).

Christine de Pizan, *The book of fayttes of armes & of chyualrye*, trans. William Caxton (Westminster: William Caxton, 1489), STC 7269.

Copland, Robert, trans., *The life of Ipomydon*, An adaptation of Hue of Rotelande (London: Wynkyn de Worde, c.1522), STC 5732.5.

——, (London: Wynkyn de Worde, c.1527), STC 5733.

Copland, Robert, *Robert Copland: Poems*, ed. Mary Carpenter Erler (Toronto: University of Toronto Press, 1993).

Dante Alighieri, *Divine Comedy*, ed. Charles S. Singleton, 6 vols. (Princeton: Princeton University Press, 1970–75).

——, *De monarchia*, ed. Pier Giorgio Ricci, trans. Prue Shaw (Florence: Società Dantesca Italiana, 1965). Electronic version Princeton Dante Project, http://etcweb.princeton.edu/dante/pdp/.

Elyot, Thomas, *The boke named the Gouernour, deuised by [Sir?] Thomas Elyot knight* (London: Thomas Berthelette, 1531), STC 7635.

Erasmus, Desiderius, *Bellum Erasmi translated into englyshe* (London: Thomas Berthelette, 1534), STC 10449.

——, *The Correspondence of Erasmus: Letters 842 to 992, 1518 to 1519*, Vol. 6 of *Collected Works of Erasmus*, trans. R. A. B. Mynors and D. F. S. Thomson, annotated by Peter G. Bietenholz (Toronto: University of Toronto Press, 1982).

——, *The Education of a Christian Prince*, trans. Neil M. Cheshire and Michael J. Heath; with the *Panegyric for Archduke Philip of Austria*, trans. and ed. Lisa Jardine (Cambridge: Cambridge University Press, 1997).

Feylde, Thomas, *The contrauerse bytwene a louer and a Iaye* (London: Wynkyn de Worde, 1527?), STC 10838.7.

Given-Wilson, Chris, ed. and trans., *Chronicles of the Revolution 1397-1400: The Reign of Richard II* (Manchester: Manchester University Press, 1993).

Goodwyn, Christopher, *The maydens dreme* (London, Robert Wyer, ?1542), STC 12047.

Gower, John, *Confessio amantis* (Westminster: William Caxton, 1483), STC 12142.

——, *Jo. Gower de confessione amantis* (London: Thomas Berthelet, 1532), STC 12143.

——, *Confessio Amantis: Confessions of a Lover*, ed. Reinhold Pauli, 3 vols. (London: Bell & Baldy, 1857).

——, *The Complete Works of John Gower*, ed. G. C. Macaulay, 4 vols. (Oxford: Oxford University Press, 1899–1902). Vol. I, The French Works; Vols II and III, The English Works, published simultaneously for the Early English Text

Society as Vols I and II, Extra Series 81–82 (London: Oxford University Press, 1901); Vol. IV, The Latin Works.

——, *The Complete Works of John Gower*, ed. G. C. Macaulay, 4 vols. (Oxford: Clarendon Press, 1902).

——, *The English Works of John Gower*, ed. G. C. Macaulay, EETS ES 81–82 (London: Kegan Paul, Trench, Trübner, 1900–01).

——, *Confessio Amantis*, ed. Russell Peck, 3 vols, Latin trans. Andrew Galloway (Kalamazoo, MI: Medieval Institute Publications, 2003–13).

——, *The French Balades*, ed. and trans. R. F. Yeager (Kalamazoo, MI: Medieval Institute Publications, 2011).

——, *John Gower: The Minor Latin Works*, ed. and trans. R. F. Yeager, with "In Praise of Peace," ed. Michael Livingston (Kalamazoo, MI: Medieval Institute Publications, 2005).

——, *Poems on Contemporary Events: The Visio Anglie (1381) and Cronica Tripertita (1400)*, trans. A. G. Rigg, ed. David R. Carlson (Toronto: Pontifical Institute of Mediaeval Studies, 2011).

——, *The Major Latin Works of John Gower: The Voice of One Crying and the Tripartite Chronicle*, trans. Eric W. Stockton (Seattle: University of Washington Press, 1962).

Greene, Belle de Costa, Belle de Costa Greene to James F. Bell, 21 December 1932, UNC-CH Incunabula 532.5 Curatorial File, Wilson Library, University of North Carolina, Chapel Hill.

Gringore, Pierre, *The castell of laboure*, trans. Alexander Barclay (Paris and London, c.1503–28?), STC 12379–82.

Hawes, Stephen, *The comforte of louers* (London: Wynkyn de Worde, 1515), STC 12942.5.

——, *The conuercyon of swerers* (London: Wynkyn de Worde, 1509), STC 12943.

——, *The example of virtu* (London: Wynkyn de Worde, 1504?), STC 12945.

——, *The exemple* (sic) *of vertu* (London: Wynkyn de Worde, 1530), STC 12947.

——, *A joyfull medytacyon* (London: Wynkyn de Worde, 1509), STC 12953.

——, [*The Pastime of Pleasure*] (London: Wynkyn de Worde, 1509), STC 12948.

——, *The passe tyme of pleasure* (London: Wynkyn de Worde, 1517), STC 12949.

Hunt, Richard W., Falconer Madan, P. D. Record, *Summary Catalogue of Western Manuscripts at the Bodleian Library* (Oxford: Clarendon Press, 1895–1953).

Legge, M. Dominica, ed., *Anglo-Norman Letters and Petitions from All Souls MS. 182* (Oxford: Blackwell, 1941).

Leland, John, *Laudatio pacis. Ioanne Lelando antiquario autore* (London: Reyner Wolfe, 1546), STC 15442.

——, *Principum, ac illustrium aliquot & eruditorum in Anglia virorum, Encomia, Trophaea, Genethliaca, & Epithalamia* (London: Thomas Orwin, 1589), STC 15447.

——, *De uiris illustribus: On Famous Men*, ed. and trans. James P. Carley, with the assistance of Caroline Brett (Toronto: PIMS, 2010).

Letters and Papers, Foreign and Domestic, of the Reign of Henry VIII, eds J. S. Brewer, J. Gairdner, and R. H. Brodie, 21 vols. (London: HMSO, 1862–1932). Online at http://www.british-history.ac.uk/search/series/letters-papers-hen8.

Lydgate, John, *The chorle and the birde* (Westminster: William Caxton, 1476), STC 17008.

267

——, *The chorle and the birde* (Westminster: William Caxton, 1477), STC 17009.
——, *The falle of princis* (London: Richard Pynson, 1494), STC 3175.
——, *The falle of princis* (London: Richard Pynson, 1527), STC 3176.
——, *The horse the ghoos & the sheep* (Westminster: William Caxton, 1476), STC 17018.
——, *The horse the ghoos & the sheep* (Westminster: William Caxton, 1477), STC 17019.
——, *The hystorye, sege and dystruccyon of Troye* (London: Richard Pynson, 1513), STC 5579.
——, *The lyf of our lady* (Westminster: William Caxton, 1483), STC 17023.
——, *The lyf of our lady* (Westminster: William Caxton, 1484), STC 17024.
——, *The prouerbes of Lydgate* (London: Wynkyn de Worde, 1510?), STC 17026.
——, *The prouerbes of Lydgate* (London: Wynkyn de Worde, 1520?), STC 17027.
——, *The temple of glas* (Westminster: William Caxton, 1477?), STC 17032.
——, *The testament* (London: Richard Pynson, 1520?), STC 17035.
Mancinus, Dominicus, *The myrrour of good maners*, trans. Alexander Barclay (London: Richard Pynson, 1518?), STC 17242.
More, Thomas, *St. Thomas More: Selected Letters*, ed. Elizabeth Frances Rogers (New Haven: Yale University Press, 1961).
——, *Morus ad Craneveldium Litterae Balduinianae Novae: More to Cranevelt: New Baudouin Letters*, ed. Hubertus Schulte Herbrüggen, Supplementa Humanistica Lovaniensia XI (Leuven: Leuven University Press, 1997).
The myrrour of the worlde, trans. William Caxton (Westminster: William Caxton, 1481), STC 24762.
Nevill, William, *The castell of pleasure* (London: Henry Pepwell, 1518), STC 18476.
——, *The castell of pleasure* (London: Wynkyn de Worde, 1530?), STC 18475.
Pace, Richard, *Oratio Richardi Pacei in pace nuperime composita et foedere percusso inter inuictissimum Angliae regem et Francorum regem christianissimum in aede diui Pauli Londini habita* (London: Richard Pynson, 1518), STC 19081a.
Philippe de Mézières, *Le Songe du Vieil Pèlerin,* 2 vols, ed. G. W. Coopland (Cambridge: Cambridge University Press, 1969).
——, *Letter to King Richard II: A Plea made in 1395 for peace between England and France*, trans. G. W. Coopland (Liverpool: Liverpool University Press, 1975).
Pickles, J. D. and J. L. Dawson, *A Concordance to John Gower's 'Confessio Amantis'*, Publications of the John Gower Society, 1 (Woodbridge: D. S. Brewer, 1987), https://middleenglish.library.jhu.edu/search/.
Sargent, Michael G., ed., *Nicholas Love's Mirror of the Blessed Life of Jesus Christ: A Critical Edition Based on Cambridge University Library Additional MSS 6578 and 6686* (New York: Garland, 1992).
Shakespeare, William, *The Merchant of Venice*, in G. Blakemore Evans, *et al.*, eds, *The Riverside Shakespeare*, 2nd edn. (Boston: Houghton Mifflin, 1997).
Skelton, John, *The bowge of courte* (Westminster: Wynkyn de Worde, c.1499), STC 22597.
——, *The bowge of courte* (London: Wynkyn de Worde, c.1510), STC 22597.5.
——, *A goodly garlande or chapelet of laurell* (London: Richard Faques, 1523), STC 22610.
——, *The Complete English Poems of John Skelton*, ed. John Scattergood, revised edition (Liverpool University Press: Liverpool, 2015).

Bibliography

Usk, Adam, *The Chronicle of Adam Usk, 1377–1421*, ed. and trans. C. Given Wilson (Oxford: Clarendon Press, 1997).
Walsingham, Thomas, *The Chronica Maiora of Thomas Walsingham, 1376–1422*, trans. David Preest; notes and intro. James G. Clark (Woodbridge: Boydell Press, 2005).
Walter, William, *Guystarde and Sygysmonde* (London: Wynkyn de Worde, 1532), STC 3183.5.

Secondary Texts

Adams, Robert P., *The Better Part of Valor: More, Erasmus, Colet, and Vives, on Humanism, War, and Peace, 1496-1535* (Seattle: University of Washington Press, 1962).
Alvar, Manuel, "Prólogo" to *John Gower: Confesión del Amante. Traducción de Juan de Cuenca (S. XV). Edición Paleográfica. Anejos del Boletín de la Real Academia Española (45)*, ed. Elena Alvar (Madrid: Real Academia Española, 1990).
Alves Moreira, Filipe, "Notas sobre a convivência de línguas em Portugal no século xv e a tradução da *Crónica de Alfonso X*," *e-Spania* 13 (2012).
Amado, Teresa, "O projecto histórico de um Infante," in *Lindley Cintra. Homenagem ao homem, ao mestre a ao cidadão*, ed. Isabel Hub Faria, 303–09 (Lisboa: Cosmos, 1999).
Annan, Noel, *The Dons* (London: Harper Collins, 1999).
Anon., "George Campbell Macaulay," *Modern Language Review* 10 (1915): 392.
Anon., Review of G. C. Macaulay, ed., *The Works of John Gower*, Volume I, *The Athenaeum*, 7 September 1901, 305–06.
Arens, William, "The Divine Kingship of the Shilluk: A Contemporary Reevaluation," *Ethnos* 44 (1979): 167–81.
Arias Guillén, Fernando, "El linaje maldito de Alfonso X. Conflictos en torno a la legitimidad regia en Castilla (*c.* 1275-1390)," *Vínculos de Historia* 1 (2012): 147–63.
Ashdowne, R. K., D. R. Howlett, and R. E. Latham, eds., *Dictionary of Medieval Latin from British Sources* (Oxford: British Academy, 2018).
Bagshaw, Samuel, *History Gazeteer, and Directory of the County Palatine of Chester* (Sheffield: George Ridge, 1850).
Bahr, Arthur W., "Reading Codicological Form in John Gower's Trentham Manuscript," *Studies in the Age of Chaucer* 33 (2011): 259–62.
——, *Fragments and Assemblages: Forming Compilations of Medieval London* (Chicago: University of Chicago Press, 2013).
Bakhtin, M. M., *Rabelais and His World*, trans. Hélène Iswolsky (Cambridge, MA: MIT Press, 1968).
Barkham, Michael M., "The Spanish Basque Irish Fishery & Trade in the Sixteenth-Century," *History Ireland* 9, no. 3 (2001): 12–15.
Barolini, Teodolinda, "The Wheel of the 'Decameron'," *Romance Philology* 36 (1983): 521–39.
Barrington, Candace, "The Trentham Manuscript as Broken Prosthesis: Wholeness and Disability in Lancastrian England," *Accessus* 1 (2013): 1–33.

Bennet, J. A. W., "Caxton and Gower," *Modern Language Review* 45 (1950): 215-16.

——, ed., *Selections from John Gower* (Oxford: Clarendon Press, 1968).

Benskin, Michael and Margaret Laing, "Translations and *Mischsprachen* in Middle English Manuscripts," in *So meny people longages and tonges: Philological Essays presented to Angus McIntosh*, eds Michael Benskin and Michael L. Samuels (Edinburgh: Middle English Dialect Project, 1981), 55-106.

Benskin, Michael, Margaret Laing, Vasilis Karaiskos, and Keith Williamson, *An Electronic Version of A Linguistic Atlas of Late Mediaeval English* (Edinburgh: The University of Edinburgh, 2013), http://www.lel.ed.ac.uk/ihd/elalme/elalme.html [revised online edition of McIntosh, Angus, Michael L. Samuels, and Michael Benskin, *A Linguistic Atlas of Mediaeval English*, 4 vols. (Aberdeen: Aberdeen University Press, 1986).

Benson, C. David and David Rollman, "Wynkyn de Worde and the Ending of Chaucer's *Troilus and Criseyde*," *Modern Philology* 78 (1981): 275-79.

Blades, William, *The Life and Typography of William Caxton* (London: Joseph Lilly, 1863).

Blair, Ann, "Reflections on Technological Continuities: Manuscripts Copied from Printed Books," *Bulletin of the John Rylands Library* 91, no. 1 (2015): 7-33.

Blake, N. F., "Caxton's Copytext of Gower's *Confessio Amantis*," *Anglia* 85 (1967): 282-93; reprinted in *William Caxton and English Literary Culture* (London: Hambledon Press, 1991): 187-98.

——, "Manuscript to Print," in *Book Production and Publishing in Britain 1375-1475*, ed. Jeremy Griffiths and Derek Pearsall, 403-32 (Cambridge: Cambridge University Press, 1989).

——, "Early Printed Editions of the *Confessio Amantis*," *Mediaevalia* 16 (1993 for 1990): 289-306.

Blayney, Peter W. M., *The Stationers' Company and the Printers of London, 1501-1557*, 2 vols. (Cambridge: Cambridge University Press, 2013).

Blodgett, James E., "William Thynne (d. 1546)," in *Editing Chaucer: The Great Tradition*, ed. Paul G. Ruggiers, 35-52 (Norman: Pilgrim Books, 1984).

Bly Calkin, Siobhain, *Saracens and the Making of English Identity: The Auchinleck Manuscript* (New York: Routledge, 2005).

Boffey, Julia, *Manuscript and Print in London c.1475-1530* (London: The British Library, 2012).

——, "From Manuscripts to Print: Continuity and Change," in *A Companion to the Early Printed Book in Britain 1476-1558*, eds Vincent Gillespie and Susan Powell, 13-26 (Cambridge: D. S. Brewer, 2014).

—— and A. S. G. Edwards, eds, *A New Index of Middle English Verse* (London: British Library, 2005).

—— and Carol Meale, "Selecting the Text: Rawlinson C. 86 and Some Other Books for London Readers," in *Regionalism in Late Medieval Manuscripts and Texts*, ed. Felicity Riddy, 143-69 (Cambridge: D. S. Brewer, 1991).

Bone, Gavin, "Extant Manuscripts Printed from by W. De Worde with Notes on the Owner, Roger Thorney," *The Library*, 4th ser. 12 (1932): 284-306.

Brody, Nathaniel, *The Disease of the Soul: Leprosy in Medieval Literature* (Ithaca, NY: Cornell University Press, 1974).

Brown, Cynthia J., *Poets, Patrons, and Printers: Crisis of Authority in Late Medieval France* (Ithaca: Cornell University Press, 1995).

Brown, Harry J., "For Worldes Good," in *The Crusades: Other Experiences, Alternate Perspectives: Selected Proceedings from the 32nd Annual CEMERS Conference*, ed. Khalil I. Semaan, 179–91 (Binghamton, NY: Global Academic Publishing, 2003).

Brusendorff, Aage, *The Chaucer Tradition* (Oxford: Clarendon, 1925).

Bühler, Curt F., *The Fifteenth-Century Book: The Scribes, the Printers, the Decorators* (Philadelphia: University of Pennsylvania Press, 1960).

Bullón-Fernández, María, "Engendering Authority: Father and Daughter, State and Church in Gower's 'Tale of Constance' and Chaucer's 'Man of Law's Tale'," in *Re-Visioning Gower*, ed. R. F. Yeager, 129–46 (Asheville: Pegasus Press, 1998).

——, *Fathers and Daughters in Gower's* Confessio Amantis*: Authority, Family, State and Writing* (Cambridge: D. S. Brewer, 2000).

Burke, John, *A Genealogical and Heraldic Dictionary of the Peerage and Baronetage of the British Empire*, 6th edn. (London: Henry Colburn, 1839).

Burrow, John A., "Gower's Poetic Styles," in *A Companion to Gower*, ed. Siân Echard, 239–50 (Cambridge: D. S. Brewer, 2004).

——, "Scribal Mismetring," in *Middle English Poetry: Texts and Traditions: Essays in Honour of Derek Pearsall*, ed. Alastair J. Minnis, 169–79 (York: York Medieval Press, 2001).

Butterfield, Ardis, *The Familiar Enemy* (Oxford: Oxford University Press, 2009).

Campbell, Tony, "Portolan Charts from the Late Thirteenth Century to 1500," in *History of Cartography*, vol. I: *Cartography in Prehistoric, Ancient, and Medieval Europe and the Mediterranean*, ed. J. B. Harley and David Woodward, 371–463 (Chicago: University of Chicago Press, 1987).

Carley, James P., "John Leland in Paris: The Evidence of his Poetry," *Studies in Philology* 83 (1986): 1–50.

—— and Ágnes Juhász-Ormsby, "Survey of Henrician Humanism," in *Oxford History of Classical Reception in English Literature*, Vol. 1: 800–1558, ed. Rita Copeland, 515–40 (Oxford: Oxford University Press, 2016).

Carlson, David R., "Woodcut Illustrations of the Canterbury Tales, 1483-1602," *Library*, 6th series 19 (1997): 25–67.

——, "Greeks in England, 1400," in *Interstices: Studies in Late Middle English and Anglo-Latin Texts in Honour of A. G. Rigg*, ed. Richard Firth Green and Linne Mooney, 74–98 (Toronto, University of Toronto Press, 2004).

——, "Gower on Henry IV's Rule: The Endings of the *Cronica Tripertita* and Its Texts," *Traditio* 62 (2007): 207–36.

——, "The Invention of the Anglo-Latin Public Poetry (circa 1367-1402) and its Prosody, Especially in John Gower," *Mittellateinisches Jahrbuch* 39, no. 3 (2004): 389–406.

——, "The Parliamentary Source of Gower's *Cronica Tripertita* and Incommensurable Styles," in *John Gower, Trilingual Poet: Language, Translation, and Tradition*, ed. Elisabeth Dutton with John Hines and R. F. Yeager, 98–111 (Cambridge: D. S. Brewer, 2010).

Carter, P. R. N., "Tuke, Sir Brian (d. 1545), administrator," *Oxford Dictionary of National Biography* 23 September 2004; https://doi.org/10.1093/ref:odnb/27803.

"Caxton's Chaucer," *British Library*; https://www.bl.uk/treasures/caxton/homepage.html.
Cioffari, Vincenzo, "The Conception of Fortune in the *Decameron*," *Italica* 17 (1940): 129–37.
——, "The Function of Fortune in Dante, Boccaccio, and Machiavelli," *Italica* 24 (1947): 1–13.
Clark, John W., "A New Copy of Caxton's Indulgence," *Speculum* 9 (1934): 301–03.
Coffman, George R., "John Gower in His Most Significant Role," in *Elizabethan Studies and Other Essays in Honor of George F. Reynolds*, ed. E. J. West, 52–61 (Boulder, CO: University of Colorado Studies, 1945).
Cole, Andrew, *Literature and Heresy in the Age of Chaucer* (Cambridge: Cambridge University Press, 2008).
Coleman, Janet, *Medieval Readers and Writers, 1350-1400* (New York: Columbia University Press, 1981).
——, "Property and Poverty," in *The Cambridge History of Medieval Political Thought, c. 350-c.1450*, ed. J. H. Burns, 607–48 (Cambridge: Cambridge University Press, 1988).
Coleman, Joyce, "Lay Readers and Hard Latin: How Gower May Have Intended the *Confessio Amantis* to Be Read," *Studies in the Age of Chaucer* 24 (2002): 209–35.
——, "Philippa of Lancaster, Queen of Portugal – and Patron of the Gower Translations?" in *England and Iberia in the Middle Ages, 12th-15th Century: Cultural, Literary, and Political Exchanges*, ed. María Bullón-Fernández, 135–65 (New York: Palgrave Macmillan, 2007).
Connolly, Margaret, "The Edited Text and the Selected Text and the Problem of Critical Editions," in *Editing and Interpretation of Middle English Texts: Essays in Honour of William Marx*, eds Margaret Connolly and Raluca Radulescu, 229–47 (Turnhout: Brepols, 2018).
——, *John Shirley: Book Production and the Noble Household in Fifteenth-Century England* (Aldershot: Ashgate, 1998).
——, "What John Shirley Said About Adam: Authorship and Attribution in Trinity College Cambridge MS R.3.20," in *The Dynamics of the Medieval Manuscript: Text Collections from a European Perspective*, eds Karen Pratt, Bart Besamusca, Matthias Meyer, and Ad Putter, 81–100 (Göttingen: V&R Unipress, 2017).
Cooper, Jeff, *Edward Thomas: Towards a Complete Checklist of his Writings* (Blackburn: White Sheep Press, 2004).
Copeland, Rita, ed., *Oxford History of Classical Reception in English Literature*, Vol. 1: 800–1558 (Oxford: Oxford University Press, 2016).
Cornelius, Ian, "Gower and the Peasants' Revolt," *Representations* 131 (2015): 22–51.
Cortijo Ocaña, Antonio, "La *Confessio Amantis* en el debate del origen del sentimentalismo ibérico: un posible contexto de recepción," in *Actas del VIII Congreso Internacional de la Asociación Hispánica de Literatura Medieval (Santander, 22-26 septiembre, 1999)*, eds Margarita Freixas, Silvia Iriso Ariz, and Laura Fernández, 583–601 (Santander: Asociación Hispánica de Literatura Medieval, 2000).

Costomiris, Robert, "Some New Light on the Early Career of William Thynne, Chief Clerk of the Kitchen of Henry VIII and Editor of Chaucer," *The Library*, 7th ser., 4 (2003): 3–15.

Curtis, Catherine, "The Social and Political Thought of Juan Luis Vives: Concord and Counsel in the Christian Commonwealth," in *A Companion to Juan Luis Vives*, ed. Charles Fantazzi, 113–76 (Leiden: Brill, 2008).

Curtis, Cathy, "More's Public Life," in *The Cambridge Companion to Thomas More*, ed. George M. Logan, 69–92 (Cambridge: Cambridge University Press, 2011).

Da Costa, Alex, "'That ye mowe redely fynde…what ye desyre': Printed Tables of Contents and Indices 1476-1540," *Huntington Library Quarterly* 81, no. 3 (2018): 291–313.

Dalché, Patrick Gautier, *Carte marine et portulan au XIIe siècle: le Liber de existencia riverarium et forma maris nostri Mediterranei (Pise, circa 1200)* (Rome: Ecole Française de Rome, 1995).

———, "The Reception of Ptolemy's *Geography* (End of the Fourteenth to Beginning of the Sixteenth Century)," in *The History of Cartography*, vol. 3: *Cartography in the European Renaissance*, ed. David Woodward, 285–364 (Chicago: University of Chicago Press, 2007).

Dane, Joseph A., *Who is Buried in Chaucer's Tomb? Studies in the Reception of Chaucer's Book* (East Lansing, MI: Michigan State University Press, 1998).

Daniels, R. Balfour, "Rhetoric in Gower's to 'King Henry the Fourth, in Praise of Peace'," *Studies in Philology* 32, no. 1 (1935): 62–73.

Delano-Smith, Catherine and Roger J. P. Kain, *English Maps: A History* (Toronto: University of Toronto Press, 1999).

Devereux, E. J., "John Rastell's Text of *The Parliament of Fowls*," *Moreana* 27/28 (1970): 115–20.

DeVries, Kelly, "The Lack of a Western European Military Response to the Ottoman Invasions of Eastern Europe from Nicopolis (1396) to Mohács (1526)," *The Journal of Military History* 63 (1999): 539–59.

———, "The Effect of Killing the Christian Prisoners at the Battle of Nicopolis," in *Crusaders, Condottieri, and Cannon: Medieval Warfare in Societies around the Mediterranean*, eds Donald J. Kagay and Andrew Villalon, 157–72 (Leiden: Brill, 2003).

Dilke, O. A. W., "The Culmination of Greek Cartography in Ptolemy," in *The History of Cartography*, vol. 1: *Cartography in Prehistoric, Ancient, and Medieval Europe and the Mediterranean*, eds J. B. Harley and David Woodward, 177–200 (Chicago: University of Chicago Press, 1987).

Doran, Susan, and Glenn Richardson, eds, *Tudor England and Its Neighbours* (Basingstoke: Palgrave Macmillan, 2005).

Doyle, A. I., and M. B. Parkes, "The Production of Copies of the *Canterbury Tales* and the *Confessio Amantis* in the Early Fifteenth Century," in *Medieval Scribes, Manuscripts, and Libraries: Essays Presented to N. R. Ker*, eds M. B. Parkes and Andrew Watson, 163–210 (London: Scolar Press, 1978).

Driver, Martha W., "Printing the *Confessio Amantis*: Caxton's Edition in Context," in *Re-Visioning Gower*, ed. R. F. Yeager, 269–303 (Asheville, NC: Pegasus Press, 1998).

———, *The Image in Print: Book Illustration in Late Medieval England and its Sources* (London: British Library, 2004).

Du Boulay, F. R. H., "Henry of Derby's expeditions to Prussia 1390-91 and 1392," in *The Reign of Richard II: essays in honour of May McKisack*, eds F. R. H. du Boulay and Caroline M. Barron, 153–72 (London: Athlone Press, 1971).

Duff, E. Gordon, *William Caxton* (Chicago: The Caxton Club, 1905).

——, *Printing in England in the Fifteenth Century. E. Gordon Duff's Bibliography with supplementary descriptions, chronologies and a census of copies by Lotte Hellinga* (London: Bibliographical Society, 2009).

Duffell, Martin J., *A New History of English Metre* (London: Maney for the Modern Humanities Research Association, 2008).

——, and Dominique Billy, "From Decasyllable to Pentameter: Gower's Contribution to English Metrics," *Chaucer Review* 38, no. 4 (2004): 383–400.

Dust, Philip C., *Three Renaissance Pacifists: Essays in the Theories of Erasmus, More, and Vives* (New York: Peter Lang, 1987).

Eastwood, Bruce, *Ordering the Heavens: Roman Astronomy and Cosmology in the Carolingian Renaissance* (Leiden: Brill, 2007).

Echard, Siân, "Pretexts: Tables of Contents and the Reading of John Gower's *Confessio Amantis*," *Medium Aevum* 66 (1997): 270–87.

——, "With Carmen's Help: Latin Authorities in the *Confessio Amantis*," *Studies in Philology* 95, no. 1 (1998): 1–40.

——, "Dialogues and Monologues: Manuscript Representations of the Conversation of the *Confessio Amantis*," in *Middle English Poetry: Texts and Tradition: Essays in Honour of Derek Pearsall*, ed. Alastair Minnis, 57–75 (York: York Medieval Press, 2001).

——, "Last Words: Latin at the End of the *Confessio Amantis*," in *Interstices: Studies in Late Middle English and Anglo-Latin in Honour of A. G. Rigg*, eds Richard Firth Greene and Linne R. Mooney, 99–121 (Toronto: University of Toronto Press, 2004).

——, "Gower in Print," in *A Companion to Gower*, ed. Siân Echard (Cambridge: D. S. Brewer, 2004), 115–35.

——, *Printing the Middle Ages* (Philadelphia: University of Pennsylvania Press, 2008).

Edwards, A. S. G., "The Circulation of English Verse in Manuscript after the Advent of Print in England," *Studia Neophilologica* 83, no. 1 (2011): 67–77.

—— and Carol M. Meale, "The Marketing of Printed Books in Late Medieval England," *The Library* 6th ser. 15 (1993): 95–124.

Edwards, Robert R., "Gower's Poetics of the Literal," in *John Gower, Trilingual Poet: Language, Translation, and Tradition*, ed. Elisabeth Dutton with John Hines and R. F. Yeager, 59–73 (Cambridge: D. S. Brewer, 2010).

——, "Gower's Reception," in *The Routledge Research Companion to John Gower*, eds Ana Sáez-Hidalgo, Brian Gastle, and R. F. Yeager, 197–209 (London and New York: Routledge, 2017).

Eisenstein, Elizabeth L., *The Printing Press as an Agent of Change: Communications and Cultural Transformations in Early-Modern Europe* (Complete in One Volume) (Cambridge: Cambridge University Press, 1979).

Erler, Mary C., "Early Woodcuts of Skelton: The Uses of Convention," *Bulletin of Research in the Humanities* 87 (1986–87): 17–28.

——, "Printer's Copy: MS Bodley 638 and the *Parliament of Fowls*," *Chaucer Review* 33, no. 3 (1999): 221–29.

Evans, James, *The History and Practice of Ancient Astronomy* (Oxford: Oxford University Press, 1998).
Evans-Pritchard, E. E., *The Divine Kingship of the Shilluk of Nilotic Sudan* (Cambridge: Cambridge University Press, 1948).
Faccon, Manuela, *La Fortuna de la* Confessio Amantis *en la Península Ibérica: el testimonio portugués* (Zaragoza: Prensas Universitarias de Zaragoza, 2010).
Fantazzi, Charles, ed., *A Companion to Juan Luis Vives* (Leiden: Brill, 2008).
Federico, Sylvia, *New Troy: Fantasies of Empire in the Late Middle Ages* (Minneapolis: University of Minnesota Press, 2003).
Ferster, Judith, *Fictions of Advice: The Literature and Politics of Counsel in Late Medieval England* (Philadelphia: University of Pennsylvania Press, 1996).
Fideler, Paul A. and T. F. Mayer, eds, *Political Thought and the Tudor Commonwealth: Deep Structure, Discourse and Disguise* (London: Routledge, 1992).
Fisher, John H., *John Gower: Moral Philosopher and Friend of Chaucer* (New York: New York University Press, 1964).
Forni, Kathleen, *The Chaucerian Apocrypha: A Counterfeit Canon* (Gainesville: University Press of Florida, 2001).
Förster, Max, "Über Benedict Burghs Leben und Werke," *Archiv für das Studium der neueren Sprache und Literaturen* 101 (1898): 29–64.
——, "Kleine Mitteilungen," *Archiv für das Studium der neueren Sprache und Literaturen* 102 (1899): 213–14.
Fox, George, *The Mediaeval Sciences in the Works of John Gower* (Princeton: Princeton University Press, 1931).
Fredell, Joel, "The Gower Manuscripts: Some Inconvenient Truths," *Viator* 41 (2010): 231–50.
——, "John Gower's Manuscripts in Middle English," in *The Routledge Research Companion to John Gower*, eds Ana Sáez-Hidalgo, Brian Gastle, and R. F. Yeager, 91–96 (London and New York: Routledge, 2017).
Fryde, E. B., *et al.*, eds, *Handbook of British Chronology*, 3rd edn. (Cambridge: Cambridge University Press, 1996).
Furnivall, Frederick J., [untitled], *The Athenaeum*, 18 February (1871): 210.
Galloway, Andrew, "The Literature of 1388 and the Politics of Pity in Gower's *Confessio Amantis*," in *The Letter of the Law: Legal Practice and Literary Production in Medieval England*, eds Emily Steiner and Candace Barrington, 67–104 (Cornell University Press, 2002).
——, "Reassessing Gower's Dream Visions," in *John Gower, Trilingual Poet: Language, Translation, and Tradition*, ed. Elisabeth Dutton and John Hines with R. F. Yeager, 288–303 (Cambridge: D. S. Brewer, 2010).
Ganim, John, "Gower, Liminality, and the Politics of Space," *Exemplaria* 19 (2007): 90–116.
Gardham, Julie and David Weston, *The World of Chaucer: Medieval Books and Manuscripts* (Glasgow: Glasgow University Library, 2004).
Gaskell, Philip, *A New Introduction to Bibliography* (Delaware: Oak Knoll Press, 1972).
Giancarlo, Matthew, "Gower's Governmentality: Revisiting John Gower as a Constitutional Thinker and Regiminal Writer," in *John Gower: Others and the Self*, eds Russell A. Peck and R. F. Yeager, 225–59 (Cambridge: D. S. Brewer, 2017).

Gillespie, Alexandra, "Poets, Printers, and Early English Sammelbände," *Huntington Library Quarterly* 67, no. 2 (June 2004): 189–214.

——, *Print Culture and the Medieval Author: Chaucer, Lydgate and their Books, 1473-1557* (Oxford: Oxford University Press, 2006).

Ginsberg, Warren, "From Simile to Prologue: Geography as Link in Dante, Petrarch, Chaucer," in *Through a Classical Eye: Transcultural and Transhistorical Visions in Medieval English, Italian, and Latin Literature in Honour of Winthrop Wetherbee*, eds Andrew Galloway and R. F. Yeager (Toronto: University of Toronto Press, 2009), 145–64.

Goff, Frederick R., ed., *Incunabula in American Libraries; a Third Census of Fifteenth-Century Books Recorded in North American Collections* (New York: Bibliographical Society of America, 1964).

Gorman, M. M., "The Diagrams in the Oldest Manuscripts of Isidore's 'De natura rerum' with a Note on the Manuscript Traditions of Isidore's Works," *Studi Medievali* 42, no. 2 (2001): 529–45.

Gow, A. S. F., Review of G. C. Macaulay, ed., *The Works of John Gower*, Volume IV, *The Classical Review* 18 (1904): 62.

Grady, Frank, "The Lancastrian Gower and the Limits of Exemplarity," *Speculum* 70 (1995): 552–75.

——, "Gower's Boat, Richard's Barge, and the True Story of the *Confessio Amantis*: Text and Gloss," *Texas Studies in Literature and Language* 44 (2002): 1–15.

Graeber, David, and Marshall Sahlins, *On Kings* (Chicago: Hau Books, 2017).

Griffiths, Jane, "What's in a Name? The Transmission of 'John Skelton, Laureate' in Manuscript and Print," *Huntington Library Quarterly* 67 (2004): 215–35.

——, "Gower's *Confessio Amantis*: A 'New' Manuscript," *Medium Aevum* 82 (2013): 244–59.

——, *Diverting Authorities: Experimental Glossing Practices in Manuscript and Print* (Oxford: Oxford University Press, 2014).

Griffiths, Jeremy, "Book Production Terms in Nicholas Munshull's *Nominale*," in *Ashgate Critical Essays on Early English Lexicographers*, Vol. 2: *Middle English*, ed. Christine Franzen (Farnham, Surrey: Ashgate, 2012), 333–56.

——, "*Confessio Amantis*: The Poem and its Pictures," in *Gower's Confessio Amantis: Responses and Reassessments*, ed. A. J. Minnis (Cambridge: D. S. Brewer, 1983), 163–78.

——, "The Manuscripts," in *Lollard Sermons*, ed. Gloria Cigman, EETS OS 294 (Oxford: Oxford University Press, 1989), xi–xxix.

Grundmann, Hermann, *Der Typus des Ketzers in mittelalterlicher Anschauung* (Leipzig and Berlin: B. G. Teubner, 1927).

Gura, David, "A Critical Edition and Study of Arnulf of Orléans' Philological Commentary on Ovid's *Metamorphoses*," PhD dissertation, The Ohio State University (THE:CLA2010PHD873).

Hall, J. J., *Cambridge Act and Tripos Verses*, Cambridge Bibliographical Society Monograph no. 15 (Cambridge: Cambridge Bibliographical Society, 2009).

Hamm, Robert Wayne, "A Critical Evaluation of the *Confisyon del Amante*, the Castilian Translation of Gower's *Confessio Amantis*," *Medium Aevum* 47, no. 1 (1978): 91–106.

——, Peter G. Beidler, and R. F. Yeager, "Gower," in *A Manual of the Writings in Middle English*, ed. A. E. Hartung (New Haven, CT: Connecticut Academy of Arts, Sciences & Letters, 1986), 7: 2399-2418.
Hanna, Ralph III and A. S. G. Edwards, "Rotheley, the De Vere Circle, and the Ellesmere Chaucer," *Huntington Library Quarterly* 58:1 (1996): 11–35.
Hanna, Ralph and David Rundle, *A Descriptive Catalogue of the Western Manuscripts in Christ Church, Oxford* (Oxford: Oxford Bibliographical Society, 2017).
Harley, J. B. and David Woodward, "The Foundations of Theoretical Cartography in Archaic and Classical Greece," in *History of Cartography*, vol. 1: *Cartography in Prehistoric, Ancient, and Medieval Europe and the Mediterranean*, eds J. B. Harley and David Woodward (Chicago: University of Chicago Press, 1987), 130-147.
Heal, Felicity, "The Bishops and the Printers: Henry VII to Elizabeth," in *The Prelate in England and Europe, 1300-1560*, ed. Martin Heale (York: York Medieval Press, 2014), 142-69.
Heffernan, Carol F., *The Orient in Chaucer and Medieval Romance* (Cambridge: D. S. Brewer, 2003).
Hellinga, Lotte, ed., *A Catalogue of Books Printed in the XVth Century Now in the British Library. Part XI: England* ('t Goy-Houten, The Netherlands: Hes and De Graaf Publishers, 2007).
Hellinga-Querido, Lotte, "Reading an Engraving: William Caxton's Dedication to Margaret of York," in *Across the Narrow Seas: Studies in the History and Bibliography of Britain and the Low Countries Presented to Anna E. C. Simoni*, ed. Susan Roach (London: The British Library, 1991), 1-15.
Heng, Geraldine, *Empire of Magic: Medieval Romance and the Politics of Cultural Fantasy* (New York: Columbia University, 2003).
Herrero Jiménez, Mauricio with Tamara Pérez-Fernández and Marta Gutiérrez Rodríguez, "Castilian Script in the Iberian Manuscripts of the *Confessio Amantis*," in *John Gower in Iberia: Manuscripts, Influences, Reception*, eds Ana Sáez-Hidalgo and R. F. Yeager (Cambridge: D. S. Brewer, 2014), 17-31.
Hiatt, Alfred, *Terra Incognita: Mapping the Antipodes before 1600* (Chicago: University of Chicago Press, 2008).
Hocart, A.M., *Kingship* (London: Oxford University Press, 1969 [1927]).
——, *Kings and Councillors: An Essay in the Comparative Anatomy of Human Society*, ed. Rodney Needham (Chicago: University of Chicago Press, 1970 [1936]).
Hodnett, Edward, *English Woodcuts 1480-1535*, 2nd edn. (Oxford: Oxford University Press, 1973).
Hollinshead, Janet E., "Chester, Liverpool and the Basque Region in the Sixteenth Century," *Mariner's Mirror* 85, no. 4 (1999): 387–95.
Hook, David, ed., *The Arthur of the Iberians: The Arthurian Legends in the Spanish and Portuguese Worlds* (Cardiff: University of Wales Press, 2015).
Horobin, Simon, *The Language of the Chaucer Tradition* (Cambridge: Boydell and Brewer, 2003).
Horobin, Simon and Daniel Mosser, "Scribe D's SW Midlands Roots: A Reconsideration," *Neuphilogische Mitteilungen* 3/106 (2005): 289–305.
Houghton, L. B. T. and Gesine Manuwald, eds, *Neo-Latin Poetry in the British Isles* (London: Bristol Classical Press, 2012).

Hudson, Anne, *The Premature Reformation* (Oxford: Oxford University Press, 1988).
——, *Selections from English Wycliffite Writings*, Medieval Academy Reprints for Teaching, 38 (Toronto: University of Toronto Press, 1997).
——, ed., *Wyclif: Political Ideas and Practice. Papers by Michael Wilks* (Oxford: Oxbow Books, 2000).
Hutton, James, "John Leland's *Laudatio Pacis*," *Studies in Philology* 58 (1961): 616–26.
——, *Themes of Peace in Renaissance Poetry*, ed. Rita Guerlac (Ithaca: Cornell University Press, 1984).
Irvin, Matthew W., *The Poetic Voices of John Gower: Politics and Personae in the Confessio Amantis* (Cambridge: Boydell and Brewer, 2014).
James, Mervyn, *Society, Politics and Culture: Studies in Early Modern England* (Cambridge: Cambridge University Press, 1986).
James, M. R., *A Descriptive Catalogue of the Manuscripts in Pembroke College, Cambridge* (Cambridge: Cambridge University Press, 1905).
——, "The Salomites," *Journal of Theological Studies* 35 (1934): 287–97.
Jefferson, Judith, "The Hoccleve Holographs and Hoccleve's Metrical Practice," in *Manuscripts and Texts: Editorial Problems in Later Middle English Literature*, ed. Derek A. Pearsall (Cambridge: D. S. Brewer, 1987), 95–109.
Jones, Terry, "Did John Gower Rededicate His *Confessio Amantis* before Henry IV's Usurpation?" in *Middle English Texts in Transition: A Festschrift Dedicated to Toshiyuki Takamiya on His 70th Birthday*, eds Simon Horobin and Linne R. Mooney (Woodbridge, Suffolk: York Medieval Press/Boydell and Brewer, 2014), 40–74.
Justice, Steven, *Adam Usk's Secret* (Philadelphia: University of Pennsylvania Press, 2015).
Kane, Brian, *Sound Unseen: Acousmatic Sound in Theory and Practice* (Oxford: Oxford University Press, 2014).
Kantorowicz, Ernst H., *The King's Two Bodies: A Study in Mediaeval Political Theology* (Princeton: Princeton University Press, 1957).
Kaylor, Noel Harold Jr., "The Orientation of Chaucer's 'Canterbury Tales'," *Medieval Perspectives* 10 (1995–96): 133–47.
Kerby-Fulton, Kathryn, "'Langland in his Working Clothes'? Scribe D, Authorial Loose Revision Material, and the Nature of Scribal Intervention," in *Middle English Poetry: Texts and Traditions: Essays in Honour of Derek Pearsall*, ed. Alastair J. Minnis (York: York Medieval Press, 2001), 139–67.
—— and Steven Justice, "Scribe D and the Marketing of Ricardian Literature," in *The Medieval Professional Reader at Work: Evidence from Manuscripts of Chaucer, Langland, Kempe and Gower*, eds Kathryn Kerby-Fulton and Maidie Hilmo (Victoria, BC: University of Victoria, 2001), 217–37.
Kirby, J. L., *Henry IV of England* (London: Constable, 1970).
Knapp, Ethan, "The Place of Egypt in Gower's *Confessio Amantis*," in *John Gower, Trilingual Poet: Language, Translation, and Tradition*, eds Elisabeth M. Dutton, John Hines, with R. F. Yeager (Cambridge: D. S. Brewer, 2010), 26–34.
Knight, Stephen, "Places in the Text: Topographicist Approach to Chaucer," in *Speaking Images: Essays in Honor of V. A. Kolve*, eds R. F. Yeager and Charlotte C. Morse (Asheville, NC: Pegasus Press, 2001), 445–61.

Kobayashi, Yoshiko, "Lament to Prophecy in Book I of John Gower's *Vox Clamantis*," in *Through a Classical Eye: Transcultural and Transhistorical Visions in Medieval English, Italian, and Latin Literature in Honour of Winthrop Wehterbee*, eds Andrew Galloway and R. F. Yeager (Toronto: University of Toronto Press, 2009), 339–62.

——, "Letters of Old Age: The Advocacy of Peace in the Works of John Gower and Philippe de Mézières," in *John Gower: Others and the Self*, eds Russell A. Peck and R. F. Yeager (Cambridge: D. S. Brewer, 2017), 204–22.

Krummel, Miriamne Ara, "Globalizing Jewish Communities: Mapping a Jewish Geography in Fragment VII of the Canterbury Tales," *Texas Studies in Literature and Language* 50 (2008): 121–42.

Kuskin, William, ed., *Caxton's Trace: Studies in the History of English Printing* (Notre Dame, IN: University of Notre Dame Press, 2006).

——, *Symbolic Caxton: Literary Culture and Print Capitalism* (Notre Dame, IN: University of Notre Dame Press, 2008).

Lahey, Stephen E., *Philosophy and Politics in the Thought of John Wyclif*, Cambridge Studies in Medieval Life and Thought, Fourth Series (Cambridge: Cambridge University Press, 2003).

——, "John Wyclif's Political Philosophy," *Stanford Encyclopedia of Philosophy* 2006; rev. 2013, https://plato.stanford.edu/entries/wyclif-political/.

Lass, Roger, "Phonology and Morphology," in *The Cambridge History of the English Language, Volume II, 1066-1476*, ed. Norman Blake (Cambridge: Cambridge University Press, 1992), 23–155.

Lavezzo, Kathy, *Angels on the Edge of the World: Geography, Literature, and English Community, 1000-1534* (Ithaca: Cornell University Press, 2006).

Lee, Sidney and A. S. G. Edwards, "Thynne, William (d. 1546), literary editor," *Oxford Dictionary of National Biography* 23 September 2004, https://doi.org/10.1093/ref:odnb/27426.

Lefanu, Sarah, *Rose Macaulay* (London: Virago, 2003).

Logan, George M., ed., *The Cambridge Companion to Thomas More* (Cambridge: Cambridge University Press, 2011).

Longo, Pamela, "Gower's Public Outcry," *Philological Quarterly* 92, no. 3 (2013): 357–87.

Lowe, Ben, "Peace Discourse and Mid-Tudor Foreign Policy," in *Political Thought and the Tudor Commonwealth: Deep Structure, Discourse and Disguise*, eds Paul A. Fideler and T. F. Mayer (London: Routledge, 1992), 108–39.

——, *Imagining Peace: A History of Early English Pacifist Ideas, 1340-1560* (University Park: Pennsylvania State University Press, 1997).

Lozovsky, Natalia, *The Earth is Our Book: Geographical Knowledge in the Latin West ca. 400-1000* (Ann Arbor, MI: University of Michigan Press, 2000).

Lubac, Henri de, *Medieval Exegesis: The Four Senses of Scripture*, 3 vols, trans. Mark Sebanc and E. M. Macierowski (Grand Rapids: W. B. Eerdmans Pub. Co., 1998–2009).

Lutz, Cora, "Manuscripts Copied from Printed Books," *Yale University Library Gazette* 49, no. 3 (1975): 261–67.

Lynch, Kathryn, ed., *Chaucer's Cultural Geography* (New York: Routledge, 2002).

Macaulay, George C., "A Local Historian [Agostino Giustiniani]," *MacMillan's Magazine* (April 1891): 464–73.

——, ed., Arnold, Matthew, *Poems* (London: Macmillan, 1896).
——, "Beaumont and Fletcher," in *The Cambridge History of English Literature*, Volume VI, eds A. W. Ward and A. R. Waller (Cambridge: Cambridge University Press, 1908), 107–40.
——, ed., Berners, Lord, *The Chronicles of Froissart* (London: Macmillan, 1895).
——, "Eton as it is," *Eton College Chronicle*, 9 November 1871, 683.
——, *Francis Beaumont, a Critical Study* (London: Kegan Paul & Co., 1883).
——, "Froissart the Lover," *MacMillan's Magazine* (January 1895): 223–30.
——, "Froissart the Historian," *MacMillan's Magazine* (March 1895): 384–92.
——, *Graduated German Reading-Book* (London: Rivingtons, 1888).
——, ed., *Herodotus. Book III* (London: Macmillan, 1890).
——, *James Thomson* (London: Macmillan, 1910).
——, ed., *Livy: Books XXIII and XXIV* (London: Macmillan, 1895).
——, ed., *Livy: The Hannibalian War* (London: Macmillan, 1880).
——, "Note on Chaucer's borrowings from Benoit de Sainte Moire," in *Three More Parallel Texts of Chaucer's* Troilus and Criseyde *from MS. Li in St John's College, Cambridge; MS No. 61 in Corpus Christi College, Cambridge, and the Harleian MS. 1239 in the British Museum*, put forth by F. J. Furnivall, Part I, Books I–III, Chaucer Society Publications, 1st series, LXXXVII (London, 1894).
——, "Notes on some MSS of Herodotus," *Transactions of the Cambridge Philological Society* III, part III (1890): 135–39.
——, "On Horace *Ars Poetica*, ll. 128-30," *Classical Review* 26 (1912): 153–54.
——, "Shakespeare's *Tempest*, Act I, sc. II, l. 29," *Modern Language Review* 11 (1916): 75.
——, ed., Tennyson, Alfred Lord, *The Marriage of Geraint. Geraint and Enid* (London: MacMillan, 1892).
——, ed., Tennyson, Alfred Lord, *Gareth & Lynette* (London: Macmillan, 1892).
——, ed., Tennyson, Alfred Lord, *The Holy Grail* (London: Macmillan, 1893).
——, "The Ancren Riwle," *Modern Language Review* 9 (1914): 63–78, 145–60, 324–31, 463–74.
——, "The Capture of a General Council, 1241," *English Historical Review* 6 (1891): 1–17.
——, "The *Confessio Amantis*," in *The Cambridge History of English Literature*, vol. II, eds A. W. Ward and A. R. Waller (Cambridge: Cambridge University Press, 1908), 166–76.
——, "The English Bible," *Quarterly Review* 215 (1911): 504–30.
——, "The Lost French Works of Gower," *Academy* 13 April 1895, 313–15.
——, "The 'Speculum Meditantis' of John Gower," *Academy* 27 July 1895, 71–72.
——, "The 'Speculum Meditantis' of John Gower II," *Academy* 3 August 1895, 91–92.
——, trans., *The History of Herodotus* (London: Macmillan, 1890).
——, "'Troilus and Criseyde' in Professor Skeat's Edition," *The Academy* 6 April 1895, 297–98.
——, "'Troilus and Criseyde' in Professor Skeat's Edition," *The Academy* 20 April 1895, 338–39.
——, "Walt Whitman," *Nineteenth Century* 70 (December 1882): 903–18.

—— and M. R. James, "Fifteenth Century Carols and Other Pieces," *Modern Language Review* 8 (1913): 68–86.
MacCulloch, Diarmaid, ed., *The Reign of Henry VIII: Politics, Policy and Piety* (Houndmills: Macmillan, 1995).
Machan, Tim William, "Thomas Berthelette and Gower's *Confessio*," *Studies in the Age of Chaucer* 18 (1996): 143–66.
McDonald, Nicola F., "'Lusti Tresor': Avarice and the Economics of the Erotic in Gower's *Confessio Amantis*," in *Treasure in the Medieval West*, ed. Elizabeth M. Tyler (York: York Medieval Press, 2000), 135–56.
McIntosh, Angus, "Word Geography in the Lexicography of Medieval English," *Annals of the New York Academy of Sciences* 211 (1973): 55–66; reprinted in *Middle English Dialectology: Essays on some Principles and Problems*, eds Angus McIntosh, Michael L. Samuels, and Margaret Laing (Aberdeen: Aberdeen University Press, 1989), 86–97.
McKitterick, David, *Print, Manuscript and the Search for Order 1450-1830* (Cambridge: Cambridge University Press, 2003).
Manly, John, "Note on the Envoy of Truth," *Modern Philology* 11 (1913): 22.
Martín, José-Luis, "Defensa y justificación de la dinastía Trastámara. Las Crónicas de Pedro López de Ayala," *Espacio, Tiempo y Forma, Serie III, Hisstoria Medieval* 3 (1990): 157–80.
Mattingly, Garrett, "An Early Nonaggression Pact," *Journal of Modern History* 10 (1938): 1–30.
Meindl, Robert J., "The Latin Works," in *The Routledge Research Companion to John Gower*, eds Ana Sáez-Hidalgo, Brian Gastle, and R. F. Yeager (London and New York: Routledge, 2017), 341–54.
Merrills, Andy, "Geography and Memory in Isidore's *Etymologies*," in *Mapping Medieval Geographies: Geographical Encounters in the Latin West and Beyond, 300-1600*, ed. Keith D. Lilley (Cambridge: Cambridge University Press, 2013), 45–64.
Meyer, Karl, "John Gower's Beziehungen zu Chaucer und könig Richard II," PhD dissertation, University of Bonn, 1889.
Minnis, Alastair, "*Quadruplex sensus, multiplex modus*: Scriptural Sense and Mode in Medieval Scholastic Exegesis," in *Interpretation and Allegory: Antiquity to the Modern Period*, ed. Jon Whitman (Leiden: Brill, 2000), 231–56.
——, *Fallible Authors: Chaucer's Pardoner and Wife of Bath* (Philadelphia: University of Pennsylvania Press, 2007).
Mooney, Linne R., "A New Manuscript by the Hammond Scribe Discovered by Jeremy Griffiths," in *The English Medieval Book*, eds A. S. G. Edwards, Vincent Gillespie, and Ralph Hanna (London: British Library, 2000), 113–23.
——, "Chaucer's Scribe," *Speculum* 81, no. 1 (2006): 97–138.
——, Simon Horobin, and Estelle Stubbs, *Late Medieval English Scribes*, Version 1.0 (York: University of York, 2011), https://www.medievalscribes.com.
—— and Estelle Stubbs, *Scribes and the City: London Guildhall Clerks and the Dissemination of Middle English Literature 1375-1425* (York: York Medieval Press, 2013).
Moore, J. K., "Manuscripts Copied from Books Printed Before 1640," *Primary Materials Relating to Copy and Print in English Books of the Sixteenth and Seventeenth Centuries* (Oxford: Oxford Bibliographical Society, 1992), 1–9.

Bibliography

Morse, Ruth, Helen Cooper, and Peter Holland, eds, *Medieval Shakespeare: Pasts and Presents* (Cambridge: Cambridge University Press, 2013).

Mula, Patrick, "'Il peccato della fortuna'. La nouvelle X 1 du *Décaméron*," *Lettere italiane* 60 (2008): 43–83.

Natoli, Bartolo A., *Silenced Voices: The Poetics of Speech in Ovid* (Madison: University of Wisconsin Press, 2017).

Needham, Paul, *The Printer and the Pardoner: An Unrecorded Indulgence Printed by William Caxton for the Hospital St. Mary Rounceval, Charing Cross* (Washington: Library of Congress, 1986).

Nicholson, Peter, "Gower's Revisions in the *Confessio Amantis*," *Chaucer Review* 19 (1984): 123–43.

——, "Poet and Scribe in the Manuscripts of Gower's *Confessio Amantis*," in *Manuscripts and Texts: Textual Problems in Middle English Editing*, ed. Derek Pearsall (Cambridge: D. S. Brewer, 1987), 130–42.

——, "The Dedications of Gower's *Confessio Amantis*," *Mediaevalia* 10 (1988): 159-80.

——, "Gower's Manuscript of the *Confessio Amantis*," in *The Medieval Python: The Purposive and Provocative Work of Terry Jones,* eds R. F. Yeager and T. Takamiya (Basingstoke: Springer, 2012), 75–86.

Nixon, Howard M., "William Caxton and Bookbinding," *Journal of the Printing Historical Society* 11 (1976–77): 92–113.

Nolan, Maura, "The Poetics of Catastrophe: Ovidian Allusion in Gower's *Vox Clamantis*," in *Medieval Latin and Middle English Literature: Essays in Honour of Jill Mann*, eds Christopher Cannon and Maura Nolan (Cambridge: D. S. Brewer, 2011), 113–33.

Nuttall, Jenni, *The Creation of Lancastrian Kingship: Literature, Language, and Politics in Late Medieval England* (Cambridge: Cambridge University Press, 2007).

Oakley, Francis, *Kingship: The Politics of Enchantment* (Oxford: Blackwell, 2006).

Oldham, J. B., *English Blind-stamped Bindings* (Cambridge: Cambridge University Press, 1952).

Olsson, Kurt, *John Gower and the Structures of Conversion: A Reading of the Confessio Amantis* (Cambridge: D. S. Brewer, 1992).

——, "John Gower's *Vox Clamantis* and the Medieval Idea of Place," *Studies in Philology* 84.2 (1987): 134–58.

Oman, Charles, *The Great Revolt of 1381* (Oxford: Clarendon Press, 1906).

Painter, George D., "Caxton through the Looking Glass: An Enquiry into the Offsets on a Fragment of Caxton's Fifteen OES, with a Census of Caxton Bindings," in *Studies in Fifteenth-Century Printing* (London: Pindar, 1984), 130–37.

Palmer, J. N. N., *England, France, and Christendom 1377-99* (London: Routledge and Kegan Paul, 1972).

Parish, W. D., *List of Carthusians, 1800-1879* (Lewes: Farncombe and Co., 1879).

Parkes, Malcolm B., *Pause and Effect: An Introduction to Medieval Punctuation in the West* (Aldershot: Scolar, 1992).

——, "Patterns of Scribal Activity and Revisions of the Text in Early Copies of Works by John Gower," in *New Science out of Old Books: Manuscripts and Early Printed Books, Essays in Honor of A. I. Doyle*, eds Richard Beadle and A. J. Piper (Aldershot: Scolar Press, 1995), 81–121.

Pascual-Argente, Clara, "La huella de las *Sumas de historia troyana* en la *Confessio Amantis* castellana," *Revista de Filología Española* XCV, No. 1 (2015): 127–52.
——, "Iberian Gower," in *The Routledge Research Companion to John Gower*, eds Ana Sáez-Hidalgo, Brian Gastle, and R. F. Yeager (London and New York: Routledge, 2017), 210–21.
Patch, Howard Rollin, *The Tradition of the Goddess Fortuna in Roman Literature and in the Transitional Period*, Smith College Studies in Modern Literature 3.3 (Northampton, MA: Smith College, 1922).
Pearsall, Derek, "The Gower Tradition," in *Gower's 'Confessio Amantis': Responses and Reassessments,* ed. A. J. Minnis (Cambridge: D. S. Brewer, 1983), 179–97.
——, "The Manuscripts and Illustrations of Gower's Works," in *A Companion to Gower*, ed. Siân Echard (Cambridge: Boydell and Brewer, 2004), 73–97.
Peck, Russell A., *Kingship and Common Profit in Gower's* Confessio Amantis (Carbondale, IL: Southern Illinois University Press, 1978).
—— and R. F. Yeager, eds, *John Gower: Others and the Self* (Cambridge: D. S. Brewer, 2017).
Pérez-Fernández, Tamara, "The Margins in the Iberian Manuscripts of John Gower's *Confessio Amantis*: Language, Authority and Readership," in *Gower in Context(s). Scribal, Linguistic, Literary and Socio-historical Readings* (Special issue of *ES. Revista de Filología Inglesa* 33.1), eds Laura Filardo-Llamas, Brian Gastle, and Marta Gutiérrez Rodríguez (Valladolid: Publicaciones Universidad de Valladolid, 2012), 29–44.
——, "From England to Iberia: The Transmission of Marginal Elements in the Iberian Translations of Gower's *Confessio Amantis*," in *Text and Transmission in the European Middle Ages, 1000-1500*, eds Carrie Griffin and Emer Purcell (Turnhout: Brepols, 2018), 119–40.
Petkov, Kiril, "The Rotten Apple and the Good Apples: Orthodox, Catholics, and Turks in Philippe de Mézières' Crusading Propaganda," *Journal of Medieval History* 23, no. 3 (1997): 255–70.
Phillips, Helen, "Aesthetic and Commercial Aspects of Framing Devices: Bradshaw, Roos and Copland," *Poetica, an International Journal of Linguistic-Literary Studies* 43 (1995): 37–42.
——, "The Invisible Narrator of the *Chevalier des Dames*," in *Texts and their Contexts: Papers from the Early Book Society*, eds John Scattergood and Julia Boffey (Dublin: Four Courts Press, 1997), 165–80.
Pollard, Alfred W. and G. R. Redgrave, *A Short-Title Catalogue of Books Printed in England, Scotland and Ireland and of English Books Printed Abroad 1475-1640*, 2nd edition revised and enlarged by W. A. Jackson, F. S. Ferguson, and Katharine F. Pantzer, 3 vols. (London: Bibliographical Society, 1986–91).
Pollard, Graham, "The English Market for Printed Books" (The Sanders Lectures, 1959), *Publishing History* 4 (1978): 7–48.
Pollnitz, Aysha, *Princely Education in Early Modern Britain* (Cambridge: Cambridge University Press, 2015).
Potter, David, "Foreign Policy," in *The Reign of Henry VIII: Politics, Policy and Piety*, ed. Diarmaid MacCulloch (Houndmills: Macmillan, 1995), 101–33.
Pouzet, Jean-Pascal, "Southwark Gower: Augustinian Agencies in Gower's Manuscripts and Texts – Some Prolegomena," in *John Gower, Trilingual Poet:*

Language, Translation, and Tradition, ed. Elisabeth Dutton (Cambridge: D. S. Brewer, 2010), 11–25.

Pugh, Syrithe, ed., *Mortalizing the Gods from Euhemerus to the Twentieth Century* (New York: Routledge, 2019).

Ransom, Emily A., "*The New Notborune Mayd Vpon the Passion of Cryste*: The Nutbrown Maid Converted [with text]," *English Literary Renaissance* 45, no. 1 (2015): 3–31.

Reeve, M. D., "Manuscripts Copied from Printed Books," in *Manuscripts in the Fifty Years after the Invention of Printing: some papers read at a colloquium at the Warburg Institute on 12-13 March 1982*, ed. J. B. Trapp (London: Warburg Institute, 1983), 12–20.

de Ricci, Seymour, *A Census of Caxtons*, Bibliographical Society Illustrated Monographs 15 (Oxford: Oxford University Press, 1909).

Richardson, Glenn, "Eternal Peace, Occasional War: Anglo-French Relations under Henry VIII," in *Tudor England and Its Neighbours*, eds Susan Doran and Glenn Richardson (Basingstoke: Palgrave Macmillan, 2005), 44–73.

——, "The French Connection: Francis I and England's Break with Rome," in *The Contending Kingdoms: France and England, 1420-1700*, ed. Glenn Richardson (Aldershot: Ashgate, 2008), 95–115.

——, *The Field of Cloth of Gold* (New Haven: Yale University Press, 2013).

——, ed., *The Contending Kingdoms: France and England, 1420-1700* (Aldershot: Ashgate, 2008).

Ringler, William A. Jr., "The Nutbrown Maid (a Reconstructed Text)," *English Literary Renaissance* 1.1 (1971): 27–51.

Roberts, Jane, "On Giving Scribe B a Name and a Clutch of London Manuscripts from c. 1400," *Medium Ævum* 80.2 (2011): 247–70.

Rodríguez Porto, Rosa M., "La *Crónica Geral de Espanha de 1344* (ms. 1 A de la Academia das Ciências) y la tradición alfonsí," *e-Spania* [online] 25 (2016), http://journals.openedition.org/e-spania/25911.

Roland, Meg, "'After poyetes and astronomyers': Geographical Thought and Early English Print," in *Mapping Medieval Geographies: Geographical Encounters in the Latin West and Beyond, 300-1600*, ed. Keith D. Lilley (Cambridge: Cambridge University Press, 2013), 127–51.

Rosser, Gervase, "A Note on the Caxton Indulgence of 1476," *The Library* 6th ser., 7 (1985): 256–58.

Ruggiers, Paul G., ed., *Editing Chaucer: The Great Tradition* (Norman, OK: Pilgrim Books, 1984).

Russell, Alexander, *Conciliarism and Heresy in Fifteenth-Century England: Collective Authority in the Age of the General Councils*, Cambridge Studies in Medieval Life and Thought, Fourth Series (Cambridge: Cambridge University Press, 2017).

Russell, Joycelyne G., *Peacemaking in the Renaissance* (Philadelphia: University of Pennsylvania Press, 1986).

Sáez-Hidalgo, Ana, "Gower in Early Modern Spanish Libraries: The Missing Link," in *John Gower: Others and the Self*, eds Russell A. Peck and R. F. Yeager (Cambridge: D. S. Brewer, 2017), 329–44.

——, "Iberian Manuscripts of Gower's Works," in *The Routledge Research Companion to John Gower*, eds Ana Sáez-Hidalgo, Brian W. Gastle, and R. F. Yeager (London and New York: Routledge, 2017), 110–16.

——, Brian W. Gastle, and R. F. Yeager, eds, *The Routledge Research Companion to John Gower* (London and New York: Routledge, 2017).
—— and R. F. Yeager, eds, *John Gower in England and Iberia: Manuscripts, Influences, Reception* (Cambridge: D. S. Brewer, 2014).
Sahlins, Marshall, "The Stranger-King: or Dumézil among the Fijians," *The Journal of Pacific History* 16 (1981): 107–32.
Samuels, Michael L., "Chaucerian Final '-E'," *Notes and Queries* 217 (1972): 445–48; reprinted in *The English of Chaucer and his Contemporaries*, ed. Jeremy J. Smith (Aberdeen: Aberdeen University Press, 1988), 7–12.
——, "Chaucer's Spelling," in *Middle English Studies presented to Norman Davis*, eds D. Gray and E. G. Stanley (Oxford: Clarendon Press, 1983), 17–37; reprinted in *The English of Chaucer and his Contemporaries*, ed. Jeremy J. Smith (Aberdeen: Aberdeen University Press, 1988), 23–37.
Samuels, Michael L. and Jeremy J. Smith, "The Language of Gower," *Neuphilologische Mitteilungen* 82 (1981): 294–304; reprinted in *The English of Chaucer and his Contemporaries*, ed. Jeremy J. Smith (Aberdeen: Aberdeen University Press, 1988), 13–22.
Santano Moreno, Bernardo, *Estudio sobre Confessio Amantis de John Gower y su versión castellana, Confisyon del Amante de Juan de Cuenca* (Cáceres: Ediciones Universidad de Extremadura, 1990).
Saul, Nigel, *Richard II* (New Haven: Yale University Press, 1997).
Scanlon, Larry, *Narrative, Authority, and Power: The Medieval Exemplum and the Chaucerian Tradition* (Cambridge: Cambridge University Press, 1994).
Schnepel, Burkhard, *Twinned Beings: Kings and Effigies in Southern Sudan, East India and Renaissance France* (Göteborg: Institute for Advanced Studies in Social Anthropology, 1995).
Shogimen, Takashi, "Wyclif's Ecclesiology and Political Thought," in *A Companion to John Wyclif, Late Medieval Theologian*, ed. Ian Christopher Levy (Leiden and Boston: Brill 2006), 199–240.
Simpson, James, *Sciences and the Self in Medieval Poetry: Alan of Lille's* Anticlaudianus *and John Gower's* Confessio Amantis (Cambridge: Cambridge University Press, 1995).
Smith, Jeremy J., "The Trinity Gower D-Scribe and his Work on Two Early Canterbury Tales Manuscripts," in *The English of Chaucer and his Contemporaries*, ed. Jeremy J. Smith (Aberdeen: Aberdeen University Press, 1989), 51–69.
——, "Spelling and Tradition in Fifteenth-Century Copies of Gower's *Confessio Amantis*," in *The English of Chaucer and his Contemporaries*, ed. Jeremy J. Smith (Aberdeen: Aberdeen University Press, 1989), 96–113.
——, "John Gower and London English," in *A Companion to Gower*, ed. Siân Echard (Cambridge: D. S. Brewer, 2004), 61–72.
Smith, Julie A., "The Poet Laureate as University Master: John Skelton's Woodcut Portrait," in *Renaissance Rereadings: Intertext and Context*, eds Maryanne Cline Horowitz, Anne J. Cruz, and Wendy A. Furman (Urbana: University of Illinois Press, 1998), 159–83.
Smith, Margaret M., *The Title-Page and its Early Development 1460-1510* (London and New Castle, DE: British Library and Oak Knoll Press, 2000).
Smith, Martin Ferguson, ed., *Dearest Jean: Rose Macaulay's Letters to a Cousin* (Manchester: Manchester University Press, 2011).

Smuts, R. Malcolm, "Kynaston, Sir Francis (1586/7–1642), writer and founder of an academy of learning," *Oxford Dictionary of National Biography* 23 September 2004; https://doi.org/10.1093/ref:odnb/15822.

Sobecki, Sebastian, "*Ecce patet tensus*: The Trentham Manuscript, *In Praise of Peace*, and John Gower's Autograph Hand," *Speculum* 90 (2015): 925–59.

Solopova, Elizabeth, "Chaucer's Metre and Scribal Editing in the Early Manuscripts of the *Canterbury Tales*," *The Canterbury Tales Project Occasional Papers* 2 (1997): 143–64.

Spies, H., Review of G. C. Macaulay, ed., *The Works of John Gower*, in *Englische Studien* 32 (1903): 251–75.

Staley, Lynn, "Gower, Richard II, Henry of Derby, and the Business of Making Culture," *Speculum* 75 (2000): 68–96.

Stanbury, Sarah, *The Visual Object of Desire in Late Medieval England* (Philadelphia: University of Pennsylvania Press, 2007).

Stewart, Vaughn, "Reading Nobility: Authority and Early English Print," PhD dissertation, University of North Carolina at Chapel Hill, 2016.

Stillwell, Margaret Bingham, ed., *Incunabula in American Libraries: A Second Census of Fifteenth-Century Books Owned in the United States, Mexico, and Canada* (New York: Bibliographical Society of America, 1940).

Stone, Zachary E., "'Between tuo stoles': The Western Schism and the English Poetry of John Gower (1378-1415)," *New Medieval Literatures* 19 (2019).

Stow, George B., "Richard II in John Gower's *Confessio Amantis*: Some Historical Perspectives," *Mediaevalia* 16 (1993): 3–31.

Takagi, Masako, "Caxton's Exemplar and a Copy from Caxton's Edition of the *Chronicles of England*: MS HM136 and BL Additional 10099," *Arthuriana* 22, no. 4 (2012): 120–39.

Tarlinskaja, Marina, *English Verse: Theory and History* (The Hague: Mouton, 1976).

Taylor, Andrew, "John Leland's Communities of the Epigram," in *Neo-Latin Poetry in the British Isles*, eds L. B. T. Houghton and Gesine Manuwald (London: Bristol Classical Press, 2012), 15–35.

Taylor, Karla, "Inside Out in Gower's Republic of Letters," in *John Gower Trilingual Poet: Language, Translation and Tradition*, eds Elisabeth Dutton and John Hines, with R. F. Yeager (Cambridge: D. S. Brewer, 2010), 169–81.

Teresi, Loredana, "Anglo-Saxon and Early Anglo-Norman *Mappaemundi*," in *Foundations of Learning: The Transfer of Encyclopaedic Knowledge in the Early Middle Ages*, eds Rolf H. Bremmer Jr. and Kees Dekker (Leuven, Belgium: Peeters, 2007), 341–67.

[Thomas, Edward], "Chaucer's Mate," *Daily Chronicle*, 18 June 1901.

——, "The Poet of Southwark," *Daily Chronicle*, 29 October 1902.

Thompson, Stith, *Motif-Index of Folk-Literature. Electronic Version* (Charlottesville: InteLex, 2000), http://pm.nlx.com.proxy.lib.umich.edu/xtf/view?docId=motif/motif.02.xml;chunk.id=div.motif.v2.1;toc.depth=2;toc.id=div.motif.v2.1;hit.rank=0;brand=default.

Tillyard, E. M. W., *The Muse Unchained* (Cambridge: Bowes and Bowes, 1958).

Tomasch, Sylvia, "*Mappae mundi* and the 'Knight's Tale': The Geography of Power, the Cartography of Control," in *Literature and Technology*, eds Mark Greenberg and Lance Schachterle (Bethlehem, PA: Lehigh University Press, 1992), 66–98.

Toulmin Smith, Lucy, Review of G. C. Macaulay, ed., *The Works of John Gower*, *Archiv für das Studium der neueren Sprachen und Literatur* 110 (1903): 197–202.
Tournoy-Thoen, Gilbert and Godelieve, "Giovanni Gigli and the Renaissance of the Classical Epithalamium in England," in *Myricae: Essays on Neo-Latin Literature in Memory of Jozef IJsewijn*, Supplementa Humanistica Lovaniensia 16 (Leuven: Leuven University Press, 2000): 133–93.
Tracy, James D., *The Politics of Erasmus: A Pacifist Intellectual and His Political Milieu* (Toronto: University of Toronto Press, 1978).
Trapp, J. B., "Gigli, Giovanni (1434–1498), papal official, diplomat, and bishop of Worcester," *Oxford Dictionary of National Biography*, 23 September 2004; https://doi.org/10.1093/ref:odnb/10670.
Tyerman, Christopher, *God's War: A New History of the Crusades* (London: Allen Lane, 2006).
van Dijk, Conrad, *John Gower and the Limits of the Law* (Woodbridge, Suffolk: D. S. Brewer, 2013).
van Duzer, Chet and Ilya Dines, *Apocalyptic Cartography: Thematic Maps and the End of the World in a Fifteenth-Century Manuscript* (Leiden: Brill, 2016).
van Es, Bart, "Late Shakespeare and the Middle Ages," in *Medieval Shakespeare: Pasts and Presents*, eds Ruth Morse, Helen Cooper, and Peter Holland (Cambridge: Cambridge University Press, 2013), 37–51.
Vanes, Jean, ed., *Documents Illustrating the Overseas Trade of Bristol in the Sixteenth Century* (Bristol, UK: Bristol Record Society, 1979).
Viúla de Faria, Tiago, "From Norwich to Lisbon: Factionalism, Personal Association, and Conveying the *Confessio Amantis*," in *John Gower in England and Iberia: Manuscripts, Influences, Reception*, eds Ana Sáez-Hidalgo and R. F. Yeager (Cambridge and Rochester, NY: D. S. Brewer, 2014), 131–38.
Wakelin, Daniel, "Writing the Words," in *The Production of Books in England 1350-1500*, eds Alexandra Gillespie and Daniel Wakelin (Cambridge: Cambridge University Press, 2011), 34–58.
——, *Scribal Correction and Literary Craft: English Manuscripts 1375-1510* (Cambridge: Cambridge University Press, 2014).
Walker, Greg, *Writing under Tyranny: English Literature and the Henrician Reformation* (Oxford: Oxford University Press, 2005).
——, *John Skelton and the Politics of the 1520s* (Cambridge: Cambridge University Press, 2002).
Wallace, David, *Chaucerian Polity: Absolutist Lineages and Associational Forms in England and Italy* (Stanford: Stanford University Press, 1997).
Warner, J. Christopher, *Henry VIII's Divorce: Literature and the Politics of the Printing Press* (Woodbridge: Boydell Press, 1998).
Warner, Lawrence, "Scribes, Misattributed: Hoccleve and Pinkhurst," *Studies in the Age of Chaucer* 37 (2015): 55–100.
Watt, Diane, *Amoral Gower: Language, Sex, and Politics* (Minneapolis: University of Minnesota Press, 2003).
Wawn, Andrew N., "Chaucer, *The Plowman's Tale* and Reformation Propaganda: The Testimonies of Thomas Godfray and *I Playne Piers*," *Bulletin of John Rylands University Library of Manchester* 56 (1973): 174–92.
Wells, William, "Gower and Caxton," *South Atlantic Bulletin* 27, no. 1 (1961): 9–10.

Wetherbee, Winthrop, "Latin Structure and Vernacular Space: Gower, Chaucer and the Boethian Tradition," in *Chaucer and Gower: Difference, Mutuality, Exchange*, ed. R. F. Yeager (Victoria, BC: University of Victoria Press, 1991), 7–35.

Whitmarsh, Tim, *Battling the Gods: Atheism in the Ancient World* (New York: Alfred A. Knopf, 2015).

——, *Beyond the Second Sophistic: Adventures in Greek Postclassicism* (Berkeley: University of California Press, 2013).

Wickert, Maria, *Studies in John Gower*, 2nd edn., trans. Robert J. Meindl (Tempe, Arizona: Arizona Center for Medieval and Renaissance Studies, 2016).

Wilks, Michael, "Predestination, Property and Power: Wyclif's Theory of Dominion and Grace," *Studies in Church History* 2 (1965), 220–36.

Woodward, David, "Medieval *Mappaemundi*," in *The History of Cartography*, vol. 1: *Cartography in Prehistoric, Ancient, and Medieval Europe and the Mediterranean*, eds J. B. Harley and David Woodward (Chicago: University of Chicago Press, 1987), 286–370.

Wright, John Kirtland, *The Geographical Lore of the Time of the Crusades: A Study in the History of Medieval Science and Tradition in Western Europe* (New York: Dover, repr. 1965).

Wyatt, Michael, *The Italian Encounter with Tudor England: A Cultural Politics of Translation* (Cambridge: Cambridge University Press, 2005).

Yeager, R. F., *John Gower Materials: A Bibliography through 1979* (New York: Garland, 1981).

——, "'O Moral Gower': Chaucer's Dedication of *Troilus and Criseyde*," *Chaucer Review* 19 (1984): 87–99.

——, "*Pax Poetica*: On the Pacifism of Chaucer and Gower," *Studies in the Age of Chaucer* 9 (1987): 97–121.

——, *John Gower's Poetic: The Search for a New Arion* (Cambridge: D. S. Brewer, 1990).

——, "English, Latin, and the Text as 'Other': The Page as Sign in the Work of John Gower," *Text* 3 (1987): 251–67.

——, "Gower's Lancastrian Affinity: The Iberian Connection," *Viator* 35, no. 1 (2004): 483–515.

——, "John Gower's Audience: The Ballades," *Chaucer Review* 40, no. 1 (2005): 81–105.

——, "Spanish Literary Influence in England: John Gower and Pedro Alfonso," in *John Gower in England and Iberia: Manuscripts, Influences, Reception*, eds Ana Sáez-Hidalgo and R. F. Yeager (Cambridge: D. S. Brewer, 2014), 119–29.

Yoran, Hanan, *Between Utopia and Dystopia: Erasmus, Thomas More, and the Humanist Republic of Letters* (Lanham: Lexington Books, 2010).

Zach, S. E., "The One-Millionth Volume: Restored," *The Bookmark* 45 (1975): 9–12.

INDEX

Adams, Robert P. 238 n.27
Alcock, John 223
Alfonso, Pedro, *Disciplina Clericalis* 120 n.14
Alphonse X, king of Castile and Léon 120, 121
Alvar, Manuel 127
Alves, João José 121 n.17
Alyngton, Sir Giles 228, 229
Amado, Teresa 121 n.17
Anaximander of Miletus 100 n.27
Ancrene Riwle, Corpus MS 251
Annan, Noel 248
Arens, William 65 n.32
Aristotle 64
Arnold, Richard, *Customs of London*, 1503 211 n.31
Arnulf of Orleans 109 n.42
Augustine, St. 78

Bagshaw, Samuel 211 n.29
Bahr, Arthur W. 36, 151 n.61, 173 n.11, 233 n.6
Bakhtin, Mikhail 60
Balade moral of gode counseyl (attrib. to Gower by Shirley) *see* Gower, Shirley
Barclay, Alexander 9, 228–29
  asked to abridge the *Confessio* 228
  The Castell of Laboure (attrib.) 227
  The Introductorye to wryte and pronounce French 226–27
Barkham, Michael M. 215 n.36
Barolini, Teodolinda 77 n.9
Barrington, Candace 143 n.44, 173 n.11
Barron, Caroline M. 142 n.42
Bartholomaeus Anglicus, *De proprietatibus rerum* 98 n.26
Batkie, Stephanie L. 2, 33–53

Beadle, Richard 15 n.11, 34 n.3, 102 n.29
Bede 141
Beidler, Peter G. 260 n.48
Bell, James Ford 205, 216
Bennett, J.A.W. 207 n.22, 259
Benskin, Michael 13
Benson, C. David 224 n.19
Benson, Larry D. 33 n.1
Berners, Lord (translator of Froissart) 220 n.4
Berthelet (Berthelette), Thomas 6, 9, 55, 70, 198, 200, 233
  1532 printed edition of Gower's *Confessio* 8–9, 169–71, 181 (illust.), 185–88, 221–22, 225–30, 253
    comparison with Caxton's edition 184–88
    continuity and innovation in prints derived from MSS 8–9
    encomium on Gower 245
    Gower seen as a humanist and a promoter of the English language 184–85, 228
    Latin poem, *Carmenta iuvante*, preceding *Confessio* 184–85
    paratexts, including handling of Latin 184, 222–26
  1554 edition of *Confessio* (illust.) 8–9, 183
  Print of Erasmus, *Institutio principis Christiani* 246
Besamusca, Bart 159 n.26
Bible
  1 Esdras 62
  Matthew 20:1–16 72 n.3
  Pentateuch 141
  2 Samuel 12:6 148 n.57

Bietenhold, Peter G.   241 n.46
Billy, Dominique   18
Blades, William   196
Blair, Ann   190 n.4
Blake, Norman F.   19 n.28, 189
   nn.1–2, 190, 191 n.9, 195,
   196 n.22, 202, 207 n.22, 220 n.7,
   222 n.14
Blayney, Peter, W.M.   221 n.9,
   229 n.29, 234
Blodgett, James E.   233 n.5, 234 n.8
Boccaccio   3, 77, 196
   De casibus virorum illustrium   224
   Decameron   84
Boethius   3, 77, 196, 222
Boffey, Julia   8–9, 158 n.18, 190,
   212 n.31, 219–30, 227 n.23
Bone, Gavin   191 n.9
Bradshaw, Henry, *The Lyfe of Saynt
   Werburge*   227
Branca, Vittore   76 n.7
Bremmer, Rolf H.   106 n.30
Brett, Caroline   231 n.1
Brewer, J.S.   243 n.55
Brody, Saul Nathaniel   141
Brooke, Rupert   251
Brown, Cynthia   2
Brown, Harry J.   143
Brusendorff, Aage   160
Bühler, Curt F.   189–90
Bullón-Fernández, María   120 n.15
Burgh, Benedict   6, 159, 163–65,
   222
Burley, Simon   86
Burns, J.H.   83 n.26
Burrow, John   18 n.22, 29, 94
Butterfield, Ardis   131 n.3

Calkin, Siobhain Bly   136 n.19
Cambrai, Treaty of, 1529   243
Campbell, Tony   91 n.6
Campeggio, Lorenzo, papal
   legate   238
Cannon, Christopher   91 n.4
Capgrave, John   136, 142
Carley, James P.   231, 232 n.3, 245
Carlson, David   33, 35, 87 nn.36–38,
   88 n.40, 110, 134, 135 n.15,
   209 n.23

Carter, P.R.N.   235 n.12
Castro, Fernando de ("o Moço")   114,
   120
Cato   222
Catullus   232
Caxton, William   55, 70
   1477 (1478?) printed edition of
      Canterbury Tales   7, 198, 202,
      207 n.22
   1483 printed edition of Chaucer's
      Canterbury Tales   6, 169–70, 177
      (illust.), 186–88, 198, 219–23,
      225, 228, 230, 253
         compared with Bodleian MS
            Hatton 51   189–200
         imitation of Caxton's
            paratexts in MS Hatton
            51   190–200
         includes a table of contents
            and some short Latin
            pieces   186, 221, 221 n.1
         Latin apparatus and front
            matter   175–85
   Boethius, *Consolation of Philosophy*
      (1478)   202
   Boke of Curtesye   202
   *Boke of the fayttes of armes and of
      chiualrye*   222
   *Dicts and Sayings of the
      Philosophers*   197
   Editions of poems by
      Lydgate   222–23
   Indulgence, printed 1481 for
      Giovanni dei Gigli, papal
      nuncio   8, 204–07
   Myrrour of the Worlde   223 n.16
   Ovid's *Metamorphoses*   207 n.22
   *Recuyell of the Historyes of
      Troye*   197, 200
   Troilus and Criseyde   202
   The UNC-Chapel Hill Library,
      Incunabula 532.5, copy of
      Caxton 1483   8, 201–17
         binding filler, scraps
            now removed and kept
            separately   207–09
         Indulgence of 1381, used in
            binding   204–07

The Nut-Brown Maid,
fragmentary copy in margin   208 (illust.), 211–14
possibly in Spain in 16th century   214–16
provenance and acquisition   201–02, 216–17
readers' marks and comments   210–14
Charles V, Emperor   236, 243
Charles V, king of France   86
Chartier, Alain   229
Chastysing of goddes chyldern   223
Chaucer, Geoffrey   4, 9, 18, 89, 90, 155, 157, 188, 232, 239 nn.34,36, 245, 252
   Canterbury Tales   230
      Scribes of   48 n.26
   "Clerk's Tale"   71 n.1
   Parlement of Foules   228
   Troilus and Criseyde   2, 27, 33, 166, 234, 253 n.27
   (*"Truth"*), *Balade of gode counseyle* ("Fle fro the prees")   153–66, 164
Cheshire, Neil M.   241 n.45
Cicero   92 n.8, 222
Cigman, Gloria   211 n.30
Clark, James G.   136 n.20
Clark, John W.   205 n.13
Códice de Tristan   129
Coffman, George R.   58 n.14
Cole, Andrew   82
Coleman, Janet   83 n.26, 86 n.32
Coleman, Joyce   120 n.15, 176 n.20, 215 n.38
Colet, John   245
Connolly, Margaret   6, 153–66, 154 n.2, 157 n.14, 159 n.26, 166 nn.49,51
Connolly, Ruth   200 n.36
Constantine, emperor   132, 139–45
Constantinople, threat from the Turks in the 1390s   132–34, 139–41, 151
Cooper, Helen   246 n.72
Copeland, Rita   245 n.66
Copland, Robert   9, 226–30

print of Barclay's *Introductorye*   226
print of Neville's *Castell of Pleasure*   227
Cornelius, Ian   35 n.7
Cortijo Ocaña, Antonio   126
Costa, Alex da   193 n.15, 200 n.38
Costa Green, Belle de   205
Costomiris, Robert   233 n.5
Council of Constance (1414–18)   81 n.17, 144
Council of Florence (1431–49)   144
Council of Nicaea   144
Council of Pisa (1409)   144
Crusades, 11th–13th centuries   132, 134
call for a crusade in the 1390s   137, 139–43
Cruz, Anne J.   225 n.20
Cuenca, Juan, translator of Castilian version of *Confessio*   115, 116, 127, 129
Cuento de Tristán de Leonís   129
Curtis, Catherine   238 n.27, 239, 242 n.52, 243 n.58

Dalché, Patrick Gauchier   91 nn.5–6
Dane, Joseph   171 n.5, 220 n.5, 234 n.11
Daniels, R. Balfour   143
Dante   3, 76 n.9, 77 n.10, 95 n.22, 108–09
   De monarchia   83–84
David, Alfred   154 n.5
Davidson, Clifford   95 n.22
Dawson, J.L.   161
Dekker, Kees   106 n.30
Delano-Smith, Katherine   93 n.11, 97 n.25, 100
Devereux, E.J.   228 n.27
DeVries, Kelly   140 n.34
De Worde, Wynkyn   221
   Canterbury Tales (1498)   223
   The chastising of goddes chyldern   223
   Chaucer, *Parliament of Fowls*   228, 229
   Ipomydon   228
   Neville's *Castell of Pleasure*   226

Skelton's *Bowge of Court* and other poems by Skelton 225
Skelton's *Pastime of Pleasure* 225 n.21
Troilus and Criseyde (1517) 224
Dilke, O.A.W. 91 n.5
Dines, Ilya 98 n.26
Doran, Susan 243 n.54
Doyle, A.I. 15, 16 n.16, 17, 25–28, 28 n.56, 100 n.29, 190, 191 n.8, 197
Driver, Martha W. 192, 194 n.18, 195, 196, 203 n.7, 207 n.22, 209 n.23, 223
Drury, Sir Robert 230
Drury, Ursula 230
Duarte, Dom 120, 121
Du Boulay, F.R.H. 141 n.42
Duff, E. Gordon 197, 197 n.25, 203 n.7, 219
Duffell, Martin J. 18
Dust, Philip C. 238 n.27
Dutton, Elizabeth 35 n.7, 48 n.27, 79 n.12, 90 n.3

Echard, Siân 6–7, 14 n.6, 15 n.11, 18 n.22, 55, 94 n.18, 114 n.3, 131 n.1, 160 n.30, 169–88, 172 n.8, 173 n.11, 174 n.14, 176 n.20, 185 n.26, 186 n.30, 189 n.1, 191 n.8, 192 n.14, 194 n.17, 220 nn.4,7, 246 n.71, 258 n.40
Edwards, A.S.G. 9–10, 158 n.19, 165 n.47, 190 n.4, 196, 197 nn.25,27, 200, 230 n.31, 233 n.5
Edwards, Robert R. 94, 220 n.7
Eisenstein, Elizabeth 190
Elyot, Sir Thomas, *The Governour* 246
Epstein, Robert 2–3, 55–70
Erasmus 242–43
  Dulce bellum inexpertus 241, 244
  Epigrammata 234 n.8
  Institutio principis Christiani 241, 246
Erler, Mary Carpenter 225, 226 n.22, 229

Euhemerism 4, 93–96, 99–100, 109, 111
Eusebius 140
Evans-Pritchard, E.E. 65 n.32

Fabyan, Robert, chronicler 224
Faccon, Manuela 114 n.5, 122 n.21
Fakenham, Nicholas, *Determinatio de schismate* 144
Fantazzi, Charles 238 n.27
Faques, Richard, print of Skelton's *Garland of Laurel* 225
Faria, Isabel Hub 121 n.17
Faria, Tiago Viúla de 120 n.15
Federico, Sylvia 106 n.32
Ferguson, F.S. 219
Fernández, María Bullón 214, 215 n.38
Feylde, Thomas, *Controversy between a Lover and a Jay* 227
Fideler, Paul A. 238 n.27
Filardo-Llamas, Laura 114 n.4
Fisher, John Hurt 1, 15, 55, 85 n.31, 150 n.58, 172 n.10, 223, 260 n.48
  his idea of Gower's "scriptorium" 256–57
Fitzralph, Richard 8, 86
  De pauperie salvatoris 81 n.17
Forni, Kathleen 236 n.19
Förster, Max 163, 163 n.41, 165
Fortune, in Boethius and the Stoics 77
  Fortune and the limits of referentiality 71–88
  Fortune and the limits of ethical choice, in Gower's "Tale of the Two Coffers" (*Confessio*, V.2278) 78
Foucault, Michel 199
Fox, George 92 n.9
Francis I, king of France 240
Franzen, Christine 211 n.28
Frazer, Sir James 64
Fredell, Joel 15 n.11, 55 nn.1–2, 56, 56 nn.4–6, 85 n.31, 258 n.39
Froissart, Jean 250 n.14
Fryde, E.B. 206 n.18
Furman, Wendy A. 225 n.20

Furnivall, F.J. 157 n.15, 159, 160 n.27, 202 n.3, 253 n.27

Galloway, Andrew 35 n.7, 71 n.1, 89 n.2, 106 n.31, 113 n.1, 116 n.8, 142–43, 146
Ganim, John 90 n.3
Gardham, Julie 100 n.29
Gardner, Eileen 95 n.22
Gaskell, Philip 191 n.10
Gastle, Brian 8, 15 n.13, 85 n.31, 89 n.1, 114 n.4, 120 n.15, 201–17, 216 n.39, 221 n.7
Gerber, Amanda J. 2–4, 89–112, 94 n.19
Gerson, Jean 144
Giancarlo, Matthew 57, 61, 64, 65, 67 n.38, 71–72
Gigli, Giovanni dei, Papal nuncio 204–07
    epithalamium for Henry VII and Elizabeth of York 206
Giles of Rome, *De regimine principum* 86
Gillespie, Alexandra 15 n.8, 199, 199 nn.31–32, 220 n.5, 234 nn.8,11
Gillespie, Vincent 158 n.19, 190 n.24
Ginsberg, Warren 89 n.2
Gioffani, Vincenzo 76 n.9, 77 n.10
Given-Wilson, Chris 87 nn.36–38, 135 n.18, 138 n.29
Glossa Ordinaria 141
Godfray, Thomas, printer 229, 233, 234
Goff, Frederick R. 203 n.9, 204 n.12
Goodwin, *The Maydens Dreme* 227
Gorman, M.M. 98 n.26
Gourmont, Jean de 239
Gow, A.S.F. 260 n.48
Gower, John 232 *see* Macaulay
    Gower-as-archer xviii (illust.), 4, 35 n.6, 89, 101 (illust.), 100–05
    Gower's life 13
    ideas of kingship and secular dominion, view of Richard II 3, 72, 84

Lollardy, attitudes to 3, 83
Gower's tomb in Southwark 171
Gower's trilingualism and bilingualism 174–75, 180 n.24, 188
Gower's works in MS and print, compared 169–88
Confessio Amantis 139–40, 143, 144 n.48, 148, 177 (illust.), 185
    affiliations of MSS and treatment of text 169–200, 181
    dialogic structure and speaker-markers 185–88
    Fortune and justice in the "Tale of the Two Coffers" (*Confessio*, V.2273–2390) 72–77
    geographical texts and images 4, 89–112
    influence of metre in scribal copying and pronunciation 17–31
    kingship, sacral and divine, absolutist and constitutionalist 57
        the anthropological theory of kingship 58–70
        the *Confessio* as an exemplum of bad kingship, and of the king who became a tyrant (Richard II) 36, 45, 49, 52–53
    language, dialect, metre and use of final -e 1–2, 22–23, 26, 171–85
    Latin apparatus 82, 114–15, 176–81
    Latin marginal summaries, relation to English text 73
    layout and ink 177
    "Moral Gower" 33–53, 34, 52
    Prologue and final dedication, political significance of 85–88

293

the "Tale of Constance"
(III.1075–1148) 213–14
textual history and the
"recensions" 3, 15, 55–70
use of Ovid 42, 46–77
Confessio Amantis, in Pauli's
edition
Castilian translation of *Confessio*
(*Confisyon del Amante*) 4–5,
113–30, 215–16
    careful work of translation (by
Juan de Cuenca) 115–16,
127–29
Portuguese translation of *Confessio*
(*Livro do Amante*) 4–5, 113–30,
215–16
    examples of translation
methods 116–17
    treatment of paratexts (prose
summaries and Table of
contents) 114–15, 11
Caxton's printed edition of 1483,
compared with Bodleian MS
Hatton 51 7–8, 189–200
    comparison of MSS and
printed editions in the
transition period 6–7
Recently discovered MS 180
Balade moral of gode counseyle
("Passe forþ þou pilgryme"),
attrib. Gower 6, 153–66
*Carmen super multiplici viciorum
pestilencia* 145–46
Cinkante balades 131, 147–49,
165
Cronica Tripertita 2, 33–53, 87,
142
    added notes and
commentary 46
    allusion to Salomitic
heresy 34, 37–38, 46,
47 n.25
    like the *Confessio*, shaped as
an exemplary criticism of
Richard II 52
French poems, in BL MS
Add.59495 173

In Praise of Peace 5–6, 131–33,
135–41, 142–51, 155, 165, 173,
221
    danger of war between
England and France in the
1390s at a time of increasing
threat from the Ottoman
Turks in the East 133–44
    first use of the word
"mescreauntz" 134
In Praise of Peace in Thynne's 1532
edition of Chaucer 9, 231–46
    humanism and the promotion
of the English language in
the 1530s 9
    the threat of the Ottoman
Turks (siege of Vienna,
1529) 236, 240
    war and the Papal Schism, a
call for Christian unity in
the 1530s 5–6, 235–46
Mirrour de l'Homme (*Speculum
Meditantis*) 232, 250, 252–53
Quia unusquisque 172, 187,
194–95
Quicquid homo scribat 150–51
shorter Latin poems, including
those sometimes added in
Confessio MSS 2, 7–9, 34,
146–47, 149, 172, 173 n.12,
174–75, 181, 184
*Traitié pour essampler les amantz
marietz* 45, 131, 148–49, 161,
165, 175, 221
Vox Clamantis 3–4, 77 n.11, 87,
146
    Book I ("the Visio Anglie"),
the Beast-Vision 33–53,
107
    Book I, xvii, the
Ship-Vision 107–08,
110–11
    creative and allusive
use of geographical
history 106–12
    geographical texts and
images 89–112

similarities to and differences from the *Confessio* 38, 39 n.14, 40–41, 44–46
use of Ovid 46–47
translation into English by Eric W. Stockton 107 n.33
Grady, Frank 85 n.31, 140
Graeber 3, 58–62, 64, 65 n.32, 66–68, 70
Gray, Douglas 27 n.53
Greenberg, Mark 90 n.2
Greene, Richard Firth 135 n.15, 172 n.8
Griffin, Carrie 114 n.4
Griffiths, Jane 180 n.22, 220 n.6
Griffiths, Jeremy 189 n.1, 195 n.21, 211
Grillo, Reginald 134
Gringoire, Pierre 227
Grundmann, Hermann 83 n.25
Gui, Bernhard, inquisitor 83 n.25
Guillén, Fernando Arias 121 n.18
Gura, David 109 n.42
Gutiérrez Rodríguez, Marta 114 nn.4–5

Hall, J.J. 248 n.6
Hamm, R. Wayne 127, 260 n.48
Hammond scribe, the, designated by Eleanor Prescott Hammond as the scribe of Cambridge, Trinity College MS R.3.21, London, BL MS Add.34360, and other MSS 158
Hanes, Frederick M. (Hanes Foundation at UNC Chapel Hill) 210 n.2, 216
Hanna, Ralph W. 158 n.19, 230 n.31, 254 n.32
Harley, J.B. 91 n.6, 92 n.7, 100 n.27, 106 n.30
Hartung, A.E. 260 n.48
Hawes, Stephen
  The Example of Virtue, printed by de Worde (1504) 225
  The conuercyon of swearers, printed by de Worde (1509) 225
  The joyfull medytacyon (1509) 225
Heal, Felicity 206 n.20

Heale, Martin 206 n.20
Heath, Michael J. 241 n.45
Heffernan, Carol F. 89 n.2
Helen, mother of the emperor Constantine 139
Hellinga (-Querido), Lotte 196, 219, 230 nn.32,33
Heng, Geraldine 89 n.2
Henry IV (Henry Bolingbroke, Henry of Lancaster, Henry earl of Derby) 2–3, 5–6, 50, 67–68, 108 n.38, 131, 133, 135–37, 142–43, 145, 148–51, 172, 173 n.11, 215, 233, 236–37, 255, 257
  events of 1399 and the Deposition of Richard II 51
  Henry's ascent and claim to the throne 43, 88
Henry VIII 9, 220, 222, 229, 231 n.2, 233, 236, 238–43
Herbrüggen, Hubertus Schulte 243 n.56
Hereford *Mappa Mundi* 92
Herrero Jímenez, Mauricio 114 n.5, 115 nn.6–7, 122 n.20, 215 n.35
Higden, Ranulph, *Polychronicon* 202, 222
  translation by John Trevisa 202, 222
Hill, Richard, his miscellany, Oxford, Balliol College MS 354 171
Hilmo, Maidie 16 n.16
Hines, John 35 n.7, 48 n.27, 79 n.12, 90 n.3
Hingeston, F.C. 142 n.43
Hocart, A.M. 58 n.17
Hoccleve, Thomas 25, 28–30
  Metre 29
Hodnett, Edward 224 n.18, 229 n.29
Holland, Peter 246 n.72
Hollinshead, Janet E. 215, 215 n.36
Hook, David 129 n.30
Horace 251
Horobin, Simon 17, 17 n.18, 19–20, 20 nn.31–32, 30, 56 n.4
Horowitz, Maryanne Cline 225 n.20
Houghton, L.B.T. 232 n.3
Hudson, Anne 80, 81 n.17, 84 n.29

Hutton, James 239 n.33, 241 n.43, 244

Ipomydon 228
Irvin, Matthew W. 72 n.2, 120 n.13
Isidore of Seville
   commentary on Leviticus 141
   De natura rerum 98
   Etymologiae 98, 98 n.26
Isocrates, Greek orator 239, 245

Jackson, W.A. 219
James, Mervyn 82 n.22
James, Montagu Rhodes 251, 254
Jardine, Lisa 241 n.45
Jefferson, Judith 29
João I, king of Portugal 215
John of Garland, Ovid commentary 46
John of Gaunt 215
Jones, Terry 56 n.4
Juhász-Ormsby, Ágnes 245
Justice, Stephen 16 n.16, 138 n.30

Kagay, Donald 140 n.34
Kain, Roger J.P. 93 n.11, 97 n.25, 100
Kane, George 258
Kantorowicz, Ernst H. 65
Karaisko, Vasilis 14 n.3
Katharine of Aragon 9
Kaylor, Noel Harold 89 n.2
Keiser, Arendt de 196
Ker, W.P. 260
Kerby-Fulton, Kathryn 16, 24, 30
Kingship
   anthropological theories of 58–70, 65–66
      divine and sacral (absolutist and constitutionalist) kingship 61–70
      ideas of sovereignty 58–59
      kingship of Richard II, Gower's criticism of 35, 39–53
      Shilluk kingship 64–65
Kirby, J.L. 135 n.16
Kittredge, George Lyman 260 n.48
Knapp, Ethan 90
Knight, Stephen 89 n.2

Kobayashi, Yoshiko 9, 106 n.31, 132–33, 141, 237 n.23, 231–46
Kraus, H.P. 216
Krummel, Miriamne Ara 89 n.2
Kuskin, William 220 n.5
Kynaston, Sir Francis, translation of Chaucer's *Troilus and Criseyde* 210

Lahey, Stephen E. 81 n.17, 83 n.27, 86 n.33
Laing, Margaret 13
Langland, William, *Piers Plowman* 259
Latini, Brunetto 64, 109
Lavezzo, Kathy 90 n.2
Leche, John 210
Lee, Sidney 233 n.5
Le Fanu, Sarah 249 n.11
Legge, M. Dominica 134 n.12
Le Goff, Jacques 95 n.22
Leland, John 233, 233 n.6, 234–35, 238, 245
   De viris illustribus 9, 231–32
   Epigrammata 232–33, 235
   Laudatio pacis 244
   praise of Chaucer 235 n.14
Leo X, Pope 238
Levy, Ian Christopher 81 n.17
Lilley, Keith D. 92 n.11, 99 n.26
Lily, William 245
Linacre, Thomas 245
Linguistic Atlas of Late Middle English (*LALME*) 13–14, 18 n.26, 19, 22
Livingston, Michael 133 n.6, 156 n.12, 221 n.12
Logan, George M. 243 n.58
Lollards and the Lollard threat 138, 145–46, 150
London, Guildhall 25
Longo, Pamela 108 n.37
Love, Nicholas, *Mirror of the Life of Jesus Christ* 95 n.21
Lowe, Ben 238 n.27, 241 n.43
Lozovsky, Natalia 92 n.8
Lubac, Henri de 93 n.12
Lydgate, John 9, 17, 158 n.20, 166, 220, 230
   Fall of Princes 154
   printed editions of his poems 223

A Thoroughfare of Woe 154
"A wikked tonge wol always deme amis" 154
Lynch, Kathryn 90 n.2

Macaulay, G.C. (George Campbell), editor of Gower's *Works* 1, 6, 13, 15, 18, 20, 21 nn.39–40, 22, 25–27, 28 n.56, 34 n.4, 40 n.15, 48, 55–56, 70, 71, 83 n.24, 92 n.10, 108 n.35, 113 nn.1–2, 117, 133, 155–57, 159–66, 169–70, 172, 176, 191 n.9, 198 nn.28–29, 202 n.5, 219 n.2, 222 n.13, 247–61
  career, as a school-teacher, and at Aberystwyth and Cambridge 249–53
  descriptions of MSS of Gower 165
  his edition of Gower's Works 9–10, 247–61
  his editions of Tennyson's *Idylls* 249–50
  his life and family 9–10, 248–51
  methods as an editor 156, 160–61, 251–61
  publications 249
  his theory of textual "recensions" 85 n.31, 255, 258–59
  rejection of Shirley's attribution to Gower of the *Balade moral of gode counseyle* 155–66
  reviews of his edition of Gower 260–61, 260 n.48
  his views about metre and lexis in the *Confessio* 162–63
Macaulay, Grace (née Conybeare) 248–49
Macaulay, Rev. S.H. 248
Macaulay, Rose 248, 249 n.11
Macaulay, Thomas Babington 248
MacCulloch, Diarmaid 243 n.54
Machan, Tim William 176 n.20, 220 n.7, 228 n.26, 246 n.71
Machlinia (publisher) 223
Macierowski, E.M. 93 n.12
Mancinus, Dominicus 228 n.25

Manly, John Matthews 160, 211 n.28, 258
Manuel II Palaeologus, Greek emperor 5–6, 132, 137
  visit to England 132, 135–40, 150
Manuscripts
  Aberystwyth, National Library of Wales MS Peniarth 392 (the Hengwrt MS) 27, 30
  Cambridge University Library MS Ff.1.6 (the Findern anthology) 171
  Cambridge University Library MS Mm.2.21 177 n.21
  Cambridge, St Catherine's College MS 7 174 n.15
  Cambridge, Pembroke College MS 307 174 n.15
  Cambridge, St John's College MS B.12 174 n.15, 177 n.21
  Cambridge, Sidney Sussex College MS 63 177 n.21, 198
  Cambridge, Trinity College MS R.3.2 16, 24–30, 175 n.17, 177 n.21, 197
  Cambridge, Trinity College MS R.3.20 154
  Chicago, Newberry Library, Case MS 33.5 174 n.15, 254 n.34
  Geneva (Coligny), Bodmer Foundation MS 178 13, 172–73, 175 n.16, 177 n.21, 254 n.34
  Glasgow University Library, Hunterian MS 59 (T.2.17) 4, 100, 173 n.13, 174–75
  London, BL MS Add.12043 177 n.21
  London, BL MS Add.22718 197 n.26
  London, BL MS Add.29729 6, 158, 163, 165
  London, BL MS Add.59495 (Trentham MS) 5–6, 15 n.13, 34 n.4, 36 n.10, 131–52, 145–51, 155, 233 n.6
  London, BL MS Cotton Tiberius A.iv 4, 15 n.13, 100, 194

Index

London, BL MS Cotton Tiberius B.v 104–05
London, BL MS Egerton 913 177 n.21
London, BL MS Egerton 1991 174 n.1
London, BL MS Harley 367 159
London, BL MS Harley 2251 58
London, BL MS Harley 3490 180
London, BL, MS Harley 3869 13, 173 n.13, 175, 177 n.21
London, BL MS Harley 7184 253 n.28
London, BL MS Harley 7334 16, 26, 30
London, BL MS Royal 18.C.XXII 174 n.15
London, BL MS Royal B.XX.vi 150
London, BL MS Stowe 950 177, 179 (illust.)
London, Society of Antiquaries MS 134 174 n.15
London, University Library, Senate House MS V.88 (the Ilchester MS) 16
Madrid, Biblioteca del Escorial MS g-II-19 5, 115–17, 122, 127, 129
Madrid, Biblioteca Nacional MS 20262/19 115–17
Madrid, Biblioteca Nacional MS 22644 115–17
Madrid, Biblioteca Real MS II-3088 4–5, 114–17, 120–22, 127
Manchester, Chetham's Library MS A.7.38 177 n.21, 180 n.24
New Haven, Yale University, Beinecke Library, Osborn Collection MS fa.1 197 n.27, 254 n.33
New Haven, Yale University, Beinecke Library MS Mellon 25 197 n.26
New York, Columbia University Library, Plimpton Collection MS 265 254 n.33
New York, Pierpont Morgan Library MS 125 174 n.15, 254 n.34
New York, Pierpont Morgan Library MS 126 195, 254 nn.29,34
New York, Pierpont Morgan Library MS 690 254 n.33
Nottingham University Library, Middleton Collection MS Mi LM 8 174 n.15, 177 n.21
Oxford, Arch.Selden MS B.11 174 n.15, 197 n.26
Oxford, Arch.Selden supra MS 53 29
Oxford, Bodleian Library MS Ashmole 35 154, 158–59, 161, 164, 165, 180 n.24
Oxford, Bodleian Library MS Ashmole 59 6, 154–66
Oxford, Bodleian Library MS Bodley 294 6, 23–24, 28, 161, 173 n.13, 175, 255–56
Oxford, Bodleian Library MS Bodley 693 24, 28, 174 n.15
Oxford, Bodleian Library MS Bodley 902 23–4, 28, 161, 174 n.15, 177 n.21, 255
Oxford, Bodleian Library MS Eng. poet a.1 (the Vernon MS) 19
Oxford, Bodleian Library MS Fairfax 3 2, 4, 13, 21–24, 26–28, 113, 160, 161, 175 n.16, 176–77, 178 (illust.), 255–56, 259–60
Oxford, Bodleian Library MS Hatton 51 (copy of Caxton) 7–8, 181, 182 (illust.), 189–200
    contents and lay-out 34, 38
    imitation of paratexts in Caxton's 1483 edition of Chaucer 191–99
    notes by another hand 49–50
    speaker-markers 193
Oxford, Bodleian Library MS Hatton 92 2–4, 33–53, 48
    Emphasis on the moral and political Gower 33–53

Oxford, Bodleian Library MS Laud misc.609   13, 174 n.15
Oxford, Bodleian Library MS Laud misc.719   4, 39 n.14, 100 n.28, 104–05
Oxford, Bodleian Library MS Lyell 31   177 n.21, 254 n.33
Oxford, Bodleian Library MS Rawlinson C.86   6, 158–59, 163–64, 165
Oxford, Bodleian Library MS Selden supra 53   29
Oxford, All Souls College MS 98   48–49, 194
   compared with MS Hatton 92   48–52
Oxford, Balliol College MS 354   171
Oxford, Christ Church College MS 148   174 n.15
Oxford, Corpus Christi College MS 67   161, 174 n.15, 255
Oxford, Corpus Christi College MS 198   26
Oxford, Magdalen College MS lat.213   191 n.10
Oxford, New College MS 266   177 n.21, 195
Oxford, Wadham College MS 13   161, 175 n.18, 177 n.21
Philadelphia, Rosenbach Foundation MS 1083/29   254 n.33
Princeton University, Firestone Library, Garrett Collection MS 136   180 n.24, 254 n.33
Princeton University, Firestone Library, Taylor Collection MS 5   177 n.21, 254 n.54
San Marino, CA, Huntington Library MS EL 26 A 13   27, 166
San Marino, CA, Huntington Library MS EL 26 A 17 (the 'Stafford MS)   2, 13, 166 n.50, 177 n.21, 198, 254 n.34, 255–57
San Marino, CA, Huntington Library MS 150   4, 100 n.28
Vatican City, Biblioteca Apostolica Vaticana

MS 6428   129
MS urb.Lat.341   110
Washington, Folger Library MS Sm.1 (V.b.29)   180, 181, 254 n.34
(Private Collection) formerly Marquess of Bute MS I.17   254 n.34
Manuscripts and prints, co-existing in the post-print era   189–90
Manuwald, Gesine   232 n.3
Maps, portolans and cartography in the Middle Ages   91–112
   maps and their interpretation   4
   Mappae mundi   96
   T-O maps (*orbis terrarum*)   96–98, 100, 104–05
Marcellinus, Ammianus   92 n.8
Marchaunt, John ("Scribe D")   25–27, 173 n.13
Margaret of Austria   243
Martin, José-Luis   121 n.18
Mattingly, Garrett   239 n.29
Maw, Martin   247 n.1
Mayer, T.F.   238 n.27
McIntosh, Angus   2, 13–14
McKitterick, David   190, 191 nn.10–11, 195 n.19, 198 n.30, 248 n.4
McWilliam, G.H.   76 n.7
Meale, Carol M.   158 n.18, 196 n.24, 197 nn.25,28, 200, 200 nn.34–35
Meditationes vitae Christi (attrib. John of Caulibus)   95 n.21
Meindl, Robert   89 n.1, 108
Merrills, Andy   98 n.26
Meyer, Karl   164, 254
Meyer, Matthias   159 n.26
Mézières, Philippe de   132–35, 137
   Epistre au Roi Richard II (1395)   139, 141, 145, 150
   Le songe du vieil pelerin (1389)   133
Minnis, Alastair J.   16 n.16, 29 n.58, 82 n.23, 93 n.12, 185 n.26, 194 n.18, 195 n.22, 207 n.22, 220 n.7
Mooney, Linne R.   17 n.21, 25, 27, 56 n.4, 135 n.15, 158 n.19, 172 n.8

More, Sir Thomas 9, 239, 243, 244
  Utopia, Epigrams 234 n.8
Moreira, Filipe Alves 121 n.17
Morse, Charlotte C. 89 n.2
Morse, Ruth 246 n.72
Mosser, Dan 17 n.18
Mula, Patrick 77 n.9
Murphy, Dee 249 n.10
Mynors, R.A.B. 241 n.46

Nafde, Aditi 7–8, 189–200
Natoli, Bartolo A. 42 n.18
Needham, Rodney 58 n.17
Neville, William, *The Castell of Pleasure* 225, 227
Newton, Thomas, ed. Leland, *Epigrammata* 232–33, 235
Nicholas of Lyra 93
Nicholson, Peter 15, 56, 85 n.31, 257–58, 259
Nicopolis, battle of, 1396 134, 140
Nixon, Howard 204 n.10, 210
Nolan, Maura 91 n.4, 109, 109 n.37
Northern Homily Cycle, *Legend of St Eustace* 19
Nut-Brown Maid, The (illust.) 212
Nuttall, Jenni 138 n.27

Oakley, Francis 58, 61 n.27
Oldham, J.B. 204 n.10
Olsson, Kurt 58 n.14, 90
Oman, Charles 107 n.34
Orwin, Thomas, printer 232 n.3
Ottoman Turks, the threat they posed to the West in the 1390s 133–44
  called "mescreantz" in Gower's *In Praise of Peace* 133
  similar threat posed in the 1530s, 237–38, 240, 243
Ovid 96, 106–10, 207 n.22, 232
  Metamorphoses 6.571 42 n.18
  Metamorphoses, MSS of 96–97

Pace, George 154 n.5
Pace, Richard, Latin oration of 1518 on Peace 9, 238–43, 244, 245
Painter, George D. 204 n.10

Palmer, J.N.N. 138 n.28
Pantzer, Katharine F. 204 n.11, 219
Parish, W.D. 211 n.29
Parkes, Malcolm B. 15, 16 n.16, 17, 25–8, 28 n.56, 33 n.3, 100 n.29, 102 n.29, 190–91, 197
Pascual-Argente, Clara 120 n.15, 127, 216 n.40
Patch, Howard Rollin 76 n.9, 77 n.10
Pauli, Reinhold, edition of Gower's *Confessio* 18 n.25, 250, 255
Payn, Robert, translator of Portuguese version of *Confessio* 115–17, 119
Pearsall, Derek 15 nn.11–12, 16, 16 n.15, 29 n.57, 55 n.1, 56 n.4, 57 n.11, 160 nn.30,32, 162, 165 n.48, 171 n.6, 172, 189 n.1, 195 n.21, 207 n.22, 220 n.7, 258, 259 n.43
Peasants' Revolt, The 41–45, 107 nn.33–34
Peck, Russell 13 n.1, 55, 56 n.3, 57 n.9, 58 n.14, 70, 71, 72 n.2, 85 n.31, 116 n.8, 132 n.5, 156, 216 n.40, 237 n.20
Pepwell, Henry, print of Neville's *Castell of Pleasure* 226
Pérez-Fernández, Tamara 2, 4–5, 113–30, 114 nn.4–5
Petkov, Kiril 134, 137
Picard, Jean 144
Pickles, J.D. 161
Piers Plowman see Langland
Philippa of Lancaster 215
Phillips, Helen 212 n.31, 226 n.22, 227 n.23
Pindar 241
Pinkhurst, Adam 25–27
Piper, Alan J. 15 n.11, 34 n.3, 102 n.29
Pizan, Christine de 222
Plotius Tucca 235
Plutarch 245
Pole, Michael de la 86
Pollard, Alfred W. 200 n.33, 204 n.10, 219
Pollnitz, Aysha 242 n.49

Pontano, Giovanni   232
Potter, David   243 n.54
Pouzet, Jean-Pascal   48
Powell, Sue   190 n.4
Poyntz, William, Francis and John   230
Pratt, Karen   159 n.26
Preest, David   136 n.20
Ptolemy's *Geography*   91 n.5
Pugh, Syrithe   93 n.14, 94 n.19
Purcell, Emer   114 n.4
Putter, Ad   159 n.26
Pynson, Richard   220 n.4, 239
   print (1518) of *The Myrrour of Good Manners*, with comment on Gower in the prologue by Alexander Barclay   228
   printed edition of Chaucer in 3 volumes (1526)   224, 229
   printed editions of Lydgate's poems, including the *Troy-Book* and *Fall of Princes*   223–24, 230
   use of woodcuts   224

Queen Margaret's Entry into London, Verses on   175

Radulescu, Raluca   157 n.14
Ransom, Emily A.   211 n.31
Rastell, John, print of Chaucer's *Parliament of Fowls*   228
Redgrave, G.R.   204 n.11, 219
Reeve, M.D.   190 n.4
Ricci, Pier Giorgio   83 n.28
Ricci, Seymour de   202 n.4, 203 n.9, 205
Richard II   2–3, 134–36, 137, 138 n.27, 139, 145, 232, 255
   Richard II and the Appellant Crisis, 1387   41–44, 49, 51
   Deposition, The, Articles of, Record and Process   87
   Gower's criticism of   35, 39–53
   his kingship   71–88
   costume and fashion in the reign of   138 n.27
Richardson, Glenn   239 n.30, 240, 242 n.53, 243
Rickert, Edith   211 n.28

Riddy, Felicity   158 n.18
Rigg, A.G.   33 n.3, 110 n.44
Ringler, William A.   211 nn.31–33
Roach, Susan   196 n.23
Roberts, Jane   25 n.45
Rodríguez Porto, Rosa M.   121 n.17
Roland, Meg   92 n.11
Rolle, Richard   223
Rollman, David   224 n.19
Rosenbach, A.S.W.   216
Rosser, Gervase   206 n.26
Ruggiers, Paul G.   233 n.5
Rundle, David   254 n.32
Russell, Alexander   144
Russell, Joycelyne G.   238 n.27, 239 n.37, 240 nn.39–40

Sáez-Hidalgo, Ana   15 n.13, 85 n.31, 89 n.1, 113 n.1, 114 n.5, 120 n.14, 215 n.25, 216 nn.39–40, 221 n.7
Sahlins, Marshall   3, 58–61, 66–68
St Mary's Overey, priory   15, 132, 150
Sallust, *De bello Jugurthino*   93 n.11
Samuels, Michael L.   13, 13 n.5, 19–20, 27
Santana Moreno, Bernardo   127
Sargent, Michael   95 n.21
Saul, Nigel   86
Sawtre, William   138
Scanlon, Larry   39 n.14
Scase, Wendy   2, 13–31
Scattergood, John   219 n.1, 227 n.23
Schachterle, Lance   90 n.2
Schism, the Great Schism (between Eastern and Western Churches, from 1054)   133–44, 150
Schism, the Western or Papal Schism (1378–1417)   131–33, 144, 150, 237, 242
Schnepel, Burkhard   65 n.32
Scogan, Henry, *A Moral Balade*   155
Scribes and their methods of copying   14
   Literatim copying   14–31
Sebank, Mark   93 n.12
Seiler, Thomas H.   95 n.22
Semaan, Khalil I.   143 n.47
Shakespeare, William
   Julius Caesar   138 n.29

The Merchant of Venice 74–75, 78, 84
The Tempest 251
Shirley, John 6, 153–66
  attribution to Gower rejected by Macaulay 155–66
  his attribution of the *Balade moral of gode counseyle* to Gower 153–66
  his MS miscellanies (e.g. Bodleian MS Ashmole 59, London BL MS Add.29729) 157–58
  reliability of Shirley's attributions of authorship 159–60
Shogimen, Takashi 81 n.17
Silius Italicus 239
Simpson, James 56, 57 n.8, 62, 92 n.9
Singleton, Charles S. 77 n.10
Skeat, Walter William, Rev. 18 n.25, 155, 159, 250 n.19, 253
  his edition of Chaucer 253
Skelton, John 9, 92 n.8
  The Bowge of Court 225
  The comforte of louers (1515) 225
  The Garland of Laurel 225
  The Pastime of Pleasure 225 n.21
Smith, Jeremy 13, 16, 16 n.18, 19 n.29, 24, 27 n.53, 162
Smith, Julie 225
Smith, Margaret M. 223 n.15
Smith, Martin Ferguson 249 n.8
Smuts, R. Malcolm 210 n.25
Sobecki, Sebastian 15 n.13, 131–33, 150, 173, 236
Solopova, Elizabeth 30
Sovereignty, ideas of 58–59
Spies, H. 260 n.48
Staley, Lynn 85 n.31
Stallings-Taney, Mary 95 n.21
Stanbury, Sarah 79 n.13
Stanley, E.G. 27 n.53
Steiner, Emily 143 n.44
Stewart, Vaughn 204 n.10
Stillwell, Margaret Bingham 205 n.12
Stockton, Eric W. 107 n.33, 108 n.36, 110 n.43
Stone, Zachary E. 132, 144

Stow, George B. 56 n.5, 85 n.31
Stow, John 6, 159
Stubbs, Estelle 17 n.21, 25
Suleiman the Magnificent 236
Sylvester, Pope, and the baptism of the emperor Constantine 139–40

Takagi, Masako 211 n.28
Takamiya, Toshiyuki 257 n.38
Tarlinskaya, Marina 18
Taylor, Andrew 232 n.3
Taylor, John, *In Praise of Hemp-Seed* (1630) 188
Taylor, Karla 2–3, 71–88
Ten Brink, Bernhard 157 n.15
Teresi, Loredana 106 n.30
Thomas, Edward (the poet), reviews of Macaulay's edition of Gower 260–61
Thompson, D.F.S. 241 n.46
Thompson, James (the poet) 251
Thompson, Stith 74 n.5
Thynne, William 9, 245
  1532 printed edition of Chaucer's Works 8, 165, 219–22, 226, 229, 231–36
    containing Gower's *In Praise of Peace* 231–46
    Thynne's Prologue as a means of establishing "cultural capital" for Gower and his credentials as a pioneering humanist 220, 246
Tillyard, E.M.W. 250 n.17
Tomasch, Sylvia 90 n.2
Toulmin-Smith, Lucy 260
Tournoy-Thoen, Gilbert and Godelieve 206 n.21
Tracy, James D. 242 n.49
Trapp, J.B. 190 n.4, 206 n.19
Trevisa, John, translator of Higden's *Polychronicon* 222
Tuke, Sir Brian 9, 220, 233, 234, 236, 238, 243–45
Tunstall, Cuthbert 239, 243, 245
Turks *see* Ottoman Turks
Tyerman, Christopher 137, 142 n.22
Tyler, Elizabeth 209 n.23
Tyrwhitt, Thomas 234 n.11

Usk, Adam   135–39

Van Dijk, Conrad   56–57, 61, 66
Van Duzen, Chet   98 n.26
Vanes, Jean   215 n.37
Van Es, Bart   246 n.72
Van Kranevelt, Frans   243
Veldener, Jan   196
Vere, Robert de   86
Vienna, siege of, by the Turks, 1529   236
Villalon, Andrew   140 n.34
Villon, François   229
Virgil   96, 175

Wakelin, Daniel   15 n.8, 17, 29 n.59
Walker, Greg   9, 206 n.21, 220 n.3, 235–36, 238
Wallace, David   59 n.21, 77 n.9
Waller, A.R.   251 n.23
Walsingham, Thomas, *Chronica Maiora*   136
Walter, William, *Guyscarde and Sygysmunde*   227
War and Peace: the danger of war between England and France despite the threat from the Ottoman Turks in the East in the 1390s   133–44, 151
    see Philippe de Mézières; Schisms; Gower's In Praise of Peace; Nicopolis, battle of
    the similar threat in the 1530s   237–38, 240, 243
    see Gower's In Praise of Peace; Schisms; Vienna, siege of; Richard Pace
Ward, A.W.   251 n.23
Warner, J. Christopher   236
Warner, Lawrence   25 n.45
Watson, Andrew G.   15 n.11, 100 n.29, 190 n.4
Watt, David   5–6, 131–51
Watt, Diane   33 n.2

Wawn, Andrew N.   234 n.8
Wells, William   203 n.9
West, David   100 n.29
West, E.J.   58 n.14
Wetherbee, Winthrop   176 n.20
White, Eric   170
Whitman, John   93 n.12
Whitmarsh, Tim   93 n.15
Wickert, Maria   89 n.1, 106 n.31
Wilks, Michael   84, 85 n.30
Williamson, Keith   13 n.3
Wilton (Wylton) Diptych   138 n.28
Wolsey, Thomas, Cardinal   238, 239
Woodville, Anthony   222
Woodward, David   91 nn.5–6, 92 n.7, 100, 100 n.27, 106 n.30
Wright, John Kirtland   94 n.17
Wright, Thomas, edition of Chaucer   165
Wyatt, Michael   206, 206 n.21
Wyatt, Sir Thomas, Satire I   230
Wycliffe, John   3
    De officio regis   80
    Wycliffite ideas about kingship and secular *dominium*   72, 78–88

Xenophon   245

Yeager, R.F.   15, 15 n.13, 16 n.14, 33 nn.2,4,7, 45 n.21, 48 n.27, 57 n.9, 79 n.12, 85 n.31, 89 nn.1–2, 90 n.3, 106 n.31, 114 n.5, 120 nn.14–15, 131, 132 n.5, 133 n.6, 145 n.52, 146 n.53, 147, 156 n.12, 172 n.10, 176 n.20, 192 n.13, 203 n.7, 214 n.34, 215 n.38, 216 nn.39–40, 221 nn.7,12, 233 n.6, 237 n.20, 257 n.38, 260 n.48
Yoran, Hanan   242 n.49

Zack, S.E.   209 n.23
Zaleski, Carol   95 n.22

VOLUMES ALREADY PUBLISHED

I *Concordance to John Gower's* Confessio Amantis, edited by J.A. Pickles and J.L. Dawson, 1987
II *John Gower's Poetic: The Search for a New Arion*, R.F. Yeager, 1990
III *Gower's* Confessio Amantis: *A Critical Anthology*, Peter Nicholson, 1991
IV *John Gower and the Structures of Conversion: A Reading of the* Confessio Amantis, Kurt Olsson, 1992
V *Fathers and Daughters in Gower's* Confessio Amantis: *Authority, Family, State, and Writing*, María Bullón-Fernández, 2000
VI *Gower's Vulgar Tongue: Ovid, Lay Religion, and English Poetry in the* Confessio Amantis, T. Matthew N. McCabe, 2011
VII *John Gower, Poetry and Propaganda in Fourteenth-Century England*, David R. Carlson, 2012
VIII *John Gower and the Limits of the Law*, Conrad van Dijk, 2013
IX *The Poetic Voices of John Gower: Politics and Personae in the* Confessio Amantis, Matthew W. Irvin, 2014
X *John Gower in England and Iberia: Manuscripts, Influences, Reception*, edited by Ana Sáez-Hidalgo and R.F. Yeager, 2014
XI *John Gower: Others and the Self*, edited by Russell A. Peck and R.F. Yeager, 2017
XII *Historians on John Gower*, edited by Stephen H. Rigby and Siân Echard, 2019
XIII *Studies in the Age of Gower: A Festschrift in Honour of Robert F. Yeager*, edited by Susannah Mary Chewning, 2020

Printed in the United States
By Bookmasters